EXPAND!
The dynamic approach to international marketing development

EXPAND!...

The dynamic approach to international marketing development

ALAIN-ERIC GIORDAN

**With contributions by Sir ADRIAN CADBURY
and over 500 short case studies**

Gower

Published by
Gower Publishing Limited
Gower House
Croft Road
Aldershot
Hampshire GU11 3HR
England

Gower
Old Post Road
Brookfield
Vermont 05036
USA

Alain-Eric Giordan has asserted his right under the Copyright, Designs and Patents Act 1988 to be identified as the author of this work.

British Library Cataloguing in Publication Data

Giordan, Alain-Eric
  Expand!: Dynamic International Market
  Development Programme
  I. Title II. Mlodzik, Arlene
  658.8

  ISBN 0–566–07435–4

Library of Congress Cataloging-in-Publication Data

Giordan, Alain-Eric.
    [Exporter plus 2. English]
    Expand! : a dynamic international market development programme /
  Alain-Eric Giordan.
       p.   cm.
    Includes bibliographical references.
    ISBN 0–566–07435–4
    1. Export marketing--Management. 2. Foreign trade promotion.
  I. Title. II. Title: Dynamic international market development
  programme.
  HF1417.5.G5513   1993
  658.8'48--dc20   93–29373
                                                         CIP

Typeset in 10 point Palatino by Intype, London and printed in Great Britain at Hartnolls Ltd. Bodmin

Contents

SELECTING WAYS TO EXPAND: INVENTORY AND PRACTICAL ADVICE

Translator's Note

In addition to my responsibilities as International Relations Officer at a French undergraduate business school, and as international marketing teacher, I was the translation collaborator for *Expand !. . .*

(Incidentally, I am an English-speaking Canadian, but have lived overseas for 22 years, so my English has been strongly influenced by interacting with non-native speakers for more than two decades.)

The challenge was to take Alain-Eric Giordan's book *'Exporter Plus'*, originally written in French, and adapt it into an English form suitable for a multi-national target audience and not just the English-speaking British or American public. Consequently, there is a pluri-national linguistic approach whose results are not meant to be academic, but reflect the authenticity of international business, thus enabling the reader to identify with his familiar export English language environment.

Alain-Eric, who speaks fluent English, and I struggled and 'fought' over what we thought was the right tone, and when we could no longer see 'the forest for the trees', we badgered our business friends and colleagues into taking a look at our creation. Tom Fiorina in particular, an American pharmaceutical marketing specialist, deserves special thanks for proof-reading our material and making helpful suggestions. Also thanks go to Lucrezia Dillon-Corneck, an Australian communication specialist.

Hopefully our collective efforts, together with final style adjustments by Jeremy Thompson, one of Gower's copy-editors, have paid off.

We all wish you a good read!

Arlene Mlodzik
Paris, January 1993

Index of Short Case Studies

Introduction

How to Expand?

Everywhere in the world, millions of export* executives are seeking answers to this question. Given the increase of international competition in all fields, governments in most countries are encouraging their companies to convert this problem into an opportunity.

The means of expanding are numerous, particularly those which make up what I call *international marketing development* – which is what this book is all about.

International marketing development is so varied in its application that it is accessible to any company, large or small, in any professional activity, and often without any excessive investments being necessary.

However, rare are those executives who are familiar with, or who have mastered, the complete range of expansion means available. There are several reasons for this:

■ **Lack of training for international development**
Few people concerned with exports have had a specially adapted international development training program. Usually, they find themselves thrust onto the international scene without adequate preparation, just because of a chance career opportunity.

In addition, most export training programs are overly focused on the necessary administrative procedures for opening up commercial relations with foreign markets. They thus provide poor preparation for the next step – ensuring the expansion of these markets.

■ **Limited experience = reduced efficiency**
Not only have export executives usually received no adequate training in this respect, but their former experience (as engineers,

---

*The word 'export' is used throughout this book in its widest sense, and therefore covers the effective exporting of products (whether manufactured or not), as well as the development of foreign markets achieved with delocalized production, the performance of a service, the transfer of technology, and all other activities that do not involve the physical exporting of tangible goods.

financial controllers, sales representatives, etc.) does not really help them to master the multitude of new activities they must take on when they find themselves left to their own devices in a foreign country.

It is not easy for an engineer 'dropped' into exporting to define an international distribution strategy, or to judge the relevance of a media advertising campaign . . . nor for an export executive to deal with product marketing, or to evaluate the advantages or disadvantages of delocalized production. All the more difficult when the making of these decisions happens in a country whose language, culture, customs and market specificities are quite unfamiliar.

Having to forge their experience in the heat of the action, as it were, such executives are naturally driven to use their limited range of homemade solutions, or to implement the classical recipes used within their industry.

Although international field experience grows after a few years, large gaps in mastering the whole range of market development means and techniques are likely to endure.

■ **Inadequate structures**

Many companies set up their export departments by basing them on their domestic sales organization. Although this type of structure can ensure the opening up of foreign markets, and the follow-up of day-to-day business, it rapidly becomes unsuitable for conceiving and orchestrating further development.

■ **Overloaded export executives**

Being in charge of too many markets, most export executives have to expedite business between 'planes, and often lack the time to get organized in a more productive manner.

The sheer volume of the daily problems tends to weigh them down and absorb all their attention, thus preventing them from devoting their time and energies to expansion. As a result, they often feel bogged down in a quagmire of minor hassles instead of being involved in the building of tomorrow's strategies.

Thus, the purpose of this book is to offer practical advice, and to become a real toolkit for those executives who participate – directly or indirectly – in the management of their company's international expansion. They will find a method of development as well as an inventory of dynamic devices, combinations of which will enhance their company's foreign market shares. The generic term 'dynamic devices' (in French, 'moyens moteurs') was coined within **L'Oréal** by Robert Salmon, when General Director of their **Perfumes and Beauty Division** (at present he is Vice-Chairman of this group). It covers all procedures which can trigger the development of a company's sales. Rarely efficient when applied individually, several dynamic devices should be selected together, according to their efficiency and complementarity, in order to constitute a development action. We will see how to combine these different types of actions (product, push and pull) within the framework of an international development plan.

Getting Organized to Expand: Development Method

In the development of foreign sales, where operations have to be carried out quickly, given the multiplicity of markets* to be dealt with, it would seem reasonable to ensure a company's international expansion by keeping to a structured development method.

First, an international expansion strategy has to be defined (Study Phase) by both establishing the priorities for intervention and by targeting specific objectives, according to market opportunities and the company's capacities. Then (Preparation Phase), the means which are best adapted to the achievement of these objectives have to be selected, and brought together into the framework of a development plan; this practical organization will take into account the specific constraints of the target markets. Finally (Action Phase), the development plan's implementation has to be followed up, the results analysed, and experience reinvested to fine-tune subsequent plans.

This methodology has been designed to deal with real field situations; this might upset the marketing theory wizards, but those who are on familiar ground in exporting know that simplicity (which does not exclude innovation) far outweighs excessive conceptual sophistication.

Furthermore, there is no miracle solution or universal recipe in this method. The multitude of parameters (nature of the product, type of market plus its miscellaneous constraints, competitive environment, development phase attained, activated channels of distribution, local particularities of consumption or utilization, communication opportunities, etc.) can only lead to a multitude of specific cases.

This is a guidebook which can be adapted to the variety of situations encountered on the international scene. For clarity, I have broken down, step-by-step, certain procedures which are normally carried out simultaneously. This structured presentation is such that none of the determining factors of a market study will be omitted, nor any indispensable element to the success of a development plan neglected.

Selecting Ways to Expand: Inventory and Practical Advice

After closely examining the three development method phases – Study, Preparation, Action – the entire range of dynamic devices will be inventoried in order to enhance a company's foreign market share.

---

*When talking about exporting, the term 'markets' is deliberately used, as this is more flexible than 'countries', whose meaning is restricted by the notion of borders. There are national markets, such as Japan; supranational markets, such as Scandinavia; regional markets such as the US's East Coast, Sun Belt or California; there are even markets whose essential characteristic is not geographic, such as the duty free market.

This whole approach can be compared to a cocktail recipe book (the word cocktail could actually figure in a definition of the marketing mix). First, it offers a method for the successful composition of drinks – how to adapt them to the tastes of different nationalities; choosing and measuring the appropriate proportions of spirits and mixers; using the shaker, etc. Then, all the different possible ingredients are detailed, with practical guidelines on how to use them, descriptions of those mixtures to be avoided, and advice on the treatment of hangovers! And all this without forgetting the famous formulae of experienced barmen from all over the world.

This inventory of dynamic devices will be presented by field of application. First, dynamic devices involving the product and its adaptation to each market are considered. Then, the 'push'* dynamic devices – the company's international team, the local representative's team, and the channels of distribution are examined. Finally, the 'pull' dynamic devices, including all aspects of communication such as advertising, public relations and sales promotions, are discussed. Each type of dynamic device is featured with practical advice on its implementation, always quite delicate in an international context.

There are two final remarks. The dynamic devices described in this book are mostly those which evolve from 'international marketing development'. Other development means are not covered, or are only briefly tackled: for instance, practical advice about subsidiary companies, mergers and acquisitions, as well as the development of alliances, proposed by Sir Adrian Cadbury (see section 1.3.3.) in order to position marketing strategy within company policy decisions.

Moreover, the dynamic devices presented here obviously cannot be directly applied to every sector of professional activity. Thus, for example, the actions mentioned in the retail distribution chapter cannot all be transposed to the capital goods sector.

However, I have often verified the value of innovation by adapting development techniques observed elsewhere to the individual situation and constraints of another company, as well as to the specific character of any industry anywhere in the world. This is why more than 500 short case studies, selected from various industries and markets, illustrate the advice proposed in this book.

---

*'Push' dynamic devices are those which are applied to the distribution of products. Their role is to push these products into the hands of consumers or potential users. Such devices are: commission on turnover for salespeople; distributors' markups, etc.

'Pull' dynamic devices largely rely on techniques of communication which enhance the specific advantages of the offer, such as its specific 'plus' or its price, to directly generate demand.

These two types of dynamic devices are often combined for greater efficiency. It is rare, in fact, that the nature of a product and the characteristics of a market lead to a choice of either a total push strategy, where only the distribution exerts a driving force on sales, or a total pull strategy, where the distribution is neglected and only the demand stimulated.

Among other factors that led us to decide to launch 'CZA Paris', our first subsidiary abroad, in Warsaw, was the zloty/franc exchange rate – together with the low cost of labour and establishment expenditures – that made our total monthly operations budget in Poland as light as about $5000! ... even though our initial entry investment amounted to $70,000 in foreign currency as share capital. Then', emphasizes Bertrand des Abbayes, 'don't you think it was a more reasonable gamble to be the very first in an underdeveloped Poland, than to enter an expensive race with a crowd of more powerful competitors in a wealthy western European country? ...

With Barbara working half-time in our Warsaw subsidiary (she was, at that time, the only Polish communication expert available in Poland!) plus a staff of five, locally hired and trained in our Paris office, we managed to get a first client, the syrup and liquor producer Berger, then several other foreign companies, such as l'Express (which launched the 'Spotkania' magazine in Poland), Wagons-Lits and a few others, as well as Polish companies, for instance the confectionery manufacturer Olza ...

In 1992, we are still among the market leaders, and whatever happens with the present arrival of more competitors, our Polish drive has proven profitable and it even provided further advantages: when as the only marketing and communication agency in Poland, CZA could develop business relationships with some major western European groups that would probably never have approached us in Paris', concludes Bertrand des Abbayes.

Although quite unusual, *CZA*'s success story is based on a logical analysis: if confronted with the applicable market development potential parameters developed in the following chapters, Polish pre-selection would largely switch on 'green lights': the present gloomy Overall Economic Situation (1.1.1.2) should eventually turn into growth in this 'would-be consumer' market of 38 million people. As for the Competitor's Positions (1.1.1.5) evaluation, no competitors is a rare answer, making *CZA* the only wolf in the sheepfold. A tasty situation (even if, in such a case, some clients cannot distinguish between a communication specialist and a fake ... until they get to meet a real one) providing a strong impetus to place Poland as a priority in terms of Market Assessment (1.1.1.9), even with the Miscellaneous Constraints (1.1.1.6) to be faced in such a country.

Furthermore, the Product Development Potential (1.1.2) appears excellent in Poland, with the opportunity to place a native born specialist to lead the local subsidiary and apply the *CZA* methodology and marketing creativity techniques, unparalleled in this virgin market. Still, some Practical Parameters (1.2.1) can bring even stronger reasons to support Poland's ranking as a *CZA* priority target: with a direct monthly cost of $5000 for the Warsaw subsidiary, even pessimists would bet on a favourable Potential/Investment Ratio (1.2.1.2). More questionable was the evaluation of Return on Investment Size and Rapidity (1.2.1.3), but here again, the initial light investment made *CZA*'s Polish subsidiary quite a realistic gamble, even with no return for a few years.

The concept of Opportunities to be Seized (1.2.1.4) appears tailor-made as an additional justification for *CZA*'s solitary eastwards rush – the surest way to possess a virgin market is to get there first. But *CZA*'s trump card still has to be revealed: the key reason that drove Bertrand des Abbayes to choose Poland as the top intervention priority abroad was his agency's Personnel Qualities (1.2.1.5).

▶   *As Michel 'Mickey' Bibrowicz (CZA's artistic director) confirms, the agency's staff motivation was the deciding factor: 'Obviously, the CZA 'Polish connection', started by Barbara and myself, was a real 'plus' to get the CZA Warsaw subsidiary to take off successfully ... Another factor that Bertrand could count on was our desire to act as super-professionals in our homeland, after years of sorrowful separation ... Furthermore, all the 20 staff members working at CZA, even those who hardly cared for Poland before, felt a strong motivation to participate actively in this country's economic recovery, together with the CZA team in Warsaw* ... And you surely imagine how proud each of us can be, for tiny CZA having gone first to Poland and still being among the market leaders!'*

The notion of 'market selection' can also be found in areas where market development is not continual (as in the case of consumer goods), but is based on successive, individual contracts.

▶   *Krebs, a general engineering firm specializing in the study and realization of turnkey projects for the chemical, petro-chemical and hydrometallurgic industries, bears heavy costs for each tender's preparation. Therefore, before investing heavily in research, Krebs evaluates the strengths of its links with the potential client, and the project's feasibility and financing. By avoiding the dispersion of its resources, Krebs concentrates on valid projects and proposes competitive prices.*

1.1.1.2   Overall economic situation

A complete economic evaluation of each short-listed country is the logical first step. It is not necessary to spend too much time on this, as it should have been thoroughly undertaken when commercial relations were originally initiated; the importance of regular follow-ups of a market's overall economic situation should be emphasized, though, so that a balance between the risks of investing and the returns made through new opportunities can be struck.

A watchful eye must thus be systematically kept on international information of interest to the company, such as the general economic situation of major markets, as well as the evolution of demand, distribution and competition, particularly in research and the launching of products (see the 'Sfernice example in section 1.1.1.3) as well as commercial and promotional activities.

***CZA** Paris contact in Warsaw: Barbara Gebarzewski, ul.Elblaska 14, 01737 Warszawa, Poland. Tel: 39 89 61; **CZA** in France, Tel: (1) 47 58 74 00.

Large companies have specialized staff who scour the domestic and foreign press, key trade magazines, their competitors' publications, professional and consumer organizations, etc., and transmit a synthesis of information gathered to those in charge.

This is clearly impossible for small businesses, but they should nevertheless set up some sort of informal Documentary Service, undertaken part-time by a secretary well prepared for the job or with the help of a carefully briefed student, who will concentrate research on the major publications and trade magazines of both domestic and main foreign markets.

Many countries support their companies' export development in various ways, both in the homeland as well as overseas. Obviously, a comprehensive information service about foreign markets is the main aim of such official organizations, some examples of which are given in Table 1.1.

Table 1.1

Australia: Australian Trade Commission, GPO Box 2386, Canberra ACT 2601. Tel: (61–6) 276 51 11.
Canada: Info-Export Center BPTE, Lester Building, 125 Promenade Sussex, Ottawa, Ontario K1A 0G2. Tel: (1) 613 993 64 35.
Hong Kong: H-K Trade Department, Trade Department Tower, 700 Nathan Road, Kowloon. Tel: (852) 398 53 33.
New Zealand: Trade Development Board, PO Box 10–341, Wellington. Tel: (64–4) 499 22 44.
Singapore: Trade Development Board, 1 Maritime Square, 10–40 World Trade Center, Singapore 0409. Tel: (65) 271 93 88.
United States of America: International Trade Administration, Washington DC 20230. Tel: (1) 800 343 4300.
United Kingdom: Department of Trade and Industry's EMIC (Export Market Information Center), Ashdown House, 123 Victoria Street, London SW1E 6RB. Tel: (071) 215 5444.

Services provided by several other organizations and private companies complement those already mentioned. Different systems should cover any export requirements, whether general or specific, standard or urgent. Three examples serve to demonstrate the variety available.

■ **World Trade Centers**: there are 243 WTCs located in most main trading cities worldwide.

'A world trade center in any city is a business shopping center, complementing and supporting the existing services of private and government agencies,' explains World Trade Centers Association President Guy F. Tozzoli.

Most WTCs provide a full range of information services, including computerized communications, extensive database and library facilities covering world markets, trade opportunities, government regulations, tariffs, and other business topics. Trade research services are also available.

Contact: The **World Trade Centers Association, Inc.**
One World Trade Center, Suite 7701
New York, NY 10048, USA
Tel: (1) 212 313 4600

■ The **Economist Intelligence Unit**, a division of the British Press Group, publishes an annual report on the overall economic situation of 165 countries as well as more in-depth quarterly reports. (Contact in London: Tel: (44) 071 493 6711.)

■ **SVP International**, a telephone information system with 50 years' experience. 500 consultants and researchers in 16 countries on five continents answer 8000 business questions every working day for over 100,000 SVP cardholders. (Telephone contact in Paris (33) 1 47 87 11 11; in London (44) 71 837 66 66; in New York (1) 212 645 45 00; in Sydney (61) 2 282 30 52; in Tokyo (81) 33 294 28 71; in Toronto (1) 416 362 52 11.)

1.1.1.3   Qualitative/quantitative demand evolution

There are few industries for which such information can be collected from the sources cited above (except 'tailor made' surveys), because needs are too specific and information has to be updated too frequently. However, many companies still decide to expand in foreign markets without first trying to estimate the local potential product demand. Their investment is thus almost sure to be wasted.

▶   *A European pesticides manufacturer wore themselves out after several years in the United States because of an inaccurate preconceived idea – that their products would surely be in great demand from the world's largest agricultural producer. Unfortunately, agriculture is extensive in the US, which results in a low production cost per acre. The company's relatively expensive products are well adapted to Europe where farmers invest to obtain a high per acre yield, but they have little future in the US.*

▶   *Similarly, a French pharmaceutical laboratory wasted two expensive years in Germany and the US trying to develop sales of a treatment for liver ailments. A more detailed market study finally revealed that only the wine-loving French people suffer from liver ailments on a large scale.*

Therefore, it is important to study the demand for the product in the field itself (that is actually where product competition begins – see the introduction to Chapter 4) by updating information from available sources: the local representative should be trained to do this essential task; and distributors where information is received by talking mostly to people in direct contact with the end-users. Listening to a product's (potential) users can also be useful if put into perspective and the information is reliable (it is easier to track the evolution of demand in capital goods by directly contacting potential users than the evolution of consumer goods, whose users number in the millions).

For this field study, the executives operating in a given country should be systematically assisted by R & D and Production specialists. In addition to profiting from their technical expertise, this reinforces the mobilization of all the company's departments for international development, as well as strengthening the team spirit (see section 5.1.2.3). This is what appears in the testimony of Pierre Rigoux:

▶ '*Sfernice* [*now part of the Vishay Intertechnology group*] *manufacture passive electronic components, essentially for professional, civil or military applications but also for the electronics industry. Our international development strategy is based on direct exportations, manufacturing subsidiaries in foreign countries, transfers of technology or joint ventures.*

One of our constant concerns is to make sure our products have an inherent competitive edge from the moment of their definition and conception. Thus, we make sure that our R & D people are in permanent contact with the field.

As a result, all aspects of the search for information is a team effort shared by the Research and Sales people: surveillance of competitors' products; evolution of standards and specifications; techniques of production, machines, procedures and materials; new applications likely to ensure openings for our existing products or for products to be developed ...

The search for information is carried out in three main directions:

■ *First, technological watch of specialized trade magazines, mostly American and Japanese. For example, in 1985, the announcement of a new type of amplifier enabled us to develop a specially adapted resistor.*

■ *Then, a systematic observation of professional exhibitions and trade shows. Ten to fifteen research specialists and engineers visit the major trade shows of our industry, such as Electronica in Munich or Le Salon des Composants Electroniques in Paris. These missions are carefully prepared in advance. Each person in his field has an exact task to accomplish and has to present a report on his return. All the information collected, put together and analysed, gives a pretty good picture of the state-of-the-art.*

■ *Finally, there is a permanent dialogue with our main clients and the official organizations responsible for standardization, specifications and type authorizations to keep up to date on future prescriptions and even to participate in their elaboration. The Centre National d'Etudes Spatiales, l'Agence Spatiale Européenne, the National Aeronautics and Space Administration are examples. The French representative on the board of the Electrotechnical International Commission for resistive products is one of our company Directors.*

It's the totality of these acts of surveillance and technological observations, of field surveys and technical partnerships, which enables us to keep our position as innovator and to fine-tune the world's most advanced products, targeting future technical needs. In electronics, as in other industries, new products can't be competitive unless they respond to real needs.'

As a matter of prudence, information collected in the field should be compared and cross-checked before modifying the market development strategy. Also, information available from economic services connected to our embassies, Chambers of Commerce established in foreign countries, as well as the local representative's advertising agency, should not be neglected. A visit to specialized trade organizations can also help to verify an analysis of demand evolution in the country where we have just spent a brief time. It is common, particularly for consumer products, to find that information on demand evolution is too fragmentary to base an important decision concerning product strategy or advertising communication. This information needs to be completed by a carefully prepared market study carried out by a specialized agency. It is advisable to check on the competence of such agencies as well as their independence in relation to the local representative and *his* advertising agency (you can't run with the hare and hunt with the hounds!)

▶ *Export managers who have to constantly gather, classify, cross-check and interpret information have good reason to envy the sophisticated methods used by aircraft manufacturers to follow the needs evolution of airline companies. (But this jealousy disappears when you think of the limited number of aircraft ordered each year and the savage competition among the major manufacturers.)* **Airbus Industrie**, *for example, keep a permanently updated, very detailed computer database on the evolving profile of every airline company's fleet: type, performance, capacity and age of each plane; routes exploited; composition and characteristics of the clientele and freight carried, etc. These profiles, plus information collected by their salespeople from the airline companies concerning their needs, enable* **Airbus Industrie** *to prioritize solutions exactly adapted to their future development.*

It should be stressed, however, that the evaluation of a low potential demand for its products should not necessarily lead a company to disregard certain countries whose future evolution could lead to spectacular changes.

▶ **Club Med** *decided to move into the Japanese market as early as 1974, when holidays were still largely unknown to the Japanese. In consideration to his company, a faithful Japanese employee still refuses to take the two weeks' holidays to which he has a right, and contents himself with a few long weekends, generally spent visiting family. As a result, the majority of those interested in holidays are newly-weds on honeymoon, or young 'office ladies' still living with their parents, who use part of their salary to complete their cultural education by travelling abroad before getting married.*
After a few years, by the mid-1980s, **Club Med** *managed to have more than 25,000 Japanese members per year, and continues to grow 30% a year – quite impressive when you know that the 'products' had not yet been*

adapted to the brevity of Japanese vacations (an average of 6 days), with the closest vacation villages to Japan, in Thailand, Malaysia, New Caledonia, Tahiti and Bali, representing a 20 to 30-hour return journey!

This shows the Tchichukai Club's potential in Japan (this Japanese name corresponds to the translation of Mediterranean, literally, the sea surrounded by land), where they are now opening vacation villages (Sahoro, for instance, on the island of Hokkaïdo, a ski resort which in summer becomes a centre for golf, tennis, onsen – very hot baths – and nature walks) to get closer to their clientele and offer shorter vacation opportunities such as weekend packages.

*Thanks to this long-term development policy, **Club Med** has forged for themselves the image of being a forerunner and will be in a good position when Japan really wakes up to vacations!*

*An original idea, expressed in 1980 by **Club Med's** President Gilbert Trigano, was to reduce – in part – the 'Made in Japan' domination over the rest of the world. 'The Japanese government should encourage all Japanese employees to really take their two weeks of holidays. Thus, Japan would resemble more the industrialized countries which are both competitors and partners. And the Japanese themselves would discover the benefits of holidays which are considered generally as one of the great innovations of the 20th century . . .' Japan seems to be moving in this direction, as indicated by a law passed in 1987 to encourage people to indulge in leisure activities.*

In the same way, huge market potential may justify an interest even when a country's political situation is blocking its development.

▶ *'**Roussel Uclaf** didn't wait for the December 1991 Federation of Russia's independence, to consider how to enter this market' says Dominique Gian-carli, Director for Eastern Europe. 'Since the early 1980s, we have been contemplating a technology transfer with the official authorities that were successively in charge, during this 10-year period. With the welfare priorities that came into force in 1989, this slow process was fortunately accelerated. Then, the experience and contacts patiently established over the years paid off, and we were able to settle a joint venture in 1991 for the construction of a pharmaceutical plant near Moscow.' (For the continuation of this case, see section 4.5.1.1 in the Delocalized Production chapter.)*

Obviously, such a long-term strategy can only apply to large groups that have the financial capacity to disregard somewhat the importance and rapidity of a country's potential return on investment (see section 1.2.1.3).

1.1.1.4   Distribution network

This is another essential barometer which makes possible the assessment of a market's development potential, as it is rare to be able to 'push' for sales expansion (especially for consumer products) without a relatively structured and dynamic distribution network. The means of studying this network's evolution are similar to those previously described for demand evolution. However, every opportunity offered by the evolution of a distribution network must be exploited as soon as possible to improve the chances of success.

▶ *For a long time, **Facom** (specialists in hand tools, and the leading European manufacturer) maintained limited business connections in Finland because of the inherent market difficulties, where the channels of distribution were strict and static. But as soon as a group of distributors started setting up a national network, market development in Finland became a priority for **Facom**. The rapidity of their reaction time enabled them to sign a preferential agreement with this group, and consequently to gain control of almost 20% of the market.*

We remain in Scandinavia to emphasize, with a less fortunate example, the importance of the nature and the suitability of the distribution network among the success factors.

▶ *In Sweden the sale of beauty products is prohibited in pharmacies. As a result, **RoC** cannot use (as they do everywhere else in the world) this type of sales outlet which is perfectly adapted to advising clients on the use of low allergenic products. This explains why the sales results of **RoC** products are much lower than expected for a country like Sweden, where women generally are particularly concerned with skin care.*

1.1.1.5   Competitors' positions

This is an area in which information is even more difficult to collect and verify. Nevertheless, it is essential to know what operations the competition has carried out, is implementing or is preparing, so that the chances of success can be realistically estimated and the appropriate strategy decided upon: either investing more with appropriate dynamic devices, or playing a more defensive game to maintain the existing position while waiting for more favourable circumstances in which to counter-attack. This frees resources for other markets where an investment is more likely to bear fruit.

More generally, the areas in which competitors prefer to compete should be defined and analysed (e.g. distributors' markup, price, product quality and other advantages, after-sales service, etc.) so that the ability to reciprocate in kind can be estimated.

The search for information on the competition (general characteristics, products, results, growth distribution, development methods, etc.) relies on both a sense of observation and deduction, and can be facilitated by the contacts cultivated in and around the profession during trips, conventions, seminars, etc.

This is a permanent task for local representatives, but vigilance should be maintained in any case: it is worth maintaining direct sources of information because the local representative may have

as a springboard for following up development in other geographical areas.

▶ *The strategy favoured by Henri Micmacher,[1] founder of* **Pronuptia** *(world leader in wedding dresses) is particularly explicit concerning this point of view. 'We try to develop sales abroad by a system of concentric circles. In my opinion, you can only get established in a vast country by successive, carefully located regional development . . . We choose a region in a country and we cover this region as well as possible before tackling another. Such is our development strategy abroad: concentration first, expansion afterwards.'*

This strategy can also be successfully applied on a smaller scale:

▶ *After their success in the West Indies (see sections 1.1.1.5 and 1.2.1.3), the* **C. Marion Co.** *decided to introduce their products to Spain. Instead of attacking the country as a whole, or even selecting the capital or one of the big provinces, however, the company decided to follow a progressive strategy by starting with Spain's islands, the Canaries and the Balearics. The advantages:*

- *each island being a small market makes the distribution easier to handle for an SME without a large investment.*
- *the importance of Anglo-Saxon and Scandinavian tourism in these islands made them major importers of smoked pork (bacon).*
- **Marion's** *success in these islands gave them a credibility for the continuation of their export development in Spain, then in the UK, Scandinavia and Germany.*
- *finally, after adapting themselves to dealing with the needs and commercial follow-up of small Spanish wholesalers in the Canary and Balearic Islands, all* **Marion's** *staff were ready to work with a large Madrid broker.*

However, another anecdote illustrates the study of market development potential. It should be noted that there are cases where instinct, determination and the luck of being in the right place at the right time can bring about success which had not been foreseen by even the most sophisticated analysis.

▶ *How else can the beginnings of* **Perrier's** *American adventure be explained?*
Until the early 1970s, the presence of the pear-shaped green bottles was minimal. The President of the **Perrier Group**, *Gustave Leven, wanted to expand this market, which he felt had a solid development potential, and a study was carried out to verify his intuition. The answer was devastating: no future for* **Perrier** *in the States! Gustave Leven persisted and had two other studies done . . . with the same results.*
It is fortunate for the **Perrier Group** *that its President had the courage, despite negative studies, to concentrate on the American market with a 10 million franc investment for the first year, in 1977!*

Finally, to conclude on market assessment, the opportunities offered by different forms of 'piggy back' should not be overlooked. This enables companies that do not have sufficient means to do business directly in countries with attractive development potential to entrust the sale of their products to an already established company, whether it operates in a complementary field of activity or belongs to an international trading company.

▶ *Rhône-Poulenc, one of the world's largest chemical, agrochemical, biotechnological and pharmaceutical groups, make 77% of their turnover outside France in 140 countries, and have developed numerous export partnerships in the past ten years. As explained by Benedicte Mautin, in charge of these partnerships: 'We opened our 60-country Overseas Multidivisional Companies network to other exporting companies. This activity covers mostly products with direct complementarity to those manufactured by* **Rhône-Poulenc** *and today, it generates an export turnover of about $400 million with about 200 partner companies, 50% of which are French. This operation offers a triple interest:*

- *that of the local clientele wishing to deal with the same company for a complete line of products;*
- *that of industrial companies wishing to export, which are confronted by the choice of a trustworthy agent in faraway or difficult countries;*
- *that of our Overseas Multidivisional Companies which can test the quality of their services on principals outside the* **Rhône-Poulenc** *group, assure the development of these services and thus reduce their costs.'*

1.1.2   Product development potential

As it is necessary to define an international market development strategy to concentrate efforts on priority markets, there should also be a product development strategy to select the most interesting products to promote internationally.

In this process, however, most companies find themselves confronted with two apparently unreconcilable requirements:

- Success in exporting often means adapting products to various demands, according to the needs and special tastes of different markets, and to the various constraints imposed by local standards and regulations.
- On the contrary, healthy management theory tends to limit the number of references in a product range to a minimum. Obviously, an increase in the production of a limited number of products lowers the cost price, thus increasing profitability and/or allowing more investment for sales development.

It is within the framework of a product development strategy, where the national and international potentials for each product are studied, that the above-mentioned requirements for the best of global interests can be reconciled.

1.1.2.1 Products to 'freeze'

Periodically in the race for development, obsolete or declining products should be deleted from the range. This classic 'catalog cleanup' rarely takes place without some sobbing and gnashing of teeth at best, or much shouting and pitched battles at worst.

In fact, the normal life-cycle of a product – launching, growth, maturity, stagnation, decline – does not take place everywhere at the same speed. Multiple factors will have influenced the development of the same product in a different way in separate markets: for example, the degree of adaptability to regulations and to demand, the quality of the local representative's performance, the dynamism of the distribution, the aggressivity of the competition, etc.

When it becomes necessary to abandon the manufacture of products which are internationally obsolete, it is frequent to run into fierce opposition from local representatives and distributors in those few markets where these products are still successful. Sometimes the share these products take in their overall turnover is such that it would be fatal to cease their supply from the country of origin.

When possible, in such cases, a special stock could be constituted to supply the markets concerned until a satisfactory replacement product is ready to take over.

When putting products aside*, a flexible attitude must be taken to maintain the force of the international product development strategy without creating difficulties for any priority markets. This flexibility should correspond to the importance of the market.

After mentioning voluntary catalog cleanup above, which should be decided and carried out after a cold-hearted analysis, it is interesting to mention a case (fortunately very rare) where a company's entire production had to be overhauled in the heat of action.

▶ *Whereas Jaz** found themselves the leader in electromagnetic movements of watches and alarm clocks, the technological revolution brought about by quartz movements (1977–78) completely upset the world's watchmaking market. Almost overnight, Jaz sales fell (in the US sales of Jaz alarm clocks went from 300,000 to 0 units in one year), and their entire product policy had to be recreated on a totally new basis. (For the continuation of this case, see section 1.1.2.3.)*

---

*As for markets (see section 1.1.1.1) the expression 'put aside' is better than that of 'eliminating/ suppressing', for sometimes old products become popular again after having been abandoned for a time.
**Brand C. G. H. (Compagnie Générale Horlogère).

1.1.2.2   Availability

When it is a matter of selecting, from among the products not put aside, those which will benefit from the maximum of support and whose sales should progress spectacularly, the most elementary step is to make sure of their availability:

■   *Supplies of raw materials, components, and subcontracted parts must be secured. It would also be wise to diversify supply sources.*

▶   *In this way, **Suze** (a bitter French aperitif made from the roots of the gentian plant) had a shortage problem which risked hindering the company's development. They decided quickly to set up a program to grow this plant, native of Auvergne in the centre of France, . . . in Normandy (much to the astonishment of local farmers) so as to be in control of supply.*

▶   *Since **McDonald's**[2] want to offer their original product all over the world, it is sometimes difficult for them to find raw materials of adequate quality in the different countries/regions. In particular, potatoes grown in many countries are too small or mealy and it is hard to imagine **McDonald's** serving tiny and pasty fries . . . Importing the 'Russet Burbank' potato from the USA was too expensive and even forbidden by certain governments worried about protecting their agricultural production. Consequently, **McDonald's** have their favourite variety of Idaho potato grown in 18 countries.*

▶   *A supply problem can also appear because of economic conditions: for example, growers might decide to abandon certain fragrant varieties of fruit to devote themselves to other, more lucrative varieties. This brought the **Lenôtre** company to negotiate contracts with growers, assuring them of a sufficiently profitable selling price for their strawberries, raspberries and blackcurrants, etc. so as to guarantee the highly flavoured quality of their pastries, ice creams and sorbets.*

■   All the same, flexibility of production and capacity for its development have to be organized in such a way as to anticipate the increase in demand.
■   In the field of services, engineering, etc., there must be staff available with the necessary qualifications, or at least the possibility of recruiting and training them.

▶   ***Hewlett Packard***[3] *(for which the grey matter of the employees is the principal product source) explain that their European success was based largely on the availability of hundreds of engineers after the Second World War.*

1.1.2.3   Adaptation to international demand

Products whose universal acceptance has been proven by quantitative and qualitative results in all markets (export and domestic) should be favoured. First to be highlighted should be those products where the standard model will be universally acceptable, or almost everywhere. Those products which necessitate modification to satisfy regulations and demand should be chosen next. The importance of the cost and the difficulties in modifying the products must obviously be taken into account for the final ranking.

▶   *In the case of **Jaz** (see section 1.1.2.1) it was not simply a matter of adapting the product, but of making a dramatic entry into the new quartz technology, without preparation and at top speed, since most of the international demand was directed towards this new type of movement. To become involved in this new technology, **Jaz** invested heavily in research and development, and tried to get closer to the level of production costs available from Asia by robotizing their factories. (For continuation of this case, see section 1.1.2.4.)*

1.1.2.4   Competitiveness

Several products can seem to respond equally well to international demand, but they may have different development potentials because of a number of factors that can be called 'competitiveness': the 'plus' factors which enable them to be favourably distinguished from their rivals (innovation, performance, quality, price, originality, esthetics, after-sales service, etc.).

Certain companies manage to combine one or more of these competitiveness factors on two levels: on that of the totality of their activities/production/services, which facilitates their positioning and reinforces the coherence of their image; and on that of a few products, whose particularly efficient characteristics strengthen the competitiveness of the brand as a whole.

▶   *The originality of **RoC** in relation to almost all the other cosmetics brands is to have perfected non-allergenic products. This is possible by the elaboration of formulae having a restricted number of components (thus limiting the possibilities of an allergic reaction), selected after elaborate and rigorous clinical tests. All the **RoC** product lines thus benefit from a favourable competitive position, especially since people worldwide have become aware of the growing importance of allergy problems. In addition to this general advantage, certain **RoC** products enjoy an originality over their rivals, easily understood by their clientele in Tokyo as well as in Montreal: the shaving creams of their men's line Keops, for example, are the only ones which contain neither soap nor perfume – which gives an exclusive and forceful sales argument.*

Another basic factor, of course, is the price, whose competitiveness is a requirement for success in most sectors, except for those few where the scarcity or performance of a product, or other factors of this type, lessen its importance by overthrowing the normal price/quality ratio.

Product competitiveness*, which is based on originality, price, performance, etc., or better still, on all these factors at the same time, is indispensable to international expansion, and must be considered as early as this stage in the study of product potentials. It is the competitiveness of 'locomotive products' which will successfully move forward overall development.

▶   *The originality of Keops shaving creams brings an 'extra' to the other products in this line for men, and **RoC** naturally invest more in these shaving creams with various dynamic devices.*

▶   *If you're not in on the competition, you're out of the running. It is in this desperate situation that we find **Jaz**, despite their efforts to adapt to international demand for quartz movements (see section 1.1.2.3). This total reconversion of know-how and the retooling of the factories had been too sudden: it directly penalized the competitiveness of their first quartz products. They were not as efficient, and were 30% more expensive than the competition. For **Jaz**, the problem was reduced to a simple alternative: disappear, or find a miracle solution (for a continuation of this case, see section 1.2.2.1).*

1.1.2.5   Export profitability

Last but not least ... it is better to invest in the development of the most profitable products, among those we have already selected, without forgetting that the changes necessary to respond to export restrictions often noticeably affect product profitability in relation to the domestic market.

▶   *With the desire to make their export activity as profitable as possible (and of course, to have their production lines operating at a maximum), **Profilafroid**, who specialise in shaping steel for construction and metallurgical industries, give priority to their development efforts for finished products (crash barriers along roadsides, for example) rather than for semi-finished products with lower added value.*

1.1.2.6   Product assessment

After each product has been studied according to the criteria of availability, adaptability to demand, competitiveness and profitability, the assessment of their general development potential will also

---

*All the factors of competitiveness are reviewed as Dynamic Devices (see Chapter 4).

include the foreseeable life expectancy (many fashion-oriented products or those threatened by technical progress are in this respect in opposition to products whose lifetime is traditionally longer), and various other risks: new regulations banning or hindering product development, launching of more competitive rival products, etc.

Each assessment ranks products into a 'hit parade', according to which they will be divided into:

A: **Strategic products**: these are the locomotives of expansion, as they respond to the greatest demand segments in international markets and logically receive the priority support of dynamic devices.

B: **Tactical products**: these bring an additional dynamism to expansion. In general, they correspond to narrower market segments, and are only moderately supported with dynamic devices.

C: **Accessory products**: these are the 'wagons' of the 'expansion train', making up a complementary range of products in response to specific market needs. They receive very little or no dynamic device support.

1.2   Ranking of Intervention Priorities

A strategic organization process followed by the company **Kleber Industrie**, at the stage of ranking their priorities of intervention, is given below, and explained by Patrick Bassi, International Commercial Director.

▶ *'For a company like **Kleber Industrie**, which has a diversity of products (driving belts, pipes, transportation belts, cisterns, airplane de-icers, rubber parts, etc.) covering numerous different industries (automobile, agriculture, chemicals, mining, steel, aeronautics, military material, petroleum, etc . . .) the risk of dispersing our efforts inefficiently is high. It's even higher for exporting where the number of countries multiplies the temptation to indulge in scattered actions.*

For each country that we have enough data on, we have proceeded by the "strengths – attractions" approach for our major lines of products. Among the criteria for the strengths are:

- *competitive position of **Kleber Industrie***
- *the company's technical position*
- *commercial adjustment (local and international)*
- *image and/or recognition*
- *degree of industry knowledge (global and specialized)*

The criteria for the attractions are:

- *size of the segment*
- *growth rate*
- *competitive intensity*

■ *profitability*
■ *political and financial risks*
■ *local economic situation*

This allows us to make a strategic diagnosis for each country analysed. The totality of these country/product assessments is then passed in review within the framework of the company's development policy and according to our investment capacities, in order to group the countries together by types of action to be undertaken.

■ *countries where our products have to be consolidated*
■ *countries where our present turnover has to be developed*
■ *countries for prospection*
■ *countries for occasional visits*
■ *countries not to be visited*

For each country and each product division, we have thus been able to formalize a strategy which assures a better efficiency for our actions.'

By looking back over the method followed so far, we will study in parallel the market and product rankings that have already been divided into three groups: priority markets, priority markets on a waiting list, and secondary markets; strategic products, tactical products and accessory products.

At this stage, this parallel study remains relatively theoretical as it originates from two individual surveys carried out on markets and products. As we have just seen in the **Kleber Industrie** example, several parameters now have to be integrated (company policy and investment capacity, among others) which will facilitate the choice of those objectives best suited to ensure international expansion.

1.2.1   Practical parameters

1.2.1.1   Unjustified underdevelopment

Underdevelopment examples are common in exporting, most often explained by historic or economic causes, but appearing unjustified in relation to the potential of a market or a product. For instance, results could have been hindered by the bad choice of local agent, or they could have been subject to a quota system which has since been abolished, or the sales of a priority product could have been disappointing because of an erroneous product positioning in a given local market.

▶ *As for **Cointreau** in the USA, a few years ago priority was at first given to the development of European positions. Then, although some development potential still remained for **Cointreau** in Europe, the company decided to concentrate a large part of their efforts on the USA. Every year **Cointreau** was selling 1.4 million cases annually in Europe for 210 million inhabitants.*

The strategic conclusions are these. First, form as clear a view as you can of the overseas markets you believe your business should be in to maintain its growth into the future. Second, get your foot in the door of those markets and be prepared to take some risks in doing so. Third, keep in mind that your choice of a local ally is more critical than the precise terms of the alliance.

Finally, it is important to establish your overseas network as fast as you prudently can, because in spite of trade barriers and protectionist politicians the world is rapidly becoming one market place and you may be sure that your international competitors are already taking advantage of the opportunities which this development presents.

Mobilizing the adapted development means *(Preparation Phase)*

We have just finished the 'Study Phase' of this method of development which must be carried out by export executives. This study leads to a definition of the main objectives of development policy by taking into account the choice of intervention priorities. Consequently, it would be impractical to have the local representatives participate directly. With the exception of the managers of foreign subsidiaries and a few agents, the interests of the local representatives would often conflict with company interests, which involve planetary scale medium- and long-term objectives.

However, the development of an export market depends almost exclusively on the active participation of the local representative. Given that understandable pride makes it difficult to accept lessons in business development from a foreigner in one's own country and specialty, imposing ready-to-use plans on local representatives should be considered taboo if rejection, or worse sabotage, is to be avoided.

A more constructive attitude on the part of the export executive would be to work in collaboration with the local representative, going over those points in the Study Phase which might interest him, and thus getting him to adhere to the priorities and objectives that directly concern him and his market.

This is the point we have reached so far.

The local representative, then, must be totally involved in the next phase, that of preparing the development plan, before taking charge of the Action Phase, with the company's close or more distant assistance.

This method is sometimes difficult to put into practice within unstructured markets. However, everything should be done to follow this procedure, for even the most judicious recommendations made to an uninvolved or unmotivated local representative will vanish as soon as the export executive's aircraft has taken off.

This applies to any exporting company, whether it is represented locally by the Agent-Importer-Distributor type of structure or by its own subsidiary.

▶ *In the framework of their international sales development, **Air France** have perfected a consultative planning procedure which could be adapted and applied, at least partially, to most SMEs (small and medium sized enterprises):*

*Every year the sales managers of all **Air France** branches in the world work on the preparation of a development plan for their market.*

All of these plans, with the information and suggestions contained therein, are studied by the Head Office for the elaboration of the **Air France** world sales development policy.*

The real needs of each market are thus better satisfied. This is verifiable when the sales managers receive the general development policy plan and the instructions concerning their particular market. These instructions explain the retained orientations and the possible differences with the initial local development plan which had been proposed. Thus, general policy is better understood and adhered to locally.

Now let us see how to prepare the sales development of priority export markets in a concrete manner.

First, the dynamic devices which could make up the development plan should be 'pre-selected' (see section 2.1). In the elaboration of this plan (see section 2.2), among those dynamic devices retained in the pre-selection should be those which, when mixed together, will enable the company to reach its sales objectives in the most efficient and profitable way.

This plan will then be readjusted in the light of its practical organization (see section 2.3) and timetable (see section 2.4), so as to obtain a maximum of success factors and to master most of the hindrances which usually lead to a failure in international development.

The final part of the Preparation Phase is the budget (see section 2.5) which should be sufficiently flexible in its use and imaginative in its financing to ensure the success of the development plan.

2.1	**Search for Development Plan Components**

The first step is to gather all those elements which could help to develop sales in a market, according to selected objectives.

The most efficient method for building up this arsenal of elements for a first selection, without neglecting any, is to review quickly the set of dynamic devices displayed later in this book (see Chapters 4, 5 and 6).

This detailed review should trigger a guided creative exercise to

---

*The suggestion of the local **Air France** branches were very specific in defining the characteristics of the 'Air France Le Club' class for their business travellers.

2.1.2.1   Adaptation to objectives and constraints

The first criteria for the pre-selection of dynamic devices is obviously their adaptation to the realization of objectives. This is why it is so important to have sufficiently detailed objectives. The 'selected' dynamic devices must pass through a filter of different sorts of constraints, the export company's first, then those of the local representative: mainly investment capacity, the availability of people and competences, etc. Then follow the constraints of the target market itself: general characteristics, regulations in force, local habits and social taboos that are dangerous to transgress, established rules in the industry, structure and organization of distribution, special manufacturing processes, etc.

▶ *Let us get back to **Cointreau** in Venezuela at the moment of the dynamic device pre-selection. The legal restrictions of the country do not allow advertisements to show someone drinking alcohol or to suggest that drinking can be pleasant. The name 'Cointreau on the Rocks' cannot even be pronounced. Only a glass of **Cointreau** with ice cubes can be shown ...*

  *Because of these constraints, the pre-selection of dynamic devices concentrated on promotional activities and public relations. The final selection included: in sales outlets, posters of **Cointreau** on the Rocks were put up; ice buckets in the form of a **Cointreau** bottle were sold; free tastings of **Cointreau** on the Rocks were offered in bars, restaurants and night clubs.*

▶ *Among the dynamic devices chosen by **Air France** to encourage more Japanese businessmen to use their flights between Japan and Europe before going on to Africa, their final destination, was a welcome desk especially set up for them. These passengers often suffered from organizational problems, mostly because of language difficulties. Setting up a 'Japanese Business Desk' in the **Air France** agency on the Champs Elysées in Paris, France consequently seemed a good way in which to attract this specific clientele. Japanese businessmen could get help from Japanese-speaking personnel to take care of any sort of problem – reservations, communications with their African business partners, etc. This idea was implemented and exploited as a sales argument in Japan for the targeted clientele, and the adaptation of this Welcome Desk to the desired objective resulted in a significant sales increase.*

2.1.2.2   Coherence of the whole

The coherence of the dynamic devices with the nature of the product, its distribution and the target clientele, is a success factor for any development plan. There are few exceptions to this rule which can be justified by a calculated will to surprise or even to shock, or by a dominant position in the market which allows imposition of the leader's rules.

Thus, it is with great concern for coherence that hindrances should be hunted down, by studying the market position and the results of former development actions, and dynamic devices pre-selected to be used in future actions.

For example, it would be obviously incoherent and thus dangerous for a mineral water, whose communication campaign emphasizes its natural origin and purity, to sponsor a Formula 1 team. For a large proportion of their clientele, racing cars present an image of noise and air pollution which would have a negative effect on the image of such a product.

On the other hand, setting up a Press Relations service for the main foreign markets is a solid coherence factor. In this way, articles could appear which would lend credence to the advertising messages and the arguments of the local sales force (see section 6.4.3).

▶   *The international success of Zodiac*, inventor and world leader in inflatable boats, provides a valid example of this factor. From the crossing of the Atlantic in 1952 by Alain Bombard to the expeditions of Commandant Cousteau, world press and TV coverage have often witnessed the perform-ances of these boats. There is no doubt that these demonstrations of robust-ness and reliability stimulated both the efforts of Zodiac dealers and the interest of potential Zodiac buyers.*

2.1.2.3   'Innovation' as added value

If it is recommended to carefully study those dynamic devices gener-ally used in a market, and more specifically those developed by competitors, this does not mean that they should be imitated in every case. Despite an apparent aspect of reassurance, the 'me too' strategy offers a feeble guarantee of success, especially if too light an invest-ment capability only allows the use of minimum means compared to those of the competitors. This observation applies more to push and pull dynamic devices than to product dynamic devices, where follow-ing rival technical innovation is sometimes unavoidable. In this case, an effort should nevertheless be made to add something specific to the product to distinguish it from its model.

Numerous small budgets in export development are wasted in unproductive 'me too' copying, which outsiders hoped will help increase their sales by following in the footsteps of the market leaders. This waste is even more regrettable given the fact that these same budgets, invested in innovative dynamic devices or in classic dynamic devices used in an innovative manner, would probably generate spec-tacular results.

Thus it is not only a pre-selection of dynamic devices adapted to

---

*This group is especially known by the public for their inflatable boats. However, they are extremely diversified in their products and are among the world leaders for products which demand state-of-the-art technology for supple, composite materials (parachutes, blimps, stratospheric balloons, rubber swimming pools, end of runway barriers for aircraft, etc.).

one's own objectives and situation that has to be mixed. A good dose of innovation has to be added to this cocktail of dynamic devices, which can take many forms as long as it has a positive effect on the target clientele, as well as on the networks and relays that can reach or influence them in our favour.

Here are two cases where the effects of innovation were felt at complementary levels. In the first case, innovation reinforced the competitiveness of the product by assuring a more favourable cost effectiveness. In the second case, innovation provided a better communications support, better adapted to the needs of users by making a more effective product presentation.

► *It is not by chance that a company becomes the top European pen manufacturer, second in the world. One of the reasons for **Waterman's** success can surely be found in the constant research for technical and aesthetic innovation. These efforts, such as the setting up of lacquer workshops on an industrial scale, generated undeniable successes, which let **Waterman** win points on the international market by offering superb quality lacquer pens at extremely competitive prices (see section 4.3.3.3).*

*But this result required tenacity, as remembered by **Waterman** staff: 'using lacquer is a particularly delicate operation. One of the technical problems that had to be resolved was creating a dust-free environment, as the smallest fleck of dust creates a blister, and we had to limit the number of flawed products to a minimum. This led us to imagine solutions never before applied to our industry. Our workshops looked like hospital operating rooms, the personnel like astronauts . . . and it worked out fine!!'*

► ***Facom*** *was the first tool company to invest in a complete catalog to sell their products (more than one million copies printed in seven languages!). This tool Bible – both luxurious and informative (color photographs of the tools with specific indications on their use and even general advice on safety precautions), as well as extremely well made (reinforced binding to stand up to constant handling) – is distributed to foremen and workshop managers, and is a continual temptation for them to buy. As soon as they open it and leaf through it looking for a specific tool, they realize they need additional tools as well, usually provided to them by competitors, and order everything from **Facom**.*

All innovation runs risks, and very few companies take the chance of innovating simultaneously on several fronts; on the contrary, prudence induces managers to render their international strategy more secure by diluting innovative actions with strong doses of classic and well-tried dynamic devices.

► *Then it is stimulating to listen to Alain Dominique Perrin analyse the **Cartier** adventure and to measure the prodigious leap taken in a few years by this venerable centenarian. While observing the multitude of innovations launched by **Cartier** less than 20 years ago, many thought 'they would make or break' **Cartier**. Here is what Alain Dominique Perrin has to say: 'In this world of constant mutation, if the riposte is movement, then for*

Cartier there also had to be a revolution! Starting with the 1970s, both the company and the epoch were put into question. The chains of commercial conservatism of an industry had to be broken. In the jewellery and watch-making industries these chains aren't made of gold but of tempered steel! It was by escaping from the velvet-lined walls of *Cartier's* Parisian temple that an irreversible process of revolution was set in motion.

■ to pass from the state of a sleepy, prestigious retailer to that of an enterprise on the move;
■ to pass from the state of a historic institution, royal jeweller of the 19th century to that of a young, contemporary, international company;
■ to create products for the whole world and not just for Paris, London or New York;
■ to create products for tomorrow, to impose youth on an aging company and clientele.

Concretely, there had to be innovation without destruction of the patrimony – which gave birth to the 'Musts de *Cartier*'. A whole new marketing universe backed up by its own history set out to conquer new markets. Innovation without destruction, rejuvenating people and products. Old Lady *Cartier*, who is now 150 years old, employs 2500 people whose average age is 34. How did we do it? By permanently training and preparing young people. Every year, *Cartier* take on 60 French trainees of whom 80% are sent to foreign subsidiaries, and 20% will be hired at the end of their training programs. A pool of potential employees is thus set up. These young people become international in outlook, learn to take risks, and develop a passion for performance knowing that only the best will definitively be hired. Innovation without destruction also means renewing the products through creation and research. Behind *Cartier* today, an advanced tech-nology and an efficient industrial tool are hidden. Believe me, concerning high tech, we have no reason to envy the Japanese. However, just like them, *Cartier* gives priority to its after-sales service in order to strengthen loyalty in our foreign markets. This is the life insurance of a famous name. All over the world, *Cartier* respect their committments. In a world in constant movement, the difficulty is to keep and reinforce your positions. After the conquest, it's trench warfare.'

2.2   Development Plan Elaboration

After the 'hunt for hindrances' and the wide ranging pre-selection of dynamic devices, this is the critical moment of choice. With the best of these ingredients, the most efficient mix has to be composed within the framework of the development plan, according to the criteria of efficiency and profitability, before testing the feasibility of the whole.

As we are in full flights of fancy, let us get carried away with nightmare visions of what can go wrong. Here are a few 'disaster film' scenarios:

■ *It was a major mistake to rely on a brilliant local representative without noticing that he does not know how to operate effective delegation. He falls seriously ill after the big banquet (indigestion and other complications!) and a few weeks later it becomes obvious that his collaborators have been incapable of efficiently taking his place. Anarchy reigns, from the sales division to the delivery department. When the local representative finally recovers and comes back to work three months later, the situation is critical. A large part of the stock will have to be destroyed, since the products are perishable and cannot be sent to another country due to the special packaging. Not only has the investment in public relations and media advertising been unproductive, but Herculean efforts will be necessary to overcome this flop whose effects have spread far and wide.*

■ *The new packaging has been well prepared to respond to market demand, but the local representative did not pay enough attention to the regulations in force, resulting in the omission of a few legal notices on the labels. Hardly launched on the market, the products have to be recalled. It will take at least two months to rectify the situation – which is comparable to the preceding scenario.*

■ *At the beginning, everything has gone according to plan; more attractive, new packaging; saleswomen strongly supporting the brand (no one had ever thought to invite them anywhere before); efficient advertising support. However, after six months, sales have almost fallen back to their former low level. After investigation, it appears that the saleswomen stay at the job an average of three months. Almost none of those who were initially motivated can still promote the products now. In addition to this, competitors have mounted a violent offensive to recover their lost clientele by a massive advertising counter-attack. Result: heavy local losses for this year, and the next effort to get back into the market will be even more costly.*

■ *A final nightmare scenario! At the moment of kicking off the development plan, the market leader launches a rival product with a vastly superior investment. The advertising campaign is literally swept aside by this deluge, and products sell feebly, despite the efforts of the saleswomen to promote them. Similar results as above . . .*

2.2.2   Profitability criteria

2.2.2.1   Cost/effectiveness ratio

After measuring the efficiency of the pre-selected dynamic devices, the next step is to look into their profitability, particularly their cost/effectiveness ratio. The information and approximations on the investment to be considered for each of the dynamic devices and their expected performance will furnish an objective basis of comparison, whose importance will be essential for making up the development plan mix.

Thus, it can be ascertained, after reviewing the whole set of dynamic devices available (see Chapters 4, 5 and 6), that many can contribute efficiently to the success of the development plan without being particularly costly: in particular, certain product adaptations (characteristics, price, etc.); numerous possibilities that can be applied to the international company team, the local representative and distribution (organization, motivation, communication, assistance, training, etc.); communication operations such as advertising, sales promotion and public relations (especially unconventional actions).

Setting up a subsidiary in a promising market is a dream which all too rarely comes true for many exporting companies. However, it is often a means of development with a spectacular cost/effectiveness ratio when applied to a priority market (see sections 1.1, 1.2 and 1.3).

Still, this requires knowing how to sail around the shoals and reefs which are bound to appear so as to make the investment produce the desired results.

▶   *Let us embark with **Zodiac** to benefit from their business navigation experience. Their international expansion was, indeed, efficiently backed up by distribution subsidiaries in several countries where they already had an existing export sales volume: Great Britain, Holland, Germany, Spain (manufacturing and distribution subsidiaries), Italy, Greece, USA (two subsidiaries), as well as Canada, Australia and Japan. The results obtained by **Zodiac**, thanks to their direct establishment in these markets, are significant and confirm the interest of this formula. In Italy, for example, the country with the toughest local competition (there are more than 20 national manufacturers of inflatable boats!) **Zodiac's** turnover doubled in the first year and almost doubled again during the second.*

*Here are some of the recipes (which can be applied to many other companies) which enabled **Zodiac** to develop successful subsidiaries by maintaining a satisfying cost/effectiveness ratio:*

■   *Have one of the directors from headquarters in charge of looking after each subsidiary. Make sure this person has enough time to devote to this project. He will be, in fact, the 'godfather' of the new subsidiary, from its conception until it comes of age. This, of course, means a lot of time spent in the subsidiary itself.*

■   *At the beginning, start with the smallest possible team (a manager-salesman, a secretary, and a multi-purpose warehouseman who will take care of the stock, receive and dispatch shipments, as well as ensure after-sales service) to limit initial fixed costs to a minimum. As Didier Domange, President of the **Zodiac Group**'s 'Conseil de Surveillance' explains: 'This type of basic structure is usually enough to get started, but we're careful to enlarge it before the need is strongly felt.' In such a small team, the selection and training of the personnel are obviously essential, particularly for the manager (very often a native of the country, familiar with this very industry).*

■   *Avoid getting hopelessly lost in the myriad of legal, accounting and fiscal problems by entrusting them to experts. 'It's saving precious time for the director from headquarters "mothering" the subsidiary as well as for the local manager, who can thus devote themselves completely to totally productive work.'*

■ *Give the subsidiary enough oxygen so it can grow quickly. 'Of course, we make life as easy as possible for our new subsidiaries, especially concerning terms of payment' emphasizes Didier Domange, 'but they regularize their situation fairly quickly and they usually balance their budget from one to two years on an average after starting up. Except in the USA where it took four years, given the size and the complexity of this market.'*

2.2.2.2 Amortization capacities

Priority should be given to dynamic devices whose life expectancy will allow an amortization over a long period of time, as well as those usable or transposable on different markets. Thus, it is possible to divide the start up budget respectively, and considerably reduce the production costs.

▶ *This is why it might be more interesting to invest in the production of a technical training film, usable for several years for many different markets, rather than frequently sending out training staff. This is especially true where there is a high rate of personnel turnover. In these cases, the local representatives can organize training sessions with the film whenever they become necessary, thus reducing costs. The company trainers will only be sent out periodically to check up on procedures and to provide complementary instruction to the local trainers.*

This desire to make the most of development actions should also include the search for better exploitation of existing dynamic devices, even if some habits have to be curbed.

▶ *The prestigious Parisian fur-coat designer and manufacturer **Révillon** annually created a fur collection, at a cost of 5 million francs, and traditionally only presented it in Paris to the specialized press, as well as to French and foreign 'super clients'. A few years ago, to amortize more efficiently this indispensable but costly dynamic device, **Révillon** decided to fly the collection to their priority markets (USA, Middle East, Japan, Europe) to stimulate sales. In 1986, the collection was shown in Japan, Hong Kong, Taïwan and Korea as well as in Italy, West Germany, Benelux, Switzerland, Austria, and even in the USSR and China.*

2.2.2.3 Utilization control

Certain dynamic devices such as samples, gifts, POP material and professional literature sometimes make up the essentials of development plans, while a large part of these investments might remain unproductive because of unscrupulous use or negligence.

In certain countries, it is a well-known fact that the priority destination of samples is the salespeople, their families and friends. Worst yet, sometimes samples are even sold on a few markets, despite the 'not for sale' notices. It would probably be enlightening to know what percentage of samples are really handed out to potential clients in relation to the initial stock.

The situation is comparable for gifts, gadgets and various items used in public relations which are usually given out to everybody *except* the potential customers concerned.

Concerning POP material and professional literature, their lack of specific value protects them from this type of traffic, but this same factor also contributes to their being misused or neglected.

Any conscientious export executive who has gone to the trouble of inspecting his local representative's warehouse, and taking a quick look at the distributor's stocks or the back room of a sales outlet, has managed to recuperate dusty POP material or company brochures before they are damaged or out of date. And this is nothing compared to what is wasted by carelessness or just thrown out because it clutters up the storeroom.

The fact that these materials are furnished free or at cost price, or even sold to local representatives and distributors, does not change anything: a dynamic development plan cannot sustain too much of a deadweight.

This is one hindrance whose negative effects can only be partially suppressed. It is out of the question to eliminate these investments, even if it is probable that half are wasted. However, this necessary evil should be reduced to manageable proportions (see section 6.3.1.3).

Realism and flexibility are necessary here, when putting the finishing touches to the development plan: this type of investment in markets that cannot be easily supervised should be reduced to a bare minimum, supplying only those indispensable networks. In other markets, safe networks and those which can be secured (thanks to training and motivation efforts) should be designated and invested in normally, while networks that escape close supervision should only be frugally supplied. It is obvious that very solid field knowledge of the market is necessary to be able to set up and implement a profitable and efficient development plan which involves a large proportion of such dynamic devices.

More generally, the dynamic devices that can be 'checked up on' should receive priority at the moment of making up the development mix. The efficiency and profitability of the dynamic devices, after use, should also be estimated to improve the preparation and composition of future development mixes (see section 3.3).

importance of a trend that fortunately seems to be developing – the regrouping of exporting companies. This type of association ties means and competences together around a common international strategy.

▶ *Most often it links companies with complementary products which unite forces to speed up the expansion of foreign markets.* **Provence Export** *is a group of six firms producing up-market food products.* The President of this association, Marc Pouzet, says: 'It's a pooling together of our client files and information collected; it's mutual aid to the other companies during a mission and the organization of joint promotional operations. All this has helped the global export of the six companies to rise from $2 million in 1975 (first year of operation) to $13.5 million in 1991.'*

▶ *Rarer are the examples of rival companies who decide to work together on the international market. It is the case of two wine-makers/brokers from the Loire Valley in France, specializing in high quality Muscadet, who now make more than 70% of their sales abroad. Although direct competitors, Jean-Ernest Sauvion and Michel Bahuaud, the directors of the two companies, do more than just exchange information. There is a great deal of cooperation between the two companies to increase their international 'fire power'. Frequent meetings enable them to coordinate their actions for establishing the best synergy: during their trips or at trade shows they represent each other, and even take orders for their competitor-friend; client control and loyalty is strengthened with subsequent frequent contacts; advertising and promotional actions can be enlarged, due to cost sharing, etc.*

Thus it is not just non-competitive companies with complementary products which can associate their international ventures. But the success of the informal association of Sauvion-Bahuaud is based on many indispensable ingredients. In particular, a complete and mutual trust in their gentlemen's agreement; similar views on development strategies; respect for the same rules of organization for the quality of client service, without forgetting a shared sense of international contact. All of these ingredients enable the two companies to entrust clients and deals to their 'ally', in total equanimity for the good of both companies' world expansion.

Obviously, every company executive cannot expect to find matching partnership possibilities next door to his office. In some cases, there may not even be any company within the country that could have complementary interests in sharing a joint action. In such circumstances, the **World Trade Centers** Network can provide effective assistance to locate synergy opportunies. The WTC Network is a computer-based electronic communication system developed by the WTC Association, in co-operation with **General Electric**. It provides to WTC members an international message system classified by professional sectors, a database (directory of WTC members worldwide), as well as an electronic trade-lead system which transmits cooperation

---

*Barral, Facor, Fruidoraix, Marius Bernard, Perlamande, Reynaud.

and business opportunities through the Bulletin Board, with a potential readership of 3.7 million people.

The WTC Network system can also help to determine a potential partner's viability, and so lessen the risk of doing business with unknown companies in other countries. The system is as easy to use as a telephone, works with almost any type of computer or word processor, and can be accessed from approximately 800 cities in 61 countries via local telephone. A message can be received for the cost of a local phone call, and be sent overseas at a fraction of the cost of telex or fax. (For more information about the WTC Association see section 1.1.1.2, as well as their contact in the New York WTC headquarters.)

2.2.3   Decision and control

We have just examined the criteria of efficiency and profitability, enabling us to (approximately) estimate the hoped-for performance of our pre-selected dynamic devices which make up the mix of actions of our development plan. Now let us proceed to the choice of dynamic devices before going on to the verification stage.

2.2.3.1   Development mix choice

To select the most efficient dynamic devices, it is advisable to make a parallel comparison between their efficiency and their profitability. Whereas in international practice this evaluation is usually carried out during a meeting, where a quick comparison between the force of impact and the cost effectiveness is made without going into detail for each criterion.

In the following example, it is interesting to study the synthesis of an evaluation of dynamic devices where they are examined in relation to the two criteria of efficiency and profitability:

▶ *This example is based on the main dynamic devices used by **Générale Biscuit** (**Groupe BSN***) in Scandinavia some years ago, in the framework of an ambitious development plan. As described by Patrik Goasdoué, Director of Foreign Markets and Exports, the positions of **Générale Biscuit** were particularly dissimilar in the Nordic countries before 1982:*

■ *Denmark: distribution of three products, under the brand name 'De Beukelaer' by a traditional-type agent;*

■ *Sweden: distribution of a range of products, under the importer's brand name (manufacturer of chocolates and sweets);*

■ *Norway: distribution of a product through the Swedish importer's subsidiary, under his brand name;*

---

*In 1986, **Générale Biscuit** became the Biscuit Branch of BSN.

■ *Finland: virtually non-existent sales.*

Among the conclusions of a study carried out at that time by **Générale Biscuit** in Scandinavia, it is interesting to note in particular:

■ the important potential for development in these countries of high purchasing power with political and economic stability;
■ the relative vulnerability of the local industry (problems of production quotas linked to the exiguity of their markets);
■ the long-term opening up of the borders (the three countries are members of AELE) and the probable homogenization of these markets for communication purposes.

As a result of this study, **Générale Biscuit** decided to launch LU, their international brand, on these markets, which have become one of the priority export zones of development benefitting from heavier investment.

A quick presentation is given in grid form (Figure 2.1 on p. 68) of the dynamic devices selected by **Générale Biscuit** for their Scandinavian development plan and their evaluation according to efficiency and profitability criteria.

(Note: These dynamic devices are presented in the order of the inventory made through the second part of this book – Dynamic Devices 'Product', 'Push' and Pull'.)

The dynamic devices are evaluated for each criterion according to the estimated level of their performance: xxx = very strong, xx = strong, x = medium, – = weak. For the criteria whose differentiation is direct, the evaluation is a straight 'yes' or 'no'.

'Product' dynamic devices

General establishment of the brand LU:

■ *launching it* ex nihilo *in Finland,*
■ *transfer from the old De Beukelaer brand to the LU brand starting with an association of the two brands on packages in Denmark,*
■ *by comparable association with the LU brand with the importer's brand in Sweden and Norway.*

Renewing the range of products:

■ *starting with the existing lines, by the constitution of a 'trans-Nordic' homogeneous range of products, with basic common characteristics,*
■ *a sustained program of new product launches (with priority given to products clearly different from the local competition).*

Adapting price levels:

■ *adjusting the pricing policy to local market conditions, while keeping an up-market position.*

'Push' dynamic devices

Appointing a Scandinavian director:

■ *with the recruitment of a Scandinavian export director in charge of this zone, and the preparation for his mission by a special training program*

		Efficiency Criteria				Profitability criteria				
		Force of impact	Synergy effects	Ease of implementation	Readjustment capacity	Cost/effectiveness ratio	Amortization capacities	Utilization control	Negative effects estimation	Partnershin
Product dynamic devices	• Generalization of the Lu brand	XXX	XXX	X	–	XX	XXX	XXX	NO	Y
	• Renewal of the product range	XXX	XXX	X	X	XXX	XXX	XXX	NO	N
	• Adaptation of price levels	XX	X	X	X	XX	XX	XX	YES	Y
Push dynamic devices	• Putting in place a Scandinavian executive	XXX	XXX	XX	–	XXX	XXX	XXX	NO	N
	• Reinforcing importer network	XXX	XXX	X	–	XXX	XXX	XX	NO	Y
	• Stimulating the sales force	XXX	XXX	XXX	X	XX	XX	X	NO	Y
Pull dynamic devices	• Internationalization of communication	XXX	XXX	–	–	XX	XXX	XXX	NO	N
	• Investments in advertising media (TV)	XXX	XXX	XX	X	XXX	X	XXX	NO	Y
	• Support of consumer promotions	XXX	XXX	X	XX	XXX	XX	XX	NO	Y
	• Public relations actions	X	XX	XXX	XX	X	XXX	XXX	NO	Y

Figure 2.1 Evaluation of dynamic devices taken from the 1983/84 development plan of Générale Biscuit (Group BSN) in Scandinavia

at headquarters, as well as in several subsidiaries of **Générale Biscuit** *in Europe.*

Reinforcement of the importers' network by the homogeneous choice of partners having in common:

- *a marketing background and experience in getting leading brands onto the market,*
- *a sufficient size to enable a strong national impact,*
- *solid positions in modern distribution networks,*
- *an industrial specialization in a complementary domain, not in direct competition with the biscuit industry. Thus, the choices fell on:*
  - ☐ *a manufacturer of sweets and chocolates, having already marketed* **Générale Biscuit** *products under his own brand, in Sweden and Norway,*
  - ☐ *a food manufacturer, mainly specializing in sweets and chocolates in Finland,*
  - ☐ *a manufacturer of cereal products in Denmark.*

Sales force stimulation:

- *launching a specific incentives program,*
- *sales training and the development of adapted 'sales aids'.*

'Pull' dynamic devices

Internationalization of communication:

- *although communication was not completely standardized in Scandinavia, certain themes and styles were brought closer together within the LU international communication policy.*

Investment in media advertising:

- *in parallel to public relations and sales promotion actions, TV campaigns were launched in Finland and later (in 1988) in Denmark.* **Générale Biscuit** *started similar actions in Sweden and Norway as soon as TV advertising was authorized.*

Support of consumer promotions:

- *strong sales promotional actions are necessary in Scandinavia, due to modernization of the distribution system and the absence of TV advertising in Sweden and Norway (even recently as well in Denmark). Very ambitious promotional programs were set up (including massive use of POP material) mainly during summer, when biscuit consumption goes up.*

Public relations actions:

- *in each country, at strategic times, with the setting up of LU advertising art exhibitions to emphasize the historic origin of the brand and to reinforce the authenticity of its image.*

Today, thanks to the implementation of this development plan, LU is in second place in the biscuit market in Scandinavia, while this brand was not even present there before 1980!

2.2.3.2   Individual action effects

After choosing the development mix, it should be made sure that the plan's implementation has a good chance of reaching the fixed objectives (see section 1.3).

As talking of 'good chances' means, international development cannot be considered as an exact science. In most cases we are faced with an equation containing several unknowns, with too many parameters and variables unlikely to be within direct control.

This is a mighty task whose solution is not found only in calculations based on objective data. We also have to count on common sense, international experience, intuition, and why deny it . . . on luck that we will have managed to coerce!

It is obviously preferable to begin by trying to measure the quantitative and qualitative effects of each action provided for in the development plan, which will allow an approximate evaluation of the overall effects.

In most cases, a solid basis to start from is provided by one's own specific market results. From this, the performance study* of the dynamic devices that was drawn up for the mix selection can be used to extrapolate the effects of each action. This extrapolation will be made all the easier with some experience of similar actions already carried out on comparable markets.

This close study allows a supplementary check on the investment level decided for each action. If it is too low it will be unproductive; if it is too high, similar results might be obtained with a lighter investment.

2.2.3.3   Overall effects

It is out of the question, of course, to hope to obtain a reasonably exact global estimation of the overall effects of the development plan just by adding together the quantifiable effects that were simply defined for each action. It would be way off target!

Certain actions are in synergy on the same target (see section 2.2.1.2), just like two hunters who both fire one shot into a flight of ducks. Three fall to the ground. Each hunter can consider that he bagged three ducks, and this corresponds to the effects of each development action. However, the global hunt score (overall effects) is only three ducks and not six!

The advantage of synergy, like hunting with a group, is that the overall results often go beyond those obtained by the same actions which would be implemented individually. Let us say, to finish with

---

*Sometimes with statistical data, particularly to measure the impact force of certain dynamic devices (see section 2.2.1.1).

our 'bloody' example, that the hunters would only have shot down two ducks if they had not coordinated their efforts.

▶ *Let us return to exporting with an imaginary case of prospecting a new clientele segment in our development strategy in Atlantis. As one of the leading software designers and manufacturers, we have decided to introduce our most recent program to the 80,000 physicians and 20,000 attorneys of the country. This potential clientele constitutes a second priority target market for 1991, as in 1990 our starting year in this market, we aggressively canvassed the Atlantis small and medium-sized enterprises (SME).*

Sales figures for SME in 1990:   *1000 programs.*
Sales objectives for SME in 1991:   *1500 programs.*
Sales objectives for doctors/lawyers in 1991: *500 programs.*

▶ *Contrary to the commercial strategy used with SME, having sales staff canvass the prospects directly, we have decided:*

- ■ *to take out a double-page, colour advertisement with a response coupon in two trade journals, 'The Physicians' Review' and 'The Attorney's Tribune', which are supposed to cover the two professions;*
- ■ *to send a personalized letter (also with a response coupon) to all the doctors and lawyers two weeks after the appearance of the advert in their professional magazines;*
- ■ *to have the sales people call on all the doctors and lawyers who send back the coupon (the salesforce will have been specially reinforced for this occasion).*

Forecasting the effects of each action:

▶ *We know by experience that the response rate for coupons in trade journals is about 0.5% and is around 2% for direct mail. This corresponds to 500 coupons from the magazines and 2000 from the direct mail.*

Forecasting the effects of the actions taken together:

▶ *These two actions were planned at a two-week interval as it was determined that a more powerful synergy would be attained by using the direct mail as a reminder of the ad, rather than simultaneously with it.*
  But since it is our first experience in intersecting advertising actions, we are going to start with a pessimistic forecast of the overall effects. In retaining the figure of 2000 coupons actually sent back, we are supposing that all the coupons coming from magazines will be from doctors and lawyers who would have responded to the direct mail and we do not take into account the synergy of the combination of these actions. Knowing that at least 25% of the returned coupons bring in firm orders on our other markets, this unrealistic and pessimistic calculation adds up to 500 programs sold. Moreover, if it were verifiable, we could think that it would be possible to reach the same results with only the direct mail.
  By miraculous coincidence, this low hypothesis also corresponds to our sales objective, so there is nothing to be worried about. But we should perhaps wonder if our sales objectives could not be more ambitious. In fact,

a more optimistic forecast on the 'double action' effects of our advertising strategy can result in 2500 to 3000 returned coupons, which will lead to the sale of 625 to 750 programs.

In reality, according to the industries and the countries, there is not often access to as much specific statistical data as in this Atlantis example, despite the existence of data banks or market studies. Thus, forecasts may have to be based on more uncertain approximations to decide whether the development plan will actually allow reaching the designated objectives.

2.3   Practical Organization

2.3.1   Unforeseeable factor reduction

► *From Paris, an engineer organizes a meeting with the technical directors of several important Mexican companies, in a Guadalajara hotel. He was told he could project the 16 mm film, which is the main part of his presentation, in a meeting room. Half an hour before the arrival of his guests, he goes into the meeting room to make sure that everything is alright and to give the film to the staff in charge of the projection. The technician tells him that the sound track of his film makes it incompatible with the hotel projector. It is too late to get another projector or to change the time of the meeting . . .*

► *How many companies participating in trade shows, exhibitions or conventions abroad have received their clients in empty booths – without products, decoration, or sometimes even professional literature. Why? This material was sent too late to absorb unexpected events such as a strike, customs delays, a public holiday, which can hold up transit, or failed to take into consideration the fact that local transportation may last ten times longer than the international leg of the journey.*

► *Here is another example concerning a fashion designer who was presenting for the first time a collection in New York, to the specialized press and some buyers from up-market boutiques and department stores. A New York agency took care of selecting the models for the show, according to the required sizes. Just to be sure, twelve models instead of ten came to the rehearsal which only took place two hours before the show. Dresses, suits and coats fit perfectly, but none of the models could get into the shoes, which were too small for them. The designer had simply forgotten to mention the standard sizes of the shoes. The collection was not presented barefoot, thanks to a frantic shoe hunt. But the shoes found at the last minute could not compare to those which had been specially designed or chosen to match each outfit. The quality of the show clearly suffered from this oversight.*

Obviously, no one can think of or foresee everything. But all efforts should be made to limit the 'unforeseeable' to a minimum, or even to imagine alternative solutions for particularly important circumstances.

2.3.1.1   Entire staff involvement

We will stress the same fact over and over again: sales growth on foreign markets can only be the fruit of a team effort. Everybody in charge concerned by an action or a development plan must be informed and consulted, as well as the staff in their respective departments, before being asked to participate in its implementation (see sections 5.1 and 5.2).

▶   *This has been confirmed by the experience of **APRIL**, a French specialist in Programmable Logic Controllers (**Schneider Group**): 'Our internationalization was accelerated thanks to a development strategy worked out after consultation with all the different company departments.*

A general tendency is too often reducing international expansion to a purely commercial dimension, whereas all aspects of a company are linked together. A development plan cannot be successfully implemented unless all the company departments are implicated making the understanding of the planned actions global and adhered to by all the personnel.

Moreover, a company cannot be really efficient just in entrusting its international development to a handful of specialists. Everybody should be able to contribute directly in some capacity to the teamwork of international development and consider that normal.

That is why a six-month period of reflection took place on the theme 'the day-to-day business of internationalization'. There were half day meetings within every department: production and stock management, research & development, marketing and sales, human resources and other administrative services.

Everybody thought about his daily tasks, projecting them in an international context to see what could slow things down or speed them up, from answering the phone to after sales-service deliveries. Everything was gone over in detail.

The synthesis of these workshops was made into a video film which was shown within all departments (it is of vital importance to show people the concrete results of their efforts). This way, everybody became aware of the global situation. The implementation of the totality of the proposals is still being carried out, as the objective of total quality implies a constant renewal, especially in an international context.'

Not consulting every department means doing without a specialist's experience, such as the person in charge of advertising or transportation; the same abroad, with our local representative's field experience, which can provide an extra support. Too bad, when all this advice would have probably helped avoid the disasters mentioned in the anecdotes in section 2.3.1.

Even worse, neglecting certain people in charge can give them the impression that they are being deliberately ignored, with the risk of creating a negative attitude or even a destructive action on their part (the classic 'banana peel'), despite the consequences to the company and themselves.

This is another example of the grain of sand which can throw a machine 'out of sync'. Fortunately, this does not happen too often inside companies. It is more frequent, though, with the local representative, who feels he is being taught a lesson on his own territory.

In this latter case, the most frequent form of sabotage is passive rather than active. A local representative who was not motivated and convinced to participate in our development plan will tend to do nothing, or only to partially do what was planned, while preparing excellent arguments to prove his good faith. Obviously, this type of attitude could compromise the whole development plan.

On the contrary, hopeless situations can turn into striking successes with the committment of the whole executive team involved, which mobilizes the totality of the individual experiences and energies:

▶ *Profilafroid were aiming at supplying the roadguards for a motorway outside Riyadh, Saudi Arabia. Unfortunately, the call for tenders stipulated other standards which put **Profilafroid** partially out of the running. In fact, parts of their tooling system were totally incompatible with the required production standards. However, as it was a big contract and the export executives thought they stood a good chance, they took their problem to the engineers in the R&D department. They in turn got hooked . . . and finally managed to find alternative techniques with the **Profilafroid** material. The export executives went back to their potential clients and finished up by convincing the Saudis to disregard the advice of their consultant (who had designed the call for tenders) and to sign with them.*

Thus, it is a must to integrate the international factor into internal communication among executives. Yves Carcelle,* when he was the **Descamps** CEO, had this to say about it:

▶ *'We hold weekly meetings to keep everyone up to date on what and how we are doing on our different foreign markets. Each person can thus be ready to intervene if necessary in his speciality, as well as contribute to the general discussion if need be. Moreover, we try to only take on executives with international experience, no matter what their job is in the company. I, myself, make an effort to try to present our collection to our franchisees or journalists on our major markets in their own language . . .'*

A last word about involving the people in charge, both at headquarters and in the field, which concerns the time factor: it is easy and inexact to say 'there are no urgent problems, only delays caused by disorganized export executives'. No one can deny having occasionally delayed transmitting information or instructions, making life difficult for the departments concerned. It is thus a necessary disci-

---

*Yves Carcelle is now President of **Louis Vuitton Malletier** (see section 6.4.2.3).

pline to transmit information to the interested parties *as soon as* it is available or, at least, whenever it can be used.

▶ *Here is an example concerning the reorganization of market distribution, which is always a delicate matter. Following the decision to change the channel of distribution in an African country for their lines of office equipment, the staff in charge of **IBM** export operations immediately notified the logistics department based in France. They had six months to figure out the best approach to customs (given the new channel of distribution), to set up a system of payment by documentary credit, and to make sure everything was ready to roll on time.*

2.3.1.2   Local factor integration

After travelling in all countries, seasoned export executives' observations are usually sufficient to have an approximate idea of what is feasible, what is available, and how long it will take. Furthermore, they will not fail to consult local representatives and specialists to confirm or contradict their first impressions.

However, on the other hand, the clearer the local conditions become for the export executives, the more they tend to forget that they (local conditions) are not clear at all for the people at headquarters who have not had a chance to travel in foreign countries.

An extreme vigilance is to assure that what is being planned for a given market can accordingly be carried out. All necessary information should be passed on to the head office staff so that certain interventions of their own – which would be justified on the domestic market or elsewhere abroad – do not conflict with the unfolding of the current plan.

▶ *There is a well-known example in the pharmaceutical industry which perfectly illustrates the necessity to integrate local information. A few years ago, an American laboratory wanted to inform market influencers in an original manner of the existence of a new medicine about to be launched in Switzerland. The Americans held a brainstorming session where no one with any real experience of daily life in Switzerland attended. They decided to send telegrams (from the USA) announcing the launching of this medicine to all the medical specialists concerned. However, no one had counted on the speed with which telegrams are transmitted in Switzerland. Given the time difference, the telegrams arrived in the middle of the night. According to the various cantons, they were either phoned immediately or delivered at dawn. It is not difficult to imagine the reaction of these medical specialists being awakened for such news!*

Here is another typical example of a foreseeable ... unforeseeable incident, if local factors are methodically taken into consideration:

▶ *A European soft drinks manufacturer decided to enlarge the range of one of his product lines with a giant size bottle, primarily for sales promotions on several markets, the USA in particular. This new model was ready to be launched when someone noticed that a slight detail had been overlooked. The bottle was several centimeters too high for most American store shelves. Result: the scheduled sales promotions were cancelled, the distributors unhappy, the sales force demotivated, while waiting for a new bottle to be manufactured in a rush.*

To reduce this type of unforeseeable incident, the methods of companies which give the utmost importance to local data should be used as inspiration.

▶ *Fish* only undertakes an international mission after a detailed investigation of all the places their boats will have to operate in. This reconnoitering is of capital importance for the success of the missions (carried out far from the home bases, in difficult conditions), for it allows the choice of the best adapted vessels. For example, there was a contract with **Elf Cameroon** for drilling operations platforms which were in fairly shallow waters at the mouth of a river. A detailed study of the sea bottom was made which showed that the available **Fish** boats might run aground in the shallowest parts. Consequently, two new boats were built in time, with a shallower draught better adapted to working in deltas.*

Let us conclude on an anecdote which illustrates to what point foreseeing the unforeseeable, despite all efforts, can sometimes be a thankless task:

▶ *Having to take charge of a considerable industrial project in Africa, a big French group realistically estimated the logistics problems involved. Because of the impossibility of stocking materials at the site, the supply shipments had to arrive continuously and with great regularity. The site was 600 miles away from the nearest port and the railway was the sole solution to get the supplies over this last leg of the journey. The logistics experts of the company decided to overhaul this part of the railway, which seemed the weakest link in the chain of transport, so that it could bear the passage of convoys of a much heavier weight than the usual trains circulating. After inspecting the 600 miles of railway in the bush, the decision was taken to reinforce the bottom of the track, replace the wooden ties and shore up the bridges, over a period of months. Finally, these Herculean works in an unfriendly environment were completed and the first convoys left the dispatching center in France, reached the port of embarkation, were transported to the African port, unloaded according to special procedures, and sent on by special trains. For several months everything went like clockwork – to the great relief of the logistics staff. Until one day, when a heavy convoy derailed far from the African bush . . . but near Rouen, in France!*

---

*F.I.S.H. (Feronia International Shipping) is a subsidiary of the naval company **Worms** which outfits and operates boats auxiliary to the search for offshore oil (offshore supply vessels).

be developed. For instance, local manufacturing within certain countries might not be up to quality standards (see section 4.5.2).

▶ *How to expect that the international use of **Facom** catalogs could create any problem? Still, a few countries – like Brazil, Chile, Indonesia – consider these superbly illustrated booklets as luxury products and tax them accordingly. Up to $20 duty is to be paid on $9 cost price catalog, which makes the operation too expensive. **Facom** then have to evaluate the technical capacities of local printers to make up the catalog with the same photographic excellence, in color, and a binding as robust as the original. In countries where the printers are not up to standards, **Facom** only distribute one or several 'digests' which are adapted to local users' main needs.*

2.3.2.3 Material requirements

The inventory of material requirements should be conducted with the same rigour. Even more than for the preceding points, the respective advantages of getting supplies locally, from the homeland or from another country have to be compared in terms of quality, cost, delivery times and for the feasibility of the whole operation.

▶ *Thus, it is easily imagined how rigorous the evaluation of material needs can be for the realization of 'turnkey' projects, mostly in certain countries suffering from chronic shortages of the most common raw materials. Sometimes even the ingredients necessary for making reinforced concrete (cement, aggregates, steel rods, water) are under the control of monopolies which impose a quota system of supply.*

2.3.3 Functions to delegate

The psychological importance of having the staff in charge at headquarters as well as within the local representation participate in the organization of development plan actions has already been mentioned. This importance comes into focus when delegating parts of the preparation and realization of these actions.

2.3.3.1 Internal delegation

In theory, delegating tasks inside the company should not be a particular problem; the staff's required competence is confirmed, and there is sufficient means and time to perform the delegated actions.

However, problems sometimes arise because a mission has not been defined clearly enough. All those aspects that make an international mission different from routine domestic work (specifications, standards, style, finish, delivery period) have to be very carefully explained. One should not hesitate either to go into great detail over the importance of these characteristics and the apocalyptic consequences that will be unleashed if they are not respected.

2.3.3.2   Local delegation

Indeed, there are more difficulties inherent in delegating tasks far from home base to staff working for the local representative or distributors.

At the risk of sounding redundant, it has to be said again that before delegating anything to anybody, their capacity in successfully carrying out the mission entrusted to them has to be evaluated. (This can be done through conversation with the staff concerned, or with their managers.) This should be followed by a precise definition of the work to be carried out and a presentation of all necessary information. Things are not always done this way, of course, especially if communications cannot be directly controlled, for instance having to go through the local hierarchy or because of language problems. Using an interpreter inevitably distorts the message, and also complicates the feedback information which is necessary to make sure the staff have fully understood what they are supposed to do.

The definition of tasks should be accompanied by solid preparation, during which some sort of specialized training might be necessary, or even rehearsals or simulations.

Each participant has to be made aware of the importance of his own particular job to the success of the whole. Where possible, this importance should also be recognized by each person's professional environment.

The motivation and enthusiasm of the 'troops' should be developed during dynamic preparation sessions which can be organized – when the situation fits – with a 'commando operation' atmosphere, where the positive results of each individual performance will be shown as essential to build up the success of the unit (see section 3.1.2).

2.3.3.3   Subcontracting

There is a common tendency to underestimate the difficulty of efficiently using the services of outside specialists.

The problems are not only found in the choice of a 'good' subcontractor (see section 6.1.4.4 for the choice of local service agencies), but in the necessity of giving this specialist the means of carrying out the desired tasks.

In the home country, the subcontractor gets a specific definition of what is expected. This, together with a closer relationship and better control, makes the risk of failure much lower than abroad.

Whether it concerns the fabrication of POP, sales promotion, public relations material, or the preparation of a media plan or any other kind of subcontracted task, too many examples illustrate that when an exporter does not take the time to carefully explain what is needed and why, the results are disappointing, if not disastrous.

The collaboration of a local representative in foreign markets is logically a deciding factor to reduce such dangers. In most cases, the local representative is in charge of the subcontractors or suppliers, and it is incumbent upon the export executive only to follow up matters in coordination with headquarters. In the rare case where the export executive finds himself in direct control of local agencies without the assistance of a local representative, he should be as clear and specific as possible in his instructions, not hesitating to use models and examples to illustrate what he wants done (see section 6.1.4.3) and keeping a constant 'eye' on them as well.

2.3.4. Communication organization

'Communication' in all its meanings can be either a mine-field or a source of dynamic devices for exporters: communication between two people establishing and maintaining a relationship; transmission of information; transfers of technology; transportation of people and merchandise; transfer of funds; communication in advertising, sales promotions and public relations. The extent and multiplicity of problems in international communication are such that they could appear in almost every page of any export development book.

However, the logical place to deal with them in detail is now, with the practical organization of the development plan, as its success depends largely on the quality and rapidity of communication in the field, on a given market, and between this market and headquarters.

2.3.4.1 International communication difficulties

International communication problems make up the major hindrance to foreign sales development. This should not surprise anyone where everyday communication problems are considered – with an office colleague or the next-door neighbour. Such problems, which stem from differences of character, culture, social environment or interests, are substantially exacerbated as soon as a border is crossed.

International causes can be added to the usual communication blocks between inhabitants of the same country: obvious differences of language used in meetings, on the 'phone, in letters and telexes; differences of race, customs, lifestyles; historical, political, economic and cultural differences; plus more differences in ways of thinking, logic, organization and ways of working, etc.*

▶   *A telex from the Republic of China arrived one day on the desk of Alain Geffriaud, Export Director of the **Société Française de Brasserie** (a French brewery) addressed to **Société Française de Brassières**. Being used to the usual mistakes in telex communications, he was able to decipher that they wanted samples and a price list, which he immediately sent off, preceded by a telex indicating that he was sending them a 'bundle of 24 × 25 cl and 24 × 33 cl'. It is by return telex, where the Taiwanese indicated their perplexity with these sizes, that Alain Geffriaud realized the mistake. The Taiwanese, wanting to import women's brassieres, had simply found the **Française de Brasserie** in a trade directory under the letter 'B' and mistook Brasserie for Brassières.*

*The anecdote does not stop there, as the Chinese company very kindly forwarded the beer samples and price list to the TTAM (Taiwan Tobacco and Alcohol Monopoly), which helped accelerate negotiations undertaken by Alain Geffriaud with this country, whose access was complicated and delicate at that time. Two years later, the **Société Française de Brasserie** was finally able to export beer to Taiwan!*

The difficulty in international communications has always been felt, and has given rise to usages and codes of conduct enabling people to get on the same wavelength which is recognized as more favorable to establishing a climate of understanding and cooperation. The history of relations between tribes, peoples and nations have engendered today's rules of protocol.

In the same way, commercial rules and usages are slowly being established on an international basis. However, their influence remains superficial and limited, as the quality of international communication is based primarily on a shared desire for dialogue.

This common desire for dialogue often exists at a first contact between two foreign businessmen. Being aware of the fragility and difficulty of this communication, each person will make a special effort to develop the contact.

However, the sunny skies darken on this new-found relationship after the ritual phase 'I'll be in touch with you as soon as I get back to my office' is uttered. Once there, the exporter is submerged in work waiting for him, and neglects or even forgets to communicate rapidly as promised. His counterpart, disgruntled, will not be in the same frame of mind when he receives the promised letter two months later.

Perhaps not having completely understood this letter, he himself will put off answering, then give a very vague answer, which in turn will demotivate the exporter . . .

This scenario, and others like it, have been experienced by everyone

---

*On this subject, see *The Global Edge*, by Sandra Snowdon (Simon & Schuster, NY).[1] This book contains practical advice on how to communicate in 23 countries.

*A few years later, the Club successfully tested such a geographical segmentation of their communication operations in major Japanese cities. Taking advantage of the high density of potential clients working in the main business districts, Jean-Robert Reznik (who was then Vice-President in charge of the Pacific-Asia region) decided to concentrate his investments there, in particular on the big underground stations such as Ikebukuro, Shibuya and Yurakutcho, in Tokyo. The strong visual impact of this underground station advertising produced even more spectacular results, due to the combined commercial support of **Club Med** sales representatives in the travel agencies of these targeted areas.*

2.5.1.2 Evolution possibilities

The importance of using budgetary flexibility as a real tool has already been stressed. However, when studying the means of financing a development plan, an export company is not alone in investing, since it can also negotiate to get the biggest possible commitment from the local representative.

Knowing that the development plan will be more efficiently carried out if it can be adapted continuously to the evolution of the situation, an agreement about such amendments has to be made with the local representative while working on the budget together. If not, he might resist changing or adapting the development plan, due to evolving factors within his own market or in neighbouring areas (see the **Chupa Chups** example in section 3.2.3.2).

2.5.2 Internal financing

All three basic ways to finance an internal development plan require the cooperation of the local representative. This cooperation can manifest itself in other fields as well, but it is mainly within the framework of negotiations about investments* that the good will of the local representative can best be judged. How to motivate his desire to cooperate will be covered by specifically studying the relationship with the local representative in Chapter 5.2.

2.5.2.1 Within existing agreements

This is the case where the budget for the development plan is scheduled in the agreements already established between a company and its local representative. Many contracts specify that the local represen-

---

* Obviously, this type of negotiation is only possible when there is a local representative who can be depended upon, such as a subsidiary or an exclusive importing agent.

tative has to invest a part of his mark-up in dynamic devices. According to the industry, the investment percentage can vary between 5% and 20% of the turnover before tax, which can be enough to cover the development budget of a market, especially when 'cruising speed' has been reached with a sufficient sales volume to finance expansion efforts.

The case of representation abroad by a foreign subsidiary can also be considered: then, even if its turnover is not high enough to finance a development plan, the general management of the group will decide (often in lively debates among the managers of the different companies, each pleading his cause) how to divide up the necessary investments.

2.5.2.2   In addition to existing agreements

This is the most frequent case to rapidly take advantage of a market potential, where more needs to be invested than has already been agreed in the contract with the local representative. Given that both the company and its local representative are sure to make profits in the near future with a common development plan, negotiations can be successful, as demonstrated by the **Blédine-Phosphatine** example in Egypt (see section 2.5.1.1).

However, this negotiation can be facilitated if, logically, the agent* can hope to receive a fair return for his efforts, which depends on the conditions made in his contract.

Let us imagine that to reach the desired sales level, the agent in Market X is to spend 10% of his profit margin for two years, in addition to the 15% mentioned in his contract for dynamic devices, while the export company will match this investment effort with the same budget. There is little probability of the agent accepting such a deal if his contract expires in three years time, because he would only have one year to recoup his investment if the contract is not renewed.

This fairly simple example illustrates the hidden (or exposed) worry of many importing-distribution agents who think (quite often rightly) that too successful a development of a product line in their territory increases the temptation for brand owners to establish their own subsidiary, after getting rid of the now useless agent.

This most important point for an agent's motivation will be reviewed in section 5.2.1.1. Therefore, supposing that he is sufficiently

---

* We are talking here of an agent or representative having the exclusivity for distribution in a certain territory. In the case of non-exclusive agents, all distributing the same products in the same or in overlapping territories, the preparation of a common development budget is far more difficult. Besides pure negotiation, the multiple agents have to be motivated in relation to their individual interests, and sometimes the carrot and stick strategy has to be employed.

motivated, it still has to be considered how to finance the 'extra' investment necessary for mutual market development.

The division of this supplementary budget between an export company and its local agent can vary considerably according to the recognized market potential of the products, the size of mark-ups, locally recognized practices in the industry, and numerous other parameters and variables of which the personality and negotiating talents of each party are of vital importance. In practice, though, supplementary development budgets are often shared 50/50.

It would be in the exporter's obvious interest to finance 'in kind' the maximum of his part of the investment, and encourage his agent to look after local costs (reinforcing the sales team, commissions or bonuses for the trade, advertising, etc.).

The practice of financing 'in kind'* has quite a few advantages: it avoids siphoning off a large part of the company's finances, reduces the real amount of investment (providing products or free POP material whose value is based – with a possible reduction – on the selling price and not on cost price), or is even included under headings already accounted for in operating expenses (overseas assistance missions made by technicians, trainers, executives, etc.).

2.5.2.3   Ex nihilo

Certain contracts with local representatives do not include an advertising margin in the local price structure. This is usually the case for non-exclusive agents and distributors whose mark-up only covers overhead expenses and a profit margin.

In this case, it is usual for pull development costs (essentially advertising, sales promotions, public relations) to be covered entirely by the exporting company, since the advertising margin is retained at headquarters, thus having higher export prices in the market concerned.

However, even here there is no fossilized rule, and there is nothing to stop a company that wants to expand its sales in a certain market from asking its local distributors to contribute to the necessary financial costs. This leads to the same type of negotiation described above, where the final decisions will be made in direct relation to the interests and motivations of those parties involved.

Last but not least, unhoped for sources of finance sometimes only need a little imagination to be exploited. The idea is to track down all the ways of reducing costs that are built into the price structure (transportation, distribution, etc.).

If such reductions are not used to reduce the local selling price,

---

* This practice will not weaken the initial development plan, since the budget takes into consideration the cost of all the dynamic devices foreseen. A large part of these dynamic devices is often made up with products, materials or services originating from the exporting company.

they can finance some of the development budget and thus reduce the necessary investment.

▶   *In this way, a small French company discovered that by shipping the three components of its product separately to Brazil, they were able to get into more favorable customs duty categories, and thus reduce the duty paid CIF value of their products by almost 30%.*

2.5.2.4   Investment control

We have just seen (section 2.5.2.2) that it is advantageous for exporters to contribute 'in kind' to the development budget. Some go much further by overestimating the cost of supplies entering into the budgetary framework so as to lighten their actual participation even more. On their side, certain agents (whether or not taken in by this manoeuvre) do not hesitate to have recourse to similar manipulations, exaggerating the cost of certain items entered into their budgetary framework, or making up phony invoices for supplies or services. It is worth checking the costs borne by agents, either by random surveys or parallel investigations, to be conducted more carefully – if proven positive – before taking the appropriate measures.

Under-the-table commissions on certain services or supplies are more difficult to uncover, until chance plays a role:

▶   *The administrative manager at the headquarters of a French exporting company had to call up the advertising agency which worked with their importer in Holland. Several details had to be settled after a computer change in invoicing procedure had taken place. Speaking to the agency's accountant – who was not particularly bright – she was surprised to be asked 'Now, what about the commission, shall I still transfer the 5% to your importer, or to your company?'*

Another sneaky manoeuvre used by certain agents is simply not to carry out the actions projected in the development plan, but to bill for it anyway. It is hard to find out whether 15 or 12 saleswomen were really hired for a two-week sales promotion, or if the radio commercials were really broadcast as planned! There have even been cases where agents have set up phantom advertising agencies so as to more easily produce the (phony) invoices required.

Fortunately, this kind of swindle does not happen too often, but prudence requires random checks of a local representative's activities (see section 5.2.1.6).

2.5.3   External financing

These external means should be looked for every time the agreements (already existing or to be concluded with the local agent) do not allow sufficiently rapid self-financing for the development plan launch. This will also be the case when market conditions impose local manufacturing or the acquisition of a distribution company. Indeed, if such actions can sometimes be envisaged at lower costs (manufacturing under license, for example), it might be necessary to be the total or part owner of the production or distribution companies.

2.5.3.1   For a development plan

Often, the cost of an international development plan goes beyond the export company's available funding, especially when it involves supporting a relatively long effort (two to five years). In this case, it would seem normal to consider the costs incurred as a real investment in a financial (and not commercial) sense, and thus to look for financing which can be paid back by the expected profits. This clearly supposes that the hoped for profits can be freely repatriated without excessive taxation.

Banks are now well used to granting this kind of middle-term financing in the framework of 'credit' which takes the overall company needs into consideration, and not just the financial aspects linked to international activity.

2.5.3.2   For a subsidiary

After having assessed the funding needed for a foreign start up or acquisition, the company management should look for the best adapted financing for the implementation of the project within the framework of their international development strategy.

According to its nationality, the company could search for funding among the country's government or financial institutions, as well as the banks and investment companies intervening in the country where the subsidiary is to be opened (see examples in section 2.2.2.5).

The possibilities are many and various, but access conditions may considerably limit the choice of funding.

3

Making a success of actions undertaken
(Implementation Phase)

3.1   Development Plan Realization

At last, time for action! . . .

For months we have patiently studied how to develop a market, then meticulously prepared the offensive with our allies in the field: the local representative will obviously be in the front line, possibly assisted by staff seconded from headquarters, or by his local suppliers; the company will also be there in the background to supply more essential logistics support.

Now the moment has come for the offensive. However, it must be remembered that the quality of communication is a major factor for success – as already said (see sections 2.3.3, 2.3.4). If we mention it yet again, it is because the quality of communication (rapidity, clarity, precision, dynamism, sympathy) has far more importance in the heat of the action than during the preparation stage, where there was still time to delay matters or to clarify a misunderstanding.

To illustrate this seemingly obvious fact, and to better realize how difficult it is to establish clear and efficient communication between two people of different nationalities, let us see how we can adapt to international relations the 'communication funnel', a well known process to sales specialists. Suppose one person is the exporter and the other his agent in Taïwan, to whom he is giving instructions about the use of promotional items (see the chart on page 98). Both are speaking in English, which is not the mother tongue of either person. When two people are in direct contact, the more approximate and inaccurate the language, the greater the distortions and the misunderstandings. Fortunately, a substantial part of the basic message usually gets through in most cases.

On the other hand, the higher the number of intermediaries (who

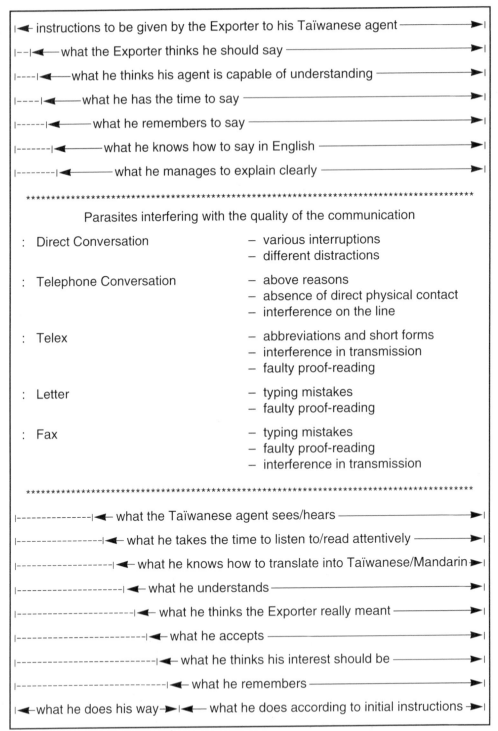

|◄─ instructions to be given by the Exporter to his Taïwanese agent ────────►|

|──|◄──what the Exporter thinks he should say ─────────────────────►|

|────|◄──what he thinks his agent is capable of understanding ─────────►|

|────|◄───what he has the time to say ───────────────────────────►|

|──────|◄──── what he remembers to say ──────────────────────►|

|───────|◄──── what he knows how to say in English ────────────►|

|────────|◄────── what he manages to explain clearly ──────────►|

****

Parasites interfering with the quality of the communication

: Direct Conversation   – various interruptions
                                – different distractions

: Telephone Conversation   – above reasons
                                – absence of direct physical contact
                                – interference on the line

: Telex   – abbreviations and short forms
                                – interference in transmission
                                – faulty proof-reading

: Letter   – typing mistakes
                                – faulty proof-reading

: Fax   – typing mistakes
                                – faulty proof-reading
                                – interference in transmission

****

|───────────────|◄─ what the Taïwanese agent sees/hears ────────────►|

|─────────────────|◄─ what he takes the time to listen to/read attentively ───►|

|───────────────────|◄─ what he knows how to translate into Taïwanese/Mandarin►|

|─────────────────────|◄─ what he understands ───────────────────►|

|───────────────────────|◄─ what he thinks the Exporter really meant ───────►|

|─────────────────────────|◄─ what he accepts ─────────────────►|

|───────────────────────────|◄─ what he thinks his interest should be ───────►|

|─────────────────────────────|◄─ what he remembers ──────────────►|

|◄─what he does his way─►|◄─ what he does according to initial instructions ─►|

Figure 3.1 International Communication Funnel

act as filters) between two people, the more unrecognizable the message becomes.

▶

*To lauch 'Tamango' in an English-speaking country, **Léonard Parfums** had their agent tell the saleswomen to use the international slogan 'Tamango de **Léonard**: a flowery, romantic fragrance by the most exotic French couturier.'*

Before launching this very exclusive product in a limited number of specially selected outlets, the agent's representatives were supposed to invite the saleswomen to a cocktail party, where they would become acquainted with this new perfume.

A week later, however, many of the saleswomen were presenting Tamango in a banal manner, such as 'a lovely French perfume'. Explanation: the Marketing Director did mention this very slogan at a meeting, but had forgotten to send his representatives the cards providing a presentation summary of Tamango together with the other POP material for the saleswomen. Without this material support, the original message got lost somewhere between the Marketing Director, the Sales Director, the regional development managers, the sales representatives and the saleswomen.

3.1.1   Operations management

The responsibility of running operations should, of course, be left to the local representative, as the export executive's presence will only be episodic – except when the stakes are so high that he remains in place for weeks or months, devoting himself almost entirely to a 'super priority' market, and following his other markets from afar.

Also, because it is the local representative's territory, the export executive's presence may undermine the representative's authority, demotivate him, or worse, create hostility. This would certainly be tactless!

On the other hand, leaving the local representative to his own devices when it is known that he has management weaknesses in certain areas would also be risky. The export executive is, in fact, on the local representative's territory, but it is still a question of developing the company's products and future.

Obviously, the export executive's role in assisting will be made easier by establishing a relaxed, team-spirit oriented working relationship, where condescending attitudes (paternalistic, professorial or dictatorial) are avoided. This will create a balance between the local representative's thorough market knowledge (and any other qualities), and the export executive's experience in the international distribution of his company's products.

The main point is not to 'short-circuit' the local representative in relation to his staff (except on rare occasions), for his authority must never be questioned. The more it becomes necessary to manage operations behind the scenes, the more discreetly it has to be done, with the local representative's cooperation and in his shadow, unless a part or all of his authority is officially delegated temporarily.

Between a tactless and irritating interventionism and the granting of an unchecked free hand, the export executive has to find the optimum position for each market's local representative.

This approach can be found in company directors who want to undertake international development by limiting the risks of deviation, especially for products where brand image is an important driving force.

▶   *The **Waterman** export field staff involve themselves completely in their markets, rather than drafting long reports back at headquarters. Every export executive cooperates regularly with his markets' local representatives, whether they be subsidiary managers or agents, thus constantly assisting and checking up on actions undertaken.*

3.1.1.1   In the field

Whether the field operations are being run by the local representative, with or without the export executive's participation, the latter is to check up on each stage of development. This obviously has to be done in a motivating manner (see section 3.1.2), where the carrot is more visible than the stick.

It is better to be realistic and suppose that, even with the most meticulous preparation, a few grains of sand will get into the development plan's mechanism and cause problems. This will help to keep cool heads all around when figuring out where to put a few drops of oil to get the machine running smoothly again.

Let us suppose that a few sales reps did not carry out their mission in the way laid down in the development plan with a detailed memorandum . . . or the advertising agency is late with the POP material production, or that they did not get the priority advertising space they were supposed to for the beginning of the media campaign . . . or that the sales promotion/public relations agency is not providing the expected outstanding performance. No matter how irritating these irregularities can be, reactions should not be violent, except in cases of obvious bad faith.

Harsh criticism may only inhibit the motivation of the local sales staff, who are sometimes confronted by difficulties that were underestimated. Also, in certain countries, people are even more sensitive to criticism if it comes from a foreigner. As for service agencies, given that it is not very easy to change them in the middle of implementing a development plan, the most sensible action to take is *not* to shout and threaten. Otherwise, the agencies in question will think they have lost their client's confidence, and that this job will be given to another agency at the end of the present campaign. They will thus only invest a minimum amount of energy so as to fulfill their contractual obligations, devoting more time and energy to their other accounts.

It would be better to study carefully with those concerned the causes for the discrepancies between the instructions given, the timetable, the desired quality and what was effectively accomplished. This usually helps to excuse collaborators and suppliers. It can then be seen together how to act to achieve the objectives despite the setbacks.

3.1.1.2   From afar

If it is not possible to frequently visit a market where a major development plan is underway, interest, nevertheless, can be demonstrated by following events from afar.

Besides a basic check on operations (see section 3.2), it is fundamental to remain in contact with the market (without overdoing it) to motivate the key staff in the field, and to be ready, if necessary, to intervene rapidly.

In addition to the usual forms of communication like mail, fax and telex, the less formal nature of the telephone gives a good chance to 'get a feel' of the situation at a distance.

▶ *Clarins, for example, maintain normal contact with their markets by letter and reports but make a special effort to have at least one 'phone contact per month with each of their local representatives. For Christian Courtin-Clarins, President of the international division, 'the telephone enables you to regularly sum up the situation and to get a feeling of what's going on much better than a letter. Between two trips, you remain closer to your markets for a proportionally negligible cost. But 'phoning doesn't mean improvising. Before these 'phone meetings, our local representative and the **Clarins** export service prepare a list of subjects to be dealt with, to make the conversation as profitable as possible for both parties. The importance of these conversations makes it often useful to summarize the major points in a memorandum which is then handed out to the persons concerned.'*

3.1.2   Effort stimulation

A development plan inevitably involves a lot more work, both in terms of quantity and quality, for the participants. According to their position in the company, those in charge and their staff ought to be sufficiently motivated by participating in a development plan because they know that the plan's success will bring them added satisfaction, be it financial, honorary or otherwise.

The motivation of local staff responsible for the practical execution of the plan also has to be assured. There is usually a special bonus for those directly or indirectly involved in selling (sales reps, demonstrators, sales ladies), but the efforts of the sales staff would not be enough for the success of the plan without the support of other services both outside (window dressers, deliverymen, etc.) and inside (administrative staff, dispatching, invoicing, after-sales service, etc.) the company. For these people, the compensation is rarely more than a few paid hours of overtime and (sometimes) thank you's.

Special means can be used to stimulate the efforts of the local representative, and he should also encourage his own department heads to transform their staffs into 'winners'.

Thus, the day-to-day routine has to be dropped, the development plan transformed into a battle plan, and the different actions translated into a commando offensive. Beyond the development plan itself (which particularly interests us), the overall atmosphere at the local representative's company should be charged with energy, and as a result it should become more efficient.

It would appear that the stimulation methods described below are especially applicable to sales teams. In fact, heads of administrative services can use them as models and adapt them to their own personnel with the same success.

It is an undeniable fact that the international success of many companies has been built on the motivation of their personnel as a whole, at headquarters as well as in the field.

▶ *In the **Group Bouygues**, for example, a charter written by its President-Founder, Francis Bouygues, expresses well the spirit of mobilization which is permanently maintained. 'Article 6: We are a combat community, ready for any challenge. Article 7: We love challenges which generate progress . . .' To meet these challenges, always difficult in the construction industry, people especially motivated by the **Bouygues** charter, contribute to reinforce the group spirit. The 'companions du Minorange' (contraction of 'minium orange', the colour of machines on construction sites) make up about 5% of the manual workers of the company. They get material benefits worth the equivalent of 6% of their salary in the form of workclothes with the insignia of the brotherhood, plus their rank and name . . . as well as annual trips to Dubrovnik, Palerme or Istanbul . . . They make up Francis Bouygues' pretorian guard, the faithful of the faithful, actors in and witnesses of the highlights of **Bouygues** history. There is no difficult worksite nor major project without a handful of Minorange companions.*

▶ *In the **Doublet** company, the motivation and stimulation of the personnel for its international development is based on long-range projects, such as developing an avant-garde technology (see section 1.2.2.2), the constant search for quality and the investment in training and internal communications. The company has six quality circles. It is the workers who push for the purchase of more elaborate, sophisticated equipment and ask for additional training to be able to use it properly.*

But the salaries are not higher than anywhere else. How to explain this Japanese-like company spirit? Luc Doublet answers: 'There is no particular bonus system for the personnel. They are motivated only by their interest in their jobs. The company trains them, gives them responsibilities and

3.2.2.1   Forecasts/results comparison

Such a comparison may indicate certain trends, and the chances of success of the development plan, but conclusions should not be reached hastily. For instance, quantitative results might be following the forecast results, or even exceeding them, but this does not necessarily mean that the plan is working well. It is obviously more difficult still to compare forecasts and results of qualitative objectives, where there are even fewer statistics to interpret.

3.2.2.2   Explanation of variations

The decision as to whether to modify or maintain the development plan is too important to be made lightly, and efforts should be made to uncover the real explanations of its first effects on the market. Thus, the comparison of forecasts and results should often be supported by more study, including organized or (at least) random field surveys.

Before drinking champagne with the local representative who has proudly announced a sales volume 50% higher than forecast for the first two months of the development plan, and getting carried away with his enthusiasm, it could be useful to clarify a few points. For example:

■ Could this brilliant result be explained by reasons outside company performance, such as the collapse of the main competitor's sales due to temporary problems (stockouts, strikes, etc.), or massive purchases by unscrupulous distributors who intend to re-export the products (offered locally at a promotional price) to higher retail-priced markets?

■ Another classic cause of apparently high sales: the local representative's sales force has opened up more 'doors' than forecast, and has loaded them all up with a lot of stock. If sales on a retail level do not follow in the same proportion, the local representative's turnover will soon go into freefall. Worse still, in some markets, retailers can send back stock that does not 'move' quickly enough (in the USA, for example); then a fantastic turnover can sometimes become negative.

On the contrary, initial results which are not so encouraging do not necessarily mean that the company is barking up the wrong tree. Certain dynamic devices do not always produce, rapidly enough, effects that were hoped for with overoptimistic forecast figures (for example, actions concerning the brand or product image such as reorganizing an after-sales service).

Besides interpretation errors, it is necessary to be careful not to be influenced by explanations of positive or negative results proffered, usually in bad faith, by certain people in charge who place their personal interests before those of the company.

Not to be forgotten, either, is the danger of generalizing observations which are too fragmentary to be really representative. The flattering remarks about the new advertising campaign, heard by chance when talking with two potential clients in an aeroplane, should not become the keystone of any analysis. Neither should the disparaging remarks of a saleswoman about the present sales promotion. In both cases, a more detailed study should be made.

3.2.3   Possible development plan modifications

After each check point meeting conducted during the development plan, it has to be decided with the local representative if any changes should occur. If, by a miracle, everything hums along according to the forecast, things might be left alone. However, if any modifications are necessary, caution has to be used before proceeding.

3.2.3.1   Change of course

Let us forget about minor modifications to concentrate on the major course changes which, for various reasons, can become necessary:

- ■ discrepancies between actual and forecast figures. The natural tendency to react only at the announcement of bad results should be distrusted, whereas the reasons for a sales progression exceeding by far the fixed objectives might not be analysed properly (some people do have a ready-made explanation: 'Why, we're the best! . . .'). Nevertheless, a quick analysis reinforced by information collected from the local representative or from the trade, could bring about certain fundamental changes: were forecasts simply too conservative . . . or perhaps there is an opportunity to take advantage of, while there is time, and in any case before the competitors?

▶ *'It's in 1986 that our sales in West Germany really took off' explains Alain Giroud, then Export Director of **Evian**. 'Of course, we were undertaking development actions on this market, but not to the point of explaining such a sales progression which was on its way to doubling our turnover for 1985. After checking things out with our local representative and the major distributors, as well as a thorough market study, we were able to determine that the consumption habits of the West Germans were slowly moving towards still water. Up until then, the market had been dominated (the contrary to France) by sparkling waters which represented 97% of the sales. According to our information, still water sales had progressed from 3 to 5% of the market during 1986, which explained our good results. This progression seemed to be continuing, so West Germany became a development priority which implied changing its dimension by reinforcing our local sales* *force and investing more in media advertising. Four months later, we opened a sales subsidiary at Mayence to better implement our strategy and to enlarge our position on this expanding market.'*

- Market evolution in an unexpected direction, thus rendering most development actions unsuitable.

▶ ***Dubonnet*** *came across this situation in England, where they drastically reduced their investments planned for 1980 in the middle of the year, as the decline in English purchasing power observed at that time was making them unproductive.*

- New constraints or regulations putting some dynamic devices out of action (see the example of **Löwenbräu** in Turkey in section 4.4.2.2).
- Negative reactions from the distribution, the clientele, or even from the local representative's sales force concerning certain development actions. (This usually indicates incomplete preparation, with insufficient testing or motivation activities.)

Whatever the reasons, it is of paramount importance that the modifications are accepted positively at all levels, and are not received as a sign of worrysome indecision, which can be a major demotivation factor.

For this purpose, the local representative has to transmit a well prepared, dynamically styled brief to all those involved, explaining all the (good . . .) reasons why there have been modifications, and what benefits are expected as a result.

3.2.3.2   Investment redistribution

Changing course in the middle of a development plan automatically involves rebalancing investments. This should not be a problem if the careful planning ahead of the check point meetings allows decisions to be made before irreversibly committing investments (see section 3.2).

Leaving such leeway makes it possible to modify the relative importance of each media in the framework of an advertising budget, to give priority to a new distribution channel with a greater investment, etc.

▶ *Greece, 1980. In the middle of an ambitious **Chupa Chups** development plan, imports were severely reduced by a government measure obliging importers to get licenses and to make a guarantee deposit in a bank for six months. The development plan was immediately interrupted, particularly the advertising media which was 100% financed by **Chupa Chups**. A part of this investment was redirected for their agent's use, who was thus able to cope with the new situation. In parallel, periodic promotional actions were organized in the retail outlets to maintain interest in **Chupa Chups** while waiting for better days.*

After deciding to change course, rebalancing investments in the framework of the same market does not usually pose other problems – though a consensus still has to be reached with those in charge locally. However, matters may become more complicated when investments committed in a market have to be reallocated, for instance, because a major offensive of a competitor has made development efforts completely ineffective.

In such a case, a good deal of diplomacy is needed to convince the local representative to redirect investments to more immediately productive markets, before coming back to support his efforts with a greater chance of success.

3.3   Follow-up

Our development plan was a stunning success – quite obviously – but we have not finished with it yet. A plant needs more than water and fertilizer for just a few months to become a Baobab tree, as many weekend gardeners know.

3.3.1   General assessment

3.3.1.1   Study of overall results

The obvious starting point is comparing all the final figures with forecasts and results from years before, in order to analyse them and extract extremely precious information to ensure business development.

But the general comparison of the results and forecasts is not the only source of information necessary for an effective analysis. This comparison should be pursued in greater detail to get results on each line of products, and to estimate the importance of each in the final results.

Performance is also to be compared to that of competitors and to the general evolution of the market. Another barometer worth consulting regularly is the average turnover per retail outlet, to confirm the evolution of real sales progression.

Finally, it could be interesting to compare some of these results to those of other countries with relatively similar characteristics, after having adjusted results to a common denominator – the number of inhabitants or the number of households, for example, for consumer products.

3.3.1.2   Analysis of success and failure factors

This analysis appears to be quite different from those made in the heat of the action, during the course of the development plan, to modify some actions if needed. Most of the information now being accessible and the necessary distance (in time) being acquired, it is possible to establish more objectively and precisely, the determining factors of success or failure (see **Air France** example in section 5.3.1.1).

Usually, there is a tendency to look only for the reasons for failure, to make a few heads roll, or for the reasons for success, to hand out a few medals. By doing this, export executives forget to congratulate those who fought with courage in the face of adversity, and whose dynamism should contribute a lot to the next offensive, as well as stimulating those who let themselves be carried along by the victory won by others.

More generally, it should be considered that both success and failure are provoked by complex factors whose specificities should be discovered for each market so as to stimulate a faster sales development.

The most brilliant results do not dispense anyone from this analysis (a good dose of self-criticism should also enter into it), for it is possible to discover, even after a spectacular success, that results could have been even better.

Then, instead of basking in the warmth of success, the chance should be taken to improve future performance, while there is still time, as confirmed with the **Dim** example of the mid–1980s, in the US:

▶ *Whereas the sales of the leading French manufacturer of pantyhose seemed to be progressing in a satisfying manner, their management were surprised to learn, thanks to the results of a routine focus group, that their advertising films which were received so well in Europe did not go down so well with their American clientele. (For the continuation of this example, see section 4.1.2.2).*

3.3.2   Continued exploitation

After completing the development plans in all priority markets, their continued exploitation can have the comparable effect of adding a turbo compressor onto a car engine; the experience, energy and information accumulated during their implementation should be used again before the generated stimulus diminishes.

3.3.2.1   Re-utilization of committed means

A development plan often serves as a test base for one or more original dynamic devices. Their success within this framework should encourage using certain of them again on the same market, and transposing them to other markets after possible modification or adaptation.

▶ *One hundred year birthdays are not a common occurrence. An anniversary is a productive source of dynamic devices which can be used – and re-used – in an efficient development action. In this way, **Waterman** concentrated the effects of important complementary dynamic devices to celebrate their 100 years of existence:*

■ *The collection of historical **Waterman** writing instruments emphasized their professionalism as the forerunner of the great penmaker. There were pens, POP material, posters, as well as a portrait gallery of famous **Waterman** product users. Certain of these pens were themselves instruments of historical events: it was a gold **Waterman** which signed the Treaty of Versailles, June 28 1919, in the hand of Lloyd George, British Prime Minister.*

■ *The launching of a new line of pens, the 'Man 100', of which the aesthetic aspects as well as the performance attest to the brand's masterful technology.*

■ *Taking advantage of the centenary celebrations, **Waterman** chose a new logo with different type and colours, underlining the desire to be dynamic in their continuity.*

■ *This desire was reinforced by a multi-media advertising campaign with a resolutely new style: Watermania.*

The totality of these actions was organized, from their conception, as a 'centenary circus', each element being transposable to each country where this birthday was celebrated: Belgium, Germany, Italy, USA, etc.

In the same way, information or experiences having sufficient general interest (gained from the preparation or realization of a development plan) should be circulated to other markets concerned.

3.3.2.2   Maintenance of motivation

Lack of time, not planning ahead, or worse, rudeness, all contribute to forgetting to thank those who participated in a plan any way and, at all levels, in the realization of a development plan. By not showing appreciation of their work, this results in losing a significant (and relatively inexpensive) way of maintaining both morale and motivation.

The slightest actions can serve as a pat on the back to thank people for their efforts, thus assuring even more dedication for future development plans: a letter of congratulations or a gift to a salesperson; a story published in the company newsletter about the results obtained, with a photograph of the staff involved; these are just a few ways, among many others, of showing gratitude (see section 5.2.1.3 – examples of ideas needing large or small budgets).

3.3.2.3 Institutionalization

It is important to take advantage of the energy created by the first development plan in order to accustomize the local representative to preparing a new one every year.

Even when the desired position in a market has been attained, and its development will have ceased being a priority, within a company's world expansion strategy, efforts have to be maintained to avoid a gradual nibbling away of its market share by competition.

It is advisable to proceed using the same steps – Study, Preparation, Implementation – for any of the following development plans (and avoid calling them 'maintenance plans', which is far from motivating!). They should then be followed with an even greater interest as turnover and profits reach the level of market leaders ...

The institutionalization of a development plan can be broken down into four main phases:

- March/April
  check point meeting for the current plan
  possible modifications
  brainstorming about next year's plan
- June/July
  check point meeting for the current plan
  possible modifications
  main decisions for next year's plan
  start of dynamic device preparation
- September/October
  check point meeting for the current plan
  possible modifications
  detailed definition of next year's plan
  check up on dynamic device preparation
- December/January
  assessment and follow-up of the current plan's end
  possible modifications and launching of the new plan.

This rough timetable is more suited for a market of medium importance, and can be obviously broken down into monthly planning sessions for a larger market having a sufficiently structured local representative.

Selecting ways to expand: Inventory and practical advice

Introduction

Just a few remarks before going on to attack the second part of this book, where we shall conduct a systematic inventory of the dynamic devices in each field: product, commercial chain, communication.

The point of this inventory is to present the total arsenal available (with practical advice on how to use it), whose multiple resources are sometimes forgotten in the heat of the action. Because of both a lack of time and training (which cannot compensate for the acquisition of fragmentary experience in the field), many exporters tend to resort to the same techniques in developing their foreign markets. Thus, they master the application of *these* techniques, but their efficiency remains limited, like great pianists who restrict their playing to two or three octaves instead of the whole keyboard.

This is what makes it so important to review *all* of the dynamic devices available during the preparation of a development plan, so as to select those most adapted to the given market and circumstances (see sections 2.1 and 2.2).

Such a rapid review also provides a good opportunity to bring out into the open many of the hindrances and brakes to development (see section 2.1.1).

4

Reinforcing supply competitiveness: 'product' dynamic devices

It is logical to consider the product* as the first source of dynamic devices. The point of this chapter is to study how results abroad can be developed by playing on every characteristic of the supply, according to the nature of the market's demand.

This inventory of 'product' dynamic devices will be completed in the following chapters by analysing how to make international expansion more vigorous at each stage of the 'push' chain (international team, local representative, distribution channels), and how to stimulate it within the 'pull' communication activities (advertising, public relations, promotions).

Before studying those dynamic devices specifically linked to the product and its environment, it is necessary to look at two apparently unreconcilable requirements within this matter:

- the closest adaptation possible of the product to each market's needs, tastes, standards and specific constraints, as requested by the sales and marketing staff, to increase sales;
- the product's maximum standardization required by the management and production staff to obtain the lowest production cost and highest profit from economies of scale.

Beyond the internal bickering that is often provoked by defending one or other of the above points of view, all companies wanting to expand into foreign markets have to come to terms with this problem.

This is only a small issue when the necessary adaptation concerns a product's subjective characteristics and/or an objective but minor characteristic, without having to resort to a modification of the product itself, e.g. re-positioning of a product, or the addition of a legal notice.

---

*The term 'product' is used throughout this book in its widest sense: material goods (durable or nondurable consumer products, capital goods, raw materials, semi-finished goods) as well as services, technology transfers, etc. (see section 1.1).

This becomes far more serious when the desire to develop export sales forces company executives to envisage a major product transformation. Even if this does not necessitate a total retooling, with the purchase of new machines and tools, the decision to embark on 'special manufacturing projects' can lead to disturbances in production schedules; whether it means developing a 'new look', conforming to a standard variation in order to respond to a country's specific regulations, or proposing a different product quality to match the specific expectations of a market.

Thus, the strategic interest of each adaptation should be carefully examined, as well as the sales potential that such changes can be expected to generate.

It should be noted that dynamic companies which try and conform to major trends in international demand also benefit on their domestic market. The development of international business implies a constant search to improve a product's cost effectiveness in order to resist fierce competition. Certain adaptations and innovations initially carried out for foreign markets can then be incorporated into the home market (such as 'borrowing' from foreign competitors – a more astute manufacturing procedure – or a cheaper supply source, etc.). It is no surprise, then, to see that in most cases, innovative companies are also champion exporters.

A last remark emphasizes the necessity of remaining in close contact with the field: it is out of the question to undertake any 'product action' on a market (adaptation of certain characteristics, modification of price, etc.) before getting and double checking precise information. In particular, a clientele breakdown, major purchase motivations (what are the most efficient sales arguments; the most appreciated product characteristics?), its main weak points (what inhibits purchases, and how much does this slow down sales development?) and, of course, up to date information about the local competition's activities.

However, when it comes to adapting existing products, or even conceiving new ones, many companies seem to work blindfolded, without sufficient knowledge of the demand evolution on major world markets, and in almost total ignorance of their competitors' tactics.

Product innovation can pop up in a laboratory, after solitary exercise in fundamental research, whereas product competitiveness takes root in the field and implies teamwork (on this subject see the **Sfernice** example in section 1.1.1.3) between most company departments – in particular, sales, marketing, production and R & D. More assistance is needed to complete the required information from various services: the local representatives, agencies specializing in field surveys and opinion polls, other private consultants, and as well as student market surveys carried out abroad. Indeed, students specializing in marketing and export can undertake such 'field' missions when it would otherwise be too costly to have the same surveys conducted by professionals.

The lack of adequate product information in a large number of companies (linked to insufficient presence in the field – see the Introduction) seems like such a hindrance to their expansion that it is useful to demonstrate, at the very start of the chapter, that carrying out a product study in a foreign country is within the reach of any company, whatever the size – and that it pays off!

▶ *Here is the testimony of Michel Jonchère, former CEO of **Etablissements Salmon**, and Anne-Olivia Lévy and Florence Longeault, students at the Institut Européen des Affaires, concerning a field study they performed in Europe for this company:*

■ *Michel Jonchère: 'Salmon is a company of 650 people located near Cholet, France. It is the French leader in gifts for newborn babies. Our turnover is 190 million francs ($34 million), representing three million gifts: clothing, layettes, bath towels, soft toys, dolls, etc. In 1986, exports represented 10% of the turnover, realized mainly in Belgium, England and Italy. However, we had the impression that these markets were underdeveloped – which is why we were interested by the students' proposal concerning a market survey in these countries.'*

■ *Anne-Olivia Lévy: 'At our business school, l'Institut Européen des Affaires, practical field experience is part and parcel of the curriculum, along with more classical subjects (management, marketing, international commerce, etc.). We have to embark on an 8-month 'world tour' in five different countries, representing one or several companies. We set up a team, with Florence, to carry out our mission on consumer products for which we contacted 350 companies. It's with the Salmon Co., specialists in gifts for newborn babies that we signed a contract for an 8-month mission whose objective was to realize a product study to develop their sales in five European countries: Switzerland, Spain, Belgium, Luxemburg and England.'*

■ *Florence Longeault: 'After being solidly prepared by the Salmon Co., we broke this mission down into three distinct studies:*

> *(i) a consumer study in the streets of the cities visited; 1400 people were surveyed.*
> *(ii) a distribution study; 51 buyers or department heads of supermarkets, shopping centres and department stores were interviewed;*
> *(iii) an exhaustive study of competitors' products and retail prices was carried out in 150 sales outlets.*

> *Then, we presented the synthesis of these studies to the Salmon Co. management, and together we worked out a strategy of product positioning and the choice of channels of distribution for each country. On a second trip to these countries, we implemented these strategies by making appointments with buyers to test on them the concept of a special "baby village" corner, as well as the whole new collection.'*

■ *Anne-Olivia Lévy: 'Very often these appointments concluded with an* order, thanks to the unusual style of our approach: we introduced ourselves in the trade as students working for a French company which was sending us round, not as professional salespeople, but specifically to show the collections and get advice. In most cases, we were able to get appointments very quickly and were warmly welcomed. Then, it was the buyers themselves who wanted to order our products which had been adapted to their market's demand after our first survey.'

■ *Michel Jonchère:* 'This study was of immense value to us in countries where we were already established (England and Belgium in particular). It gave us concrete and specific information on the demand and distribution of gifts for babies which was totally unknown by our local agents. In Switzerland, the results were more immediate, since our sales volume, which was next to nothing in 1985, grew to 400,000 FF in 1986, and will reach about 1 million francs (about $200,000) in 1987.'

■ *Florence Longeault:* 'With the passing of one year, I think four main reasons can explain the success of our mission:

  (i) a constant readaptation of our survey organization according to the customs and particularities of each country;
  (ii) the autonomy and responsibility entrusted in us by the company was a major motivation;
  (iii) the availability and assistance of about a dozen executives of the **Salmon Co.**;
  (iv) the support they provided us in the field, coming over to help our work when an opportunity presented itself.'

■ *Michel Jonchère:* 'The success can also be explained by the method followed by this student-company project which created a dialogue leaving behind the standard clichés and refrains of people who think they know it all. All the persons contacted on our foreign markets were particularly open because they were dealing with students. Within the company, this operation excited our international ambitions and proved to us that we could export more to certain countries, whereas not everybody was totally convinced at the beginning . . .'

If this example is a good introduction to product dynamic devices, it does not mean that the use of students is adapted to solving *all* the problems encountered in international development. However, this type of mission can be very useful, particularly for field studies with a budget that any company can afford (NB: the cost of the 8-month mission of the two students from IEA, 150,000 FF, was largely devoted to travel expenses.).

Under such circumstances, this type of mission has nothing in common with a 'tourist trip'. On the contrary, it can be very profitable for the company and very instructive for the student. To attain these ends, the company has to propose a survey which answers a real need, both to give responsibility to the student and to justify the time spent by company executives, as well as the budget invested. Then, the preparation, checkpoints and follow ups will be carried out as seriously as with a classic 'professional' mission.

4.1   Product Perception Valorization

This is an essential operation to be carried out on both the product's image and positioning, and whose effect will be boosted later on by 'push' and 'pull' dynamic devices.

This operation could be compared to the re-launching of a rocket from its launch ramp. This rocket, which has already flown, is the image that the company (or brand) and products project, developed since their initial introduction on the given market. The launch ramp is the positioning given to the products so that they can reach their target clientele.

We shall carefully inspect all the elements of this image-rocket to make sure they are in working order and can function coherently together. Certain elements which did not work well during previous flights will be reinforced or replaced.

Then, there is the check to make sure that the image-rocket is still well adapted to the launch ramp positioning used until then. Flight incidents could have distorted some features, and could prevent take-off from the same ramp.

Finally, we shall study a sky chart of the market's evolution and the movements of the rival rockets and satellites in orbit. According to their movements, it could be decided either to retain the same launch ramp position, or to modify its angle of ascent to ensure the best trajectory towards the target clientele.

4.1.1.   Image

The perception of image in each market is probably one of the exporter's most delicate tasks. During too short a stay in a foreign country, he must try to discern how the different audiences of interest (distributors, users or consumers, various influencers, etc.) perceive the company, brands and products. This means, for each audience, dissecting the global image into its different facets. This feat becomes all the more perilous in major markets when the necessary backup of recent market studies is not available.

Nevertheless, with such a subjective matter, this should not drive the export executive into pure extrapolation about what is going on over the border, where each market can furnish the most unexpected surprises; particularly if the local representatives have a free hand to position, adapt and distribute products as they see fit, as well as to implement their own local communication strategy.

Sometimes, however, a significant resemblance in a product's image evolution from one country to another can be observed:

► The example of **Club Med** is of special interest, considering that its image has followed an identical transformation in all the markets penetrated over the years, despite the extreme complexity of the **Club Med** 'product' which offers a large variety of destinations, styles and activities. This phenomenon originates in the revolutionary concept of a vacation club which lets holiday-makers throw off most of the habitual, every-day constraints, to take better advantage of leisure activities. This concept is succinctly expressed in one of the slogans which was used to promote the **Club** in the United States: '**Club Med**, the antidote for civilization.'

In this context of the free, uninhibited vacation, the initial facet of the **Club's** image to be promulgated in each country (through the grapevine) is always the 'spiciest' and is expressed by moderate or excessive clichés such as:

'the relationships between men and women are very free'
'you can make love as much as you want'
'a real orgy' . . .

Then, with the increase in membership, other facets of perception started developing, thus eventually rebalancing the **Club's** image:

'non-stop sports'
'great food'
'ideal for children' . . .

After this phase, the **Club's** image reaches maturity in a country when it is perceived as the answer to each person's individual vacation needs.

4.1.1.1   Holistic analysis

This analysis leads to identifying the main currents of perception for the company, brand and product images, as perceived by the public concerned, and to differentiating between those with a beneficial influence on development and those with a negative one:

► '**Rhône-Poulenc** contributes to and participates in, to a significant extent, the changes taking place on a planetary level in the chemical and biotechnolo-gical industries. But who is aware of this? To know the answers to this type of question and measure our recognition in France and the rest of the world, we set up an in-depth image study a few years ago' explains André de Marco, Group Communications Director. 'What perception of **Rhône-Poul-enc** did opinion influencers, economic and financial leaders, government officials, present and potential clients have? What did the general public think of us?

These are fundamental questions when you know the Group is confronted every day by international competitors who have similar products, techno-logies and networks. However, these rivals enjoy a superiority because they are known under the same name all over the world, thus taking advantage of a recognition built up over the years which cements all their activities together, no matter how diversified they are.

This study was carried out in France, the United Kingdom, Germany, the United States and Brazil; 2200 people were interviewed both within and without the Group, of which more than half outside France. The results were obvious: the image of the **Rhône-Poulenc Group** was unclear. Professionals had an incomplete perception of the group and the general public were not really aware of the nature of the Group's activities. One person out of two linked the name **Rhône-Poulenc** to ecology and medicine, activities which represent a quarter of their turnover. Identified as a chemical group, they were very often attributed textiles as the major activity, whereas in reality, this only represents 1.2% of the turnover. Concerning chemicals, the public thought that **Rhône-Poulenc** still produced fertilizers, a sector which was abandoned long ago. On the other hand, people ignored the fact that the Group is the world leader for numerous high-tech products and new materials. The variety of products, often unknown by the average consumer, blurred the name **Rhône-Poulenc** for the general public. The **Rhône-Poulenc** group development was being masked by their multiple banners.

To rectify this blurred image, which did not truly reflect the company, **Rhône-Poulenc** launched a corporate campaign in France and Europe. This campaign represents the major fields of activity of the Group (medicine, vaccines, plant protection ... natural science applied to man, animals, plants ... chemical products for high tech materials ...) and shows how **Rhône Poulenc** contributes to everyone's well-being by mastering scientific and technical progress. This campaign brings all the subsidiaries and all the various activities together under the same roof, and reveals the amplitude of their fields of activity as well as the excellence of their performances. This unified tone is reinforced by a single signature, the **Rhône-Poulenc** logo, hereafter used by all the different companies in the Group.

In addition to the press campaign 'Bienvenue (welcome) to ...', which had eight basic themes (Welcome to a world of ... health, ... freedom, ... safety, ... etc.), an advertising film was made on the same themes, a real 'hymn' to life, where **Rhône-Poulenc** welcomes a newborn baby to a world that this group is helping make more hospitable.

It is thanks to a rigorous image analysis that we were able to determine our external communication strategy whose actions, like the 'Bienvenue' campaign, have four major objectives:

- to develop a strong and homogeneous **recognition** by a rigorous identification policy (one name, one logo);
- to clarify the Group's **identity** by making its new activities known;
- to build an **attractive image** of a young, enterprising, dynamic, efficient, innovative Group which creates products with high added value technology:
- to establish the image of a company which has adopted a **responsible** attitude towards its surrounding environment (ethics, security, integration into each country where it is present, etc.)'.

Before coming back to this specific point in the chapter on media advertising (see section 6.2.2.3), it is important to emphasize the double universalism used in the **Rhône-Poulenc** campaign described by André de Marco: that of the concept 'Bienvenue' and its geographical application 'to a world ...'. Obviously, this message can cross borders without any difficulty, a very important aspect for an international campaign. The adoption of 'Bienvenue' *by **Rhône-Poulenc**, one of the world's oldest and best-shared messages, reminds us of the choice of the tree by **Bull** (see section 6.1.4.3), which is another universally appreciated symbol.*

*As a final commentary, the 'Bienvenue' campaign is not only limited to media advertising but is also applied to the **Rhône-Poulenc Group** communication supports which can be adapted to its use, such as the telephone switchboards. Obviously, hearing 'Bienvenue to **Rhône-Poulenc!**' from telephone receptionists in the local language throughout 140 countries, what globetrotter would not feel he has entered a more convivial, professional world?*

Certain currents of perception identified in the image diagnosis emanate directly from the product's own characteristics (see sections 4.2 and 4.3), depend on the nature and quality of distribution channels (see Chapter 5), or have been shaped by earlier communication actions (advertising, public relations and promotions – see Chapter 6). Because of this, these currents are, to a certain extent, controllable and adjustable. Theoretically, modifying certain factors should allow harmful currents to be removed and the company's image improved. In practice, however, the difficulty of precisely determining the nature and importance of the modifications necessary, of getting them accepted without adverse reactions, and finally, of managing to achieve the required transformation, should not be underestimated.

Studies can obviously refine the diagnosis and enable one to make a decision whose results will justify the means invested:

▶ *After an 'identity study', **Taco Bell** (a chain of Mexican restaurants belonging to the **PepsiCo** Group) removed the traditional sleeping Mexican from their signs and replaced this figure with a more classic and stimulating bell. This change, together with a renovation of the restaurants' interior and exterior decoration lead to a 10% increase in turnover.*

Other currents of perception remain completely out of control when determined by factors outside the company's direct influence. For example, a product that has obviously been imported is passively subject to the negative or positive currents of perception linked to the image of its country of origin. This type of current can hardly be influenced (see section 4.1.1.4).

4.1.1.2   Coherence

The overall image analysis allows negative and positive perceptions to be determined, the sum of which constitutes the brand and product image. According to this analysis, those dynamic devices that are most likely to give the image the best possible dynamism should be triggered (see section 4.1.1.3). But before this occurs, the analysis also allows verification and improvement of the coherence of the image's different facets. In most cases, this implies looking for the causes of negative perceptions.

Common examples of incoherence include:

■ an after-sales service whose deficiency will eventually degrade the image of an excellent brand, all the more vulnerable because it is imported;

■ for capital goods, comparatively low prices offered without sufficiently comforting testimonials and a convincing, technical presentation, paradoxically might have a negative effect on sales, because they are making quality doubtful;

■ salespersonnel/demonstrators who are too young, lacking distinction or careless in their appearance, or insufficiently trained, can seriously harm the image of an upmarket cosmetics brand.

The image incoherence factors usually result from a launch, hurriedly prepared, on a market not well known by the exporter, or from the local representative's lack of control in often tending to limit costs so as to make the most profit in the shortest time. The dynamic effect of actions reinforcing the image coherence are of utmost effectiveness, as a couple of examples illustrate:

▶ *Among the numerous dynamic devices used by* **Yoplait** *to develop their position in the USA, one included a catchy advertising headline which brought in a subtle guarantee of French gastronomy: 'Get a little taste of French culture'. This milk product brand also reinforced their image as a natural and dynamic 'in' product by organizing bicycle races in ten American cities with unprecedented success (2000 participants in Los Angeles alone!). The choice of investing in amateur cycling, which is perceived as healthy, up-to-date and French by Americans, is obviously very coherent with the image's positive facets. In the same way, the hot air balloons used by* **Yoplait** *to 'cover' bicycle races and promotional activities around shopping centres are coherent with the brand image, as they are recognized as being of French origin and are considered to be a natural sport . . . flying high on the trendy winds of change.*

As another **Yoplait** *example we take their 1987 launching in Thailand, with the development of an innovative new channel of distribution with their local franchised partner,* **Thai Dairy Industry**. *A small army of young Thai girls in pale pink uniforms, on bicycles equipped with refrigerated ice cream containers, toured the streets and visited companies and even private homes (see section 5.3.1.3). These 'moving oases of coolness', their dynamic visual style, as well as the pleasant originality of this new selling distribution formula, was totally coherent with* **Yoplait's** *international image.*

4.1.1.3   Dynamics

During this book's second part, we shall inventory a great variety of dynamic devices, selecting those of most interest. According to the markets and industries, choices will be different, as given dynamic devices used successfully in certain circumstances should be completely avoided elsewhere.

Among the rare dynamic devices which must be employed in all circumstances are those which ensure satisfying image dynamics. Without this, the most vigorous development actions will be wasted, as trying to push a car with the handbrake still on . . .

After conducting a holistic image analysis (see section 4.1.1.1), the positive and negative currents of perception could be differentiated. Thus, the dynamic devices considered to be of priority are those which will limit or eliminate the braking effect on sales development caused by the image's negative perceptions:

▶ *A few years ago, many concording observations gathered from retail outlets helped the **Cristalleries de Baccarat** to become aware of a danger to their image in the Caribbean. This was caused by a lack of information on their products, whose very high price was explained quite brutally, as well as negatively, 'it's expensive just because it's French!' **Baccarat** was able to reverse this current by training the retailers' sales staff (see section 5.3.3) and by press releases which transmitted simple messages, emphasizing the irreproachable quality that justified their prices. For example, quality control at **Baccarat** is so severe that 40% of the production is destroyed to keep only the perfect pieces (see section 4.2.1.2).*

The next step is to select proper dynamic devices that will highlight the most positive image facets, particularly those responding most accurately to market needs, and those differentiating the product from the competition, in order to produce the best acceleration effect on sales.

▶ *For launching the **Perrier** development plan in the United States in 1977, Gustave Leven and Bruce Nevins, President of the American subsidiary, decided to respond to a starting awareness on the part of the American consumers (that was still hardly felt by then) of the harm caused by the accumulation of too many calories, too much sugar, alcohol, chemicals, pollution . . . An active minority of Americans were becoming interested in health foods, jogging on the beaches of Malibu or Marina del Rey, then in Central Park and even on Madison Avenue. Following the pace of this trend, Americans had a potential need for purity, nature, health, slenderness. **Perrier** was going to bring them all this, as well as 'a touch of class'.*

4.1.1.4   Country of origin

The country-of-origin image is obviously one of the key facets of an imported product image.

▶ *The **Méridien Hotels** support the positive perception their country-of-origin enjoys in this industry by offering around the world a hotel service and a life style which is resolutely French.*

This image can be a powerful dynamic device, but dependent in each market on currents of perception which escape individual company control. Consequently, this dynamic device is to be employed with discernment, playing up the nationality of a product when it is favourable to its development, or playing it down if it is harmful.

On this same point, there is no question of generalizing one or other of these attitudes for the same product, everywhere in the world:

▶ *Japanese companies only use the dynamic effect of the image of state-of-the-art technology 'made in Japan' in cases where the reinforcement of the Japanese signature does not come into conflict with national brands or remind people of recent, painful history. Thus, brands of Japanese cameras do not hesitate to emphasize their nationality or their leadership position on the Japanese market, since they are almost by now the only producers of these items.*

On the contrary, in the domain of automobiles, Japanese companies are very careful about waving their flag in countries with local production. In periods of economic crisis and unemployment, this would irritate nationalism and make potential buyers feel guilty. The communication concentrates, instead, on the technical qualities and performance, without reference to Japan. Besides economic reasons, the same phenomenon is found in southeast Asia, this time for historic reasons, as these countries were invaded by Japan during the Second World War.

▶ *When running head-on into a strong local production, a judicious communication campaign can get around negative reactions or chauvinism. Dutch cheesemakers knew how to do this in France by taking off their hats to French cheeses: 'Holland, the other cheese country'.*

▶ *Snobism linked to imported products actually rages in many countries, especially for luxury items, whose producers literally 'surf' on this wave of popularity, with more or less dexterity.*

For instance, French fashion, gastronomy and perfumes, whose brands do not hesitate to emphasize their nationality by including 'Paris' or 'France' in their names, when they do not place an Eiffel Tower or a French flag somewhere on display near the product.

But if the image of France tarnishes somewhere, for one reason or another, 'Paris', 'France', the Eiffel Tower and the French flag will be quickly packed away to avoid implicating the product. This is exactly what happened when there were major anti-France campaigns in Australia and New Zealand (see section 1.1.1.6) which made French products become very discreet and modest about their origins!

▶ *Here is another example – especially relevant – taken from the pharmaceutical industry. With the similar objective of facilitating product information for consumers of certain developing countries, some American and French laboratories decided to print their packaging and instructions in the local languages. Contrary to their forecasts, their sales fell considerably, for the consumers thought the products were now manufactured locally. To bring* out the foreign origin of their products, and to distinguish them from locally made products (which had a very mediocre image), these laboratories went back to printing the packaging and instructions in their own language, with only a succinct translation. Very quickly, sales rose to their previous levels.

▶ For Japanese clients, the image of luxury products depends mostly on the country of origin. For designer clothes in Japan, Paris or Milan are considered the capitals. However, for furs, New York holds the floor. High quality pelts 'made in the USA' enjoy such prestige that **Révillon** was able to take advantage of this phenomenon. After trying to develop sales in Japan from their Paris base without encountering the hoped for success, **Révillon** decided to play its American trump card. Given the predominant position of North America in the world production of furs, **Révillon** had opened a subsidiary in New York as of 1878, which creates its own collections and manufactures its own fur coats. To develop sales in Japan, **Révillon** counted on its American subsidiary. The image of the label **Révillon New York** worked wonders, since sales have multiplied twelve fold in the first five years.

▶ The image of a Japanese Parisian designer, such as **Kenzo**, is not particularly easy to transmit and to establish. As told by Christian Regouby[1], CEO of **Concept Groupe**, consultants in global communication, 'the purpose was for **Kenzo** in the mid–1980s to create a distinctive and exclusive brand identity, which is in itself a real communication concept and not just a successful graphics exercise.

We wanted to secure the basis of a brand image which would be communicated all over the world. This image had to integrate the idea of Paris fashion, exported by a Japanese designer whose inspiration is transnational.

For the logotype creation, we used a fine paintbrush, the instrument used to write Japanese ideograms, to draw exclusive print characters for the brand. The final design is inserted into a cartouche surrounded by a border rule. The logo calls up a Japanese origin as well as the classic sophistication of French design.

Given the **Kenzo** collections are noted for their outstanding play on colours, a certain joyous non-conformism and lots of humour, we created a concept that transmits this spirit. The logo changes colour according to predefined standards in relation to the type of medium it is made for.

Then we created, for Europe and the USA, a series of advertisements which catered to a specific esthetic emotion for the brand, through strong close-up shots, through the force of the style mixing materials and colours, and finally through the general tone that implies mystery and exoticism.

In five years, **Kenzo** has become a brand with an international awareness, enjoying a very sophisticated image. This image-capital made the development of numerous other products, such as perfumes, under the **Kenzo** brand possible.'

4.1.1.5   Preservation

More and more companies are realizing the importance of maintaining the consistency of their image and that of their products all over the world.

This started within consumer product and service industries, due to their higher visibility to international business travellers. But it is interesting to notice that even heavy equipment manufacturers, whose production remains unknown to the general public, now feel the need to have their products stand out in the context of the companies' international expansion.

It is indeed difficult to control all the numerous facets of an image, for the reasons already mentioned. However, a company can manage to greatly influence its image around the world by imposing its own specific style over the brands' and products' objective representations.

There is a simple and efficient way to do this, one which is little used by small and medium-sized enterprises, of such a low cost that this dynamic device can be included in even the tightest development budgets: this is a company 'Bible', where all its possible graphic representations are shown. It should be given to all local representatives with the obligation to conform to it. The existence of such a bible constitutes an additional support for the local representative and the trade, despite the application difficulties of certain instructions, because this bible enables them to benefit more directly from the effects of synergy provoked by the company products' recognition by its past, present and future actions throughout world markets.

There is no obligation to print and bind a luxury bible such as those of large multinationals for small companies present in only a few markets, with a development budget too limited to even invest in all those dynamic devices that are indispensable.

While waiting to become world leader in their speciality, they can make up a more modest version of a company bible just by collecting the following applicable elements in a company folder:

- symbol, logo, type character and colour models applicable to the firm, its brands and products;
- samples of letterheads, visiting cards, price lists, order forms, invoices, wrapping paper, ribbon etc.;
- photographs and patterns of personnel uniforms with samples of the material, buttons and insignia;
- photographs of signs, display units and standard shelf layout of the products in a retail outlet;
- photographs of different vehicles in the company fleet;
- standard telephone reception formula, as well as background music used for people waiting on the line;
- any other support used to valorize the company image and to distinguish it from the competition.

In professional domains where international development is based on a chain of franchised outlets, the existence of a carefully conceived bible is essential to reinforce the durability of the original concept:

▶ *In addition to the elements mentioned above,* **La Porcelaine Blanche**** also gives its future franchisees very precise instructions on the interior decoration of the outlets, the lighting, the colours, the shelf design for product displays, etc. Thanks to this exactitude, the boutiques of* **La Porcelaine Blanche** *in Frankfurt, Geneva or Dusseldorf are exactly the same as those found in Paris, Brussels or Cannes.*

It would be wrong to think that a bible is only useful for luxury and certain consumer products. Its use is also justified for capital goods and industrial products, as well as in all sectors of the service industry.

▶ *It is important for clients of a large, international bank to be able to find and recognize it in different foreign countries. This helps the clients feel secure. This is why the Communication Division of the* **Crédit Lyonnais** *has been using a visual identity manual for years which established the basic bank symbols, such as logos, emblems, basic colours . . . all the 'general significance vectors', that is to say, all the visual elements which contribute to the company identity.*
   This 'book of standards' is distributed to all the branches in the 70 countries where **Crédit Lyonnais** *is present, as a veritable visual and nominal 'identity charter' of this bank, the fundamental instrument of a homogeneous, global communication program which would be impossible without a basic, coded, reference volume.*

▶ *For the same reasons, the* **Méridien Hotels** *have published a bible:* Towards a New Meridien Image. *It presents all the visible elements of this chain's brand image (the guidelines for media advertising are proposed in another document – see section 6.1.2.4). For example, the descriptions of a new line of printed matter (brochures, catalogues, etc.); the specific places for the 'welcome toiletries' in the bathrooms; a design of the breakfast tray and table set up; the styles of china, glassware, trays, silverware and table linen to be used in 'the Brasserie' restaurant and in the more upmarket 'Restaurant de France' of each hotel; finally, models of the uniforms designed by Nina Ricci for the assistant managers, receptionists, cashiers and housekeepers, as well as the uniforms by Daniel Hechter for the head bellman, porters, and maîtres d'hôtel. Everywhere, the traveller finds the environment he has chosen, whose standardization all over the world creates client loyalty.*

In addition, it is important to note that:

■ for advertising, public relations and sales promotions, a communication bible will be proposed later on in this book (see section 6.4.4.3);

■ in the case of delocalized fabrication, a special technical file

---

*A small company which under this name launched a concept of distributing kitchenware, tableware and, by extension, general interior products.

should be established to transmit, with maximum precision, the method of production and the required standards (see section 4.5).

4.1.2   Positioning

Contrary to what can be observed at headquarters, where marketing executives spare no efforts to refine the positioning of their product lines on the national market, it is surprising to see to what extent this question is neglected on foreign markets where there is a tendency to let the products position themselves under the sole influence of the local representative.

Already satisfied to have established their brand on a new market, too many exporters then adopt a passive attitude (come what may!) hoping that products will 'find their niche' – which is for international marketing what playing blindfolded is for darts.

The exactitude of positioning on *each* market is, however, essential to attain the maximum sales potential, given that the most dynamic client segments are often different from one country to another* for the same product.

▶   *Mineral water is a mass consumer product in France, Germany and Italy, whereas its positioning in the USA and in most Anglo-Saxon countries is in a segment of semi-luxury products, and luxury products in developing countries.*

Beyond this distinction between mass and luxury markets, it is important to refine the product positioning as much as possible by choosing the clientele to target in priority, particularly in advertising and promotional communication actions.

▶   *'For 'Prince' (a double biscuit filled with chocolate or vanilla cream, of the **LU** range – **Groupe BSN**), determining the choices of positioning was logically based on the consumption habits of each country. Because of this, there are different 'bull's eyes' (in relation to the targets) in three neighbouring countries:*

■   *In Belgium, as in France, the positioning of Prince is centred on children, for their afternoon snack, with advertising adapted to this target.*

■   *In Germany, 'Prince' is offered as a snack to adolescents and young adults. Its advertising shows them playing sports and this biscuit is present as the necessary complement to their well-being.*

---

*These differences of positioning, necessary from one market to another, make it all the more important to maintain a sufficient unity of the international brand image, by preserving its objective representations (see section 4.1.1.5).

■ *In Sweden and Finland, adults are the 'bull's eye' of the target market, with communication campaigns that show 'Prince' in the convivial atmosphere of the afternoon coffee break, receptions and picnics.*

▶ *Going further with an example, the direct influence of the positioning choice on the results can be seen. Knowing that most women have naturally curly hair in Brazil, this could lead to the conclusion that there is no market in this country for permanents, whose purpose is to make straight hair curly. However, thanks to a judicious positioning of this product, an international cosmetics brand was able to exploit a latent need successfully. It was aimed at women who wanted to discipline their hairstyles: 'for curls where you want them, like you want them . . .'*

The three preceding examples apply to consumer products. Certain readers whose companies address a professional clientele might not see any relevance in looking for the best positioning of their products or services in foreign markets.

This error can be fatal for a young company which has to position itself very quickly on the most promising segments, to balance its financial commitments with sales conforming to (or even by-passing) sales forecasts.

▶ *It is with great care that Alain Letourneur, CEO of **B+ Microsystems**, and Jill Ayasse, Export Director, studied how to position on their potential foreign markets the Physiostim VS1, an electrotherapeutic appliance without rival, which can treat both men and women for incontinence (frequently occurring in people over the age of 60) or various sexual problems, such as premature ejaculation, pain or insensibility after childbirth.*

*According to their first observations, it seemed that this appliance would be positioned for incontinence in Anglo-Saxon countries (where sexology remains a taboo subject and the majority of patients still do not discuss it with their physicians), and for sexology in the Latin countries, traditionally more liberated in this field. However, since the investment capacities of **B+ Microsystems** only enabled this small company to attack one or two countries efficiently, a more detailed positioning study became necessary, in parallel with an evaluation of potential user networks:*

  (i) *The Middle East: As soon as **B+ Microsystems'** launch was announced in a medical journal, several requests came in concerning its importation to these countries. This could have led the company to believe that there was market potential in the Middle East, and taken **B+ Microsystems** on a 'wild goose chase', given the costs of promotion and training in this remote region. Furthermore, the feminine market is blocked there by secular traditions which even forbid a genital examination. As for the masculine market, the approach is difficult given the lack of preparation of the majority of physicians in using this type of machine for electrotherapy.*

  (ii) *The United Kingdom: The narrowness of the sexology market is largely compensated for by the importance of geriatrics in this country, which is very concerned about the well-being of elderly people. However, the treatment of incontinence by machines which stimulate the muscles and the nerves being usually reserved for physiotherapists, it* seemed it would take too long for physicians to become interested and invest in the Physiostim VS1.

(iii) Italy: *This is the market that **B+ Microsystems** decided to attack as a priority, given that the treatment of sexual problems is a growing activity, and the presence of 400 sexologists would allow a rapid distribution of the Physiostim VS1. Moreover, the treatment of incontinence is an interesting market segment to develop later, thanks to a network of modern hospitals and the existence of equipment subsidies. This choice of priority positioning in relation to sexology in Italy was even smarter given the proximity of this country to the headquarters of **B+ Microsystems** near Marseilles, which could only facilitate communication and accelerate success.*

(iv) Germany: *This market seemed so vast for the treatment of incontinence that **B+ Microsystems** decided to invest there afterwards, by setting up a distribution subsidiary, thanks to the revenues of their Italian sales.*

Let us now see how to play on the positioning of products to ensure development.

4.1.2.1   Target market adequacy

First, it should be checked that products are actually positioned in the most favourable market segments. A quick study will confirm this, particularly a comparison with the positioning of traditional competitors. However, prudence should be exercised in not following the herd spirit with the rest of the sheep, which might have led several competitors to incorrectly position their products by placing themselves in the same segment of the market; on the contrary, full advantage is to be taken of such mistakes.

Indeed, after surveys of this kind, even slight changes in positioning can have a dynamic effect on market development by distinguishing products from the competition. (This will be more fully developed in section 4.1.2.3.)

If the present positioning seems satisfactory, the coherence of the whole still has to be tested. To do this, a series of questions should be favourably answered:

- Do the products respond to the needs of the clients within the target segments?
- Do the product advantages, aiming most precisely at these clients, appear sufficiently explicit for them?
- Are the products distributed by those channels best adapted to their targeted clientele?
- Are the retail prices in line with buyer/user expectations?
- Is the perceived cost/effectiveness ratio favourable in relation to competitors?

■   Are the advertising actions actually presented in the media which best cover the targeted clientele?

In practice, it is rare for this short list of questions to receive a frank and massive 'yes', and any alterations which will adjust products to have a closer positioning with the targeted market segments can be considered as extra-powerful dynamic devices.

4.1.2.2   Image and positioning

The comparison of image and positioning to a rocket and its launch ramp (see section 4.1) emphasizes the closely-knit interaction of these two factors on the results trajectory. Coherence and harmony between the product image and positioning should, therefore, be maintained to ensure an optimum propulsion effect.

Only disastrous effects result from the discordance image/positioning, as illustrated in the following caricature:

▶   *Let us take a line of luxury watches, internationally positioned as a 'status symbol' of success reserved for the elite of elites. Bordering on a nervous breakdown, the local representative in an important market launches a media campaign where these watches are shown on the wrists of a group of punks. This campaign surely will not pass unnoticed, but its effects would be negative.*

However, given the narrowness of the target clientele in a specific market, it is often necessary to distinguish one's products from those of competitors who have a similar product positioning. It is possible to play on the perception of certain image facets without changing the whole positioning itself.

▶   *To continue with the watch example, the same positioning could be kept while at the same time projecting a younger and less conservative image (without resorting to a punk!) by radically changing the visual stereotype of an energetic, tanned, 40-year-old man accompanied by a gorgeous, elegant, young woman – both obviously wearing the right watches – getting out of a Rolls Royce, boarding a private jet or drinking a cocktail on a yacht.*

After this caricature, here is a real case where *Dim* rectified the image given to their pantyhose by its media advertising,[2] thanks to the survey of a focus group carried out in the USA, where their products were apparently selling well (see section 3.3.1.2.).

▶   *'Ridiculous!' This was the verdict given by a group of American women after viewing the two TV commercials that *Dim* launched in the USA as soon as they arrived in 1982. Even the women who buy the products criticize the image of 'the *Dim* girl'. However, it is the same tangly-haired adventuresses who have made the *Dim* fortune for the past 25 years. Nothing works. The skirt of 'the *Dim* girl' is too short for an ambitious career woman who has no time to be seductive. The model is too young for the* *aging baby boomer to identify with. The scenario is too fanciful for practical logic. In brief,* **Dim***, which was targeting working women – queen of consumers – was projecting a 'junior' image. Once the initial shock of incredulity wore off ('in Paris, they didn't want to believe me' reminisces the Marketing Director in New York),* **Dim** *changed direction for its 1985 spring campaign. If they were going to spend 50% of their turnover on advertising, they had to get it right.* **Dim** *started by simplifying the jingle of the new commercial, keeping just the refrain. Then, to emphasize the label 'French product in the USA', they used every cliché in the book. Result: 30 seconds in the daily life of a Parisian woman, between 30 and 40, with a Dallas-type hairstyle – sort of an American version of a French woman. Evening romance on a Seine boatride, rendezvous at the Café de la Paix, running to catch a bus to get to work at an art gallery.*

4.1.2.3   Evolution or change

Changes in positioning are envisaged when, for example, an initial error has made the company aim at a non-priority target, when the evolution of a market hints at the growth of a more favourable client segment, or if one or more competitors have just smothered development chances by positioning themselves on the same client segment with means which eclipse yours. A justified change of positioning can assuredly get the company back on a successful trajectory, but watch out for mistakes! Lady Error rarely forgives in this domain, as a radical change in positioning implies the commitment of important investments, given the mandatory modifications which follow for numerous 'push' and 'pull' elements.

It is more usual and less perilous to enlarge the positioning over neighbouring clientele segments, a move which should logically augment turnover (see section 5.2.1.6, an example of the widening of **Perrier's** distribution).

A traditional example of widening positioning, as a dynamic device, is made up by the development policy of many luxury product brands on most of the large world markets: launching a new product is done with a very precise positioning only concerning, theoretically, the most fortunate of the consumer elite. For that, after a very sophisticated presentation evening where the 'happy few' are present, the products will be distributed according to draconian selectivity, in a very few prestigious boutiques, for prices that are obviously quite high. If these products have a celebrity's label – a well-known designer, for example – this guarantee of quality will be exploited by trendy public relations campaigns. Finally, advertising will reinforce an image of inaccessible luxury for the crowds dreaming of possessing such products.

Needless to say, the launch phase represents a heavy investment for the brands or the local representative, which will only pay off if they have managed to forge a golden image for the trade and the public as a whole.

Then, progressively, distribution will be enlarged by opening new outlets, and retail price increases limited so as to make the products more accessible. However, care will be taken to keep this widening of distribution quite separate from the positioning of the luxury brand image – which will still be reinforced by different forms of communication.

Thus, on the perfume market in the USA, new imported luxury brands generally start by establishing themselves solidly in 100 or 200 'doors', then opening up their distribution each year to reach 1000 to 2000 outlets in two to five years. Many brands stabilize (at least for a time) their distribution between these figures, while others continue to open retail outlets with the growing risk that their image will converge with their positioning, and make a free fall into mass marketing.

▶ *The exploit of* **Chanel***, leader of foreign brands of perfume on the US market, has to be mentioned here. They managed to keep an upmarket image (maintained with talent by multi-media advertising campaigns in which the pure archetype of classic 'made in France' beauty – Catherine Deneuve – appeared then Ines de la Fressange and Carole Bouquet with the launching of 'Coco'), while at the same time using as vast a network of distribution and promotional techniques almost as aggressive as most mass market brands.*

Much rarer are examples of positioning in which a mass market type of product goes upmarket.

▶ *The French paper tissue market is one of the most dynamic in the world. It is a strategic market in terms of volume for the* **Kimberly Clark Group.** **Sopalin***, their French subsidiary, developed, with the design division of the agency* **Concept Groupe***, a new product starting from a packaging concept. The graphic creativity of* **Concept Groupe** *tried to strongly implicate their target clientele by means of visual codes referring to their actual or would-be life styles (tennis, sailing, golf, polo motifs).*

The choice of an elitist name for this product, 'Kleenex Club', and the concept of its packaging enabled this paper handkerchief to evolve from the banal and functional dimension of a 'useful product' to that of 'fashion accessory'.

Thanks to this new product, **Sopalin** *enlarged the generic market of paper handkerchiefs by developing their sales. Given the success of 'Kleenex Club' in France, this concept was used afterwards in other European countries.*

Here is another example of enlarging positioning, but this time linked to age-group.

▶ **Chupa Chups** *studied, tested and launched in Australia a lollipop specially designed for adults. This project was successful because it was well reinforced by push/pull dynamic devices, which included a TV advertising campaign. About 30 million units were consumed by adults during the year of launch, i.e. 50% of the* **Chupa Chups** *sales in Australia, a market of 16 million inhabitants. After this 'first', the positioning of the lollipop for adults is being applied in other markets.*

Often dynamic devices are meant to extend a positioning through a 'despecialization' process. It means that a given product which was designed to operate efficiently for very special requirements can do even greater wonders for normal users:

▶   *This concerns numerous products, developed at first for industry or a particular professional sector, which are then offered to the general public (many examples from the tool, construction and maintenance industries), or ordinary consumer products whose target clientele is widened (gentle shampoos for babies are now sold worldwide to their mothers; will this new positioning spread over the next market segment, by also proposing the same gentle shampoos to the fathers!?).*

4.2   # Product Adaptation

▶   *In Hong Kong, as in most Asian countries, liqueurs were almost unknown, to such an extent that it was called wine, under the general generic name. For* **Cointreau***, the development of this market began by its creation.*

A local study showed that the main interest in **Cointreau** *was essentially due to its orange-based composition, as for the Chinese the orange fruit projects a strong image of health.*

Consequently, it was decided to centre communication on this fruit: rather than an orange, drink **Cointreau***, the spirit of orange.*

On the back label of the bottles, a Chinese name – Kwando – was selected, which means 'gentleman manners', to translate **Cointreau***, and an orange was depicted.*

In addition to these product adaptations, the **Cointreau** *development plan in Hong Kong included, among other dynamic devices, the organization of special tastings during huge receptions (500 to 1000 people, which involved more than 100,000 people over the period). At the same time, a big TV advertising campaign was launched with a film whose theme was based on the orange associated with* **Cointreau***.*

The results were impressive: before this development plan, 90% of **Cointreau** *sales were made to Europeans (tourists or Hong Kong residents). Afterwards, sales increased by five times, and the Chinese population represented 80% of the* **Cointreau** *buyers.*

With this example, we are getting into a more objective domain of product dynamic devices. Here again, we will select ways to stimulate results, either by reducing or eliminating the hindrances caused by the negative characteristics of products, or by developing their positive aspects.

The task is, then, to adapt products so that they are closer to the expectations of international markets by responding to needs already felt and expressed, or better still, by anticipating the emergence of a need, and placing the company in an advantageous position, in advance of its rivals.

As Michel-Henri Carriol* says succinctly, 'To export more, you've got to produce what sells and not only try to sell what you produce.'

In light of this, before further studying all the means to adapt a product to foreign market demands, it is important to be reminded to 'think international' from the conception stage of a product, which will often spare the company from having to make costly modifications later. Obviously, an international product will have the significant advantage of being able to respond well to the demands of its main (home and export) markets, with only possible minor modifications needing to be made.

▶ *The interest of this procedure can also be verified for products destined for professional use, as confirmed by* **April**, *a specialist in programmable logic controllers. 'It's not when the product reaches the shelf that adapting it to different markets should be considered, because you end up with a 5-legged sheep; then bad translations of printed material (catastrophic in the domain of high technology) often go along with a too national concept of ergonomics, definitely killing the product on the markets it was supposed to conquer.*

This is why **April** *organizes marketing think-tanks with all our representatives in the targeted markets, for their programmable logic controllers to be conceptually international. If a special modification is required, it will be taken care of by the country concerned. Numerous misunderstandings are thus avoided and everyone is motivated by a product they know the origin of.'*

To carry on the inventory of dynamic devices linked to product adaptation, we will quickly go over all its characteristics, analysing results from its launch on a specific market or since the preceding development plan.

4.2.1   General characteristics

4.2.1.1   Product and brand names

Before launching a product on a foreign market, it is a must to make sure that the product and the brand names are well accepted, and do not give rise to any unfortunate connotations.

▶ *This is why, in Brazil,* **Kellogg's** *changed the name of their Frosted Flakes to Sucrilhos and Cocoa Krispies to Crokinhos. In the same way, Bran Buds had to be rechristened in Sweden, so that people would not think they had bits of 'grilled farmer' in their cereal bowls at breakfast.*

There is too much of a tendency to forget about names, as if there

---

*President of the French Chamber of Commerce in Sydney; founder and director of **Trimex Pty Ltd**, a company which represents several major French companies in Australia.

were no longer the possibility of changing anything. This is often the case, because it is generally not worth changing a name that has already been invested in and which enjoys a certain recognition. However, there are established cases where an error of appreciation before the launch or a situation changing, should lead to a decision on modifying the name to facilitate business development.

▶ *A short time after **Léonard Perfumes** had already successfully launched 'Tamango' on the US market, the career of a young black boxer, called Sugar Ray Leonard, skyrocketed and he eventually became world champion. This could have led to some kind of a confusion between the boxer and the designer/perfumer. Fortunately, in this case, it was not too difficult to find a solution: an accent was put on the E of LÉONARD (written in capital letters) to differentiate the French name from the American.*

▶ *On the contrary, it can pay off to integrate a product name into the tradition of a country. This is what **Bongrain** succeeded in doing in the USA by rebaptizing one of their cheeses 'Alouette', a name which has the advantage of being that of a French song that most Americans know as a traditional nursery rhyme, a double 'plus' for this cheese: a guarantee of French gastronomy and the fame of a name carrying a high emotional value.*

Equally important, the advertising slogan appearing as the end line, under the logo or the brand name, deserves attention.

▶ *Although fully delegating communciation strategy (see section 6.1.3.1), to adhere perfectly to their markets' specific features, **Sony** succeed in maintaining a worldwide slogan coherence. Whenever different, their end lines provide in every country both a strong, enhancing capability of high tech qualities, as well as a great flexibility to adapt to any product of this Japanese group's wide range: in Australia, New Zealand and Malaysia, **Sony** is 'the one and only': in Singapore, **Sony** stands 'one step ahead'; in Oman, **Sony's** 'research makes the difference'; in Spain, **Sony** introduces 'a fascinating world' (un mundo apasionante); in France, the end line positioning **Sony** as 'the creator' provides, in all product advertisements, quite an effective synergy to the common headline 'if you can dream it, **Sony** can do it' (also shared by all product ads.)*

There are other choices to be considered concerning names: which is the more interesting, to emphasize the name of the brand rather than that of the product, or the contrary? Or both together, as a good many companies have astutely managed to do in very different domains, from **Boeing 747** to **Chanel No 5**.

Moreover, it might have been necessary to use a well-known local name to facilitate the introduction of a product on a market, often the name of a distributor or a brand belonging to the local representative. This practice has certain advantages, particularly for products which have a short life-cycle, thus benefiting from pre-established recognition as soon as they are launched, at a far lower cost. On the other hand, for products which have a long life-cycle, or for a brand which constantly develops new products to launch, this practice can be dangerous in the long run, as it subjugates brand and products under the local partner's banner. If an escape clause were included in the contract with this local partner, it would be of interest to sail under one's own flag as soon as possible, even if his name has to be used in parallel during a transitionary period to enable the clientele to follow the shuffle (see the **LU** example in section 2.2.3.1).

▶ *The American adventure of a French firm is an interesting example of the dangers of using a local name. This company had distributed their food processors in the USA under their exclusive agent's brand name. Sales developed slowly at first, then exploded. 'But we were very quickly copied as the machine had been patented badly. In one year, about 20 cheaper, rival products appeared' says the firm's General Manager. Furthermore, hampered by the exclusivity of his contract, the American agent managed to get a similar appliance manufactured in Japan at a lower cost. 'The US market represented more than half of our sales. We couldn't refuse', explains the exporter sadly. Result of this competition: sales fell by 80% in two years!*

Obviously, he did not renew his agent's contract, and set up his own foreign subsidiary. 'Our problem was to explain to American householders that the food processor which we were now selling ourselves was nothing other than the one they had known for the past six years under an American brand name.'

In spite of an aggressive advertising campaign, it was far too late for such a counter-attack; eventually, the French firm had to give up any hope of restoring its position within the US market.

4.2.1.2   Aesthetics

Here is another delicate subject which can be the source of many surprises. Listening to and taking on board all the advice proffered throughout foreign markets would probably lead to the launch of several product versions for each market. This is obviously out of the question for management and production reasons, but also to protect the uniqueness of the international product image. However, there is such a strong dynamic effect of aesthetics on sales in most professional sectors, that it is useful to observe reactions to aesthetics (shape, proportion, colour, etc.) within each major market, to reach three main decision possibilities:

■ To retain the product's overall presentation, particularly if a modification is too costly in relation to the expected extra turnover. If the aesthetics of the presentation is a hindrance to sales, it is probable that this disadvantage can become a 'plus' by enabling the product to be set apart from the mass of others (we've got to fight with what we've got!)

▶ *Moreover, tradition can be a powerful dynamic device in aesthetics, and thus justify not changing a product presentation. **Grand Marnier** can be* mentioned on this subject as champion of long life, given that the shape of the bottle, its packaging (and of course, the liqueur itself) have not been modified since 1827!

■ To adapt the product's presentation so that it becomes closer to local tastes while trying not to betray its international image and to keep a sufficient originality.

▶ *The design of a wall-clock remains strongly influenced by local styles of interior decoration. This led **Jaz** to decorate wall-clocks differently according to major market tastes. In Germany, these clocks are mounted with ceramic tiles. In the USA, where there is a trend to appreciate old-fashioned designs, **Jaz** proposed a line of traditional French wall-clocks, that existed only in the dreams of Americans! In other words, they are models of clocks that have never existed in France, but which respond perfectly to market expectations. The identity of the brand was not lost because of these adaptations, as the **Jaz-Paris** signature remained visible on all the clocks.*

▶ *In the food industry, it is difficult not to take local preferences into consideration, especially in the case of a raw material where there is no chance to educate consumer tastes about its particular characteristic, as can be done with finished products. This happens, for example, for candied fruits used by pastrycooks and confectioners both in industrial and small-scale production, which are mixed in with the dough as filling or decoration. There is no problem to worry about, of course, for the international image of the product in this context, where the most appreciated originality resides in the taste of the fruit, so that manufacturers can adapt the products to market demands on the subject of colour: in Hong Kong as in Australia, candied angelica used with ice cream and cakes has to be a very dark green, whereas Japan requires light green and Saudi Arabia forbids the use of the green colour, light or dark, completely . . .*

■ To conceive or modify the product's aesthetics to give it an edge on its rivals.

▶ *This is the case, for example, of **Cognac Bisquit X.O.**, whose shiny, golden cap was especially designed for this purpose (see section 2.4.1.1).*

Within industrial circles, investment in product aesthetics is often still only considered justifiable for consumer products or household appliances. The rapid development of industrial aesthetics in the last few years has fortunately demonstrated the opposite: however, most of the applications concern 'high visibility' professional installations whose design comforts the eye of the user. For semi-finished products and certain raw materials, although destined to be swallowed up in the conception of a final product, aesthetics can be a particularly efficient 'plus' in relation to competitors, because it is rarely used.

▶ *This is what Jean-François Zobrist, Director of **Favi** (a company specializing in the smelting of copper alloys), demonstrates when he renders his products more attractive for a modest investment.*
In this way, a clutch throw-out fork from a gearbox usually has an

unattractive, blackish surface. At **Favi**, a quick treatment gives it a shiny look, which can seem superfluous for a part which will become invisible once the gearbox is assembled. But this surface treatment (which costs very little) is justified by the image of the 'visible quality' that is brought to the product, in comparison with the competitors' unrefined foundry products. There is another, less subjective reason: the treatment makes possible tooling flaws more apparent (they would remain undetected on an untreated part), thus ensuring far better quality control.

Here is a second example applied to brass bars destined for smelting. Adding a bit of magnesium during the fabrication gives them a more attractive, golden hue. Again, this effort to find an aesthetic 'plus', still quite unusual in this sector of activity, reinforces the global competitiveness of **Favi's** products, enabling this company to develop its foreign sales. (See section 5.1.2.3 for some other dynamic devices used by **Favi**).

Let us conclude this theme with an anecdote illustrating that a 'divine' aesthetic is not always the key to success:

▶ *The story begins in Alsace, France, at the **Lemaître S.A.** company, one of the French specialists in workshoes. Last year, orders from the Middle East stopped suddenly without explanation. To clarify the situation Jean-Michel Heckel, CEO of **Lemaître**, sent out a commercial executive. After contacting a few local distributors, the troubleshooter discovered the problem . . . which was hidden on the soles of one of the **Lemaître** models, the Maxeco 84. In fact, the design on the top part of the shoe sole – by an extraordinary coincidence – had a meaning in Arabic: Allah! Thus, **Lemaître** quickly had another design worked out for the soles of this model, and sales in the Middle East resumed normally.*

4.2.1.3   Qualities and performances

The decision to buy a consumer product, or even capital goods, is based essentially on their apparent qualities and performance. We have just looked specifically at those which stem from aesthetic adaptations, but numerous other possibilites facilitate the promotion of a product in this domain:

- This first concerns adaptations* destined to place the product at a level of quality and performance which responds best to the expectations of the target clientele:
- Adaptations designed to get people to try, then to use (or consume) the product according to the habits, tastes and usage which apply to consumer products, as well as to capital goods and services.

  Thus, in the food industry, it is regular practice to resort to special doses of ingredients to respond better to market prefer-

---

*The majority of these adaptations often suit groups of countries with comparable needs, thus enabling a company to amortize them on a sufficiently large global market.

ences. Obviously, this type of adaptation poses more problems when the products are made in their country of origin (forecasts, manufacture, special stocks) rather than locally.

▶ *For fresh products, yoghurt for example, whose production plants are set up in each country, it is possible to take local tastes into consideration with great precision. This is why there are quite noticeable differences between yoghurt of the same brand all over the world: quite liquid in Columbia, where people like to drink them; fairly liquid in Ireland; liquid or firm in the USA, because of divergent tastes; thicker and creamier in Japan and Spain, and even more so in Australia; not too sweet in Anglo-Saxon countries (USA, Ireland, UK, Australia, etc.) and in Japan; very sweet in Latin countries (Spain, Portugal, Belgium, North Africa, Brazil); a high fruit content responds to an almost universal expectation (particularly in Brazil, but less so in Japan where more delicate flavours are preferred), which often creates difficult production cost problems.*

▶ *In the case of the biscuit branch of the **BSN Group**, whose products are manufactured in France or in its international subsidiaries, the search for adaptations to different markets is a constant preoccupation, and has given rise to the creation of 'taste zones'. Before launching major products, tests take place in the priority countries, enabling the company to adjust its products and to confirm the adopted formula. This organization ensures an excellent adaptation of new products as soon as they are launched, and facilitates their development: the **LU** biscuit, Spanish **Marie LU** for example, is not only adapted to the general taste, but its firmer texture lets people dunk it in milk or coffee, according to local habits. This research by 'taste zones' was instrumental for the launching of international products which correspond to the major markets' demand, like **Pims**, whose name is as well adapted as its composition (a biscuit covered with a thick layer of orange marmalade and a thin one of chocolate).*

▶ *The necessary adaptation of the product sometimes leads to the modernization of ancestral traditions: 'On the Swedish market, three classes of beer exist which are differentiated by the amount of alcohol', explains Dr. Johann Daniel Gerstein, former Export Director of **Löwenbräu**. 'The beer that we've been brewing in Munich for six centuries belongs to class three. Because of this, we began producing beer of this class in Sweden, and we did this during the introduction period of our brand on this market. Then we considered, with our licensee, that our sales volume wasn't big enough yet and we decided, together, to enlarge our range of products to include a beer from class two, with a lower alcohol content. We were responding to the expectations of consumers who wanted a 'lighter' drink. (The fact that for drivers in Sweden, a much lower rate of alcohol in the blood is tolerated by the police than in Germany, largely explains the need of Swedish consumers for this light beer). We were careful, though, that this specific beer was still recognized as belonging to the **Löwenbräu** range of products and preserved the character of this Bavarian beer, whose origins went back to 1383.'*

▶ *For **Lenôtre**, adaptation to market preferences is also the occasion for fruitful exchanges in questions of taste and dietary research. 'It wouldn't be very* *productive running all over the world arrogantly imposing the rules of French gastronomy as untouchable principles', explains Gaston Lenôtre. 'It's better to co-operate by applying our know-how to the particular case of each country, without hesitating to use new ingredients'. This attitude does a lot to explain their success in Japan (11 boutiques in 1987). Lenôtre's Central Research Laboratory, situated near Paris, France, worked hard for the Japanese market developing original recipes that took Japanese standards of health foods into consideration, and used such recognized 'healthy' ingredients as tofu, pumpkin, carrots, avocado, etc. Moreover, it is remarkable to notice that the effects of this cooperation are not uni-directional, since the research of the Lenôtre laboratory to lower the sugar content in certain Japanese recipes enabled them to do the same in France and Germany, without modifying the taste of the ice creams and pastries.*

Here is an anecdote emphasizing that the need for adaptation to habits, tastes and usages of different markets is not always obvious, especially when differences are hiding in unexpected quarters. Here is the *Dim* experience in the USA (see section 4.1.2.2 for more on this case):

▶ *Luckily, an informal conversation brought us quite a major piece of information: American women do not wear panties under their pantyhose, and wanted cotton inserts. Everyday wear-and-tear also showed that the Dim pantyhose with a slim-line panty – a growing market segment in the USA – is a lot less slimming than its local competitors. This was far from the preoccupations of the first focus group organized for the market test in Chicago, to adapt the packaging, which was considered the major obstacle.*

Contrary to consumer products, the relatively limited number – by comparison – of users of capital goods makes more fundamental adaptations possible, even going so far as offering 'tailor-made' solutions. In this case, the adaptation to client demands will have a double effect: influencing his decision to purchase, then creating brand loyalty for future needs.

▶ *Nixdorf Computer* build their minicomputers and office automation equipment around a single flexible design and tailor the machines to the unique needs of each customer. For that, Nixdorf spend 10% of their R&D budget sending research teams of salesmen, product developers, and production people to talk to customers. The tactic cements the relationship between company and customer. As Klaus Luft, former Nixdorf Chairman, used to explain: 'When you sell integrated systems instead of off-the-shelf hardware, your customer is married to you for ten to 15 years . . .'*

The adaptations destined to facilitate the integration of a product by taking into consideration local constraints: different standards, of course, but also the nature of the environment into which the product will be inserted.

---

*Nixdorf Computer is now part of Siemens Nixdorf Information Systems, whose Chairman is Hans-Dieter Wiedig.

▶ *In the case of **Renault Véhicules Industriels** trucks, it can be a question of adaptations responding to a multitude of constraints all together: in addition to legal standards (pollution, noise, brakes, lights and signalling, weight, dimensions, etc.), geographical and climatic environmental conditions should be mentioned (special equipment for coping with tropical climates or very cold weather conditions, the dust of dirt roads, high altitudes), as well as economic conditions (needs of developing countries for relatively unsophisticated, but robust and dependable vehicles at reasonable prices) etc.*

▶ *With **Sève International**,* here is a 'mission impossible' style of adaptation, since they had to adapt to the unworkable constraints imposed on the realization of a grass-covered playing field: nearing the end of the construction of a huge olympic stadium (1.5 times the size of le Parc des Princes in Paris, France!) and a training field, Sheik Zayed d'Abu Dhabi expressed the desire to have natural grass turf growing in both stadiums three months later, so that his country could host a qualification soccer tournament for the World Football Cup.*

Needless to say, competition was fierce for the project, but nobody wanted to commit himself on the delivery date, as classic grass-growing methods take a minimum of nine months, without even taking into consideration the inherent climatic problems of this region.

Sève International, nevertheless, looked for a solution adapted to this particular problem. Finally, the method chosen for the two stadiums was to install the lawns on two giant 'Riviera-style' self-watering planters of 7500 square metres each!!! More exactly, grass slips were specially flown in from Kenya and transplanted by hand onto specially prepared compost, which was continually moistened by an underground irrigation system controlled by programmed electronic valves.

*This daring project enabled **Sève International** to get the deal. Three months later, the objectives had been met: the Sheik presided over the inauguration ceremonies, and the grass withstood the studded shoes of the soccer players.*

▶ *In the pharmaceutical industry, obtaining an authorization or approval to sell on the market from officialdom (very fussy in certain countries) can be a serious handicap for exporting companies. Still, beyond the costly constitution of files conforming to local regulations and the necessary perseverance to obtain results, the preoccupations of adapting products to demand remain of utmost importance. In Japan, for example, American and European laboratories specially reduced the size of their tablets to ease their ingestion, as Japanese have narrower throats than 'gaïjins'.*

On the contrary, when an adaptation is not rendered obligatory by constraints of utilization or specific standards, care has to be taken not to rush ahead too quickly with changes without having a serious study done beforehand: first, because this kind of adaptation can be costly; second, because in many domains (food products in general,

---

*A young French company which conceives and implements parks, grass covered playgrounds, irrigation systems and forestry projects.

sophisticated appliances) an import image constitutes an advantage, and to appear nonstandard in the eyes of the purchaser is a simple way of emphasizing the product's foreign origin.

■ To the number of dynamic devices which stimulate the decision to purchase a product, there are those which develop a product's competitiveness by giving it 'pluses' – the equivalent of boosters which improve an aeroplane's normal performance at specific moments. They are of various kinds:
  □ The specific advantages of the product (usually resulting from a technical innovation), whose influence on sales will be all the stronger as they will be considered an appreciable 'plus' of consumption or use, and the product's cost-effectiveness will compare favourably to that of competitors.

These dynamic devices are obviously powerful, but their mobilization requires both time and solid investment.

▶ *Zodiac were not satisfied with just inventing inflatable boats. In addition to this, the Group's determination to give priority to technological investment has enabled them to always keep ahead of their international competitors. It is thanks to an 80-person R&D department that **Zodiac** have always been able to bring 'pluses' to their products: major advantages such as the use of new highly resistant materials for the manufacture of boats, the inflatable keel, the intercommunication/surpression valves, the 'Futura' hull (which considerably improves the manoeuvrability and comfort), the anodized aluminium floorboards, etc.; minor advantages as well, which assist the purchase decision because of the amenities they provide for the use and maintenance of the boats.*

  □ Services regularly offered (installation, maintenance, warranty, after-sales services; see section 4.2.3).
  □ Special offers, such as promotional activities (see section 6.5).
  □ Different kinds of 'pluses' whose purpose is to offer the client an advantage he is sensitive to, which will influence his decision.

▶ *Thus, since its founding in 1957, **RoC** remains one of the few brands of cosmetics to indicate an expiry date on their skincare and makeup products. This is expensive for the company, as they systematically destroy and replace unsold products whose dates of use have expired. However, such a practice provides an extra purchase motivation for the clientele, who are sure of buying 'fresh' products.*

■ At each link of the commercial chain, there are numerous means to provide a 'plus' to products by reinforcing distributor motivation to give priority to their sales development (see section 5.3.2).

▶ *In the fast growing travel industry, a sophisticated communication system can be considered a major plus for business development. Holidex 2000 is the world's largest privately-owned computerized hotel reservation system.*

*It links over 1600 **Holiday Inn** properties in 54 countries with 24 **Holiday Inn** central reservation offices, over 40 corporate implant Holidex terminals, as well as over 240,000 airline and travel agent terminals worldwide. More than 70,000 room nights are booked each working day, a total of over 30 million bookings annually – more than all other hotel chains combined. Individual reservations through Holidex can be processed and confirmed in 142 seconds.*

■ Another 'plus', which is tending to become a 'must' in a majority of countries: countertrade applied to very different products such as . . . offering tourists in exchange for TV sets!

► *'Whether it pleases the G.A.T.T. or not, countertrade still has some fine days ahead. **NEC**, the Japanese electronics firm, has just crossed the threshold of sophistication by offering Egypt a new exchange currency, as it were: the tourist.*

*Penalized by the rise of the Yen, and more still by the financial difficulties of Egypt, this firm set up a Machiavellian plan baptized 'Cleopatra': in exchange for sending 5000 Japanese tourists who will spend about one billion Yen (about $7.87 million), i.e. 200,000 Yen per person ($1575), Egypt will buy 260,000 TV sets from **NEC**. This will notably increase **NEC**'s Egyptian market share. 'We hope to carry this plan on for ten years, as both parties will profit from it' specified Junji Kobayashi, who is in charge of the plan. A third partner will also profit from the windfall: the travel agency **Nittsu Express Co.**, which organizes the visit to the Pyramids.*

200 Japanese have already walked along the banks of the Nile for the great benefit of the Japanese company, and 600 others are expected from now until the end of March. The 'Cleopatra' plan should bring over 10,000 Japanese visitors to Egypt.'[4]

First announced in Japan by the daily Asahi Shinbum, *this news had nothing revolutionary about it, since several companies – including the French group **CGE** – already practised this form of compensation with Romania 15 years ago. **CGE**, for example, bought seats on a charter flight, nights at hotels and guided tours, to better sell their transformers and electric meters.*

However, to know more about this question, often unfamiliar to company executives, here is some information from a specialist, Hans Hoomans, Export and Countertrade Director of the *Philips* Group in France:

► *'In fact, countertrade isn't new since it is a modern version of the oldest form of commerce: barter. But today, of course, countertrade covers the whole range of sometimes very complex techniques, both to activate the most adapted international negotiations networks to a particular case, and to ensure a better financial structure.*

However, with the possible assistance of specialized advice, countertrade is accessible to even medium sized companies (certain countertrade contracts are as small as a quarter million dollars). Far from creating a problem, this technique can be a 'plus' which should be offered spontaneously when circumstances seem to call for it.

Moreover, a minimum of 100 countries are having such economic difficul-

ties that all or part of their importations can only be accomplished thanks to countertrade. As an example, among others, **Philips** was able to carry off a large telecommunications deal in Czechoslovakia by offering to have $5 million worth of kitchen stoves manufactured there, destined to be re-exported. This way, we were able to beat a Japanese offer, for despite the exchange of 'tourists for TV sets', Japan is not the only country using countertrade techniques . . .'

■ As for capital goods and services, the notion of the 'plus' concept is also largely widespread:
  □ Special conditions, or even exemption from payment for certain services involved with the product environment (training, technical assistance, etc.).
  □ Assistance offered to the clientele in addition to the usual services.

▶ *Crédit Lyonnais, for example, help their clients to find partners in the 70 countries where this bank is present. In the biggest markets (notably Europe, the USA and Japan), **Crédit Lyonnais** has set up a special 'Welcome Service' for small- and medium-sized companies. These 'Lion Export Bureaux', real export offices, offer different kinds of support: market studies, research for partners and business opportunities, as well as various other assistance (commercial, financial, legal, fiscal, logistics).*

*Moreover, **Lion Export** has set up a data bank which contains, besides general information on the bank's services, products and insurance, about 100 files on different countries whose information can provide the basic elements for a pre-market study.*

  □ Here are other examples of 'pluses' in many different fields:

▶ *All of the **Fish** boats are equipped with a fire pump whose range averages 100 metres, as well as anti-pollution equipment that enables them to bring help quickly to the drilling platforms, in addition to the services included in their assistance contracts. Only a minority of supply and assistance vessels are equipped with this kind of safety material (a fire pump alone costs about $200,000!) and it is easy to understand that many international petroleum companies prefer **Fish**, given the 'plus' safety features their presence brings to offshore drilling platforms.*

▶ *In the framework of turnkey projects, engineering companies often propose 'pluses' with their tenders to make them more attractive: search for project financing, commitment to local subcontractors for a certain percentage of the realization; sometimes, they even find production opportunities for a future factory by ensuring its commercial start up.*

▶ *When an airline wants to open up a new route, the 'pluses' play an important role in getting the sales off the ground and ensuring rapidly a satisfactory percentage of filled seats.*
*As Jean-Michel Masson, **UTA Airline*** CEO, recalls: 'When we launched*

---

*UTA is now affiliated with the **Air France** group, and mainly specializes in aeronautical maintenance and industrial affairs.

our new Tokyo-Noumea route in 1973, we had had a study of Japanese tourists done, particularly the motivations of newlyweds who represented a big segment of this market. We learned that newlyweds wanted to leave on a trip as soon as possible after the official ritual wedding ceremony of the weekend, and they wished to have a European ceremony upon arrival at their destination. This is why France had started to welcome a clientele of 'honeymooners' in prestigious and traditional places (churches, cathedrals, chateaux).

UTA airline, with Club Med and Japanese tour operators, thus organized wedding ceremonies (white dress and tuxedo, not forgetting, of course, the photographers) with the competent authorities in New Caledonia. And all this with sun and palm trees...

The widening of our classic transportation product-offer has been very successful since then: more than 1500 young Japanese couples 'got married' in Noumea in 1991.'

▶ *Manufacturers of cutting tools have always received shipments of standardized, flat, square sheets of metal from all their international suppliers. The Commentryenne des Aciers helped them save up to 20% on the weight of steel by offering products specially processed to have their dimensions matching the size of the tools to be manufactured. With this important advantage, the Commentryenne des Aciers were able to become regular suppliers for many manufacturers (particularly in the USA, Japan and Germany) and with this 'Trojan Horse', to introduce the rest of their product lines.*

The flowering of product 'pluses' galore in all domains has led to savage bidding on international markets, which tends to grow with product sophistication. It makes watching competitor initiatives and clientele reactions closely even more indispensable, together with finding a sufficiently original approach to ensure the success of this type of dynamic device.

4.2.1.4 Consumer/user satisfaction

After the decision to purchase is made, client satisfaction depends essentially on the capacity of the product to meet given needs. It is, therefore, curious that this obvious fact does not lead more exporting companies to establish rigorous procedures of quality control. Indeed, the cost of this investment is amortized on several levels, even more so on international rather than domestic markets:

- Taking into account what it cost to 'gain' a new client (initial contact, business establishment and development) on the other side of the world, it's crazy to risk losing him by delivering a product of dubious quality.
- For products under warranty, the losses caused by inefficient quality control are heavier still: to the client's dissatisfaction are added further costs (replacement of faulty parts, repairs, etc.),

obviously much higher for Djakarta or Berlin than within the homeland.

■ Quality control directly influences the image of reliability projected by a brand or a country, and it can give a supplementary added value for this highly profitable investment: German industrialists are still reaping rewards in this field! It is Japan, though, that gets the 'Oscar' for having managed – in less than 30 years – the trick of transforming an image as a gadget manufacturer (who today remembers Japanese watches sold by the pound?) into that of the inventor of high-quality, dependable products (without mentioning other facets of Japanese industry's image such as its technological advances, among others). Moreover, this result is not based only on the perfectionist mind and legendary discipline of Japanese workers, but also on rigorous quality control legislation for products 'Made in Japan', which emphasizes the importance of this problem. In fact, a sort of examination exists that all companies willing to export their products must undergo. Only those products of sufficient quality will be confirmed as 'good for export', meaning that they do not risk harming Japan's brand image. The procedure and organization of these national quality controls are delegated to the professional associations of this country's targeted priority products, among which can be found the great successes of Japanese technology: automobiles, photography, watchmaking, televisions, videos, optics, machine tools, games and toys, household appliances, etc.

Given that the self-discipline of national companies is insufficient to maintain a satisfactory quality of products 'Made in X', setting up a similar national quality control system could be a good idea, despite the costly and irritating aspect of such a system, to help improve the image of national production.

Fortunately, there are many companies for which quality control is an important element of commercial policy.

▶ *In the case of **Baccarat**, it is a question of ancient tradition, since the manufacture of crystal objects is based on an organization – almost ceremonial – that has evolved very little since 1764. Thus, following the steps in the fabrication of a crystal glass, there are two main series of quality checks:*

(1) *The 'major choice' takes place after the 'hot work' where the molten crystal takes its definitive shape: the objects are attentively and severely checked by the 'choosers'. These guardians of **Baccarat** quality verify that the dimensions have been respected within the limits of handmade specifications, the thickness, the fine finish, the clean attachments of stem to base, the general balance of the glass, the absence of air bubbles or dust imprisoned in the crystal, or any other flaws which will disqualify it.*

(2) *After this 'major choice', the objects which have passed inspection are*

then checked at each phase of the 'cold work' (cutting, reheating, trimming, engraving, polishing) to verify: possible tool marks, the regularity of chiselled angles and the equality of their dimensions, the regularity of designs (rosettes, diamonds, wide or narrow ribs), the precision and finesse of the stars on the base, the engraving designs, the décor, the polishing, etc. The extreme rigor of these quality controls can lead to 30% or 40% of discarded, flawed glassware.

Other dynamic devices can be triggered to help the client in choosing and maintaining a privileged client-product relationship. This will have the dual result of creating product loyalty and transforming the client into a benevolent market influencer within his professional and personal circles.

This approach has applications in all professional fields, and is aptly illustrated by an example taken purposely from the travel industry.

▶ *For an executive, the decision to make a first reservation in a **Méridien** Hotel could have been influenced by a multitude of factors, among others, his knowledge of the 'pluses' of this chain, the recommendation of his travel agent, a friend or his local business contacts. As soon as he arrives at the hotel, every successive impression of the '**Méridien** product' can transform him into a faithful client and market influencer. This is why **Méridien** **Hotels** want to offer tailor-made service to their 'business' clients, particularly by setting up around them the logistics assistance they are accustomed to within their companies ('Business Centres' with services like secretarial, communications, documentation, translation, reservations, etc.).*

In general, given that product quality and performance live up to their promises, the purchaser will know how best to use/consume them. There are two essential means for that: training the sales personnel (see section 5.3.3), and providing information with the product (see section 4.2.2.2), to which will be added – in an industrial environment, or for certain services – training for the users as well as technical assistance.

The simplification of maintenance is also a solid dynamic device to create loyalty among clients, which can be efficiently completed by the organization of an energetic after-sales service (see section 4.2.3).

Another possible added value, especially adaptable to consumer products, is to offer clients information that is not necessarily linked to the products, in various domains: history, geography, culture, etc. Other ideas, recipes, user or consumer tricks can also be suggested (see section 6.3.2.2). This type of initiative can be materialized in more or less original ways in the product environment (as part of the packaging), and cannot help but reinforce links with the client, to whom is given a means to enrich his knowledge and to better take advantage of his purchase.

▶   *In this way, even if rusks are now a daily consumption product in France,* ***Heudebert*** *had to come up with a special packaging on foreign markets where they were not as well-known. First, the packages are smaller because of a lower consumption rate, and to encourage impulse purchases. The front of the package gives information about the product's main uses as a support to put sweet things on, such as jam, or salty toppings such as ham, salmon, tomatoes, etc. Finally, on the back of the package, more detailed information is provided with advice and recipes.*

For major capital goods which have long life-spans, users greatly appreciate that their suppliers offer them the improvements resulting from technological evolution.

▶   ***Airbus Industrie*** *is particularly attached to this type of client assistance, so that each airline can use their aircraft in the best conditions of efficiency, use and maintenance. This assistance is without doubt one of the most powerful dynamic devices to incite a company to remain loyal to the same manufacturer when the time has come to extend their fleet.*

4.2.2   Packaging

The further away products are from direct control, the more their capacity to overcome obstacles and to sell themselves has to be reinforced. This is why it is so important to consider packaging as a fundamental source of dynamic devices which can efficiently reinforce most development plans, and no longer merely as a necessary evil.

We will make a distinction* in this domain (by order of appearance on the international scene) between the *packing* used for dispatching (and protecting) the product, which will wind up somewhere in the chain of distribution on a foreign market, and the *packaging* which accompanies the product into the consumer/ user environment.

4.2.2.1   Suitability to local environment

Protection, which is the essential function of packing used to dispatch merchandise, is not always considered holistically. This often creates problems which could easily have been avoided by keeping a few things in mind:

■   First, the resistance and weight of the packing will be chosen in

---

*This distinction is more applicable to consumer products, durable or otherwise, than to industrial products or capital goods, where *packing* and *packaging* are often one and the same thing.

relation to the fragility of the product and the transportation means used.

■ According to the nature of the product, the adaptation of the packing to the climatic conditions has to be foreseen (heat, cold, dampness), as well as the dust factor.

▶ *This need led the **Hesnault Group** (international transports) to assist their clients in this domain:*

— *Thus, for numerous shipments of 'sensitive' materials (electronics, laboratory equipment, medical materials, etc.), **Hesnault** came up with a special packing made of several layers of plastic folds, completely independent of each other, rendering the crates watertight, airtight and dustproof. This packing is particularly adapted for protecting the shipped material from the vagaries of the climate (humidity, dust storms, etc.) in many countries: in Togo, for example, where the Harmattan wind blows from the north onto the Gulf of Guinea, carrying along with it a 'fog' of red sand which gets into any standard packing.*

— *The same concept was implemented for the north of Japan, where **Hesnault** developed special packing, which included several thicknesses of isolating fibres, for cold climates. This technique is now regularly used for almost all shipments to countries with similar climates.*

■ Products must be given an extra chance to survive the treatment of handlers, who have a worldwide tendency to throw them around without too much care from a truck to the cargo compartment of a plane – to a hangar – to another truck – to a hold – to another truck – to a warehouse. For this, the word 'Fragile' is not enough: this mark appears on so many bales and crates that nobody pays attention; furthermore, few handlers speak other languages, and most of them are illiterate in many countries anyway. It would be better to put a sticker on the crates with a symbol/diagram (broken glass, for example), and better still to have a funny drawing which attracts attention and modestly contributes to the inalienable right of workers to share a joke now and then.

■ For the same reason, it is advisable to put handles or at least handholds on oversized crates which otherwise offer no easy grip, and perhaps use adaptable outer casings which enable handlers to pile them up easily inside any transport environment (containers, for example).

■ Finally, there is no reason to facilitate the work of cargo looters by clearly showing a brandname on cases containing valuable products. Despite security improvements due to the use of containers, it is obviously far better to use a neutral and hermetic packing.

Adapting the packing to export protection constraints often allows a company to keep the standard individual packaging used on their domestic market. An increased resistance to dust and particular climatic conditions can be imagined, however, for the most sensitive product categories.

Particular changes are occasionally imposed by the standards enforced on certain markets, or by distributors' required specifications. It is frequent, for example, that the distribution in superstores (especially for food products) requires exporters to adapt their packaging to correspond to standard shelf dimensions.

The nature of the packaging can also enhance the product image.

▶ *The RoC image of 'beauty in safety' is reinforced by the choice of packaging destined to avoid pollution risks to its products during use. Jars with large openings are replaced by capped tubes that avoid contact with air and fingers. Glass bottles and aluminium tubes have been chosen for all the fragile emulsions.*

4.2.2.2   Communication capability

The 'communication' function of packing cases is usually limited to information concerning the precautions to be taken during handling that were mentioned above, and to stocking instructions, of utmost importance for fragile or perishable goods. Here as well, efforts should be made to render these instructions comprehensible: again, use of diagrams, or if the instructions cannot be reduced to a graphical design, the text should be written briefly and clearly in the required languages.

This same principle should also be applied to individual packaging and, whenever applicable, to the product itself.

▶ *Jaz replaced most instructions by symbols which greatly limited the text shown on the packaging and allowed a simultaneous translation into four or even six languages. On the backs of the clocks, each control button is explained by a symbol, without any text.*

Moreover, individual packaging is a major communication medium whose role becomes particularly important for products distributed in supermarkets so that it is justifiably called the 'silent salesman', as is POP material (see section 6.3). However, it is rare to be able to measure the direct effects linked to a change of packaging in a product's sales development, which is often explained as well by the use of other dynamic devices. This makes even more interesting the case reported by[5] **IG Design** about a mission carried out for the **MAPA Co.** (**Hutchinson Group**), leader in the European disposable glove market.

▶ *'Attacked on the thin glove market segment, the manufacturer wants to improve his sales results while at the same time creating an event for the distribution, to demonstrate the vitality of the brand.*

By replacing the old, classic, polyethylene bag containing ten vinyl gloves

designed for short use (changing wheels, repairs, painting), **IG Design**
produced a PVC box. This modification has multiple advantages.

*The reduction of the package volume by half means a gain in shelf space
for the distributors. The consumer buys a box of gloves that operates like a
tissue dispenser, thus facilitating its use.*

*Benefits for the brand: a 40% jump in sales volume. In one year, they
reached one million units sold, even though the retail price went up by 10%
because packaging costs increased by 60%. In addition, this better product
rotation emphasized* **MAPA's** *vitality to the distributors.*

*Another advantage, which should not be neglected, linked to this packag-
ing transformation: the brand's signature, which disappeared before as soon
as the bag was opened, remains visible until the glove box is empty, with
the effect of reinforcing brand loyalty. All this only cost a research and
design budget of about $30,000, without any advertising support.*

*'This packaging improvement was obviously a major plus for stimulating
export markets as well,' reported Didier de Lalande,* **MAPA's** *International
Sales Manager for consumer products, a few years later. 'We are now the
German market leader only three years after launching this new presentation. In Spain and Italy, we reached this same 'pole position' even faster, in
1991, after the 1990 launch. And these results sound even more impressive if
you know that the* **MAPA** *box of gloves retail price is about double the
competitors' classic products!'*

After this example, which explicitly confirms the interest of investing
in packaging development, here is some advice concerning the adaptation of individual packaging to foreign markets:

- ■ It is likely that the packaging of all products destined to be on
  view in sales outlets on the domestic market has been designed
  to attract attention, interest the potential consumer and facilitate
  identification when surrounded by a mass of competitors. But
  what about foreign markets? It is possible that our codes of visual
  communication (shape, colour, graphics) are poorly adapted to
  local tastes, or that other products capture attention better and
  are more attractive to consumers. In this case, packaging modifications should be considered for enabling products to be more
  combative abroad, while at the same time trying not to fundamentally change their international image – a difficult but feasible
  exercise.

- ■ The packaging design can greatly facilitate the positioning of
  products sold in supermarkets in many countries.

▶ *This becomes even more obvious when considering two products of fairly
close size, shape and composition such as, for example,* **Boudoir** *and* **Champagne** *biscuits by* **LU***. Although the packages are of similar size, and there
is a photograph of an almost identical biscuit on each box,* **LU** *has managed
to clearly position each biscuit by playing on the package design. The box
of* **Boudoir** *biscuits is a basic white/light blue colour and the presence of a
fluffy rabbit indicates fairly plainly the destination of the biscuits, while
adding an emotional connotation capable of enticing both mother and child.*
Champagne *biscuits, with an 'adult' taste, are presented in a basic gold*

and white box; the rabbit is replaced by . . . a glass of champagne and a silver chandelier, thus situating the age of their consumers as well as projecting a sophisticated image for this product.

■   The ideal packaging should obviously valorize the product on both domestic and international markets, while bearing in mind that their shelving practices and selling conditions may vary considerably according to countries and distribution networks.

In this respect, an efficient action is not necessarily gaudy and expensive.

▶   *In several countries, **Evian** was suffering from a lack of visibility on super-market shelves where cartons of bottled water are placed in bulk for customer self-service. Often the boxes are unopened, and there is not even room for any POP material. This is why instructions were added: a dotted cutting line was printed on the top third of the carton along with a drawing of a pair of scissors. Thus, the stockman often think these indications are shelf instructions and cut off the carton tops, revealing the bottle caps and labels of the **Evian** bottles, which, of course, increases sales.*

A close look at the final customer attitude and needs often leads to adaptations which can strongly influence sales results. Years ago, such a packaging improvement was introduced in the Duty Free sales on board airlines, which illustrates the importance of this type of action.

▶   *The first manufacturer of ties and scarves to have come up with a transparent plastic window on the traditional packages rapidly outdistanced their compe-tition, who ended up by copying. Indeed, the passengers were able – at last – to see the design and colours of the ties and scarves, which cannot be displayed as easily in aircraft as they usually are in 'ground' bou-tiques.*

The same approach, based on surveying more closely the expectations of the local distributor's clients, also appears to be very effective for industrial products.

▶   *'We spend quite a lot of time out in the field, within our export markets, watching how the end-users are handling and machining our chromium plated bars', says Joël Tarit, International Sales Director of **URANIE**, an SME based north of Paris, whose export turnover exceeds 85%.*
    'This means many different types of application, since our bars are inte-grated into various equipment, such as cylinders or hydraulic/pneumatic systems. However, our frequent market surveys generate important technical improvements. For instance, we noticed some difficulties of the end-users in handling, cutting and re-stocking our bars because of the bulky cardboard packing, which was not easily re-usable after being removed.
    After testing several other packing alternatives, we had the simple idea to dress up our bars just like gigantic sausages! No more cumbersome cardboard sleeves now: the bars look slim and fit under the protection of an extra strong retractable plastic film, which makes them easier by far to

manipulate and store. This adaptation was very effective, as well, to spur our sales . . .'

The aesthetics of the packaging can also be linked efficiently to a better protection of product quality in the channels of distribution.

▶ *If champagne bottles have been objects of creation for three centuries, the decoration of the first **Taittinger Collection** bottle did not go unnoticed.*

*Entrusting Victor Vasarely, one of the most audacious of contemporary painters, with the mission of creating an original bottle, **Taittinger Champagne** pulled off a double innovation, aesthetic as well as protective: transfigured into a golden flask with a turquoise blue rectangular label displaying a spheric relief, which suggests the concept of an 'eternal beginning', the traditional bottle became a work of art; moreover, the gold layer is a natural protection for this precious wine against the retail outlets' neon lighting, rich in ultra-violent rays which pierces the glass and penetrate the wine, provoking an undesireable premature aging phenomenon.*

■ When the nature of the packaging allows, the printing of precise information about the product and its use is logically much appreciated (possibly with diagrams) in the languages best adapted to the priority target markets. It can even be worth printing specially adapted packaging for key importing countries. The writing of these texts should then be checked quite carefully by the local representative and/or his advertising agency, as certain translators living far away from their home country for many years may have lost contact with the evolution of their mother tongue. In addition, they might use expressions which are totally inadequate for the potential clientele's style, and others may hand in a hurried or only approximate translation.

▶ *To illustrate this recommendation, an example take from a German cosmetics company will be very effective, as well as soothing most exporters' complexes, since it shows that our German friends' reputation for efficiency is sometimes over-rated. Here is the exact reproduction – complete with heaviness of style, improper terms, spelling mistakes and misprints – from the trilingual label of a shampoo bottle. No commentary. . . .*

☐ *'Reinigt Das Haar mild und pflegend. Wertvolle Natur substanzen in Verbindung mit modernen Pflegesubstanzen wirken wohltuend und belebend. Nach jedem Waschen ist das Haar wieder geschmeidig, glänzend, gut gepflegt und hat einen angenehm natürlichen Duft.*

☐ *Cleans your hair soft and preserving. In combination with modern preserving compounds, precious natural-substances cause comfortable and stimulated. After having washed your hair it is again elastic, natural sparkling and good preserved.*

☐ *Lave les cheveux mornaux. Les substances naturelles de grande valeur en combinaison avec les compositions modernes donnent une sesation agréable et rafraichissante. Après chaque lavage, la chevel-*

ure est de nouveau légère, brillante, soignée et sent naturellement bon.'

■ Where packaging is specially made for one or several markets (special fabrication in the country of origin; local fabrication or packaging), it is worth highlighting the information printed on the package by emphasizing the product's specific advantages which correspond most directly to the local clientele's needs and expectations; as well as those which most favourably distinguish the product from the major competitors in the given market.

■ The packing and the packaging can also serve as an 'extra service' communication medium that furnishes interesting information about the product's environment, or inventive suggestions on its consumption/use (see section 4.2.1.4), or perhaps information on complementary products provided by the brand.

■ Finally, for markets where certain legal notices must figure on the products, it is advisable to check on the way in which the local representative intends to take care of this, both in terms of accuracy and presentation. Neglecting this precaution might, for instance, lead to the product's name or essential information being covered by labels stuck on by packagers left to their own devices.

4.2.2.3   Added value

There are other possibilities to develop sales thanks to packaging and/or packing which confer added value on the products. The last link in the chain of distribution will take advantage of the added value of the packing. Thus, the consumer/final user will be motivated to buy a product whose packaging brings him 'a plus.'

■ The most essential of these possibilities is promotional actions applied to the packaging, described later on (see section 6.5).

▶ *If a 6-ton truck can be considered as 'packing', the picturesque example of a French brand of apéritif (before-dinner drinks) can be cited. With the objective of gaining recognition from Italian distributors, they offered several distributors the actual truck as a gift if they ordered a full load of the French drink. Profit margin on shipments of this size is so substantial that it allowed the brand to recuperate their 4-wheeled gifts. This gesture was so spectacular that it is still talked about in Italian bars and restaurants.*

■ It can be noted that the notion of added value for the receiver is perfectly compatible with the improvement of the transportation function of the packing.

▶ *To facilitate and standardize the embarking of a multitude of small packages for their clients, the **Hesnault Group** designed a metallic box – sort of an improved chest – especially adapted for container traffic. In addition, these* boxes were also studied for possible reutilization: this is how one of **Hesnault's** biggest clients, a pharmaceutical broker established in Tokyo and in the major Japanese cities, converted them (provided as used packing) into industrial shelving in certain of their subsidiaries. The effect this kind of advantage has on client loyalty is obvious.

■ For all 'image' products, luxury items in particular, the packing is obviously a powerful dynamic device, whose overall importance must be exploited in every possible way.

▶ *Baccarat's action in this domain is an excellent illustration:*

☐ *The beauty and quality of the protective packaging brings an added value to the product which influences the purchase decision and reinforces the pleasure of the receiver in the case of a gift. This is why **Baccarat** packages can be compared to those used for jewellery.*

☐ *For the distributor (upmarket department store or 'tableware' retailer), **Baccarat** packaging has two functions: each piece or set of crystal is delivered in its final, show-case packaging, ready to sell. This packaging is also conceived to serve as a base for a window display. This allows the piece to be exhibited in the environment created for it, while remaining easily identifiable by the **Baccarat** colour and signature.*

☐ *The protective packing given to the client to transport his purchase (a flexible cardboard or plastic shopping bag) is a communication medium offering an excellent cost/visibility ratio, as it is often re-used after the purchase, if it is practical, robust and valorizes the image of its user. **Baccarat** has thus logically created large shopping bags in their colours, in glossy, flexible cardboard, to meet this need.*

☐ *The interest of **Baccarat** in their packaging, and more generally in the overall world image of the brand, is illustrated again by a courageous decision made in January 1983. The logo and colours chosen by **Baccarat's** American subsidiary in 1948, which had been used since then in the US, gave way to the institutional logo and colours of **Baccarat Paris** presented in the communication bible given to their distributors all over the world. This decision marked the end of the 34-year 'mini-schism' which had been limited to a question of form; a minor distortion within the tradition of this company founded in the 18th century!*

Here is another example, this time taken from the food industry:

▶ *In 1982, after taking control of the American company **Motts**, specializing in apple juice, the **Cadbury Schweppes Group** decided to make the product presentation more dynamic by using a 'Tetrapack' type of packaging. This was a 'first' for the USA, where fruit juices were still often packaged in glass or plastic bottles. **Mott** sales developed rapidly thanks to this multiple-advantage innovation: on an aesthetic and information level, as these cardboard packages offer a better medium for graphics, colour and text than bottles; and the new packs benefited from a consumer liking for novelty, as* *well as their appreciation of a substantial weight reduction in comparison with glass bottles. There were also distribution advantages: particularly the reduced cost of transportation due to a volume and weight reduction, plus the ease of stocking the product in warehouses and of alignment on store shelves.*

■   Other possibilities, linked to technical innovation, sometimes bring an unexpected value to the packaging: for example, that of saving the distributor money, while at the same time satisfying clients.

▶   *A brand of whisky, **Whyte and Mackay**, managed a breakthrough on the airline market by offering their whisky packaged in a bottle made of a new plastic material that resembles glass (PET = Poly-Ethylene Teresthalate): the half-litre flasks of **Whyte and Mackay** have an empty weight of 37 grams instead of 393 grams for glass. This makes an appreciable difference for a passenger already burdened with hand luggage. For an airline, this means a weight reduction of an average of 54 kilograms on a Boeing 747 or DC 10 (bottles sold on-board and miniatures for the bar service), which leads to a saving in kerosene of £12000 (about $25,000) per plane per year. Quite a sales argument!*

A good knowledge of special purchase motivations for a product can enable the company to better employ the added value of the packaging's aesthetic qualities.

▶   *Thus, it is undeniable that the unusual green **Perrier** bottle was one of the keys to their international success. We know also that their sales development, first based on this natural water's specific qualities, was reinforced on numerous international markets by a certain '**Perrier** snobism' because it is considered an 'in' drink everywhere. To profit better from this situation, **Perrier** suggested to bars, restaurants and nightclubs that they place the bottle beside the glass instead of taking it away after serving the customer. A small bit of advice = a powerful dynamic device, in which everyone finds advantage. The consumer is valorized by his choice: he does not have an anonymous glass on his table, but a recognized status symbol which enhances his good taste at a distance. The bar is trendy because they serve **Perrier**, and its presence on the tables encourages newcomers to order it, thus accelerating stock rotation. As for **Perrier**, they have everything to gain from the visibility of those hundred-million tiny advertisements all over the world.*

4.2.3   Consumer/user services

It is, to say the least, paradoxical to note – on foreign markets as sometimes on the home market – the disproportion which often exists between the enormous investments (in energy, as in capital) spent to attract attention and woo potential consumers or users, and the little interest that is shown them after they have joined the ranks of clientele.

The importance of consumer/user services varies, obviously, according to the field of activity, but should concern more widely the majority of products, in particular certain non-durable consumer products, all durable consumer products, as well as capital goods and services.

For all these types of products, the quality of consumer/user services (free or even paid) is a *sine qua non* condition of market share retention and a mine of dynamic devices capable of contributing greatly to sales development.

Then, rather than considering after-sales-service as an obligation to be perfunctorily administered by a mediocre personnel with limited means, exporters should systematically treat these services as privileged opportunities to maintain contact with their final clientele. They can, indeed, profit from these occasions to create loyalty among their existing clientele, and to bring them to consume or use their products more.

This determined attitude regarding after-sales-service will not just have direct repercussions, for satisfied clients make excellent communication relays through the grapevine. The positive effects of this phenomenon represent a powerful purchase inducement for all satisfied customer environments. On the contrary, bad service can transform a disgruntled client into a furious one, who will do everything in his power to broadcast negative feedback.

4.2.3.1   Accessibility

Would a Norwegian still be tempted to acquire an appliance after hearing that the brand's nearest after-sales centre is in Brussels? Hardly more than a Taiwanese would envisage sending a broken machine to Hong Kong for repairs, or a Brazilian living in Recife to Sao Paulo.

A foreign brand is naturally subject to a certain suspicion regarding the quality of its after-sales service (see section 4.2.3.3); consequently, it must avoid reinforcing this suspicion with too great a distance between its potential clients and its service centres.

Through several examples in professional fields where the notion of service is paramount, the attention brought to this product dynamic device by those companies cited makes it clear that their international success is not just due to chance.

▶ *On a worksite (construction of buildings, civil works projects) cranes permanently play an essential role. They must not break down. In this respect, the **Potain Group** does not neglect any factor, from the design to user training (see section 5.2.4.1). Technical salespeople regularly visit all the worksites to make sure that the machines are being used and looked after properly. Moreover, **Potain** has 300 service centres all over the world where technicians and spare parts are at the users' disposal.*

▶ *An automobile manufacturer had a clear success when experimenting with an original after-sales formula with the companies whose Directors and sales executives drove their cars. Instead of continuing to oblige these people to bring their cars in and leave them for servicing and possible repairs, the carmaker regularly sent repair trucks to every company. The users are delighted with this service, which saves them time and effort; the carmaker reduced their after-sales service costs, and this innovation enabled them to lighten the workload of several jammed service centres.*

▶ *More than 30% of **Airbus Industrie** personnel is assigned to after-sales service: upon delivery, each aircraft is accompanied by maintenance specialists. As the airline technical crews get used to looking after the Airbus, the number of maintenance specialists diminishes. But **Airbus Industrie** leave a specialist at the permanent disposal of their clients to provide technical advice and coordinate communications.*

▶ *For **IBM**, the rapidity of an after-sales service call is one of the major commercial trump cards that reinforces the famous reliability of **IBM** products: any client must be looked after no more than 24 hours after alerting **IBM**, which means using the fastest means of transport, including special air charters. Here is one example among many: an alert is sent out as a result of a problem with the 'process control' computer of a sea-faring vessel; less than three hours later, a technician boards a plane for Oslo where a helicopter is waiting to fly him on-board the ship after an hour's flight. **IBM** after-sales service is assured 24 hours a day, 365 days a year.*

These four examples concern very large companies, and are applied to 'strategic' products. A simple reduction in scale is not enough to render such services adaptable to small- and medium-sized companies. It can be noted, however, that the organization of an after-sales service represents an investment whose cost/efficiency ratio could only be positive in a normal product/market environment. There are, moreover, areas where simple ideas and modest means can lead to efficient solutions:

▶ *In their tender for the parks project of the Libyan University of Marsa el Brega, **Sève International** innovated in foreseeing a particularly well-adapted after-sales service formula: they proposed integrating six Libyans into their set-up crew, who would afterwards be in charge of the plant and tree maintenance. This formula was one of the 'pluses' which enabled **Sève** to get the contract, given that they offered a solid guarantee of a serious follow-up of the project. Indeed, since the six Libyans participated in the plantings and installation of the irrigation system, and received special training, they could easily look after the general maintenance.*

▶ ***Clarins** perfected an original communication link with their clients, who, thus literally dispose of an after-sales service. It is made of a card, packed with each product, which invites the customers to transmit their impressions and questions. Many clients send in these cards (an average of 2000 a month) given that written answers enable them to mention personal aesthetics problems without embarrassment.*

*Thanks to this system, **Clarins** keep a permanent contact with their clientele all over the world, despite the distances. Although the information gathered only furnishes a partial image of market evolution, its exploitation brings an undeniable 'plus' to the brand. 80% of the cards sent in contain compliments, suggestions or ask for beauty tips. The remaining 20% bring up problems that are examined with great attention. For example, it is in this way that **Clarins** can learn that product information given by the saleswomen of certain retail outlets is inexact. Then, an investigation enables **Clarins** to set things right rapidly. Another example: everyone knows that the application of any product (even natural water), no matter how simple and pure, can provoke a rash on certain sensitive skins; by way of response cards, a user sometimes indicates an allergic reaction to **Clarins** products. In such a case, the company, together with their client, try to isolate the substance responsible for the allergy and advise the customer about which products are more suitable. The seriousness and efficiency of the follow-ups given to the minority of response cards carrying complaints satisfy the clientele in almost every case, and reinforce the brand's quality image.*

▶ *This desire to enable the clientele to communicate their comments about the product is found in the **Club Med** questionnaire sent to all Club members during their holidays. They find it when they get back home and relive their holidays when completing it, which explains the high response rate (25%).*

*This questionnaire obviously emphasizes the **Club's** excellent organization by demonstrating the interest they bring to the well-being of their members. Moreover, the precision of the questions (which cover all aspects of **Club** life) and the marking scheme (which varies from 'remarkable' to 'very bad') constitute an extemely precise satisfaction barometer: a lowering of marks by a majority of **Club** members over a week often indicates their irritation due to the weather, which is confirmed by weather reports; in the same way, average marks coming exclusively from members of one nationality indicate, in general, the absence of or temporary indisposition of certain entertainment counsellors speaking their language.*

Clear and sufficiently detailed information about the after-sales service organization is an investment which pays off, provided it appears reasonably close and accessible.

▶ *Every year, **Renault Véhicules Industriels** publishes an international guidebook in four languages, providing some general business information on each country and details of the **RVI** outlets, along with the names of the people in charge locally. With the mention of 1500 service centres in 100 countries, the reading of this guide is quite convincing for any potential client.*

In the case where the size of a market and the small number of clients make it too expensive to run several autonomous service centres, reception/delivery points (on distributor's premises, for example) can be linked to a single centre. The essential thing is that the potential client feels the comfort and security of nearby after-sales service.

▶ *In the fur trade, after-sales service is of paramount importance for creating customer loyalty and thus influencing new sales. But this service requires an expensive and complex organization when, like **Révillon**, more than 30 boutiques have to be taken care of in a country the size of the United States. This is a highly specialized service of impeccable quality: the furs have to spend their summer vacation in cool storage, protected as if they were in Fort Knox, while delicate maintenance, cleaning and transformation operations are carried out. **Révillon's** after-sales organization allows their American customers to benefit from this service in their local sales outlet – where they bring their furs in the spring-time and pick them up again in the fall (thus also providing two excellent occasions to show off the latest models). However, the cost of this service is reduced by regrouping activities into regional centres.*

The positive aspect of proximity can be seriously reinforced by making *one* person or *one* specialized service the principal client contact for after-sales service. This contact thus becomes the client's intermediary (even his defender) for the different company departments. In this way, the client is not shunted around, and does not have to explain his case to several different people.

This type of organization is highly recommended to local representatives as its development does not necessarily require immediate investment: often at the beginning, one or two people suited to the job can be trained to provide the after-sales service in parallel to their usual jobs.

After having spoken about official after-sales service, a word has to be said, in the form of an anecdote, about the parallel circulation of replacement parts that exists for all sorts of devices.

▶ *Countries under embargo generally figure out very quickly how to keep an adequate stock of spare parts for their military 'planes, but fortunately these underground distribution networks are interested in peace-time products as well. **Moulinex** does not have an official distribution in Pakistan, nor in India where a local brand, Moulimex, tranquilly manufactures counterfeit products. Despite this, millions of smuggled **Moulinex** kitchen appliances are used in the country and shipments of spare parts follow along with astonishing efficiency for totally unofficial networks.*

Finally here is an example where the concept of investment in quality service is particularly emphasized:

▶ *The **Potain Group** did not hesitate to assist on a construction site in Algeria for a Yugoslavian building company. The point of this example is that the material to be repaired was an Italian-made crane. This demonstration of their maintenance service quality applied to a competitor's aging material (and thus on the point of being replaced) put **Potain** in a privileged position for the next order from their Yugoslavian customer.*

4.2.3.2   Welcome/reception reinforcement

The client is king only until he actually buys something ... then he very often finds himself in the position of a simple citizen whose vote has helped bring a democratic monarch to power: he can only hope that the promises will be kept.

In fact, individual clients (also, to a lesser degree, company clients) feel that they are in a weak position, and start worrying when they have trouble with a device, even under warranty.

It has to be said that the immediate inconvenience brought on by the malfunction or defect in a product is not the main problem for clients: they mostly fear that they have made a bad purchasing choice, that they will be badly received when they go to complain, that the warranty will be contested and, if the product has been imported, that there will be additional problems – a foreign brand no longer having a local representative, nor replacement parts, nor experienced technicians, etc.

For example, imagine the case of a Malaysian, Swedish or Chilean client who brings a defective product to the after-sales service desk of a British/American manufacturer – in the state of mind described above.

Now, let us dream. He is received in a pleasant place by a smiling receptionist who welcomes him by apologizing for the inconvenience and hoping the problem is not serious. After listening with an almost religious intensity to the client's explanation, she will surprise him again. Instead of the inevitable 'call or come back in a week, it should be ready', she offers to have the appliance quickly examined by a technician who will decide if he can repair it there and then, or inform the customer exactly when it will be ready for pick up.

If the client wants to wait, he will be treated like a VIP: comfortable chair, reading material, music, of course, and why not a little more imagination? This after-sales service waiting room could be used as a sort of show-room for products, models or photographs. A permanent slide-show or film could familiarize the client with the company's manufacturing facilities, its products' success story throughout the world, etc.

The client's comfort could be further improved by offering something special from the homeland to drink or eat as a snack – a good example of exterior support to development actions (see section 2.2.2.5), which will bring the client to 'seventh heaven', while at the same time providing another British/American company the opportunity of sampling a well-targeted clientele.

In a more general way, the investment required to polish up a company image by the quality and efficiency of after-sales service could be advantageously shared with other companies also represented in the given country by the same non-exclusive agent.

It is, in fact, a matter of getting the most out of the contacts linked to after-sales service, which will be talked about in the dwellings of

Kuala Lumpur, Stockholm and Santiago! It is quite easy to gain points in this field as clients are generally badly treated by the suppliers' personnel; the importance of the after-sales service welcome is, thus, a powerful dynamic device to increase the clientele and create brand loyalty.

There is, however, a small detail which should not be overlooked: the quality of the after-sales service itself!

4.2.3.3   After-sales service quality

The importance of this dynamic device is so obvious that there is no need to spend too much time on it.

Whether these services are rendered under warranty,* and they concern maintenance, repairs or technical assistance, the maximum effort must be made to fully satisfy the customer and thus strengthen brand loyalty. Efficient organization will ensure better speed and punctuality without neglecting the quality and seriousness of the work. This organization could be emphasized by certain exterior signs, according to the professional fields, which will be sure to be noticed: cleanliness of the workshops, impeccable uniforms, etc. Rigorous stock control of replacement parts will also avoid major client problems.

To take full advantage of the relationship opportunity with the client through after-sales service, the contact is to be further cultivated by an efficient telephone follow-up: the receptionist can confirm the pick-up dates or inform the client with appropriate explanations, in case of delay.

The importance of the staff's charm and psychological know-how in charge of client relations does not have to be insisted on. The local representative should be assisted, if necessary, on this particular point, as well as for the whole organization of customer/user services. Here is the experience of **Moulinex** on this matter:

▶ *'Having a quality after-sales service is fundamental for the brand image, especially when positioned as an up-market product, as is the case of **Moulinex** abroad. In fact, a well organized after-sales service gives credibility and reassurance for the first purchase and establishes loyalty afterwards. In addition to this, it is an important information source on the real appliance use by customers, on the satisfaction index as to the quality and performance that we offer them, and on the modifications they desire.*

Consequently, we have helped all our distributors (technically, and sometimes even financially) to set up a quality after-sales service. Very quickly, they observed afterwards that this service is profitable, not only thanks to the image it projects, but also financially.

Many of our distributors can carry out small repairs immediately. A good

---

*The warranty is obviously an extremely powerful dynamic device, but its nature is too specific to each product type to go into at any great depth here.

market opportunities related to a desire for international expansion – tariff rigidity corresponding to profitability and/or image preservation strategy, which can sometimes be seen as excessively short-term.

Company policy on prices is also limited as they cannot master all those parameters which enter into the calculations, and which differ considerably from one market to another (exchange rate, customs duty, taxes, distribution structure and margins, etc.). All of this involves inevitable variations in retail price levels, that the company can sometimes lessen but never wholly eliminate, and which often give rise to parallel grey markets for 'sensitive' products.

Besides these parallel operations, which can be limited by a strict control of the distribution, inter-market price variations are not a major problem given that all international competitors are subject to them. Whatever price positioning has been decided internationally (high prices, mid-range, low), it is most important to protect the entire brand image identity by maintaining this same positioning – more or less – on all markets.

4.3.1.2   Cost price and other product qualities

It is logical that the cost price focuses attention at the moment of establishing the export price, since this involves the company's profitability.

However, in addition to the cost price, it is important to estimate the influence that the product qualities (see section 4.2) can have on the establishment of export prices: thus, for example, the fact that a product proposes 'a plus' that responds to priority client needs and which reinforces the product's position in relation to the competition, is a solid encouragement to decide for a price increase.

4.3.1.3   Market characteristics and constraints

There are essential factors to be considered in this area for establishing the export price: constraints concerning market access (customs duty, miscellaneous taxes, etc.), constraints imposed by each country's economy (fluctuations of exchange and inflation rates, price controls), relationship between supply and demand, market sensitivity to price, notion of psychological price, distribution networks, competitors' positioning and price, attitude toward imported products, country of origin image. The synthesis of all these factors can be found in the definition of a market price range that should be kept permanently up-to-date.

4.3.2   Preliminaries to price adjustments

After this brief reminder of how an export price is established, let us get back to the international development situation of products already on the market, to produce a checklist of everything that should be done before launching a price action, whether it be an increase or a decrease in the framework of a development plan. As for an aeroplane, this checklist is so important that it can lead to a 'no go' that prohibits proceeding towards the planned action (see section 4.3.2.5).

4.3.2.1   Perceived quality/price ratio

We are going to try to measure client satisfaction, and by this, the degree of client loyalty. This operation is generally easier in professional fields, where the number of clients is limited, and where the contact with them is direct (capital goods, business-to-business services, etc.), than in the case of mass consumer products where information has to be gleaned from sales outlets, or a consumer survey has to be carried out, if warranted by the problem's importance.

Here is a brief example to illustrate the possibility of finding, by way of the above-mentioned operation, effective dynamic devices to bind the client more securely to the company, other than direct action on price. Whatever the professional field, competitiveness should not be based exclusively on price.

▶   *Thus, as particularly emphasized by **Bull**, it is of utmost importance that services reinforce the computer manufacturer's proposal and make them a real partner for the client. These services have to go further than the systematic response (and thus standard) to client needs, by helping them analyse, then define, their needs, and finally, by building up a wholly tailor-made proposal.*

*To do this, **Bull** have rendered their offer of services more flexible. A personalized collection of services, 'Services Plus', enables each client to find the best option corresponding to his needs, given the organization as well as the physical, economic and financial environment. The proposed services range from site preparation to how-to-use assistance, passing by on-site or off-site hardware and software maintenance, at the same time respecting the different timetables and delivery dates adapted to the different constraints of client markets. The **Bull** structure responsible for these evolutions takes into consideration not only the geographical aspect, but the linguistic and personal relations aspects as well.*

*To remain close to their customers, **Bull** have set up 'Centres de Compétences' that respond to these constraints. Linked to these centres are the 'Centres d'Expertise' grouped around production, which provide an essentially technical support system. These 'remote control' services are at the* *disposal of **Bull** personnel as well as **Bull** customers. Thus, **Bull** Teleservices (an electronic mailbox to collect client messages, questions, problems, supply orders, training program enrolments, etc. 24 hours a day) is being expanded to cover the major **Bull** Group subsidiaries.*

4.3.2.2 Competitors' situation

No pricing decision can be made before a specific analysis of the competition has been carried out: the positioning, aggressivity and prices of substitution products.

In many industries – particularly in consumer goods – a comparative analysis of competitor prices for a specific market is a heavy task given the different channels of distribution and the number of retail outlets to check on, as well as the number of references for each brand.

As a result, only a minority of companies will have the means to carry out this sort of survey with their own international team, or have it done by their local representative. Because the cost of having a 'tailor-made' comparative price analysis done by an outside specialized organization is out of the question for many exporting companies, it should be recalled that this kind of project can be entrusted to students as 'an export mission'. This can be of great interest, as illustrated by the example in the introduction to Chapter 4.

It is also necessary to foresee the competitors' reactions to a price readjustment on our part (this action will, without doubt, be the competition's first observation on the company's development plan, should we hold a sufficient market share to be 'under surveillance').

It can be seen in the capital goods sector that price comparisons of different tenders are not the only determining numeric factors for the buyer, who will also try to define the exact running costs of the proposed material/goods. Including a specific study of this point along with the prices is definitely a 'plus' that could be introduced into sectors where this is not standard practice.

▶ *Nobody will be surprised to hear that in aeronautics, studies are very detailed and precise: **Airbus Industrie** (as well as **Boeing** and **McDonnell-Douglas**) write several simulations of running costs for each individual airline. Detailed running and maintenance costs are listed in every **Airbus** proposal. It is not surprising either to notice that different parameters are selected or magnified so that each manufacturer can demonstrate the superiority of their own 'planes!*

4.3.2.3 Demand elasticity

Study of the two preceding points serves as a basis for anticipating client reactions to the increase or decrease in product prices, given the dynamic devices involved in the other development plan actions.

Here are two examples concerning the same company, one illustrating a price increase, the other a decrease:

▶ *A few years ago, after a market survey, **Grand Marnier** concluded that the price positioning of their X.O. Cognac was too low in different countries where there is a huge demand for up-market cognacs. A noticeable increase in sales of XO was seen on these markets thanks to a significant price increase supported by new luxurious packaging, as well as advertising and promotional activities.*

▶ *On the contrary, in Japan, **Grand Marnier** ran into the problem of inelastic demand caused by the parallel importation of their products which were sold at prices lower than those of the brand's 'official' representative. **Grand Marnier** decided to lower their export price so that their representative could offer more competitive prices and thus neutralize the illicit sales of the brand range. This price lowering operation on the Japanese market, accompanied by dynamic field promotions, was a major success: official sales increased by more than 50% between 1986 and 1987.*

4.3.2.4   Distributor attitude

In the case of products which are not sold directly to end-users, the trade should naturally attract interest, especially more than usual before a price action, as distributor attitudes will be of the utmost importance. It is not only vague approval that is needed, but active support (see section 5.3.2).

There is a simple and obvious, but indispensable, condition for this: the price action and the development plan as a whole must appear profitable to the distributors. If this is not the case, all projects will probably flop.

Consequently, the most elementary prudence leads to testing a distributor's reactions *before* finalizing price modifications foreseen in the development plan. To do this, a few easily accessible decision-makers in the trade should be discreetly approached and sounded out for their opinions, as well as their support.

This type of procedure is sufficiently important in a priority market to merit the personal participation of the export executive alongside his local representative: it also presents an occasion to check up on how the development plan is presented, and to get a feel for the field, as well as to maintain direct contact with the local distributors.

▶ *One of the reasons for **Pepsi-Cola's** stunning take off in 1987, after changing representatives in the UK (see section 5.2.2.1) is undoubtedly their new franchised bottler's (Britvic Corona) very close relations with distributors in the major channels. But this strong position would not have been enough to ensure **Pepsi's** success if the trade support had not been sought out and acquired, thanks to the dynamism that Britvic Corona was able to share with them.*

*In fact, Britvic Corona and **Pepsi-Cola International** logically wanted* *to take advantage of setting up their partnership to launch an ambitious development plan in the UK. In this plan, it can be noticed that the considerable increase in retail prices was well accepted by the distributors, who felt supported by the entirety of the other dynamic devices being used, especially in advertising, as well as by the actions that concerned them more directly: for example, Britvic Corona started providing a more frequent delivery service than their competitors, with 150 **Pepsi-Cola** trucks turning up on British roads.*

4.3.2.5 *Status quo* prolongation

Where tests and studies of clientele, distribution and competition lead to the conclusion that price modifications will have a negative effect on sales, there is still an alternative:

■ In the case where price adjustments are unavoidable (e.g. inevitable repercussions due to production cost increases, transport costs, or a necessary realignment of the price structure, etc.), go ahead anyway, with a maximum of precaution to try to limit the damage.

■ Keep prices at their present level, whenever possible. Here is an example of a delayed price increase: the last increase took place so recently that it is necessary to wait for competitors to raise their prices so as to be able to take advantage of the situation and readjust ours. The following is an example of delayed price decrease: this decrease is made possible by a reduction of the industrial cost of goods, but it would be interpreted by the clientele as a weakening of product quality and badly received by the distributors, even though it is economically desirable. Thus, it can be temporarily put off, but in the near future, we shall raise our product prices more moderately than those of the competition to reach the company's desired price level without drawing attention to the manoeuvre.

Studies and tests prior to a price adjustment can also lead to the decision to maintain the present level. It can be seen that the dynamic effects of prices on international development are not exclusively carried along by increases or decreases, but also by the *status quo*: what is important for the price to be the driving force in the development plan is that its structure provides for a satisfactory margin at each stage of the product 'chain', from manufacture to distribution on foreign markets, while at the same time remaining attractive for the consumer or end-user.

4.3.3   Price decrease actions

On a market where an offensive position is started by launching a development plan, a price decrease action can serve two major types of strategy: vitalizing a push and/or pull, and enlarging the target clientele, as well as a third, which is the combination of these two. It should not be forgotten, with the mention of each offensive action, that a price decrease is very often a defensive measure made necessary to realign product prices on those of competitors:

▶   *This was the case for **Jaz**, whose products were priced out of the market, 30% higher than their rivals, and who managed to survive by finding a way (see section 1.2.2.1) of bringing their prices down to a competitive level.*

4.3.3.1   Push–pull stimulation

In this case, the decrease will be made somewhere in the price structure, but without repercussions on the retail price, which will remain the same.

Thus, for example, the export price can be lowered on a market, clearing a bigger margin to devote to sales development: this allows the local representative to invest more in push dynamic devices (reinforcing his sales team, motivating distributors, etc.) and/or pull dynamic devices (advertising, public relations, promotions); another possibility could be devoting all or part of this extra margin to an improvement of the brand's profitability for the local representative and/or distributors, thus motivating them to push product sales.

4.3.3.2   Target clientele enlargement

Here, there is a decrease in retail price, thus rendering the product accessible to a wider target clientele. This decrease in retail prices is often accompanied by enlarging the local distribution (number of outlets) and using other push/pull dynamic devices.

▶   *The historic launching of the **Perrier** development plan in the USA provides a perfect example of this strategy. Until 1977, **Perrier** was sold only in 'Gourmet and Speciality shops' at a price of about one dollar (for a 23-oz. bottle). To enter the new channels of distribution dramatically, **Perrier** managed to compress their cost structure and lower the retail price by 30%, for a bottle to sell at 69 cents. Although still very high, this price was acceptable to a much larger clientele, and it simultaneously received solid support from other dynamic devices: as for push, a large sales force, promotional incentives for distributors to break into supermarkets more easily, etc.; and the pull, with a big media advertising campaign (two million* *dollars for the Los Angeles and New York areas – a budget not to be sneezed at, at that time), efficient consumer information in retail outlets, well-orchestrated public relations, etc.*

4.3.3.3   Means to lower prices

These various means can be applied to the exporting company, or can concern the local representative or distribution on international markets:

■   Compression of the price* by reducing manufacturing costs. Obviously, this cost reduction is facilitated by increasing the number of units produced, particularly due to the development of export sales, but it most often implies serious efforts in technical innovation and financing.

▶   *In the case of **Waterman**, the determination to produce pens presenting the best quality-price ratio and to offer an 'accessible luxury' to their clientele, is based on unceasing research: new manufacturing methods, automation, aesthetics, writing comfort, etc. Thus, with the setting up of the first lacquer workshops on an industrial scale (see section 2.1.2.3), **Waterman** was able to offer prices 50% lower than those of their traditional competitors for lacquer pens of comparable quality.*

▶   *In the service domain, it is the operating costs that have to be reduced, with the same innovative determination. For **Fish**, the necessity of finding means to 'squeeze' their prices presents itself for each tender submitted to oil companies. Confronted with international supply vessel competition, it has become fundamental for this company, as salaries and social costs (health insurance, pensions) for French crews are among the highest in the world. In general, however, **Fish** manage to overcome this handicap thanks to various technical solutions which lower operating costs. Thus, several of their ships were specially equipped with three engines instead of two, resulting in 40–60% savings in fuel consumption. Indeed, these ships can run only on their central motor at a speed of 9 knots for routine transportation; for urgent cargoes, they run at 13 knots using the two exterior engines, with the central one shut down; it is only for anchoring manoeuvres or towing oil platforms that the three engines (4000 HP) are used simultaneously.*

■   Local manufacturing, which is obviously a way of reducing the price structure, often spectacularly, by eliminating almost entirely the transportation costs (as well as insurance) and customs duties. There might also be lower production costs (see section 4.5).

---

*It should be noted that the more a company goes international, the more it can have recourse to means liable to reduce production costs (discovery of cheaper sources of supply; manufacture in countries offering lower production costs and a lighter tax burden; unit cost price reduction brought on most often by an increase in the number of units produced and/or the modernization of the production methods: automation, robotization).

■ Reduce the margin percentages (that of the exporting company and/or of the local representative) if sales development, provoked by lowering retail prices and enlarging the number of sales outlets, provides a satisfactory profit in absolute value.

■ Reduce distribution costs by eliminating an intermediary or by changing distribution channels (for example, switching from traditional retail distribution to mail order selling), or by reducing certain transport costs by a more rational logistics organization (see section 5.2.3.2).

▶ *Years ago **Baccarat's** position on the Canadian market had become worrisome, and the company decided to take special measures to get back into the running. The major hindrance to their development was a very high price, due to a 35% customs duty and a big margin taken by **Baccarat's** Canadian agent. The second hindrance was ... the agent himself, who had little enthusiasm and energy, so much so that the distributors lacking support and motivation made little or no effort to sell the **Baccarat** crystal at such high prices, and completely neglected the brand. After prudently making direct contact with the main distributors, **Baccarat** dismissed their agent and did not replace him, proposing instead to work directly with 25 distributors (a nice example of exclusive distribution!). This enables the company to lower prices to a more accessible level, and to finance some push dynamic devices to support the distributors: training for sales personnel, setting up POP material, organizing promotional events, etc. The distributors, delighted at finally being understood, co-operated with **Baccarat**, whose sales turnover increased by eight-fold in two years.*

*We can see, then, how this price decrease, made possible by eliminating an expensive intermediary, was able to bring oxygen to a market that was slowly suffocating. It is interesting to see that after this transitionary period, **Baccarat** are represented in Canada by an importer who efficiently follows up the distributors without weighing down the price structure too heavily.*

▶ *Transportation costs of bulky capital goods traditionally handicap their competitiveness. This is why the **Gabillard** company (manufacturer of scales and weighing machines) rethought the conception of their products. After studies, the manufacturer was able to make the table of the scales in two moveable parts, instead of a single fixed one, and was thus able to diminish its volume by half during the transportation phase.*

The significant decrease in the landed cost, brought on by this technical adaptation, was of course a determining factor for product sales development in Africa and the Middle East.

4.3.3.4   Precautions to take

It would be wrong to suppose that a price decrease automatically triggers a sales increase, even if other dynamic devices are committed at the same time in the framework of a well thought out development plan.

For the majority of products on world markets, a price decrease will generally be more warmly welcomed than an increase. Nevertheless, varying accompanying measures can often ward off certain negative effects provoked by a decrease which might hinder expansion.

For instance, an efficient information campaign for the distributors, or an advertising campaign for the clientele, will anticipate the kinds of negative interpretations which can harm brand image: 'at that price, they're getting rid of old stock' ... 'to sell at such a price, they must have skimped on quality' ... 'they probably want to clear out their stocks before launching a new product' ... 'huh, they're lowering their prices ... they must be having problems' ... , and other such nonsense.

Moreover, it is worth making sure that the price decrease is applied in a coherent manner to the entire range to avoid upsetting the sales balance of each product. There can obviously be exceptions, if they are justified and the logistics follow, particularly concerning the stocks.

Finally, it should not be forgotten that for certain types of product, a price decrease in one country might cause problems on neighbouring markets where, for example, black marketeering can upset distribution. If necessary, all precautions should be taken (order follow-up, check-ups of distributer stocks, etc.).

4.3.4   Price increase actions

Let us put aside price increases brought on by inflation or a specific direct cause (increase of certain costs, application of a new tax, etc.), to only consider price increases that play a role in the development plan.

4.3.4.1   Push–pull stimulation

Given that prior surveys are confirmed by facts, and that the increase does not provoke any particularly dissuasive repercussions on demand for company products, the increase in turnover – and thus in margins – at all levels of distribution will allow further development results by reinforcing investments in push and/or pull dynamic devices; energizing push–pull actions will be comparable in this case to that already described above, following a price decrease which benefits one or more stages in distribution without affecting the retail price (see section 4.3.3.1).

▶ *In 1977, **Grand Marnier** already occupied a respectable position in Italy, selling more than 400,000 bottles a year. But a study of the brand's development potential in this country revealed that a strong progression was possible, on the condition that the product be positioned in a more sophisticated way. The new strategy was audacious, since it planned giving up **Grand***

Marnier Cordon Jaune, and selling only *Cordon Rouge*, a prestigious cognac-based, up-market liqueur, which is much more expensive. All development actions were thus concentrated on *Grand Marnier Cordon Rouge* and its price rose sharply. In parallel, the sophistication of *Grand Marnier* was accentuated in many ways: partnered actions (media advertising and window displays) with big names in clothing and jewellery design, such as Versace and Bulgari, public relations events in fashionable nightclubs, etc. Result: *Grand Marnier* is today the leader in Italy after their sales almost quadrupled, reaching 1.5 million bottles in 1991.

4.3.4.2   Increase advantages

The decision to raise prices on a foreign market often has two contradictory justifications:

- ■ Product impact on the target clientele is so minimal that a price increase is in no danger of provoking a riot, but enables the company to mobilize more development means.
- ■ The products already benefit from an awareness and characteristics which distinguish them clearly from the competition; this means that client loyalty is sufficiently strong to resist the shock of a planned price increase, which can sometimes even allow reinforcement of the exclusive positioning of an imported brand together with client loyalty, as we have just seen with *Grand Marnier.*

Finally, international commerce is surely the realm of the unexpected and paradoxical: nobody should thus be surprised by a 100% increase, wholly justified by . . . a lack of coins; nor to ascertain the exploitable development potential when resolutely plunging into a situation which peevish but polite people would qualify as . . . troublesome.

► *A few years ago in Italy,* **Chupa Chups** *found themselves confronted by the following problem: the local margin on their lollipops was getting too low, but a retail price (50 lire) increase of the necessary 10–15% was impossible because of a shortage of coins. The only coins circulating normally were those of 50 and 100 lire.* **Chupa Chups** *decided to double their retail price by fixing it at 100 lire, while at the same time arranging for sufficiently powerful dynamic devices so that their clientele would not turn to the competitors' less expensive products:*

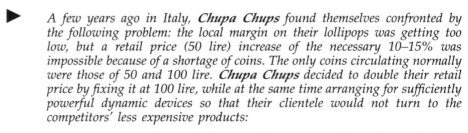

- ☐ *The most punchy push dynamic device was undoubtedly a solid conditioning of the distributors with a fantastic proposal: buying at the former wholesale price, selling at the new retail price. Needless to say, the ploy was quite successful and retailers stocked up!*
- ☐ *Among the pull dynamic devices which supported the sell through, the most interesting was a particularly clever double-televised action: the American series 'Kojak' was scheduled to be shown on TV every week a bit later on, and* **Chupa Chups** *obviously know that Kojak likes sucking on. . . . a lollipop. An investment in TV advertising (never seen*

*before in Italy for lollipops) scheduled to start during the same period as the Kojak series, had effects multiplied tenfold, for the association worked perfectly in the public's mind: Kojak was indeed sucking **Chupa Chups** lollipops!*

The results of this price increase operation: Italian sales rose from 35 to 115 million lollipops per year.

4.3.4.3 Precautions to take

Whatever motivations and justifications exist for a price increase, its preparation should be carefully carried out so that its introduction provokes a minimum of negative effects.

Besides other actions provided for in the development plan which will support product expansion, it is worth foreseeing certain means which are specifically designed to get the clientele and/or distributors to admit this increase rapidly.

At first, the 'increase' dynamic device should be linked if possible to the exterior causes, which made another increase unavoidable (inflation, exchange rate, customs duties), the one enabling the other to pass unnoticed.

This message is to be transmitted to the distributors while at the same time stimulating their interest for our products by drawing their attention to their enlarged profit margin, generated by the development plan as a whole, and by the price increase in particular. Concerning the end-user, the sales personnel's task will be to inform the clientele, with a persuasive demonstration, that the purchase is still of interest despite the increase. The sales force will be seconded by dynamic devices possibly planned for in advertising, promotions and public relations.

Finally, as in the case of a decrease (see section 4.3.3.4), it should be checked that the increase does not upset the necessary price coherence in the company's product range, nor create problems on other markets.

4.4 New Product Launches

There are relatively few sectors where single product international development is possible without leading to a diminishing market share or a premature decline.

▶ *Confronted with the competition of **Boeing** or **McDonnell-Douglas** mid-range aircraft, which were part of a homogeneous product family, the Caravelle, an aeroplane 'on its own', suffered from the fact that airlines wanted to economize substantially on maintenance costs by standardizing their* *fleets. This experience was visibly fruitful for **Airbus Industrie**, which present a complete aircraft family, from 124- to 186-seat short/mid-range 'planes, to long-range, four-engine, 260–300-seat aircraft, also including – among others – two-engine, short or long-range 'planes seating 220–330 passengers, according to the model. This comprehensive range is one of the main reasons for the international success of the different **Airbus** products.*

▶ *The same observation can be made for consumer products. In perfumes, for example, a new fragrance will have a more limited development potential if it is not rapidly backed up by launching complementary products: deodorant, soap (a must in Japan), bath oil or salts, talcum (still widely used in Anglo-Saxon markets), body creams, etc.*

This strategy is not only reserved for consumer or capital goods; it also works for services:

▶ ***Crédit Lyonnais** are following up on their international development with the recent opening of new branches in Eastern Europe, Africa and Asia. This makes almost 1700 branches in 80 countries outside France.*

In general, launching new products is a direct means of generating additional sales, while at the same time responding better to the evolution of international demand trends, as well as maintaining an offensive position in relation to the competition. However, the variety of world markets seriously complicates launching new products, as well as integrating them into well-balanced and adapted existing product lines. Therefore, launching new products presents a great choice of powerful development tools, which must be used with care, as failures are expensive and their negative effects take a long time to dissipate.

Here, again, studies done beforehand can increase the chances of success:

▶ *If the unit cost of a new product is considered, a large luxury hotel is indeed a 'heavyweight'. When being interviewed on the secrets of success for a new hotel, Conrad Hilton used to answer: 'First of all, the location; then the location; finally, the location!' It is not surprising, then, that the location of the future 'palaces' was the object of numerous studies, as should be the definition and positioning of many products whose conception and launch costs justify investing in a survey budget.*

To accentuate the 'specificness' of each type of launch (strategic or tactical products), it is obviously preferable to cite examples existing within well-known product lines.

We now follow the tracks of the Sochaux Lion and the most sporting of crocodiles throughout this section with the examples of a **Peugeot Automobile** and a **Lacoste** product as an introduction to each type of launch.

4.4.1   Strategic launches

This applies to products which are supposed to rapidly constitute a large part of the company's turnover (general export sales or priority market sales), and thus to liberate corresponding investments. In the majority of cases, this involves products or product lines whose life-cycle is expected to last for years.

For strategic launches, there must be strategic products (see section 1.1.2.6), the real locomotives of expansion. These products are so important that the launch of a new strategic product on to a market can sometimes be dissociated from the development plan to be carried out in parallel, meriting special attention and a distinct budget.

4.4.1.1   Products of universal vocation

▶ *For 50 years, the white **Lacoste** shirt apparently never changed: a lovely example of stability, it was the tennis shirt. Then, in parallel to this 'great classic', **Lacoste** provoked a mini-revolution by launching a line of coloured shirts, renewed each season, whose sales have not ceased to develop through-out the entire world because of the shirt's perfect adaptability – not only for sport – but also for weekends and leisure activities in general.*

▶ *In the car industry, the conception and manufacture of a new model takes four or five years, and monopolizes enormous investments. For **Peugeot**, each launch is strategic, and every new car has an international vocation, because it is thought of in international terms from the moment of its conception. Thus, the 205 (of which more than two million were exported between 1983 and 1991) is a standard model suiting almost all the markets, offering four variations (from basic to luxury) with four different engines. Still, adaptations can be decided on according to local preferences and constraints (for example, taxes linked to the horsepower of the engine).*

Products with a universal vocation are those which seem destined for a career as a strategic product, given their potential demand everywhere in the world.

The origins of these marvels are various: they are usually the direct result of observing demand evolution itself (market studies, client suggestions, as well as ideas emanating from the export executives, without forgetting imitating and adapting competitors' successful products), for which applied research specialists in the R & D department will find an adaptive answer.

More rarely, a totally new product is born thanks to fundamental research, before being adapted for the conquest of world markets.

▶ *In the case of **Diépal's** 'Cracottes', an original manufacturing process was at the origin of this cracker, whose texture is very light and whose taste is adapted to all consumer habits. Given that such a new product would* *inevitably be copied, **Diépal's** problem was to take advantage of their competitive edge by getting 'Cracottes' well established on their priority export markets, before being hampered by the competition. This was carried out in record time thanks to simultaneous use of different approaches: exportation and distribution in Benelux, Denmark and Switzerland of products manufactured in the new French factories; production under a licensing agreement, in Italy, UK, Sweden and Finland; plus local manufacture and distribution in Germany by one of **Diépal's** German subsidiaries.*

<h2>4.4.1.2.   Specific products</h2>

▶ *Exporting to Japan is never an easy venture, especially when cars are concerned. This makes the development of specific versions one of the only ways in which to enter this market, which is strongly defended by powerful local competitors, as Philip E. Mead, **Peugeot** Director for Asia and Pacific operations, recalls: 'Even a car like our 205, which met an international commercial success, widely enlarged by its impressive competition records, required a tailor-made Japanese launch. We decided to select a very precise target market: young, affluent company executives. This meant we could concentrate our efforts, starting with two 205 versions, the 3-door hatchback and the convertible, which were duly 'Japanized'. Besides the classical adaptations to this market, such as the right-hand-drive and a non-polluting engine, we transformed these cars into specific Japanese yuppy versions, after carefully studying their major expectations. This involved, for instance, special interiors and paintwork treatment for the body, sporty extra large wheels, plus brakes with ventilated front and rear disks, automatic gearbox, a sophisticated hi-fi system with four speakers, electrical soft roof for the convertible, etc.*

*As per mid–1992, over 10,000 205s had been sold, placing **Peugeot** among the most popular imported car manufacturers.'*

▶ *To meet the specific German market demand, **Lacoste** adapted a zipper into their original jersey. The German launching of this 'zippered jersey', which transforms a turtle-neck into a V-neck, enabled **Lacoste** to develop strong sales in this product category.*

It frequently happens that exposing a powerful demand trend, particular to one or several priority markets, justifies creating an original product. This type of product will be considered strategic, despite the geographical limitation of its diffusion, given that it is destined to become a best-seller in one or several major markets.

▶ *After tripling sales of **Gauloises** and **Gitanes** in Germany between 1970 and 1978 (more than half of which were unfiltered **Gauloises**), **SEITA** (the French tobacco group) felt that their sales growth had slowed down quite a bit: there seemed to be little hope of the German cigarette market not following the general European trend towards blond tobacco and filter tips. At this same time, Dutch manufacturers were reinjecting energy into the German pouch tobacco market and were attracting young people interested in the 'ecological' aspect of this type of product. Consequently, the **SEITA*** *export department thought about launching a **Gauloise** 'roll-your-own' tobacco on the German market.*

*In fact, 'it appeared that the **Gauloise** cigarette clientele were not too far from that of the Dutch pouch tobacco. There was a lot of positive feeling for **Gauloise** and we thought we could come up with a dark tobacco product compatible with both the roll-your-own market and with the existing cigarette.' However, as the **SEITA** export department recalls, this was a risky operation: 'the most serious danger being a big hit of **Gauloise** pouch tobacco to the detriment of the cigarette. Moreover, the launch of any tobacco product in Germany is risky, the failure rate being particularly high. The long and meticulous perfecting of the product was carried out in close collaboration with our distributor. We can say that the product was created to please the German consumer, while at the same time keeping up a certain **Gauloise** family resemblance in the packaging and taste.'*

*From then on, **SEITA** have gained more than 1% of the pouch tobacco market, which places this product in 20th position in Germany and keeps it listed within the basic assortment of the retail outlets, which is quite successful in such a traditional market. A study showed that if the pouch tobacco drew smokers from the cigarette, they were in the minority and this operation contributed to overall **SEITA** general sales development, reinforced additionally by launching a blond **Gauloise** cigarette (see sections 5.3.2.3 and 6.2.1.4). In conclusion, it can be noted that because of its success, the pouch tobacco, developed initially for the German market, is now sold in France.*

In many countries there are traditional products which seem to be almost untouchable, national institutions. However, when the market potential for these products is justified, it can sometimes be very profitable to find a way into these private hunting grounds.

▶ *It is easy to imagine the patience that Daniel Tribouillard had to have to win the following wager: to launch **Léonard Fashion** kimonos in Japan! Indeed, what could be more traditional than the kimono whose history goes back 26 centuries? To accomplish this, Daniel Tribouillard had an ace in the hole: **Léonard Fashion** enjoys an excellent image in Japan, where their silk outfits and dresses, often in flowery prints of 20, 25 or even more than 30 colours, are greatly appreciated. For years, Daniel Tribouillard studied every facet of kimonos (the different kinds of kimonos specific to each ceremony, the symbolism of the embroidered or painted patterns and designs, the manufacturing methods, etc.) to discover how the **Léonard** style could rejuvenate this garment without running counter to tradition. Finally, **Léonard** kimonos came into being in 1982, after an agreement had been reached with the Sankyo Seiko group, whose directors, at first incredulous, were won over by the enthusiasm and talent of the French designer. The kimonos are designed in the **Léonard Fashion** studios in Paris, then hand-made and hand-painted in ancestral workshops in Kyoto. The presentation of the first collection had quite an impact in Japan, as well as being a major commercial success, despite an average price of $5000. This type of exploit has been repeated since then by other French fashion houses following this example in designing kimonos for their Japanese partners.*

However, it should be said that in exporting, as for everything else, excess is detestable, and in adapting products to the specific demands of foreign markets the line has to be drawn somewhere.

▶   *It can easily be understood that* **Cointreau** *did not follow up a demand from Denmark to launch a new variety of Camembert cheese flavoured with this liqueur.*

As a conclusion of this specific products study, it is worth mentioning that even very traditional products can sometimes be exported. This is the case – less usual but very pleasant – where a foreign market is made to adapt to a product, and not vice versa.

▶   *Chocolate Easter eggs sell in considerable quantities in the UK, where* **Cadbury** *sells more than 200 million units each year (about four eggs per head of the population!). It might have seemed risky to put a major selling effort behind such a traditionally British product in an overseas market where it was unknown, especially since sales – obviously very seasonal – are only spread over a few weeks. 'But when a product is so successful on the home market, it would be a mistake not to introduce it to other markets with similar characteristics,' related Sir Adrian Cadbury, then Chairman of the* **Cadbury Schweppes** *group. 'The* **Cadbury** *USA directors doubted that our Easter eggs would be successful in their country, but we insisted that they carry out a market test. After studying its favourable results, we launched our Easter eggs aggressively the following year. Four years later, we were selling 100 million eggs a year, despite a retail price which was higher than in the United Kingdom.'*

4.4.1.3   Synergistically propelled products

▶   *In this category of products can be found stationwagons and vans which are meant to broaden the range of a passenger car line. They are both elaborated versions of a basic model, furnishing the possibility of very versatile use which enlarges the original product's market.*

▶   *In the wake of their short-sleeved white shirts, followed by their coloured shirts,* **Lacoste** *launched a line of long-sleeved shirts which responded to a different type of need, particularly that of wearing a cotton sports shirt under a pullover.*

Being in a dominant position in a market – or even simply enjoying a good image and market recognition – represents a development 'capital' that can be further exploited by launching different product lines to attract other client segments, or by launching lines of complementary products for the client segment already being served. The chances of success for this type of diversification are obviously reinforced by the synergistic effects of the group and/or the brand: structure already in place, a developed commercial organization, open distribution channels, support of corporate advertising, established awareness, etc.

▶ *Moulinex is a perfect example of this, since they largely owe their international expansion to constant product innovation. It is remarkable to note, in passing, the interest with which the consumers respond to these innovations (like the mini-oven, the juice extractor, and the automatic deep fat fryer), which illustrates that these appliances have nothing in common with useless gadgets. Moreover, quantities of 300,000 to 400,000 units have to be sold per year to reach an acceptable cost price by amortizing the manufacturing cost of a new product.*

▶ *Perrier's introduction in the USA caused the explosion of the mineral water market. To get the maximum out of this success, Perrier logically pulled behind them in their wake the other French brands of the group (Volvic and Contrex, in particular) and reinforced their position by taking control of American mineral water springs (Poland, Calistoga, Oasis, then Zephyr Hills and, more recently, the springs of the Beatrice Foods group mineral water division, such as Arrow Head and Great Bear) to profit fully from the growth of the lower-priced local mineral waters.*

Outside this sector of consumer products, the synergistic effects of product lines is also felt in the 'turnkey' sector. For example, the fact of being able to intervene at any level, to take charge of the different phases of an operation one after another, enables the company to reinforce their position, and makes it more difficult for a competitor to get a toehold.

▶ *As Jean Commelin, then president of Inter G, explained, the first phase is the determining factor. If the company in charge of the project's technical study hands in an excellent report and presents solid references, there will be a good chance that they will be entrusted with the next phase: carrying out the project. The client will see the possibility of saving a year or more (as well as considerable sums of money) by not having to call for international tenders and selecting a company after studying dozens of bids. The same reasoning can be applied to the project's following phases: technical assistance for the start up, personnel training, maintenance and repairs, which can all be looked after by specialized services included in the range of the proposed interventions.*

4.4.2   Tactical launches

Tactical launches are a source of product dynamic devices whose importance is more adapted to the development plan elaboration than strategic launches.

They apply to products or product lines which will only generate additional sales and/or whose life-cycle is short.

First, there are tactical product launches (see section 1.1.2.6) to energize expansion, which will benefit from an investment in push and/or pull dynamic devices. Then there are simple complementary products to an existing line which do not necessitate any particular investment.

4.4.2.1   New tactical products

▶ *The fact that **Lacoste** launched tennis rackets can be explained by the company's desire to counterbalance their diversification into sportswear by the production of high quality sports equipment. Everyone knows that the tennis racket market is really tough (fierce competition, after-sales service, etc.), but **Lacoste** developed this activity, even though it is marginal, as it reinforces the brand's technical credibility, their sporting positioning and dynamic image.*

▶ *On this point, **Peugeot** follow a similar procedure to **Lacoste** with their more sports-oriented models: first, the GTI models reinforce the sporting image of the 205 line and remind clients of the numerous successes carried off by this car in races (the choice of engines offered by the 205 GTIs – 105, 115 and 130 HP – was meant to create loyalty among the exacting clientele of this type of model by responding to their demand evolution); the 205 Rally model's engine (103 HP) also satisfies the demand for sports-like driving, but at a more accessible price than the powerful GTIs.*

The launch of new tactical products stems from a study of product line coherence, the adaptation to demand evolution, and the positioning compared to the competition.

This study, regularly carried out on priority foreign markets, should lead to the launch of universal tactical products, as well as products specially designed to respond to the particular needs of several markets taken as a whole.

Contrary to strategic products, launching a tactical product specifically conceived for just one country rarely pays off. A noteable exception: priority markets whose potential justifies this investment, even if it means taking advantage of a local opportunity rapidly.

Launching tactical products, which improves the coherence of product lines by completing them, is an efficient way of creating client loyalty:

■ the offer of a complete range of products or services seriously reduces the risk of losing customers;

■ this offer leads to a sales increase to existing clients by converting them to the use of complementary products; for a brand already enjoying a large customer base, this type of sales development presents the advantage of being cheaper than having to look for new client segments;

■ a well-structured range of products makes client progression towards the more sophisticated product easier. This is particularly noticable in the automotive industry.

The judicious launching of a tactical product on a market niche badly defended by the competition is another way of enlarging clientele.

▶ ***Club Med's** launch of theme weeks (golf, tennis, bridge, etc.) during the off-seasons enabled them to attract fans of these sports or cerebral activities,* *people who might normally never have come on a **Club Med** holiday, and to show them a good time. The **Club** also offer companies an interesting 'convention product': all or part of a village at the disposal of the company personnel, as well as the organization of many 'tailor-made' activities. Given the geographical locations of their villages all over the world, the **Club** can compete with traditional hotel chains by offering a reception style, varied activities, and an atmosphere particularly well adapted to reinforcing distributor loyalty or to motivating a sales force.*

On the contrary, a tactical product might also have to be launched rapidly to counter-balance a competitor's new product.

▶ *However, the point here is not to over-react too quickly; a cosmetics company provides an unfortunate example. Having learned that one of their major competitors was working on a product for a so far untouched market niche, they set their R & D and marketing departments to work. These services were so efficient that the two rival products appeared at about the same time. The follower firm's product, whose formula had been tested and considered excellent in the laboratory and in small quantities, was a huge flop once on the market: going from laboratory production to industrial production had been done too quickly, and the final formula had not been perfected! There was another, paradoxically aggravating circumstance. The marketing plan had been a success, so that the retailers' and consumers' disappointment was as big as their initial enthusiasm. Consequently, the cosmetics company had to accept the return of thousands of jars.*

4.4.2.2 Product line synergy

▶ *In this domain, **Peugeot's** launch of limited series on specific market niches (a few thousand models according to the number of countries interested) can be cited: let us begin, of course, by the fortunate crossing of our examples, with the 205 Lacoste, white with green upholstery, designed for a young, sporty and refined clientele; the 205 Green and 205 Open, obviously inspired by golf, were in synergy with **Peugeot's** sponsorship in this sport; as for the 205 Junior and Chorus (called 'Accent' in the Netherlands, where this name was better accepted), their purpose is to be the first automobile for young drivers.*

▶ *The image and reputation of **Lacoste** enabled them to launch many tactical products and accessories which gained recognition by the simple presence of the famous crocodile: socks, head-bands and wrist-bands delighted **Lacoste** fans, and contributed to the turnover of both distributors and manufacturer. Moreover, the multiplication of these highly-visible 'trademarked' products reinforced brand awareness.*

As in the case of strategic products (see section 4.4.1.3), it is possible to take advantage of the synergetic propulsion, on a smaller scale, to develop the sales of a product line.

This can be done without much risk through enriching a line of products briskly towed along by one or two locomotives (strategic products), by launching several judiciously chosen tactical and accessory products.

This type of dynamic device covers client needs in a more satisfying manner. For consumer products, this will be the means to stimulate sales of the product range as a whole by taking up more shelf space.

To these 'classic' reasons for having recourse to launching tactical products with a synergetic bent, it might also be necessary to adapt to local constraints, as the example of Bavarian brewer **Löwenbräu** illustrates:

► *'A few days before launching **Löwenbräu** in Turkey,' explains Dr. Johann Daniel Gerstein (then Export Director), 'a new law forbade all beer advertising on TV and radio. To cope with this situation, we reorganized our media plan (see section 6.2.3.5)' replaced the TV and radio commercials by posters, which were still allowed, and reinforced them by press relations support.*

*However, having established that these measures were insufficient, we decided to launch a non-alcoholic **Löwenbräu** beer, thus going in the same direction as the Turkish government to reduce the consumption of alcoholic beverages. This enabled us to carry out a big radio and TV advertising campaign, and to acquaint the public better with the name **Löwenbräu**.'*

There is another advantage to this tactic: augmenting the investment capacity for push/pull dynamic devices, thus better promoting the product line as a whole thanks to the increase in turnover that can be expected as a result.

Here is a final important point: the judicious choice of new products to be launched, mentioned above, is meant both to avoid the overlapping of products within existing product lines, and to nibble away at the clientele of rival products. A tactical launch is thus often an efficient offensive means against competitors.

4.4.2.3   Product rejuvenation

It is not unusual for a company to find themselves confronted with the following delicate international problem concerning the development of a product line: in several markets, certain signs of lassitude on the part of both the clientele and distribution have been noticed – sales are stagnating, and shelf space is being reduced in retail outlets. All this is happening despite the efforts of sales staff, whose own motivation is flagging. Regular investment in dynamic devices is shrinking as well . . . There seems to be a premature decline in this product line.

Let us imagine that this worrisome diagnosis has caught us by surprise, without a replacement strategic product in our pool ready for action, or that after a study, we decide to prolong the product's life-cycle, which still has an appreciable sales potential despite its aging. Moreover, this can bypass the need at present to support the necessary heavy investment required for the launch of a new product.

In both cases, a simple intensification of the classic push/pull dynamic devices (promotional actions included) will not always be enough to maintain the product-line's market position for the desired length of time.

It is then possible to turn to the tactic of a mini-relaunch of the product-line, by upgrading the product itself (which can be justified in many different ways: various improvements, increasing output, reducing running costs, etc.) or its appearance (adding an appealing label, renewing the packaging, or even if the length of the product's life-cycle makes it necessary, modification of the exterior, sometimes including a complete repackaging, etc.)

It is of the utmost importance to be sure of the positive reception of this tactic on the part of the distributors and clientele, as improvements decided upon too hastily can finish off products they were supposed to save!

The tactic of rejuvenating a product, if seriously considered to be adaptable without losing customers in different markets, and carried out with enthusiasm in the field, can be an efficient and cost-effective means of relaunching a flagging product line, and defending it against competitive offensives.

Moreover, there are also product actions which can be explained by tradition, even before being propelled forward by the desire to develop sales.

▶ *Grand Marnier* bring out a special blend to commemorate the great events of the English royal family: 'Coronation' for the coronation of Queen Elizabeth II, 'Royal Celebration' for the wedding of Prince Charles and Lady 'Di'. *Grand Marnier's* interest in the British royal family is reciprocal, as can be seen in its historical origins (see section 6.5.2.4).

4.4.3   Dangers to avoid

When launching new products on the vast, constantly moving, international 'ocean'*, a course has to be carefully charted so as to sail equidistant between Scylla (product concentration) and Charybdis (product dispersion). Or briefly, it is just as risky to remain immobile as it is expensive to accumulate flops.

Here is a quick reminder of the main dangers to avoid in launching a new product.

---

*The reader is kindly asked to excuse this heavy metaphor, which is only aimed at refreshing the perusal of this arid book with a breath of open sea air . . .

4.4.3.1   Dispersion

Dispersion is a classic excess committed by companies new to exporting who want to cut corners by trying to ensure their international expansion with the launch of products adapted to each market's specific demands.

If care is not taken, the number of special products will briskly outnumber normal product references, and the financial controller's nervous breakdown will brutally attract attention to the dangers of haphazard launches. In particular:

- wearing out export executives who are in charge of developing too great a number of product lines;
- overworking the export administrative service, which is overwhelmed by the subsequent multiplication of specific problems to be dealt with;
- inexorable disorganization of production;
- a logical consequence of what went on before, a total 'mess' in preparing and dispatching orders; in other words, what is being successfully exported is . . . a creeping gangrene to all the markets as a whole;
- . . . without forgetting the financial aspects: high costs in designing and manufacturing a limited series; the risks of accumulating obsolete and hence unsellable products; the cost of maintaining stocks, etc.

This slightly dramatic picture can bring us back down to earth before we get carried away by the fugitive delights of product inflation. It obviously does not mean, as we will see in the next section, that product launches for export have to be limited; but it is important to control them according to the criteria best adapted to industry. Generally, it would be logical to modulate the number of launches within a product line, according to the different product life-cycles. Thus, an increase in the number of product references is more justified during the growth and maturity phases than in the decline, where it is necessary to reduce the number of offerings in a product-line in synchronization with international disinvestment.

4.4.3.2   Concentration

Too much conservatism concerning launches can lead to an excessive reduction in product lines and an aging catalogue, as illustrated in another apocalyptic situation:

- progressive demobilization of export executives;
- lowering of the local representatives' motivation, as well as that of the distribution channels; this, of course, is to the advantage of competitors who have a more dynamic product policy;

■ strategic products losing steam because they lack the support of tactical and accessory products to impose themselves on the markets (as escort vessels accompanying an aircraft carrier): the clientele will be obliged to choose complementary products from competitors' lines to satisfy their minor needs for which there is no adapted product in company lines; seduced by competitors' tactical and accessory products, our clientele will end up being tempted by their strategic products as well;

■ company image tarnishes, and initiative is lost on international markets;

■ the logical consequence: sales collapse. At headquarters, the support staff plays endless games of gin-rummy, while the factory workers go fishing in the stream next to the plant . . .

4.4.3.3   Launch control

The conclusion of the above leads to the idea of control, the difficulty of which is to know, with the same discernment, how to temper certain creative outbursts on the part of the most imaginative export executives, and to encourage or assist those who hesitate so that they bring to their markets the new products necessary for development.

This control can only be efficiently exercised by staff having a minimum of field experience . . . and a lot of down-to-earth common sense, whether it be the General, Sales, Export, Marketing or Technical Managers, and by regular meetings of all these services. Thus, they will be able to estimate the utility of the export executives' suggestions for launches.

Obviously, this control must be carried out at a sufficient decision level, so that a synthesis of product trends, demands and needs can be consolidated for the whole international market together with the home market.

Choosing the right moment to launch a product is another key factor, mainly for strategic products, given their weight in the company's future sales volume, the importance of investment, and all the risks involved.

There are no fixed rules here, but again there are two excesses to avoid:

■ wanting to impose a quasi-simultaneous launch everywhere at the same time can seriously compromise the chance of success, as world markets are never 'ripe' all at the same time: either for reasons linked to the degree of need felt for the product from one country to another; or for reasons due to the local representative's situation (it would be suicidal to have a new strategic product launched by an agent whose contract will soon be terminated – or on the contrary, by an agent who has just started working with the company – or by an agent whose organization has just

been restructured); or for different economic reasons: unfavourable season for sales, glutting of the local distribution channels,
major launches by more powerful competitors, etc.

■ leaving the choice of the moment to launch the product on each
market wide open,* without trying to provoke an effect of international synergy (particularly effective for highly visible
products) and, thus, risking being copied by a swifter competitor
who will place a similar product on other markets ahead of us.

In the case where the advantage of non-simultaneous launches have
prevailed, there is a supplementary advantage that should give benefit: the launch on the first markets will serve as real field tests whose
results can be transposed to comparable markets.

▶ *This was why the **Gauloises** pouch tobacco launched in Germany by **SEITA**
(see section 4.4.1.2) was first tried out regionally in Bavaria. The success
of this regional test was the basis for the national launch the following
year. The experience acquired with this new product in Germany was then
transposed to several other European countries.*

4.5   Delocalized Production

Rare are industries where delocalized production does not have to
be envisaged for part of the production in order to make sales headway on one or more markets. According to the specific case, manufacturing in a certain country will concern either all the company's
products, or only a few of them; it could be the total manufacture of
a product from A to Z, or just the assembly of component parts,
manufactured in the country or not. In the same way, legal structures
can be varied, and enable a company to find a form well-adapted to
expansion needs on a market or in a specific region.

Let us take a look at the different propulsive effects that local
production can have, and how to offset the major risks inherent in
this type of dynamic device.

4.5.1   Propulsive effects of delocalized production

Recourse to local manufacture is usually justified for two reasons,
whether it be a *sine qua non* condition of access to a country because
of strict rules banning importation or high customs duties, or a

---

*We intend to forget the fierce complaints from the Financial Director, incapable of getting sufficient
sales forecasts to plan for a competitive selling price, or the groans of the Technical Director, who can
hardly set up coherent production programs.

means of accelerating market development which until then has been slowed down by obstacles of a varied nature.

4.5.1.1   Obligation on certain markets

Many countries, purely and simply, prohibit the importation of various product categories. Faced with such a ban, the alternative is obvious: manufacture locally or cross the country off the world map, while waiting for its import legislation to change. (Just a reminder, that parallel networks exist to get into these closed markets, but then this book is not meant to include a chapter on 'How to get into smuggling'!)

▶ *India is one of the best examples of a country where local manufacture is often an obligation, as described by François Perret,[6] CEO of **France Ebauches** (number one in Europe and sixth leading world manufacturer of watch components): 'Second in world population, this country will have over a billion inhabitants before the end of the century. By the very nature of its economic organization, the importation of watches is prohibited and the development of domestic production is favoured in all consumer industries. Our choices were either to submit to the situation, that's to say, to completely bypass this market, or to get involved in smuggling, which is highly developed in this region – which wasn't our vocation – or to follow the rules set down by the Indian government. We went for the last solution in which we had to collaborate with several Indian groups to set up a production plant.*

Finally, we reached an agreement with two partners, bringing them all the necessary elements for the manufacture of watch parts: the manufacturing technology, the training of the supervisory staff, technical assistance for the realization of this project in India, as well as the engineering know-how for the layout of the buildings.

The contract, as a whole, generated a very big turnover; moreover, this technological transfer accelerated our own progress by obliging us to formalize our know-how, which was usually passed on orally and was not described in a detailed and methodical manner.'

*By 1992, five years after this interview, it is worth confirming the success of the **France Ebauches** delocalization strategy in India, where a joint venture with the **Tata** Group produces yearly sales of over two million watches. (Source: Les Echos, April 8 1992.)*

The situation of import restrictions can be assimilated with the case of countries where a quota system of distribution crushes all hope of sales development, which leads to envisaging local manufacture to make headway:

▶ *In Morocco, the sales of **Airelec Radial Distribution**,* made by an exclu-*

---

*The **Airelec Radial Distribution** group manufacture and distribute electric heaters (leaders in the French market).

*sive importer, were limited by a quota system and licenses granted sparingly. To develop their sales on this market, **Airelec Radial** decided to adapt one of their appliances so that it could be exported in unassembled parts, and to set up an assembly plant in the country. Thus, the product got around the quota/licensing regulations and sales were then only limited by the market demand. In other words, the local assembly plant solicited government protection which became, in fact, a ban on importing finished, competitive products.*

Sometimes, the obligation to delocalize production takes the form of various pressures that are finally as efficient as a ban or a quota control on imports:

▶ *For years, **Monsanto** (one of the world's largest producers of agricultural chemicals) exported a herbicide to Brazil in bulk, performing final manufacturing and packaging there. The Brazilian government, worried about their trade balance, pressured **Monsanto** to build a plant capable of handling the entire manufacturing process. **Monsanto** resisted, so the government allowed a local company to turn out a herbicide that **Monsanto** claim violates their patents. **Monsanto** finally built a plant, but now they have a local competitor and are embroiled in a patent-infringement suit in the Brazilian courts. Says Thomas Gossage, Managing Director of **Monsanto International**[7]: 'If we had to do it over, we'd have made our investment earlier and avoided all this.'*

Furthermore, the market potential obtainable with obligatory delocalized production can be such that it will lead to major exceptions within a group's industrial strategy.

▶ *The construction of a pharmaceutical plant in Russia by **Roussel Uclaf** illustrates such necessary contradictions. As Dominique Giancarli, Director for Eastern Europe, comments: 'Although our group was concentrating and rationalizing production in Western Europe, we decided to open up delocalized industrial facilities in Eastern Europe . . . Our Russian joint venture is the best way to make a strong entry into this 160 million inhabitant country that urgently requires modern technology to build up a pharmaceutical industry. Indeed, for decades, the former USSR has been swapping medicines against oil, at quite favourable terms, with Poland, Czechoslovakia, Hungary, East Germany and Bulgaria, which explains why young Russia's demand appears now so vital.'*

4.5.1.2   Price structure contraction

Frequently, local manufacture is the only solution to ensure a satisfactory turnover by efficiently parrying a price problem.

This price problem can, at first, have its origin in transport costs which are too high in relation to the value of the merchandise; this is obviously the case of many heavy goods such as cement, which has to be mixed as close as possible to the worksites.

Into this category can also be assimilated perishable goods that have to be transported . . . in a Concorde especially converted into a refrigerated cargo plane, and whose transport costs would provoke a drastic 'jump' up to the FOB price!

▶   *The example of fresh products such as yoghurt comes immediately to mind, especially after firms like **Yoplait** and **Danone** have made it a solid export product, covering the world with local manufacturing plants, from the USA to Japan.*

Another traditional reason for an unbearable increase in the price structure is customs duty and other taxes, or dissuasive measures levied in certain countries against various categories of imported products.

This sometimes makes the coefficient CIF-retail price go way beyond 5, even 10, which consequently places many products out of reach for most users or potential consumers.

▶   *The **Brune** company (manufacturer of saw blades for woodcutting machinery in sawmills) held a large share of the African market, when a blade-producing plant opened up in the Ivory Coast. Very quickly, the Ivorian competitor took over the market and **Brune** was only able to get back on their feet in Africa by having their blades manufactured in Gabon by an industrial partner.*

Finally, we must not forget that delocalized production can indeed have a positive effect on the selling price.

▶   *The most common example is probably found in the garment industry: many brands, particularly German, American and French, have their clothes made in various countries (within Asia, as well as in Portugal, Morocco, Turkey, Mexico, etc.) whose labour costs keep the selling price very competitive, before importing the clothing into their own countries for domestic clientele or dispatching them to export markets.*

▶   *Many examples can be found for industrial products. As testifies Jacques Dirickx, CEO of **Dirickx**, an SME specializing in metallic fences; 'we started our own production in Brezova, Slovakia, after negotiating a joint venture which involves the manufacture of 3000 tons for the first year, with about 100 employees. We estimated an interesting sales potential for our products in Eastern Europe, and besides its human and industrial qualities (see previous **Dirickx** example in section 1.2.1.5), one of the reasons for the choice of Czechoslovakia – in 1991 – comes from its attractive local manufacturing costs, and its geographical position which makes it an excellent logistic hub to export towards the neighbouring countries.'*

4.5.1.3   Other advantages

Various reasons can lead companies to consider delocalized manufacture as a key to export development:

■ Certain standard requirements or product adaptations, indispensable for obtaining a foothold in a market or for really breaking through, cannot be taken into consideration by the production means in the country of origin for technical or other reasons. The solution will often be found in local manufacture in a country which can cover the targeted market and which has the necessary technical capacity.

▶ *Lacoste decided to have their products manufactured in Japan for a number of reasons. The 'crocodile' had an honorable share of this market (450,000 pieces per year) where the highly recognized trademark enjoyed a very good image, because for the Japanese, wearing a French brand of sportswear went well together with the elitist style of golf, tennis and skiing. However, it was local manufacturing in a 50/50 partnership with a big Japanese group that enabled **Lacoste** to penetrate this market deeply and to occupy extremely strong positions:*
   □ *Prices are more competitive, not having to include transport costs and customs duties.*
   □ ***Lacoste** 'made in Japan' products are better adapted to Japanese morphology, where sizing differs greatly from that of Europeans.*
   □ *These products are also designed to resist the particularly hard wear of local laundries (boiling water and caustic detergents).*
   □ *Finally, the union with a big Japanese group enabled **Lacoste** to better penetrate the labyrinth of Japanese distribution, which holds the world record for complexity!*

▶ *There is also a whole panoply of varied reasons which justified **Sève International's** decision to set up plant nurseries in Abu Dhabi to supply neighbouring countries:*
   □ *The transport costs and insurance of trees and plants were heavy for the price structure, and this decision placed **Sève International** in a very favourable competitive position in relation to their international competitors.*
   □ ***Sève International** became more reliable since the trees and plants used in landscaping are perfectly acclimatized, in comparison with those that are delivered in a weakened condition (or dead) after a long boat trip.*
   □ *Finally, **Sève International** clients like dealing with a company which did not hesitate to set up shop locally, and because they can choose their trees directly from the nursery and not from a catalogue.*

■ Delocalized production is also useful for dealing with unforseeable sudden spurts in demand which cannot be absorbed by the home factory within a satisfactory time limit. In a busy period, these demand spurts can be dealt with in part or entirely by other plants established abroad, for one or several of the reasons mentioned above.

▶ *This is why the **Commentryenne des Aciers** decided to transform semi-finished products (hot rolled coils) into drawn bars in Spain, following the technical specifications and the exact diameters required for each order. This led to a substantial sales development for the **Commentryenne des Aciers** in Spain, where their clients benefitted from better prices and shorter delivery periods.*

■ The economic crisis and the rise in unemployment are also at the origin of local manufacturing.

▶ *The highly automated Japanese automotive industry has for a long time retained its most competitive production within the homeland; it is mostly because of the rise of protectionism in the industrialized countries, whose national production was threatened, that the Japanese carmakers started opening factories in the USA and Europe so as to be perceived as creators of employment, and thus to be better accepted. Only later did the strong growth of the Yen in relation to other occidental currencies, the dollar in particular, come to uphold this delocalization strategy.*

■ A dynamic policy of setting down industrial roots within an export market, guided by the desire to benefit both the host country and the company, is often the essential success factor in the long run.

▶ *If **Renault Véhicules Industriels** have a large share of the North African market, it can be explained by the length of their presence and by their active industrial cooperation. According to the particular case, this cooperation with partner companies in Algeria, Morocco and Tunisia is based on the integration of local companies, the building of factories, the launching of models specific to these markets, as well as the reciprocal purchase of industrial goods. Because of this, and considering that they supply Algeria with a huge volume of spare parts, **RVI** hold a market share of about 30% of these three countries for industrial vehicles over five tons.*

■ What is true in capital goods also applies sometimes to consumer products, where local manufacture can even allow the importation of finished goods! This paradox can be explained by the legislation of certain countries which grant importing licenses to exporting companies.

▶ *Thus, for instance, in New Zealand, a French perfume and cosmetics company was faced with the following problem: their sales development was greatly reduced by the small number of import licences their agent had access to; the limited size of the market itself discouraged the local production of hundreds of perfume and cosmetic references.*
Market development was thus in relation to the obtaining of more import licences. As can be imagined, these licences 'did not grow on trees', and the only way to get them was to export from New Zealand.
A solution was found to solve this problem, as well as another that the

company had in the whole Pacific area. They decided to manufacture a few of their best selling perfume references in New Zealand, to supply both the New Zealand market and mostly the Pacific Duty Free markets (huge distributors, continually visited by mobs of Japanese tourists).

In this way, the company's sales subsidiary in Hong Kong had a closer supply source which had faster manufacturing and delivery capacities than the French plant supplying the rest of the world. This strategy greatly improved the Pacific Duty Free sales, whose distributors sometimes wait to be out of stock before reordering.

As for New Zealand, the high export volume of locally manufactured perfume was rewarded by their obtaining import licences which largely covered the market needs for skincare, makeup and other 'made in France' products such as perfumes. As a result, this company quickly became one of the country's leaders.

■ There is another reason why companies of many nationalities decentralize a part of their production: the numerous advantages offered by certain countries wanting to industrialize. This often involves fiscal benefits, investment bonuses, long-term credit at low interest rates, as well as other incentives.

■ Finally, as a reminder, because this subject goes beyond the scope of this book, the takeover of an industrial company abroad enables the company to dispose of a delocalized production tool instantly, as well as to benefit from other advantages:

▶ *Zodiac acquired the American company Air Cruisers in 1987. This enabled them to integrate one of the major competitors of Aérazur, an aeronautic equipment company which is part of the Zodiac group. As Didier Domange emphasizes; 'This was the means of getting established on the biggest market in the world, right from the start, with a large company (Air Cruisers is the same size as Aérazur), with access to a valuable research and manufacturing technical capital, an active and efficient sales service, and that is already making a profit! We would probably have needed more than ten years to reach the same point if we had started out from scratch in the USA.'*

4.5.2   Risk anticipation

It would be wrong to confuse delocalized production with a panacea for international commerce.

First, difficulties dating from the 1970s have become permanent components of the world economic landscape. *Unemployment*, in particular, affects most countries, which *incites companies to have parts of their production manufactured abroad only when it is indispensable.*

Moreover, the complexity and dangers of delocalized production should not be underestimated, and risks have to be seriously anticipated. Incidentally, it is not rare to see large companies give up on delocalized production which is commercially promising, but for which the risks could not be sufficiently reduced to ensure globally positive results for the whole operation.

4.5.2.1   Royalty transfer

Certain types of local manufacture are carried out partially with components exported from the country of origin, usually the vital 'nucleus' of a machine, a pharmaceutical formula or a food product, etc. This exportation can contribute, partially or totally, to company payment.

In the case where this payment is not sufficient, or in cases where the totality of the production is local, as well as in the case of exporting various services, international franchising operations or licensing agreements, the problem of transferring royalties will be encountered. This is a complex, legal field differing from one country to another, and one which is in perpetual evolution.

4.5.2.2   Negative repercussion estimate

The risks of negative repercussions due to delocalized production are many and varied: particularly, the loss of product quality, turnover evasion due to 'black market' sales in the country where the product is manufactured, the establishment of parallel distribution networks for these products which will compete with those of the company on neighbouring markets, etc. There are, however, certain means of anticipating and preventing such risks, which are presented below.

▶ *For **Lenôtre**, the basic concern in this area is to maintain the quality level of 'haute gastronomie' which was the origin of their success. The difficulty of this requirement can be imagined when applied to the distribution of products that have to be consumed fresh, a few hours after being manufactured, to fully appreciate their flavour. This explains the meticulousness that goes into the preparation of each new production unit at all levels: nothing is left to chance, as indicated by a quick look at the existing **Lenôtre** checklist: intensive personnel training (several Canadian and Saudi trainees spent six months at **Lenôtre** in France before opening a factory and retail outlets in their own countries); choice of production equipment; selection and inspection of raw materials; production organizaton; setting up health standards and quality control; organization of distribution; specific merchandising regulations for **Lenôtre** boutiques, etc.*

Besides these measurable risks whose importance can be estimated, others are more difficult to assess because of strong psychological resistance.

Essentially, this concerns a purchase inhibition caused by negative prejudice – grounded or not – on the part of developing country inhabitants for products manufactured locally. Often, an immoderate infatuation for imports from the world's major industrialized countries can be observed, whose goods enjoy an incomparable quality image, generally reinforced by astronomical prices.

When a brand, until then imported, decides to widen its market in a country by having certain products manufactured there, it will try to use all possible means to safeguard its image. If local legislation allows, it will first hide the local origin of the goods for as long as possible. Then it will start 'flirting' with the legislation in force, which gives rise to most interesting labels, full of insinuations, such as: 'made in France, assembled in X'; 'active ingredients made in USA'; 'designed in UK', or even 'American product' on goods made entirely from local components.

Thanks to these examples, we can appreciate the different levels of hypocrisy which would be a consumer associations' delight, if they existed everywhere.

4.5.2.3   Feasibility verification

This verification should be carried out – even summarily – to confirm interest in local manufacture, which in the case of a 'no go' will avoid more wasted time.

In the case of a green light, or a flashing yellow, a company's technical expert will have to be sent out, along with the sales and/or marketing team to study the main aspects of the project's feasibility (before giving way to the legal staff who will prepare the final negotiation):

- Confirmation of the interest of local manufacture for the company from commercial and marketing angles in the short-, medium- and long-terms, without neglecting the anticipated effects on neighbouring markets.
- Desire and capacity of the local partner to invest.
- Assessment of the local partner's experience and adaptability; if an industrial project is involved, an estimate of his capacity to assimilate and use the company's technology.
- Qualification levels of local personnel. Training possibilities.
- Existence of adapted material. Equipment possibilities.
- Degree of reliability in verifying future production, both qualitatively and quantitatively.

It goes without saying that if the study of one of the fundamental aspects of the project's feasibility brings out negative results, the only thing left to do is look for another partner, or find another solution.

The determination to succeed in penetrating a difficult market can, nevertheless, smooth out obstacles which at first glance seem insurmountable. For this there is an indispensable condition: the estimate, then the integration of local constraints:

▶ *This is the example of a French company that set up an assembly plant for capital goods in India. This plant operates to the general satisfaction of both Indian and French partners, but there are some special features in the factory's organization, so that it can continue operating despite regular local problems – particularly electrical blackouts and drought. Moreover, six months of raw materials and spare parts are kept in stock.*

4.5.2.4   Quality and quantity control

We have just mentioned the importance of estimating the possibility and reliability of these checks during the feasibility study, *before* signing a contract, handing in a technical file and starting up delocalized manufacture. In fact, this involves a major aspect of the brand/trademark's future which depends mostly on – whether we like it or not – our partner's character.

If he plays fairly and the agreement is followed to the letter by both parties, we will sail together on a serene sea, hand-in-hand, gently rocked by the sales results that correspond exactly to the forecasts . . .

Even when unfavourable economic winds generate waves, a common determination will render the agreement almost unsinkable . . .

However, difficult days – or rather years – lie ahead if we realize too late that our partner is a tiny bit tricky, or even a workaholic gangster out for a quick profit.

But let us see what should really happen, beginning with quality control.

Most local manufacturing contracts stipulate that the local partner should submit to the company, for inspection and approval,* a sample of each production series *before* selling it.

If he decides to dispense with this precaution, he can start off by sending samples up to standard . . . as they were all collected from the first series produced during the start-up period under the supervision of the company's technical team. According to the type of product, this hoax can go on until the next formal company inspection.

When it is realized that the brand's local manufacturer is distributing substandard products, months or years may go by before this damaging image gangrene can be stopped. This depends on the speed of the local procedures (obviously slowed down by borders), the quality of the file the ex-partner has put together to defend his

---

*It is important that this approval is given by the quality control services as fast as possible, or else the partner's legitimate discontent might be provoked, and he may be encouraged to bypass this procedure in future. If the quality is not up to standard, a quick intervention of the technical services is necessary to enable the local manufacturer to get back on the 'quality' track.

position, and of course, the solidity of his ties with the country's authorities.

Besides choosing the 'right' local partner, the surest means of exercising control is the direct or indirect supervision of part of the supplies, which enables the company to 'turn off the tap', as it were. This is obviously not possible in many cases where alternative supply sources are available.

Checking up on quantity is not simple either, and the best way to control it is similar. The limits of this control are the same as mentioned above: if the local partner has access to other sources for those supplies required to manufacture the company's products, he can use and abuse them as he likes.*

In this case, a fraud concerning quantity is much harder to prove than that of quality: the partner can become a counterfeitor, at the same time manufacturing the official quantity on which he pays the agreed royalties, plus any quantity of 'unofficial' items which he distributes himself – without paying royalties.

▶ *A classic, notorious example of this type of swindle involved several famous French grands couturiers: their licensees for the manufacture of fashion accessories (mostly Italian) sold huge quantities of ties, scarves, etc. without paying the royalties; these quantities were becoming gigantic for the licensees who were both manufacturers and distributors, not only for Italy but for the whole world!*

▶ *There are also many examples of licensees who do not even wait for the expiry of their contracts before going beyond their territorial limits and competing directly with the licensing company.*

▶ *Here is an unusual counter-example dealing with a counterfeiting problem that led to a licensing agreement! It is not a well-known fact, but patents apply to plants, and thus to the invention of new flowers. Fortunately, for the **Meilland** group, who are continually working on the development of 300,000 rose varieties, among which fewer than ten will be selected after a few years. This research activity, which represents half the group's turnover, relies on well-oiled legal services and more than 1000 patents all over the world.*

'We had to get organized this way after the company's (more than a 100 year old) inventions were stolen both in France and abroad', explains Alain Meilland, company CEO. 'Thus, in Israel, where there is no protection for floral inventions, we had to battle for a long time to have shipments of imported counterfeit roses inspected and seized all over the world. Then, we had to start and follow up the lawsuits to win our case. Finally, the Israeli producers had so much trouble with their importers that they themselves supported a law protecting our right to invent flowers in their country and which officially allows them to export our creations: in fact, they have become licensees, pay us the agreed royalties, and help us hunt down

---

*This danger can be multiplied indefinitely if the local representative does not have his own production unit and subcontracts to an industrial company. Hence, this type of structure should be avoided.

counterfeiters of our roses so that our common interests are protected.'

Thus, it cannot be too strongly recommended to make the right choice and to remain vigilant by continual inspections, without unnecessarily harassing an honest partner.

For certain specialists of delocalized production, 'there's no hope outside of subsidiaries or permanent supervision exercised by an official representative in the country'. Although too costly for many companies, these two formulae could constitute the ultimate weapon . . . if they were not in flagrant contradiction of the inalienable right of employees to be dishonest or even negligent in the exercise of their duties anywhere in the world – even at home!!

5

Energizing commercial organization: 'push' dynamic devices

This category of dynamic devices includes all those which push products* at each stage of the export process towards end-users or consumers; basically, this process includes each major link in the commercial chain: the company's international team, plus their local representatives and the distribution channels for each market.

These three major relays are found in many professional areas: durable/non-durable consumer products, some capital goods, and services.

On the other hand, a different situation exists for heavy capital goods, professional services, technology and raw materials, which do not enter distribution channels. Indeed, for these domains, where the number of potential clients remains fairly limited in each market, exporting companies deal directly with them through their export executives, frequently even without the backup of a local representative.

Whether the number of these relays is very limited – sometimes to just two participants, the exporter and the foreign user – in some capital goods sectors, or it includes a dozen participants (as is often the case with consumer goods in countries like Japan, where the distribution is very compartmentalized), the company has to energize them so that they all contribute to stimulating sales.

In studying the components of each of these relays, their organization, as well as motivation, it would be worth bearing in mind an old saying which is particularly suitable for international distribution networks: 'a chain is only as strong as its weakest link . . .'

It is up to us as export executives to inspect each link of the

---

*Indeed, certain basic subjects are not dealt with, such as setting up an export service in a company, or the search for and choice of a suitable local representative. Two reasons are given in explanation: this book specializes in the international development of markets already penetrated, which means it is for managers whose companies already have an export organization and local representatives; thus, this chapter suggests ways of energizing and motivating them. Moreover, several books have been written on starting up an export service and choosing a local representative (for example, *How To Sell To Europe* by Peter Danton de Rouffignac).[1]

international distribution chain, to estimate its strength, to select those which will have to support more strain to ensure success, and consequently to reinforce them. Of course, we begin with the first link: our own company's international team.

5.1   International Company Team

To state the obvious, the quality and dynamism of the international team is the basis and *sine qua non* condition of wanting to develop foreign sales.

But who are these team members? Quite simply, all the company's staff who are contributing to the success of international business, even including outside contractors in services and industry, where relevant.

A first dynamic device to envisage in this area would be trying to get everybody concerned with international development to share in this team spirit: not only the 'export executives' travelling all over the world, but also the warehouse staff in the dispatching service, as well as the receptionist, etc.

More particularly, we shall also review the many means of toughening up and motivating the key team members.

5.1.1   Field staff

This is all those company staff who participate directly in developing international sales: export executives, customer engineers, etc.

5.1.1.1   Structure set up or enlargement

Before going further, it is necessary to insist on the fact that any company wanting to enlarge their foreign markets must have a sufficient number of *full-time* export executives. In a normally competitive product sector, the development of export sales will be held up if it remains a part-time activity for the manager (CEO, General Manager, Sales Manager), who has other responsibilities and preoccupations.

However, the reluctance to hire specialized personnel is a problem for most countries, even among the world leaders. Thus, France, the world's fourth-largest exporter revealed that two exporting French companies out of three did not have a full-time specialist for their international development (from a study on Export Employment that I carried out in 1986 with Institut BVA). Yet for companies which *already export,* the return on such an investment is very fast, and thus should be a top priority for any development plan.

As evidence, here is an exemplary case (specially selected from within a small company selling very classical, non high-tech products), told by the leading protagonist in the sequence of events, Marie-Hélène Ugal, export executive for **DBC**:

▶

'*DBC, a company with 40 employees, is located in the south of France at Hyères. They specialize in the sale of flowers, fruit and vegetables, and have a turnover of $16 million.*

Flower exportation started in 1974. Not having an export specialist on staff, André David (founder and manager of DBC) responded to the demand of foreign buyers without any travelling abroad, but managed anyway to develop a clientele in The Netherlands and Switzerland.

Still, André David wanted to diversify his exports, but his lack of international preparation prevented him from approaching new markets. He knew that a part of the flower consignments sent to The Netherlands was re-exported to the United States. He contacted the French foreign trade centre in Paris, as well as the French commercial attachés in several major American cities, who gave him lists of flower importers. Unfortunately, his letters in French to those potential buyers went unanswered.

It was in December 1984 that I first contacted DBC as a trainee of the EIA of Marseille, a business school specializing in international development, whose program includes a foreign mission for an interested company.

At our first meeting, André David entrusted me with a canvassing mission in the United States, and I immediately started the preparation: study of potential business, distribution channels, competitors, design of sales literature, etc.

To complete the mission's preparation, we got in touch with American buyers (thanks to the French commercial attachés' help) by sending them a letter in English, with a questionnaire testing their interest in our products, before my arrival in their cities.

Due to this thorough preparation, in July 1985 I was able to meet about fifty companies in our four targeted cities: New York, Miami, Chicago and Los Angeles. They confirmed their interest in our products, especially for our giant tulip variety grown only in the south of France, of exceptional quality and size compared with the smaller Dutch tulips. These American importers were ready to include tulips and other flowers from our DBC product lines in their catalogues, along with Dutch and Columbian products.

Back in France, DBC decided to switch into a higher gear concerning exports. From a trainee, I became their Export Manager and followed up our American prospects: selection and contacting of importers, setting up the export administrative service, as well as the logistics of getting our cut flowers to the USA in good condition and at competitive prices. There was also the preparation of everybody concerned in adapting to international requirements. For instance, we got the local flower growers together to tell them about the potential and needs of the North American market, basically to create enthusiasm and encourage them to adapt their production.

The 1985/6 season got off to a quick start; I carried out more American export missions. Our participation in the March 1986 Wholesale Florist & Florist Supplier of America trade show held in San Diego, which had participants from all over the world, was particularly important for us, as we were the only French company represented. Our giant tulip was getting to be well-known, and already makes up 80% of our American exports. Moreover, I developed contacts and consequently sales with our European clients.

- *Altogether, the efforts of the whole company enabled us to increase our flower export turnover from $800,000 to $2 million in two years.*
- *As a result of this development, **DBC** hired four more people during the same period, basically for the export service, as well as three young trainees'.*

After the first step on the way to international expansion – getting a full-time export executive in place – it is important to follow up with indispensable investments in human resources by forming an export organization with a sufficient size to develop the company's potential sales in foreign markets.

However, some company managers may react to this with the usual objection: '. . . why should I hire export executives when I have already organized a local representative network abroad (agents or even subsidiaries)?'

This type of attitude explains why so many companies occupy a much smaller share of the world market than they could actually lay claim to. Nowadays, international competition has become too tough to hope that foreign sales will develop on their own, without frequent contact to motivate, inform, train, coordinate, assist and control the local representatives (see section 5.2.1), as well as regular surveys of market evolution to keep the products well adapted.

It is strange to note that these same companies got established in their home markets by organizing sound structures to cover their country's different regions, whereas they do not feel the same need for their foreign markets, which are much more complex.

In fact, according to the results of my Export Employment study, the average French company (within the minority of exporting companies which organized an export department) has three sales managers in France for each one of their export executives.

Just for interest's sake, let us look at the ground to be covered to reverse the above situation, or to go even further (for one sales manager in France, there should be more than ten export executives), to better correspond to the world market potential in relation to that of France.

▶ *To illustrate more completely (over a 20-year period) the dynamic cause and effect relationship between investing in human resources and expanding internationally, here is the progression of company staff and sales results for **Parfums et Beauté International** (an exporting company of the **L'Oréal Group** – see section 1.2.2.2):*

- 1970: 10 people (5 export executives)   sales: $1 million
- 1975: 50 people   sales: $10 million
- 1980: 200 people (including foreign subsidiaries' staff)   sales: $80 million
- 1987: 700 people (including foreign subsidiaries' staff)   sales: $290 million
- 1990: 1200 people (including foreign subsidiaries' staff)   sales: $420 million

*As Jean-Yves Frolet, General Director of **PBI**, reminds us: 'We have always anticipated our personnel needs (sales force, training and demonstration, marketing, administration, coordination, etc.) in relation to our development ambitions . . .'*

In other words, contrary to most companies, **PBI** did not wait for increased turnover to hire more staff. Instead, they develop their staff first in order to expand more quickly.

Having had the pleasure of working with Jean-Yves Frolet on the **PBI** team from 1972 to 1979, I remember the sarcastic remarks from several other managers of French brands of perfume and cosmetics. When meeting on business trips, some would ask how many more employees we had taken on and what we could possibly give them to do. I hope they have figured things out after a dozen years! If not, they should compare the spectacular progression of **PBI**'s figures with those of their own export structures (which often have not evolved much since then: a few export executives to cover the world, like **PBI** in 1970) and their own turnover, which has only progressed moderately as a result.

5.1.1.2   Responsibility and profile type

According to company size, export potential and the number of markets to be covered, field staff usually receive a geographical posting: generally a zone including several countries with similar characteristics – Latin America, the Far East, etc. Occasionally, a single country's importance justifies the exclusive attention of one or more people; but usually, on the contrary, a single export executive will have to look after . . . the whole world!

An efficient international organization might also include non-geographical postings: countries with subsidiaries, markets with state-controlled buying centres, Duty Free markets, etc.

Whatever the territory covered by an export executive, this person should be fully responsible within the framework of established sales objectives and budgets.

This is an important condition for both motivation and supervision, and it also gives the export executives credibility on their markets: without the power of decision in proportion to their hierarchical position and their specialty, export executives will not be efficient enough, especially when considering the cost of a day's work abroad. The local representatives will not take long in bypassing them altogether and dealing directly with the person who is really in charge, the actual decision-maker. In such a situation, we could wonder if the latter does not know how to delegate, how to train people, or even how to choose collaborators.

All of this does not mean that the field staff should have total and absolute power of decision on their markets. It is not incompatible to be in charge of a territory while at the same time being followed from afar by the manager and supported by the company's administrative and technical services.

▶ *Here is a delegation example from the **CGH (Compagnie Générale Horlogère)**, where the export department is entirely responsible for its activities: this department works as a small business within the parent company's yearly plans. This, for instance, would allow the design of a new line of **Jaz** or **Yema** watches – specially adapted to priority foreign markets – but the R&D costs will be attributed to the export department, as well as the financial costs of manufacturing the initial stocks.*

Since export executives should be given full responsibility for their territories,* they have to be chosen from men and women with a good general background, enabling them to master a great variety of tasks. In international fields, the typical super-salesperson loses lustre compared to a marketing-sales hybrid with other varied capabilities – management, production, law, logistics, etc. (see section 5.1.1.3).

The export executive's basic capabilities should enable him/her to be fully in charge of his/her markets.** It would be overly fastidious to list all those qualities necessary in an export executive. Let us just say that this person needs to be adaptable to people and countries, and possess talent and patience in negotiations (to convince and not to impose); he/she also needs to be able to communicate enthusiasm to individuals or groups, as well as have a good sense of humour.

In addition, all those qualities stemming from honesty should not be neglected, even if there is a tendency to forget them or to underestimate their long-term importance. The international domain is vast, yet each industry is a small world where everybody ends up knowing everybody else and exchanging information, opinions and, sometimes, unflattering anecdotes about each other. Common sense, if not personal conviction, should bring every executive to develop a perfectly transparent image of honesty, both for himself and his company. This implies loyalty, rigour, scrupulousness in respecting business

---

*Here we mean export zone or area managers, and not the more specialized type of field personnel such as technical sales staff.
**Sometimes, if necessary, with the assistance of a company expert or a local consultant who could help clear up a particular problem (technical, legal, financial, etc.).

commitments, courtesy and fair-play with competitors and even (! . . .) with company colleagues, as well as honesty in the proper sense of the word. The international arena is riddled with 'wheeler-dealers' and grey-market operators of all sorts. But none of this has any more favourable long-term interest compared to an impeccable personal and professional reputation.

More and more, companies are setting down behaviour standards for their personnel, with clients as well as suppliers, to back up their corporate image:

▶ *Hewlett-Packard were one of the precursors on this subject. From their foundation, HP cultivated the honesty and integrity of their personnel all around the world. The HP guide for business behaviour appears as a real moral code for environmental communication. It is beyond doubt that this attitude strongly contributed to the maintenance of Hewlett-Packard's excellent image (often referred to as a 'straight arrow') and style 'the HP way', which is a reference even outside the computer industry.*

This brief listing of some necessary capabilities is unlimited, given the capital importance of the export executive's role for a company's international sales development: in some ways it can be compared with an 'orchestra's conductor', getting the maximum cooperation and harmony out of all the players (whether they be within the markets or at headquarters).

5.1.1.3 Training investment

Nobody would think of questioning the fact that for all sports, success in international competition depends on the quality of the athletes' training.

With the toughening rivalry in all professional sectors, this applies to international trade, where success also largely depends on the efficiency of company executives, and thus on their training and experience.

This involves a wide variety of know-how, since long-term international development requires going much further than the old time sell-in to control all the 'sell-through' factors as well. Consequently, far more than an international salesman, an export executive should be a multi-talented development specialist who can manage – with the faraway assistance of headquarters – most types of issue: from negotiating the renewal of a contract with a local representative and checking the preparation of a media advertising campaign, to coordinating all kinds of specialized activities between homeland and foreign markets (product marketing, salesforce training, production management, etc.).

Continuous professional training is thus an indispensable investment to ensure international development, and to avoid getting the company involved in expensive errors, inevitable when newly appointed or even more seasoned export executives are blundering along on their own.

Besides receiving outside training, an export field executive should also get solid in-company training, so he can be well versed in company philosophy before setting out on his target markets. This also applies to professionals lured from rival companies: their acquired professional and field experience does not excuse them from learning all about their new company, and this lessens the serious risk of unintended mistakes abroad.

In fact, according to a new export executive's prior experience, several months or more might be necessary in preparing him/her to become a good company 'missionary'. This preparation includes – obviously – an intensive study of the products and their markets, and a practical knowledge of the whole company's policy, organization, methods and constraints.

For company managers hoping to equip their firms with an integrated training department, let us daydream while visiting the **Accor** Academy. It appears as a dream because this academy was obviously founded with a desire for excellence, as well as with the financial support of a very large international group (over 144,000 employees in 105 countries; 1992 turnover =$6.3 billion). However, certain aspects of this dream can be adapted to smaller companies, if not the size and organization:

▶ *Located near Paris, this 'Université du Service' reflects the group's convictions: company success is in direct relation to the progress and enrichment of the company employees. This academy is the real **Accor** cultural melting pot, essential for the diffusion of company values. In 1992, it gave seminars in different languages to 14,000 trainees from all over the world, on new technology, human relations, management, computer science or sales techniques. Management training is very highly developed for team building and performance.*

Because of its human dimensions and modern infrastructure, this campus allows the students to complete their classroom knowledge by concrete examples, making them better prepared to handle reality once back at work. The campus infrastructure includes: a 95-room hotel complex with restaurants and cocktail bars, 15 classrooms and meeting rooms, a kitchen amphitheatre, a professional reference library, a specialized video library, a gym, parks and sports facilities. Learning and leisure are in optimum equilibrium on this campus.

As emphasizes Christian Mure, the Academy's Managing Director, what could have been a major hindrance turned out to become a continuous improvement factor: 'The Accor expansion in the last two decades was not only worldwide, with many acquisitions driving our Group into new business sectors. Just to name a few, from our original speciality which involves now about 2000 hotels with the variety of a full range (Sofitel, Pullman, Novotel, Mercure, Formule 1, Motel 6 . . .), we operate as well about 6000 restaurants, we issue company restaurants vouchers for over 6 million employees, we offer a car rental fleet of 100,000 vehicles with Europcar, we

propose the services of 1000 travel agencies with Wagons-Lits Travel . . .
The specific experience and requirements of these new activities stimulated
a constant reflexion about the concept of global service, for the development
of our training programs'.

   *To diffuse competence and share know-how, **Accor** has 40 full-time*
instructors who teach at the academy or around the world. Moreover, a
team of consultants analyses each particular need to be able to design specific
programs. To this professional team can be added state-of-the-art tools, such
as training films and other audio-visual material in several languages,
designed by the production department.

   *The **Accor Group** also invest heavily in delocalized training for company*
managers and field staff abroad with – among other programs – a 'Training
the Trainer' seminar which enables participants to develop their own teams.
Finally, some centres were opened for specialized training responding to the
needs of major markets, such as in the United States. The Hotel Sofitel
School of French Culinary Skills in Bloomington, recognized both by the
Minnesota Board of Education and by the French Ministry of Education.
In Brazil, the 'Academia dos Serviços' opened near São Paulo in November
1992.

Afterwards, it will be useful to implicate the newcomer in the life of
the services he/she will be most in contact with, by setting up training programs in the Export Administration service, the Marketing
and Production Departments, without forgetting Dispatching and
After-Sales. This training period can be completed by an internship
abroad at one of the subsidiaries or with a well-established company
agent. Field experience can be acquired by accompanying a seasoned
export executive for a while, so he/she can 'get the feel' of things.

   And (need it be said?) a solid knowledge of the files for each
market is fundamental before sending a new recruit off to battle, as
it would be neither correct nor prudent to let the local representatives
brief him . . . in their own way. This specific market knowledge should
be transmitted preferably by the executive's predecessor. This 'passing
on' of information still lets the new person approach his markets
with an objective eye and bring in a different development style,
which usually has beneficial effects.

   Then, the new export executive should not be left in the closed
circuit between headquarters and foreign markets. He will need to
change rhythm regularly (at least annually) to recharge his batteries
and distance himself from day-to-day business. He should have
complementary training sessions to attend at headquarters to prevent
him from losing contact with company policy and methods because
of his frequent travels. This also enables him to enrich the administrative and production services with his field experience and market
observations. Outside company training sessions should also be
scheduled, so that the person can renew himself within different
professional sectors and through different, but often complementary,
experiences.

5.1.1.4   Personal organization

This subject does not lend itself to long discourses given that every-one has to find his/her *own* way of getting organized for professional efficiency. This search is not so easy for the travelling export execu-tive, as he is most often on his own, which means it requires solid determination and character. Whatever the recipe, it will have to make him/her anticipate rather than follow market development, which implies planning and delegating surveys or actions, and then motivating and controlling them, both at headquarters and abroad.

5.1.1.5   Material environment

Only satisfying material conditions ensures getting the maximum out of a heavy investment like the cost of export executives, enabling them to be as productive as possible.

A seriously undertaken business trip can be exhausting, especially when calendar constraints and airline timetables make night or week-end travel the most efficient choice.

It would be wise to lessen this fatigue by not considering 'charter' style flights or hotels offering just bare minimum comforts. Trying to save money by restricting travel budgets is a bad idea, which can only generate poor performance.

Moreover, the initial company image on a market is transmitted by the field staff – real ambassadors – to whom responsibility has been delegated (indeed, their personal styles and behaviour were import-ant factors in the decision to entrust a mission to them). The company has to go further in this sense by giving their field staff the ability of having the best possible impact on their markets.

Among such numerous elements contributing to company image, it would be an error not to pay the same amount of attention to them as the foreign clients will. Here are a few examples:

■ The business card, which should be perfectly composed, and printed in some cases (better still, engraved) on both sides, to give a translation which is appreciated in certain regions (Asia and the Middle East, in particular). The title on the card should be carefully chosen to give importance to the export executive and to facilitate his contacts. Instead of Export Department or Commercial Delegate, it is better to say Export Director or Export Manager. To keep some hierarchical logic among the field staff, there could be a General Export Director and several Area Export Directors, assisted by Area Export Managers. If necessary, within large export departments, each title could be extended with Assistant or Deputy.

■ The choice of hotel not only matters for the comfort offered, but also for its prestige (the first question a local businessperson asks is what hotel we are staying at), and the quality of services offered: efficient transmission of messages; secretarial, telex and fax services, etc.

■ We shall cover the company's sales literature at much greater length later (see section 6.3.2). However, this is a first opportunity to remember that company field personnel should obviously have convincing documents and be able to use them in the best way possible, not forgetting that they have to be easily transportable and practical to use.

5.1.1.6   Headquarters logistical backup

It seems incredible to invest in sending someone to the other side of the world, only to leave him in suspense for a few days before answering a specific problem which is holding things up abroad. This, alas, happens all too often because of negligence, lack of rigour in the rapid handling of correspondence, or the absence of a Director at headquarters. Any of these reasons can explain a fax going unanswered and gathering dust, which is highly damaging for the sender's morale; nevertheless, he must still try to make up plausible excuses for local clients to explain the delay in response!

Many reasons make it a must to set up a communication system at headquarters, to give priority and ultra-fast treatment to all matters coming from the field staff:

■ A quick answer guarantees better productivity on his part; any delay can slow down or even compromise a deal. Moreover, in the case of a trip covering several markets, this delay can upset a schedule carefully established in relation to specific dates in each country and the availability of local contacts, thus compromising the whole trip's profitability.

■ When these matters concern the local representatives or distributors, a rapid response from headquarters brings them another sign of efficiency that will enhance the company's image.

■ Finally, a close contact with travelling field staff is an obvious way of motivating and keeping them in check, (as we will see below).

According to a company's size and flexibility, the logistical support system of a travelling export executive can be more or less elaborate, but should necessarily cover certain essential tasks:

■ Ultra-rapid assistance, dealing directly with questions or by transmitting them to the appropriate company departments and then making sure of prompt reactions.

■ Taking care of the day-to-day business, according to instructions left by the export executive before leaving.

■ Handling important matters that arise either with the travelling executive himself, by contacting him directly abroad, or with someone who has been specifically designated at headquarters.

■ Putting aside information of interest for the executive until his return . . . or in the case of a long trip, dispatching some of it so that he/she will not suffer from information overdose on his return.

In many companies, these tasks are carried out by an Export Assistant and/or Export Secretary whom each export executive will have carefully briefed about his markets, important characteristics concerning local representatives or distributors, etc. The assistant will be used to handle routine business by working closely with his/her boss: analysis of in-coming and out-going correspondence, knowledge of important 'phone and telex communications, attendance at certain meetings (see the example in section 2.3.4.2).

▶ *This function is so important that some big exporting companies have entrusted this responsibility to seasoned administrative executives (often over-travelled ex-field staff). This is the case for **Parfums et Beauté International** (**L'Oréal Group**) who have a particularly efficient organization. Each Area Export Director (a travelling staff member) is backed up by a sedentary staff member whose role can be compared to a General Secretary or an Administrative Director, and who knows all about what is happening on the markets under the supervision of every Area Export Director's assistant; he can then interact with the Area Export Director as well as with his assistant, whether they be abroad or at headquarters, plus other company departments (Marketing, Production, Finance, Transportation, etc.) thus assuring the continuity and coherence of the area export business.*

5.1.1.7   Motivation and supervision

In addition to this, there is so often a tendency to envy 'those lucky exporters who go on those fantastic trips' – almost on vacation all the time! – that it is difficult to imagine how physically difficult this profession actually is. The idea of a 40-hour week would make people smile, especially on a business trip where there is never enough time, even when doubling the figure. Worse still, whatever is left of a personal life between two trips is seriously compromised by the obligations of business life which interfere with family life. (Company clients travel too, and organizing a suitable welcome for each one often prolongs the professional schedule with dinners, shows, or other tourist activities).

▶ *Annette Roux[2] is CEO of **Beneteau**, the world leader in sailboat manufacturing, which employs 1200 people. 'A company is like a child, it takes up all your time. With my daughter Anne-Claude, who is 11, there is no problem. She's very mature and interested in what I do. But Louis, who's 5, lets me know that he misses me.' Every week, Annette Roux travels one* *or two days in France or in Europe. Once a month she goes to South Carolina for about a week in* **Beneteau**'s *American shipyards. 'On the last trip, my son didn't want to talk to me on the phone when I called. That's hard.'*

It is not an exaggeration, then, to refer to an Export vocation, which fortunately is still attractive for those who dread routines and appreciate the pleasure of a job where there is still a zest of adventure.

In addition to these obvious compensations, as well as a sufficiently motivating salary, the general management of an exporting company should bolster up the motivation of their field personnel, who often have the impression (often more than an impression . . .) that their efforts, carried out far away from headquarters in foreign lands, are not fully appreciated.

The means of motivating field staff are many, and adapted both to individual psychology and company possibilities – be it only an encouraging 'phone call, or congratulations by telex! That warms the heart, when it is –25°C in Seoul.

▶ *Let us listen to Alain-Dominique Perrin reminiscing about something that happened 20 years ago, that even becoming CEO of* **Cartier** *has not made him forget . . . 'When I was starting out, I was in charge of launching the 'Cartier lighter' in France and Europe. Given its success in Europe in 1970, I proposed taking on the rest of the world. But the* **Cartier** *management were skeptical as to the interest of such an action. However, after insisting, Robert Hocq, our CEO, finally accepted my proposal: a three-month trip in Asia and the Pacific (where* **Cartier** *was totally unknown), then in North and South America.*

In the middle of this trip I was surprised to be recalled to Paris by Robert Hocq. I was even more surprised and delighted to discover that the reason for my return was to congratulate me for the results already realized during the mission. Robert Hocq, who had kept regularly informed of my correspondence and orders, wanted to express his personal satisfaction.

After this quick four-day visit to Paris, I left again to continue my trip with a reinforced motivation and kept up the spectacular results. This exploratory three-month trip around the world is, by the way, still the origin of 60% of **Cartier**'s *present day, non-European distribution network . . .'*

In other words, the minimum motivation necessary for the field personnel is simply to encourage their pleasure in working, to show them that their efforts are followed attentively at headquarters where they are appreciated and supported.

In addition to this minimum, every company can easily find other means to motivate their international troops.

▶ *The* **Commentryenne des Aciers** *let their field staff bring their spouses along from time to time. The effects on family life, and thus on motivation, are excellent. This can be seen in the results, given that couples socializing on a business trip or at a convention often favours the development of a more personal relationship with the clientele, especially in countries (Anglo-*

Saxon, for example) where dining out with spouses is a common business practice.

The supervision of the field personnel's activities and results should be carried out in the same spirit. They should not feel that headquarters are checking up on them, but rather trying to assist them.

The quality control of the field staff's activities can be carried out regularly during trips – with or without them – on their markets, through their correspondence and reports, as well as at headquarters where their various professional virtues can be more directly appreciated . . . and their weaknesses too.

As to quantitative checking up, this is normally carried out at meetings scheduled to study the progression of their sales volume and results, as well as each market's general evolution.

Finally, concerning the touchy subject of expense account control, it is preferable to limit the administrative hassles to what is imposed by the regulations in force. An eye should be kept open for abuse, but it is normal that the field staff find it demotivating to be called in to account for a missing taxi receipt of a few dollars, whereas they have just spent many hard days or weeks negotiating deals worth several millions . . .

5.1.2   Support staff

Why bother talking about company administrative and production staff in this book? Exactly because there is too much of a tendency to think only about exporting in terms of the field personnel. We can draw a parallel here with aviation, where the pilots and flight crews in general get all the glory, whereas the ground personnel get stuck with all the humdrum tasks. But what could a fighter jet accomplish without ground support: radar, kerosene, ammunition, spare parts and general maintenance?

It is the same for exporting. The administrative and production staff should not be considered 'nobodies' who just blindly follow the field staff's instructions without taking any risks themselves.

5.1.2.1   Support staff and exporting

Let us first look at the relationship between the support staff and exporting. This relationship will be variable, obviously, according to the structure and importance of the export service in the company. The following classification can only be applied very generally:

■ We can briefly mention the administrative staff who occasionally travel abroad (marketing executives or technicians, in particular), and can be considered similar to the field staff.

■ The specialist administrative export staff (basically, in sales follow-up, client accounts, dispatching and transportation), very aware of international tasks and procedures, at least in their field.

■ Non-specialist export staff: they work both in international as well as domestic departments, except in companies where the export organization is so big that they have their own specialists, such as Marketing & Advertising, Management, Finance, Legal, Research & Development, Production (factory and warehouse), without forgetting the general communication services – switchboard operator, telex, receptionist. Whenever these departments are not integrated into the export division, they will have in common a relative lack of knowledge of the specific needs and problems encountered abroad.

However, the growing difficulty of most export operations has led many companies to reconsider their international organization to obtain a better reliability, to accelerate the export procedure as a whole, and to compress certain costs, until then badly mastered.

▶ *The **Perrier Group** set up an export logistics team at their plant in Vergèze, south of France, with 15 administrative and production staff members specializing in specific international matters which were encountered in different areas:*

■ *Management & Product Forecasting: an export activity involving hundreds of millions of bottles in different sizes.*
■ *Follow-Up of Orders: another obviously essential service (see section 5.2.3.2).*
■ *Logistics: the importance of the dispatching can be better assessed when considering that the transport cost of a product like **Perrier** can amount to between 25–35% of the FOB value. The know-how of a logistics expert often enables a company to reduce their transport costs drastically, and thus to reinforce their product competitiveness.*

5.1.2.2   Field/support staff communication

This communication is fortunately excellent in many companies, but it is useful to emphasize the problems that can occur in certain cases, slowing procedures down, before seeing (section 5.1.2.3) how to transform this brake into a positive force for international development.

Communication problems begin here, as everywhere, with distance: the travelling export executive and the support staff at headquarters do not see each other very often (or even do not know each other, in the case of very big groups), and usually communicate via office memos, faxes and telexes, (whose brevity does not facilitate comprehension), which becomes even more difficult because of the differences in professional experience. Communication becomes even more laborious when several departments are scattered about in various places, which often happens for the production service whose factory is found far from the city where the headquarters is situated.

From this point on, any situation can develop – going from indifference to conflict to active hostility – the whole expressed by entrenched attitudes of incomprehension on both sides:

- The support staff often feel more or less jealous of the field staff who spend their time 'having fun in exotic places', leaving them in dreary weather and traffic jams, mostly when the intrepid travellers come back, brown as berries, and have the nerve to complain about how hard their jobs are!

  The irritation rises sharply when these 'good for nothings' who take it easy in luxury hotels at company expense send instructions which are always urgent, often contradictory, and hardly comprehensible, forcing the support staff into administrative acrobatics, without so much as a thank you, even when they make enormous goofs that have to be corrected at all costs, etc.

- In parallel, the field staff have the impression that it is thanks to their dynamism alone that the company expands; for them, the administrative and production staff are generally 'a bunch of complainers and fuss-pots, incapable of making an effort for an urgent problem outside working hours, who take it easy in the comfort of their office, before going home to watch TV.'

Obviously, the above caricatured clichés are a little excessive. Fortunately, the means are not lacking to improve communication and atmosphere, if certain tell-tale signs indicating similar tensions are encountered.

5.1.2.3   Team spirit stimulation

The difficulty of international business multiplies the problems, sometimes very demanding, in all company departments. This makes the creation of a real team spirit all the more important.

It is the export executives who find themselves face-to-face with the problems in the field, and it is up to them to take the initiative to have the support staff participate more actively in the determination of events.

This means that the export executives have to implicate fully the home staff in the international game, not just as 'serviceable lackeys' but as partners whose assistance is fundamental for success. This leads us to emphasize, once again, the importance of the orchestra conductor role held by the export executives:

■ First, contact should be as frequent as possible, (directly or by short memos) to enable the home staff to follow the export market's evolution, and thus to understand better the problems which arise. Good international communication can provoke miracles.

▶ *After patient efforts to enlarge their distribution in Switzerland, Alain Geffriaud, Export Director of the company **Française de Brasserie**, managed to persuade a big supermarket chain to test 'Panach', a shandy (mixture of beer and lemonade), in two of their outlets. On this small trial order of six pallets, to be delivered as soon as possible, depended a sizeable increase in the company's export sales with Switzerland. But the Swiss 'Panach' required special labels and pallets of different dimensions from French standards to fit onto the shelves of Swiss supermarkets. Mission impossible, it could have been said, in the middle of August, the busiest month where the factory had to produce 20,000 hectolitres a day. They would have to stop the production lines to retool them so as to label and pallet 30 miserable hectolitres. However, the factory manager had been kept carefully up-to-date on the international development of Panach, and after the Export Director's plea, he decided to give a helping hand to the Swiss market by integrating the six pallets into an already overloaded production program. Production staff + Field staff = the same struggle to succeed!*

■ Frequent contact would be inefficient if it did not transmit a real desire of the field staff to work hand-in-hand with the administrative and production staff. Thus, tactless formulations can give the impression that an export executive wants 'to play the field alone, keeping the ball to himself'. For example, 'Hello, Jack? . . . Can you tell me when *my* order for Jakarta will be on its way?' Or 'Hello, Pete, I was just talking to *my* Italian client on the 'phone . . .' Obviously, this unconscious personalization, very frequently on the part of field staff, is not very motivating for the support staff, who can logically think 'If it's *his* order or *his* client, how does that concern *me*? On the contrary, to speak of *our* Indonesian order, *our* foreign markets, *our* Milanese client, *our* export sales objectives, will implicate and better mobilize all company personnel.

■ If in the permanent duo, export executive-export secretary, team spirit exists most often, it can only be reinforced by emphasizing the importance of the secretary's role. For that, one of the most efficient means is to bring him/her out of anonymity outside the company, by giving his/her name to business colleagues/clients instead of speaking of 'my secretary'.

▶ *All correspondence from the International Relations service of the **Maison Sauvion**, (muscadet wines) that is signed by the Director, Marie-Paule Leroux, is counter-signed by the secretary who follows up the file and types the letters. This naturally gives responsibility to the secretaries and elicits a direct commitment concerning the client files. This system also enables foreign clients to have a 'known' company contact at **Sauvion** if Marie-Paule Leroux is away on a business trip when they call.*

- The administrative and production executives should be imperatively implicated in the preparation of development plans: their opinions and specialized advice will be greatly appreciated by the field staff who have a wider, more general experience. Thus, kept up to date and prepared to make the extra effort necessary to carry off a difficult action from time to time, the headquarters staff will be motivated by knowing the importance this effort has on the success of the whole.
- For this, the administrative and production executives should be invited to participate in strategic meetings concerning priority markets, as well as in the export conventions that some big companies organize annually to present results and develop projects. This brings the travelling export executives, the administrative and production executives and the expatriate staff all together under the same roof.

▶ *Facom* *went further in this idea, as illustrated by their Export Director, Guy Bisson: 'The best way to get the executives of non-export services involved in the development of foreign markets is to entrust them with international responsibilities. This is how the Administrative and Financial Director became CEO of* ***Facom****'s Italian subsidiary, the R & D Director the CEO of the Belgian subsidiary, and the Sales Director for France the CEO of the English subsidiary. Thus, confronted with the specifics of these markets when they go to their subsidiaries several times a month, they better appreciate the need for flexibility and adaptability. Moreover, this way of doing things has accelerated the evolution and modification of our headquarters organization.'*

- Certain export department structures facilitate the setting up of teams, including field staff as well as administrative and production staff at headquarters. Each team is in charge of a territory and the team members become jointly responsible for sales progression.

▶ *'Field staff, administrative and production staff – all are salespeople!' It is by this succinct formula that François Greiveldinger, General Manager of* ***Krebs****, explains the team spirit reigning in his engineering company. In fact, according to the needs, engineers, draftsmen, lawyers, financiers and even secretaries can be sent out into the field to present a tender or to participate in the closing of a deal. It is only regrettable that this type of organization is not applicable in all professional domains.*

- Finally, it is up to the field executives to implicate the home office and factory staff in the international successes which are carried off, by remembering to thank them directly for their help. This can be reinforced by an internal memo where the participation of the headquarters staff can be underlined. For great victories, a cocktail party or even a banquet are excellent occasions for bringing different company departments together!
- More generally and obviously, each person's motivation – head-

quarters' as well as field staff – depends greatly on career evolution opportunities, especially in a large group.

▶ *For **Accor**, today more than ever, success is intimately linked to mobility and adaptation. Their managers have to be international in their very souls and blend in with local realities. This does not hinder Americans being in Europe, Chinese in Africa, nor French in Japan. More and more, communication is becoming not only international but multi-national. It is necessary, then, to facilitate mobility, multiply experiences and cumulate the competence of all the Group's collaborators. A successful career in **Accor** means 'two professions, two countries' . . . to avoid partitioning, prejudice and singleness of mind and action.*

*To carry out this strategy, **Accor** have implemented formal and informal means; among the most efficient ones, 'Opportunity Flashes', a regular in-company employment exchange. This fortnightly newsletter contains a complete panorama of classified advertisements for all the jobs available within the Group – mentioning the countries, function, activities and necessary qualifications. Everyone is free to apply directly . . . or beforehand to receive the specific or complementary training which is needed. Finally, more informal but not less effective nor habitual, interactivity exchanges are increasing. From London to New York or from Tahiti to Los Angeles, internships and job swaps for a few months have become quite common . . . and enable the participants to immerse themselves in another local context, sometimes another language, but always with the discovery of unsuspected particularities.*

A few examples can illustrate the variety of means likely to stimulate home office staff/field staff team spirit. Such means can be based on procedure organization, unusual vacation offers, internal communication improvement, or even simply on individual initiatives:

▶ *Making their personnel aware of internal problems to increase foreign sales was the objective of **Merlin Gérin** at a company convention where all the departments involved were present. A bet that was won, thanks to the impact of a 15-minute computerized film.*

Starting from basically simple, funny drawings, the images were animated in two dimensions by the computer. The short film evoked all the aberrations likely to exist in a company, such as partitioning between services. It showed this through short scenes with funny characters. It took 15 days to make the film, which would have been impossible if the company had opted for a more classic film or cartoon. Another advantage was the reduced cost thanks to the film's simplicity, and the fact that the images were synthesized from already existing documents.

▶ *For more than ten years, **Hesnault** have organized trips to motivate and keep up morale of their administrative and production staff. These trips enable about 30 people to spend time in countries which are both strategic destinations of this transport group and very attractive, sunny vacation destinations (places already visited: Senegal, Ivory Coast, Indian Ocean, Florida, California, among others.)*

More than two thirds of the trip's cost is looked after by the company.

*The 'business' part of the holiday implies no more than a cocktail party and dinner with local clients and **Hesnault** personnel based there. There are at least four major advantages to this operation:*

■ *Exotic and interesting holidays for **Hesnault** administrative staff at fabulous prices.*

■ *Direct contact with foreign reality and perception of the particularities and difficulties which are hard to imagine sitting in an office in France.*

■ *Meeting local clients, which facilitates personalizing assistance later on.*

■ *Finally, a fantastic development in team spirit between, on the one hand, the different links in the Transport chain, at **Hesnault** headquarters in Plaisir (a Paris suburb) and in their French provincial agencies (air freight, insurance, packing, shipment, etc., all working on the same destination), and on the other hand, the overseas **Hesnault** agencies.*

▶ *During factory visits meant to impress foreign clients favourably, it is often remarkable to notice the reciprocal embarrassment of both visitors and 'visitees', whose number does not usually permit individual introductions (which would often be made inaudible by the noise anyway). Plant personnel do not particularly appreciate this type of intrusion, and feel like monkeys in a zoo! As for the foreign visitors, they might be ill at ease, encountering only fleeting, cold or even hostile glances.*
   This visit might be technically convincing, but what impression will the personnel have produced? Seeing them, the clients might think they are badly treated, demoralized, even on the verge of a strike . . .

*There again, better communication would radically change this sombre portrait and improve the company image as a whole. Before the visit, specific information should be given to the factory personnel about the coming visitors (instead of putting up a note on the noticeboard, why does the person in charge, himself, not come and make a brief announcement during a break? Why not reinforce this information by raising the visitors' national flag, which should be both an internal as well as external communication tool (see section 6.4.2.1); and finally, why not check up on linguistic competence and have some foremen or workers participate directly in the program?). Thus informed and motivated, each person can feel like an exporter and better contribute to his company's international development (see the **Favi** example below).*

▶ *A travelling field executive of a large export company by chance met a crewmember of the plane that was to fly him back the next evening from Rio to Paris. This encounter enabled him to transport for free – without paying for excess baggage – over 100 exotic plant seedlings for his company's support staff. Several years later, these seedlings have grown into luxurious plants, which are the pride and joy of the headquarters staff and have created a lively relationship between them and the Brazilian market.*

Before concluding with the virtues of team spirit for winning victories within foreign markets, here is the testimonial of Jean-François Zobrist, Director of **Favi**, which proves that success in the field does not depend on a company's size or means, but on their staff's determination.

▶ 'Founded in 1957, the *Favi* company specializes in the conception, melting down, finishing, assembling and marketing (as a subcontractor) of any machine part made of an injected copper alloy.

Today, we employ 260 people, and we have a sales volume of $24 million, of which about 35% is made up of export sales. The company project is to remain a world leader in our field.

Our ideas for implicating personnel in international development were based on something obvious: you only do well what you like, and you only like what you know well.

We wanted to give our manufacturing operators information on our international clients and their needs/products through simple actions:

- noticeboards located in the workshops informing the personnel of our foreign commercial missions, as well as client company visits;
- foreign visitors' flags raised in the factory entrance the evening before arrival, to remind everyone of the pending visit, and to welcome the client as a VIP;
- the visit is organized in such a manner that the client learns how his products are made and meets the machine operators working on them (this can sometimes lead to constructive client/operator dialogues);
- file systems set up in all workshops explaining the function of the machine parts, their destination by client and country, as well as the client's history, making sure to include interesting anecdotes and important facts, thus encouraging a personal touch when dealing with the order. For example, our operators who make the parts for one of our American clients know that the company founder's wife, grandmother of the present CEO, still takes an active role in the company (at 85!) working on an assembly line. When the CEO visited our plant, he was impressed by the warm welcome: everybody was asking him for news about his grandmother . . .

  This file system has recently been reinforced in the workshops by installing computer terminals that complete the classic files (manufacturing procedures, quality control, etc.) by describing the parts and client histories.

- organization of 'brainstorming' sessions with voluntary operators to think of commercial actions which have enabled us to come up with simple yet striking ideas such as:
  - ☐ at the end of the year, sending a lighter to each of the 5500 operators working on our machine parts, in our clients' factories all over the world;
  - ☐ according to the series, when a thousandth or millionth part has been sold, the part, finely gilded in gold-leaf, is awarded to the buyers and engineers who contributed to the product's development (average cost of the gift: $40);

☐   *to celebrate our 30th anniversary with all those who had made it possible, we sent presents made in our workshops, along with a thank you letter to all our clients, with the names and signatures of the 260 employees (certain of whom, almost illiterate, used up sheets of paper practising their signatures before they made one that satisfied them). 95% of our clients responded with a letter of congratulations, or better still, in two instances, with a case of champagne!*

To reinforce foreign client loyalty and accelerate the internationalization of personnel mentality, we take advantage of the few quality problems to intervene rapidly by having the people directly involved take charge of matters: it could be the technician who designed the part, or the founder who cast it, and not someone from the sales or after-sales departments.

*Finally, to consolidate the client/supplier relationship concretely, that is to say our machine operators and the operators using our products in our clients' factories, we organized a trip for the entire team working on a product (about 35 people) to a factory in the **PSA Group**, without supervisors or foremen, to favourize direct communication. Given the positive results of this operation, from the point of view of the work accomplished as well as knowledge of customer demands, this type of operation will soon be repeated for another foreign client.*

These actions have the double effect of reinforcing our image and client appreciation, as well as accentuating our operators' motivations, as the smallest of these actions (for example, preparing the list of 260 signatures or the design and manufacture of the 30th anniversary presents which were, in fact, real little adventures) consolidates their mobilization for international development.

It is obvious that the ultimate aim of these actions is to maintain the longevity of the company in the largest sense, and we observe that:

■   *total absenteeism (taken as a barometer of personnel motivation) is now about 2%;*

■   *returns of defective parts can only be calculated in PPM (parts per million). Many foreign customers order the totality of their supplies from us – without having a back-up subcontractor. When you know that in the automobile industry, a single missing part can stop production, you can measure the confidence they have in **Favi** and our personnel.'*

Architecture can also play a role in stimulating team spirit by bringing together field staff and support staff in a 'communicative' environment:

▶   *The first inhabited European pyramid accommodates the administrative and commercial services of the **Doublet** company, which specialize in the manufacture of flags and community equipment (grandstands, safety barriers). Higher than the Louvre Museum's pyramid (26 metres) with lots of windows, there are 1800 m² of 'interactive' offices on four levels. The building is heated by solar panels. Designed by the architect Roberto Delgado, the* *project originated from Luc Doublet, CEO of this Lille firm, for whom the monumental style of the structure is also 'the projection of the company culture towards the exterior, which enables us to make the different elements of the marketing mix more coherent.'*

There are, thus, a profusion of means to cement international team spirit. We can consider we are on the right path when everyone feels they have participated in closing a deal with our distributors in Atlantis, from the cleaning lady who polishes the desks, the receptionist whose smile warms the welcome, the worker who will have improvised a demonstration of his machine's capacities, to the secretary who will have jotted down, from last year's visit, that they take milk with their coffee and will have served them like old friends.

5.1.2.4 Training investment

Rare are those companies that think about preparing their administrative staff to integrate the international factor into their jobs, as the results of the test that I carried out on the switchboard operators of 100 French companies indicate. (This test was conducted in 1985 and, I am happy to say, things have improved greatly since then.)

Each company was contacted with the following sentence, where the word 'export' was deliberately left out: 'Would you please connect me with your overseas department?' The responses considered positive were those which were intelligible in English, even a few words meant to ask the person to wait (example, 'Just a moment, please') while the receptionist looked for someone to handle the call.

Overall results:

- positive responses: 22%
- unsatisfying responses: 78%

Of the 78 unsatisfying responses:

- Five receptionists hung up after a short, mutually incomprehensible dialogue!
- Most tried to 'force' the caller to speak in French by repeating the same thing (company name; allô, j'écoute; à qui voulez-vous parler; je ne comprends pas; je ne parle pas Anglais; etc.).
- The tone of many receptionists indicated a certain panic, even bad humour, when confronted by a situation that they could not deal with.

Apparently, at that time, a majority of French receptionists had received no instructions for handling calls in foreign languages (as it must probably be the case in English- and Spanish-speaking countries . . . and the contrary in small 'crossroad' countries like Holland, whose language is not spoken abroad, which has induced most of their inhabitants to learn at least one foreign language).

However, a few minutes would suffice to explain to the reception-ists the importance of an efficient telephone welcome for the com-pany's image, to teach them the pronunciation of a few sentences in English, and to indicate which personnel can take the foreign phone calls.*

This switchboard operator example probably applies to any other function based at headquarters or on production sites of most com-panies, which still do not feel the importance of preparing all of their employees to take an active part in their international development.

This preparation can be carried out in different ways according to the function and needs of the personnel involved. It can take the form of internal or external training, or by actions designed to inform and make people aware (see the example of **Favi** in the preceding section), or by means specifically adapted to specific requirements:

▶   *In this way, the **Sauvion** company, whose muscadet wine exports to Ger-many are made more complicated because of the large number of distributors they have in this country, did not hesitate to send one of their export department secretaries on a training program there. More exactly, it was an exchange program of a few weeks' duration with the import secretary of one of **Sauvion**'s German distributors. This enabled the two employees to become familiar with the work methods of their partner companies, and to come back to work with reinforced efficiency and motivation.*

5.1.3   Expatriates

More and more companies send executives or various specialists abroad, either for a few months of assistance mission, or for longer periods: three, five or more years.

This expatriation can take different forms: in company subsidiaries, in a local agent's company, or even without any local structures. But first, what is the purpose of investing in expatriate missions?

5.1.3.1   Dynamic effects

When the sales volume in a market and/or the sales potential justify it, it is certain that the expatriation of one or more executives is a more powerful dynamic device than the visits, even frequent, of an itinerant export executive.

The continuous presence of the expatriate in his market brings a more thorough knowledge, enabling the company to organize a better

---

*Obviously, this elementary training does not dispense with a more complete two- or three-day program (such as those organized by Sophie de Menthon, the high priestess of relationship marketing: **Multilig-nes Actiphone Conseil**, Paris – Tel: + 45 44 62 71). The switchboard is such a nerve centre for company image that it deserves this kind of investment.

adapted and more efficient development, while at the same time giving the company energizing means and direct control, which are difficult to accomplish during short visits.

Closer ties between the company, their local distribution organization and the end-user constitute a serious advantage to be well made use of.

Moreover, besides the direct dynamic effect on present business, expatriation is a means of breaking in and assessing future company directors by providing them with complimentary experience. The field personnel will acquire continuous development practice of a market and no longer in discontinuity, as they did before by hopping all over the globe. The administrative staff will also get to know the international terrain better with such direct immersions.

5.1.3.2   Problems to avoid

Obviously, it has to be certain that expatriation (often very expensive) is really justified from the strict management point of view – that recruiting someone locally would not be more expedient, and that the department from which the future expatriate has to be 'kidnapped' is not left dangerously understaffed.

Then, the choice of each expatriate has to be assessed: his/her motivation, of course, as well as experience or capacity in handling the job he/she will be assigned locally. It would be an error to expatriate a 'tenderfoot' who, when left to himself, might accumulate decision-making errors, despite all his good faith. On the other hand, as we have seen previously (section 5.1.1.3), a practical internship in a company subsidiary or a reliable agent's company can be an excellent complement to training new recruits, on the condition that the trainee is well supervised.

In addition, the personal psychological problems caused by expatriation must be taken into consideration. They are often more complex than those experienced by travelling export executives who are usually away from their usual lifestyles only a few weeks at a time.

A strong character is necessary, together with a solid faculty of adaptation to put up with the initial uprooting and isolation which await expatriates, *as well as their families*. It sometimes happens, that the expatriate himself copes well with the professional transplant, but that family balance is disrupted by all the changes, especially if the expatriate's responsibility covers huge territories where he often has to travel, 'abandoning' his family who are still poorly adapted to their new country.

For all these reasons, companies should have their candidates try out expatriation so as to limit the rejection phenomena:

- ■ If it involves putting an executive in place within a country he/she does not know, a reconnaissance trip (preferably with spouse) can indicate whether he can adapt without too much difficulty, and if he is well accepted by his local professional milieu. Moreover, he can start getting personally organized for his move, as well as for that of his family, which will simplify things later on.

▶ *Such preparation is paramount for having a good start and providing a fast return on expatriation investment, as Maha Gabbani, Associate Director of **K & G Paris Consultants**, (a service firm specialized in relocation*) confirms: 'A personal experience, 12 years ago, played a very important role in drawing the features of my professional activity. For business reasons, my father decided to buy an apartment in Paris and to transfer all our family from Saudi Arabia to France. Although things were very well organized to have us settled in without any trouble, we've only stayed for three months because of the difficulty of adapting to a different environment without the necessary information about the culture and lifestyle. This involved a serious loss with reselling the apartment, and my father had to completely reorganize his business pattern in Europe. This experience has drawn my attention on two facts: the importance of the family's adaptation on the expatriate's work productivity; and the related interest of having professional relocation experts, understanding newcomers' requirements and expectations, who can select and provide the best solutions to adapt easily and make the appropriate decisions.'*

*'You could think such situations only involve individuals, while the human resources departments of large groups can cope with solving problems and dispelling worries of the expatriated staff and their families to settle in painlessly, continues Marie-Paule Kouzmine, the other **K & G** associate director, but most of them do not have enough staff and connections to solve all the problems. For instance, a large American group was faced with a major difficulty: one of their R&D experts kept refusing the company's proposal to rent an apartment for him and transfer his family to France, instead of paying him the hotel for three months twice a year. This Mr. X was saying that he had no time to look after all the personal problems involved, and that his wife would not leave her job anyway. After I had had a meeting with Mr X proposing our help to look for an apartment, organize the kids' school admission, issue all the required legal forms, write a résumé in French for his wife and assist her looking for a job, he finally accepted the proposal; this saved lots of time, effort and cost for the company, as Mr X only had to concentrate on his new European function and was productive very quickly.'*

It can quickly be added to this expert testimony that such local support services are recommended even more to give expatriates the best chance of success wherever the environment makes a cultural gap with the newcomers and the administration formalities are difficult to deal with.

■ When expatriation concerns a large number of employees, it

---

*The Franco-Saudian **K&G** 'duo de charme' offers tailor-made business and personal services to organize a happy arrival and a pleasant life in France. Contact: 116, Avenue des Champs Elysées. 75008 Paris. Tel. +33 144 218108; Fax +33 144 218109.

would be wise to set up a special program, both for the selection of candidates and training.

▶ *The company **Ciments Français International** regularly has to send employees abroad (foremen or highly skilled workers, for example) for months at a time, to ensure the start up of new cement works. For many of them, who come from cement plants outside the major French metropoles, this is their first visit abroad where all kinds of adaptation problems can arise, especially for countries such as those in the Middle East, where the lifestyle is vastly different from that of France. The company has consequently designed a seminar where all the details on working and living conditions are fully described. A psychologist is present to detect certain inhibitions or personality blockages which could cause difficulties in the cement plants, as the expatriates have to work on teams with local workers. And the third part of the seminar gives the selected candidates general information about the country they are going to, so as to facilitate their personal adaptation and the success of the company's mission.*

▶ *This same training seminar concept is found in the vacation business, where **Club Med** takes advantage of the off-season to complete the skills of their 'Gentle Organizers' before they go off to another village. It is not surprising to find programs for teaching new sports, for the basics in management and administration, or an initiation into **Club** philosophy for the new Japanese GOs. On the other hand, the **Club** GOs are also allowed to follow longer courses in foreign universities (for example, three months at Tsukuba) studying the country's history and sociology while in total cultural immersion. It is not by chance, then, that different nationalities can integrate the **Club**'s style so well for their holidays: they meet fellow-countrymen who guide their first steps, as well as French or foreign GOs who know their country and their way of life well.*

5.1.3.3 Expatriate/headquarters communication

Having a 'company man' established somewhere abroad, in a foreign market, does not mean it is no longer necessary to be concerned about it. On the contrary, close contact has to be maintained with the company 'bridgehead' for many reasons, both personal and professional.

The expatriate practically always experiences a more or less strong impression of isolation that it is important to fight against, through showing him that his efforts are closely monitored by headquarters and that he is not being forgotten. To do this, regular communication is necessary . . . and prompt attention given to answering his letters and reports!

Some companies which have numerous employees scattered all over the world are very aware of this problem, and send their expatriate staff a special monthly newsletter.

With the development of video conferences, getting faster by now with the lowering of equipment prices, more and more companies will have this efficient communication tool, between headquarters and branches abroad, to organize far more productive and motivating meetings than with the phone/fax combination, at an uncomparably cheaper cost than those of travelling – mostly if time loss is being considered as well. But face to face meetings will still have to be maintained regularly, to provide the indispensable dose of 'human touch'.

Personal attention is also very welcome to avoid discouragement, and to maintain a conqueror's morale for company personnel at faraway frontier posts. Why not wish them a 'Happy Birthday' from headquarters?

In the case where a large number of expatriates is involved in a long-term mission (major public works projects – dams, hydro-electric plants, etc.), companies should not spare their efforts in satisfying material comforts, which becomes almost a major feat when the project is located in a difficult environment.

▶ *For their huge project in Abuja (the new capital of Nigeria in the north of the country), the **SAE** company began by building a small French city in the middle of the bush, for the expatriates and their families who would live there for three or four years. There was a medical centre, a school, supermarkets (supplied in part from France) which enabled them to retain their eating habits. For leisure time, there were tennis courts and swimming pools, libraries and video clubs where newspapers, magazines, TV news programs, best sellers and the latest films could be found, so as not to cut people off from the French way of life.*

On a professional level, close contact should be maintained:

■ Priority communication between headquarters and expatriates should enable the latter to benefit from all available company means to facilitate their task.

■ All decisions which have been made in common should be followed up and implemented (see Chapter 2's introduction).

■ Regular check-ups, which are the objective means of assessing the expatriates' work (and of correcting errors), can also anticipate (and thus prevent) any serious phenomenon of 'power fever' which affects some expatriates who find themselves – finally – almost running their own business, and behaving more and more like 'divine right' monarchs, forgetting international company policy as well as headquarters' instructions.

■ Such controls, which can be carried out as with the agents in charge of priority markets (see section 3.3.2.3), should normally take place in a climate of co-operation, given the company's 'family' framework, unless jealousy and rivalry render the atmosphere explosive. In this case, the bomb-like situation has to be rapidly defused by the Export Director or the CEO through modification of the structure to separate the hostile parties who could wreak havoc in company projects.

Contact with headquarters should, then, be frequent. The expatriates must return to headquarters every year or so, and/or should attend major meetings (export conventions, for example) so as not to be too cut off from company life and culture.

▶ *As for **Crédit Lyonnais**, with branches in 70 countries (this bank employs close to 30,000 people outside France), the necessity of having efficient internal communication can be imagined. '**Crédit Lyonnais** spirit' is maintained thanks to an internal monthly magazine, multiple intra- and inter-zone seminars, as well as a rapid rotation of expatriate personnel (every three or four years).*

These trips to headquarters, and the 'inspection' visits abroad, enable company management to discuss with the expatriates the different career possibilities which await them following repatriation. In most cases, it is wise not to prolong a foreign posting more than four to six years. Preparing a career change in advance can be a supplementary motivation for the expatriate because he knows the company has his professional interests in view.

When the expatriate returns to the fold, he has to be given every opportunity to readapt himself to his new job, in an environment which may have evolved considerably in his absence. Among the means to be used to this effect (professional training, reinsertion programs within different departments, etc.), it is worth having the 'prodigal son' prepare and host a conference on the country/countries he has returned from – his responsibilities there, market specifics, problems encountered, commercial competition, sales results, etc. – using, if possible, visual aids (graphs, slides, photographs). This conference should be for all those staff concerned, either service by service or for everybody altogether, depending on company size. There are many advantages to this kind of conference:

- The staff involved benefit from a goldmine of information collected by the expatriate, information which can be passed along much more easily in this form than in a thick report that nobody would read anyway.
- International aspects of exporting can be shared with all company personnel who will be cordially invited to attend the conference.
- The expatriate's work abroad is officially recognized by the company, and he can get back in touch with staff members he knew before leaving (and who might have forgotten him), or can meet personnel with whom he might not be acquainted.

Above and beyond questions specifically related to expatriation, all internationally-minded companies should rapidly establish a stimulating human resources policy for those people employed locally.

▶ *This is particularly the case of **Rhône-Poulenc**, present in 140 countries, since half of their 84,000 collaborators work outside France. In such conditions, what kind of human resource policy should be adopted? Each* *country has its laws, its social structure, its collective agreements with trade unions, its specific customs. 'We want to respect them' specifies Gilbert Bonneau, Director of International Affairs for the Human Resources Department. 'There is no question of harmonizing the different countries, nor of any company intervention in the way each Human Resources Director deals with local problems. On the other hand, it seemed important to establish a world **Rhône-Poulenc** policy for more general issues, such as training, career management, retirement . . .'.*

<table>
<tr><td>**5.2**</td><td># Local Representatives</td></tr>
</table>

The forms of local representation vary widely depending upon the fields of activity and the exporting companies' development strategies, as well as on the nature and requirements of each market.

In some cases, there is no real local representative, either because the company has decided to do without this intermediary by dealing directly with distribution, or because the small number of potential clients in a market does not justify it. In this latter situation, the company deals directly with the clientele, with or without a sponsor, according to the country (frequent for large engineering projects and heavy capital goods). There are also countries with a state-ruled economy, where official buying authorities cannot be compared to any sort of local representation, since a company loses all control over its products once they have been transferred (this was the classic situation in Eastern Europe until recently).

Nevertheless, it is extremely rare that a company can expand completely without a relay or a local springboard (whether it is a real representative or not) given that some dynamic devices likely to energize a firm's development plans are available.

A few dynamic devices are only applicable to specific types of representation – subsidiaries or agents, for example – but the majority are adaptable to all different forms of local representation.

Moreover, it can be seen that all the dynamic devices presented in this section and in section 5.3 ('Local distributors') offer a sufficiently vast selection to respond to local push needs, covering most eventualities, including the specific instances of franchised networks. On this subject, before starting this chapter, it is interesting to cite an example of the partnership spirit often developed by export franchisers with their foreign franchisees, which should inspire exporters in the relationships they maintain with their local representatives.

▶   *To illustrate this partnership spirit, here are a few excerpts from 'Our Bottler', **Pepsi-Cola's** bottler-franchisee creed:*

*'**Pepsi-Cola International** and their bottlers share bonds of singular strength. Independent, entrepreneurial, and community-oriented, our bot-*

tlers are at once our partners and our patrons. Above all, however, they are an integral part of the Pepsi family . . . united in the pursuit of common goals.

*Together, we strive to manufacture and market the world's highest quality beverages, to strengthen the **Pepsi-Cola** brands, and to ensure the success of our franchise network. Our destinies are intertwined. We cannot prosper unless our bottlers prosper.*

Our relationship is timeless. It is rooted in mutual trust and respect, and strengthens with every stage of our dynamic partnership.'

Obviously, the partnership spirit must replace the good old classical supplier-buyer relationship, where the sell-in conditions (such as the export price) used to be the exclusive key issue of tough negotiations. To expand quickly, the exporter and his local representative have to co-operate on the sell-through actions that will generate a successful common business for both parties: as it will often be demonstrated hereafter, this only requires acting as partners, whose proposals have to be guided by mutual interest, while planning development strategy . . . or negotiating export prices.

5.2.1   Communication with local representatives

Even though certain aspects of this vast subject have already been touched upon in earlier chapters, it is important now to deal with the matter as a whole. A general inventory of the dynamic devices based on communication with the local representatives will then be made, in order to cover all those means which are likely to encourage them to develop company business.

Throughout this inventory, it will appear that many of these dynamic devices are practically an obligation to ensure market development, in the sense that if they are forgotten or neglected, then expansion will be impeded. This will be a particularly delicate case if the local representative has other parallel activities besides the company's product development; or when the lack of a better alternative obliged the company to entrust their business to a non-exclusive agent who also looks after competing products. It could be supposed, on the contrary, that subsidiary business will not suffer from sporadic headquarters communication: but, as we have partly seen concerning expatriate staff, close contact has to be maintained with company subsidiaries, as well as with other forms of representation, to expand in foreign markets.

5.2.1.1   Motivation

Money! This short-cut, with a strong trades union connotation, reminds us – without beating round the bush – that philanthropy is no more popular in international commerce than anywhere else, and most motivating incentives for the local representative to push company products all have, as a common denominator, his interests at heart.

Theoretically, the agreement was concluded with satisfactory terms for both parties at the signing of the contract; today, it is possible that this contract still seems fair to the company, but what about the local representative? Circumstances could have changed, and unforeseen factors drastically reduced the profitability of his business with the company.

Depending upon the representative's situation and his management style, two main reactions can be imagined:

- An immediate request to revise the agreement. Obviously, this is the most desirable reaction, as it allows the company to study rapidly the complaint's authenticity; if the request is justified, it is up to the company to find an equitable solution, for example, by realigning the price structure (see sections 4.3.3.1 and 4.3.4.1), granting the representative special rates for certain materials or service supplies, and/or taking charge of all or part of the local development budgets, etc, for the general purpose of providing a more substantial mark-up (or a larger commission, if this is the remuneration planned for the type of representation that has been established*).

- Apparent satisfaction. Some local representatives prefer submitting themselves to an abnormal unprofitable situation without bringing up the subject with the company, for several reasons: either because business is not so good and they fear that by questioning the agreement they will lose the contract altogether; or, on the contrary, if representing several brands of complementary or even rival products, they consider that their operating costs are already covered by these brands, and prefer to keep our company's products under their control (sometimes, of course, to serve their own interests with competitors by limiting our own expansion); for whatever reason a local representative hides the fact that he is dissatisfied with the profit margin, it becomes a powerful obstacle which will stifle company development. The representative, obviously, will activate sales of brands bringing in more revenue, while at the same time perhaps looking for

---

*It is useful to recall here the importance of the speed with which commission is to be paid. It can be imagined how demotivating it is for a commissioned agent to see the delays in his payments getting longer and longer. Export executives *must* ensure that these payments are sent out on the agreed dates, checking up on possible company or bank administrative blockages.

another brand to replace us. Consequently, it is up to the export executive to be sufficiently perceptive in assessing the representative's degree of satisfaction with the price structure so as to rectify it if necessary.

Sufficient profit obviously ranks as the main motivating incentive for the representative* to develop company markets; then, besides some representatives' occasional exaggerated demands, here are two guidelines which can help export executives keep on the right path:

- The average level of remuneration for representatives on the given market; the export executive's regular attitude will be somewhere between a normal incentive that follows the average closely, and the need for a stronger motivating incentive that somewhat exceeds it.
- Remunerations established far above the average – which are meant in very special cases to over-motivate the company representative – involve two limits to keep at a distance: the ceiling on acceptable market prices, as well as our own bottom export price.

Besides those specific occasions where financial agreements have to be revised with the local representative for unexpected reasons, as has just been seen, it is advisable to tackle this matter openly from time to time. This will introduce a stability factor into prices and mark-ups, rendering deals more rational and efficient at each stage of distribution. Moreover, such a partnership spirit is to be established between the company and their local representative, given that the best interests of both parties must be satisfied to trigger any common dynamic actions.

Still, other motivational factors are important to directly influence the local representative's interest:

- exclusivity – most often indispensable for motivation. Here, however, three examples demonstrate that this exclusivity can be complete, shared or subdivided, and still assure good results.

▶ *The **Sogedi Co.** found themselves confronted by commercial anarchy in Belgium, when they took over exporting for a French household appliance manufacturer, who had agreed to sell his products to several Belgian importers without worrying about how this market would evolve (a market the manufacturer had never set foot in). Each importer introduced himself to the trade as being exclusive, giving retailers contradictory information*

---

*Experience shows that subsidiary managers can be as pugnacious as the most virulent representatives in defending their margins. It sometimes happens, for various reasons (difficulty in repatriating profits or royalties, for example), that the parent company decides to inflate export prices to make a maximum profit in the home country, thus logically forcing the subsidiary to operate more or less at a loss because of low margins. This inevitably illustrates the fact that human nature is such that most executives dislike not being able to demonstrate the efficiency of their work by flattering results, even for the overall interest of the Group.

and offering different prices and after-sales service. The resulting confusion can be imagined. Fortunately, the manufacturer was alerted before it was too late by requests for information or complaints received directly from several Belgian retailers. Not having an operating export service, they called in **Sogedi** *to sort matters out. Very quickly, this consulting company assessed each importer's capacities and designated one of them to be the official, exclusive company representative. With him, they prepared the Belgian Market's development plan, whose first phase was explaining the new situation to the trade and building up confidence in the brand again. Two years later, business in Belgium is sailing along without a problem, as well as regularly progressing.*

▶ *In the case of a brand unknown to the public (all communication being concentrated just on the brand's product names), there is nothing stopping the company from dividing their product lines among several local representatives. This might, of course, frustrate company partners a little, inhibit advertising or commercial synergy possibilities and double certain distribution costs. But this unusual formula does not lack interest, as* **Chupa Chups** *illustrate: in the USA, they had their whistling pops marketed by a national distributor, whereas their other products were entrusted, regionally, to local brokers. This form of dividing to better expand paid off, as putting all company products in the same distributor's basket probably would not have succeeded as well. In addition,* **Chupa Chups** *have more strategic flexibility, not being dependent on any single distributor.*

▶ **Facom's** *determination to stimulate sales directly among end-users by working closely with their distributors is demonstrated by a very direct, international sales network:* **Facom** *avoid entrusting product development to exclusive agents in each country. They prefer counting on a few, carefully selected wholesalers who have complementary clientele and territories. For these distributors, the absence of exclusivity is largely compensated for by the assistance and support supplied by* **Facom** *in different ways, especially with the regular visit of demonstration trucks (see section 6.5.2.4) to potential clients and the catalogue provided for them (see section 2.1.2.3).*

■ Another essential factor for the local representative's motivation is the way in which the brand and product image are perceived; it is of the utmost importance that this image be as positive as possible. The local representative is usually the largest buyer and/or the first influencer in his market, so much so that his confidence in and enthusiasm for the brand should be constantly maintained by time and again 'selling' the advantages of working with the company and proving product competitiveness.

■ In the same way, the local representative has to feel supported and assisted in a climate of cooperation and efficiency, as mentioned above in the **Facom** example, and as will be covered more fully below (see sections 5.2.1.2–4).

■ Many agents in precarious positions restrain from investing as much as they could do for company development, because they fear (sometimes quite legitimately) that the export company might cease doing business with them in the near future. This is a key element in motivating local agents continuously (dealt with in section 5.2.1.5).

Last, but not least, let us now leave the motivational factors directly linked to local representatives' business interests, and take a look at other, more personal motivations.

This requires observing and sufficiently knowing the local representative, as well as his executives and staff, to figure out how they can be personally* motivated, and how company sales development can be made more attractive to them.

In this area, fortunately, one essential factor is cheerfulness, which should not demand any particular effort on the export executive's part, since one of the basic qualities required is a naturally open, friendly and sociable temperament.

An export executive only has to know how to adapt himself (as always when abroad) to local cultures as well as to people's personalities, to find the communication style most suitable for both pleasant and stimulating professional/personal interaction.

This can take many and varied forms. Without being too general, let us mention the warm, friendly, colourful atmosphere of Mediterranean, Middle Eastern or Latin American clientele, whose style is 'My home is your home!' or the more reserved style met in Anglo-Saxon, Scandinavian or Far Eastern countries, where friendship is based on reciprocal esteem and only really warms up at dinner parties where drinks help to lighten the habitual reserve.

▶ *To conclude on this point, here is how **Lancôme** managed to overcome obstacles resulting from a culture gap with Korea. As Robert Salmon (**L'Oréal's** Vice-Chairman) recalls: 'We were trying to bring off the merging of a French company – where organization was flexible and responsibility individual – with a Korean pyramid-style system, with a strong hierarchy and collective responsibility. Obviously, these fundamental differences made a 'message decoding system' and a 'human relay system' necessary.*

__Lancôme__ responded to these needs by integrating bicultural Koreans, living in France and apt at understanding each cultural and behavioural specificity. In addition, we all got used to our partner's work and leisure habits, for example, the warm conviviality of Korean parties where drinks, songs and friendly atmosphere reinforce relationships and mutual confidence. __Lancôme's__ success as leader of foreign cosmetic brands on the Korean market is especially due to the effort made to understand this country: proposing without imposing and adapting without renouncing one's own values.'

---

*Money (again!) or other types of advantages in kind can be planned to motivate certain of the local representative's staff members individually. However, this practice (rather displeasing but difficult to avoid at times), which is common in distribution channels, are dealt with in section 5.3.3.2.

5.2.1.2 Activity schedule

Scheduling activities with local representatives (as described in Chapters 2 and 3) is the most efficient way of getting them to constantly provide the necessary effort to develop company markets.

Here, again, it is not a question of imposing a similar schedule on all markets: the peoples of many countries are allergic to rigorous scheduling styles, and export executives should make an effort to be more flexible. In the same way, the schedule's intensity will vary greatly according to market size and the importance of the development plans unfolding in them.

Having local representatives adhere completely to an activity schedule will only be possible if they are convinced such an organization represents an essential factor for common business development (thus, for *their* profit). In this respect, several conditions are necessary:

- The export executives must be recognized as reliable and efficient partners – which will be made easier by a good dose of professionalism, testimonials of success obtained in other markets, and a sufficient market knowledge of the specific territory – to convince the local representative that such direct assistance will be a help and not a hindrance.
- Really working as a team with the local representative, emphasizing the importance of his staff participation, who will better accept an activity schedule which they themselves have helped to plan.
- Ensure the company's support credibility all the way within headquarters. Furthermore, every company executive who travels in the same market must keep within the same strategic lines, which will not create confusion with conflicting proposals. All of this should run like clockwork if care is taken to involve the headquarters staff in development plan preparation (see section 2.3.1.1).

▶ *As explained by Gilles Bassi, when he was General Manager of the **Lainière de Picardie***: 'In order to reinforce our development in each market, we bring together our major agents/distributors and foreign subsidiary directors, as well as company executives, for a two-day international seminar every year in France. This way, we can analyse together all our results and expansion perspectives. It is undeniable that each person feels comforted by the sensation of belonging to a world organization linked with a common market expansion. This atmosphere favorizes emulation and enables us to decide collectively on our development strategy. The development plan's definition and implementation follow along then quite easily, in each country.'*

---

*An SME with 400 employees (**Groupe Chargeurs**); $110 million turnover in 1991, of which 90% is in exports; world leader for woven interlining used in men's and women's garments.

5.2.1.3   Information systematization

When one realizes how hard it is to get information circulating in the same company, even in the same department, the complexity of organizing an international system that functions regularly in two directions (between headquarters and the local representatives) can be measured.

In fact, the difficulty in perfecting this system lies in the awareness of its importance for general development, and the determination to make it work. It is usually on this last point that there are failures and blockages, up until the moment that the task is entrusted to someone who is sufficiently organized and methodic.

It will, of course, be up to headquarters to set an example by sending the local representatives all the information which can help to stimulate development and thus favourably impress them.

For companies exporting all over the world, it is in their own interest to plan for information content and dispatching frequency in relation to local development needs and potentials: for example, a complete monthly newsletter for priority markets, and a lighter newsletter every two or three months for secondary markets.

The actual form this information takes is secondary, and can be rudimentary if investment capability is limited, but it must be basically acceptable. What is important is to present the information in a clear and comprehensible manner for the interested parties.

According to the fields of activities and needs, the subjects dealt with could vary considerably, but here are a few points which could appear regularly in the company information bulletin*:

- Product information: new products being worked on, improvement of existing models, new maintenance procedures;
- Commercial information: new product launches; market openings, new contracts; sales records (presented in such a way as to provoke rivalry among representatives):
- Marketing development information: international demand evolution analysis, commentary on competitors' actions of interest, exemplary development actions implemented in various markets with the company's local representatives;
- General company information: management transfers, local representatives' visits to headquarters, updates on the state of the company's markets.

It should be noted that this latter point, which resembles a 'house organ', is also an extremely efficient internal public relations tool (already mentioned in section 5.1.3.3) for reinforcing loyalty.

---

*Obviously, to be designed for meeting any confidential requirements.

► The magazine published by **Renault Véhicules Industriels**, which appears three times a year, is an excellent example of this type of internal/external information tool. With the format of a classic news magazine, 32 pages in full colour, it gives the impression of quality which is rapidly confirmed by the content: there are superbly illustrated articles on **RVI** in the world (factories, **Renault** trucks working on spectacular sites) and on the companies using **RVI** trucks; there are celebrity interviews, a detailed story about a particular country, new products, and presentation (article and photographs) of the export staff (field staff as well as support staff covering a geographical area), a list of trade shows and exhibitions **RVI** participated in, a section on Echoes and News (**RVI** world commercial successes, visiting foreign delegations), etc. Hence, it is a pity that such a magazine is financially possible only for a minority of exporting companies.

Still for SME managers currently sighing enviously when confronted by such a 'heavyweight' of international information, it should be pointed out that they can successfully use less costly media:

► In this way, **Sauvion** (a tiny company specializing in Muscadet wines) regularly publishes the **Cléray Chronicle**, taken from the name of the company's château. Each issue has two pertinent features – originality and low cost, as one of them illustrates: three beige sheets of paper 21 × 60cm resembling parchment (sent rolled up in a cardboard tube), printed on both sides in an old-fashioned style. There are the following headings:

■ 'Gazette Review', an international press review in which it is specified that 'the Lord of Cléray is pleased to send you the following articles which tell the tales of our battles and conquests in the four corners of the kingdom and beyond the seas'. Included are 20 or more excerpts from press articles, from 'The Winnipeg Sun' to 'The Hawaii Beverage Guide' or 'The Hong Kong Daily News'.

■ 'News from our musketeers far away from the kingdom', which recounts the successes of **Sauvion** agents around the world, (in the Philippines, Newfoundland, or Finland, to name a few).

■ 'Annals: Château life, within and without', listing **Sauvion**'s numerous activities during the preceding months: the new Muscadet Selection in February; an official tasting at the Halekulani Hotel in Hawaii, a banquet dinner in Hanover . . .

■ 'Festivities to come', giving the next events in which **Sauvion** will participate

■ 'Identity Card' presents, complete with photographs (black and white) and successes, **Sauvion** agents in a world area; Asia, being featured in this particular issue, the musketeers were transformed into dragons . . .

■ 'Court pages', on the contrary, present the staff members of a **Sauvion** service (the production staff in this issue) with their specializations, in a humorous way.

It can easily be imagined how the originality in form and style of this international newsletter (whose content is the equivalent of a 12-page), *published in French, English and German, can only please **Sauvion's** French and foreign clientele. The cost is particularly modest: $5000, translations included, for a thousand copies. This low cost can be explained by a family style edition, with staff-written articles and even children participating by putting the parchment scrolls in the tubes . . .*

Let us now see how to get the feedback needed. First, something obvious has to be remembered: few local representatives have a natural inclination to become information sources, thus great patience is required on the part of export executives in training and motivating their 'informers'. A rare example from whom efficient information should naturally be expected is the local representative, who helps the company compete for a market by tender. In fact, one essential function of this local relay (sponsor, in Middle Eastern countries) is to look for information on deals 'in the making', and to get precise data on the specifications before their publication. If the relay is really well situated, he can even serve as an inspiration for drawing up the tender so that it will be better adapted to company possibilities, and thus help things along at the critical moment of choice. It should be noted that the local relay's information task will be more productive if he has been well prepared, because company choice (especially in the case of a sponsor) is based far more on his contacts with decision-makers than on his technical competence. It is thus sometimes necessary to give him general training, and clearly indicate the type of information desired.

Most forms of local representation require preparation for the transmission of information, and export executives should convince them that it is in their own interest to cooperate with the company in this matter.

To make the local representative's task easier, the export executive should prepare a form beforehand, mentioning the different headings of interest to the company:

- internal information concerning the local representative's activities: sales figures (in turnover and volume), new customers, number of outlets, stock levels, evolution of company structures, sales force, etc.
- external information: market evolution, competitors' activities and new products, etc.

Besides this information log-book (for a more complete list, see section 1.1), the representatives should be encouraged to communicate their observations and criticisms, as well as their suggestions, on the company's product performance. International markets are vast testing grounds for company products, where many new ideas can be collected with such an organization.

Having 'a market log-book' gives several advantages: it simplifies the local representative's task, as he just has to fill it in; it also simplifies the follow-up and information analysis at headquarters by using a standard form worldwide.

Here are three suggestions to get this system into operation, coming from the markets towards headquarters:

■ the pump has to be primed; that is to say, the first form should be presented to the local representative during a visit, and *never* sent. In this way, the export executive can emphasize its importance, and explain to the representative's staff how to answer each question, thus helping them fill this first form in so that the following forms should not pose any problem.

■ As for newsletters going from headquarters to the market, the frequency will be in direct relation to the size and potential of each market: monthly, bimonthly, quarterly, bi-annually, or even annually for secondary markets.

■ There should be feedback from headquarters as soon as these forms arrive to indicate to the local representatives that the information provided is both appreciated and followed up. A good way in which to stimulate motivation would be to cite certain data, mentioning the country and the local representative's name, in the newsletter. Seeing one's name making a world tour is always appreciated!

However, despite all efforts, top quality as well as homogeneous data should not be expected, as a lot of patience is required – to get the negligent or forgetful representatives to send in their forms – to make the system work smoothly. In any case, it is in the export executive's interest to follow his major market's evolution from four different sources:

■ the data sent in by the local representatives;
■ the observations and data collected directly on the markets during business trips, or by field surveys carried out there;
■ information available through secondary sources – international press, economics articles, etc. (see section 1.1.1.2);
■ fragmentary information to be cross-checked with the above, which is collected at random through informal contacts: conversations with suppliers, subcontractors, competitors, etc.

5.2.1.4   Assistance and training

The importance of assistance and training for international business development is obvious enough, so it is not necessary to belabour the point. However, a few remarks about their implementation and getting the most out of them might not be amiss.

Here is an example of practical assistance and commercial training taken from the international hotel industry – all the more exemplary as this is a domain well-known to exporters, as regular users:

▶ **Méridien Hotels** *propose to their commercial staff all over the world various dynamic devices to develop results. Among others, there is assistance for organizing sales promotions and a training program.*

■ *Sales Promotion Method (excerpts):*
- □ *Concentration on profitable sales calls only, banishing all routine ones; establishing a schedule; preparing each call by fixing objectives.*
- □ *Multiplication of qualified contacts by 'phone or organizing infor-mation meetings by sectors of activity (travel agents, airlines, com-pany executives), with ten to twenty people at a time, etc.*

■ *Training Program (excerpts):*
- □ *practical sales call exercises (face-to-face or by 'phone) carried out at information meetings;*
- □ *preparation in using sales aids (general sales presentation of the* **Méridien** *Chain, and of each hotel);*
- □ *knowledge of the hotels and the markets, by local visits.*

Apart from those particular cases of companies having their own field staff, like **Méridien,** it can be noted that the need for assistance or training is not necessarily felt by local representatives; export executives have to be sufficiently vigilant on this point to detect such unexpressed needs.

Thus, going on client calls with the agent's sales staff will provide the occasion to assess their selling competence and the quality of company product presentations. This assessment will be usefully completed by participation in local sales meetings, where field obser-vations can be dealt with in greater depth. This will help to prepare more adapted training programs for the sales force which, as a result, will improve the relationship with the trade.

▶ *This is how the export executives of the* **Laboratoire Roger Bellon (Rhône-Poulenc Group)** *adapt their pharmaceutical products' distribution experi-ence to each country's particularities, by helping some of their agents' sales staff get better organized. For example, according to local conditions, the best methods for making appointments will be defined, followed by the preparation of the most efficient presentation in the limited time (three to five minutes, on average) of a sales call on a doctor or pharmacist.*

Generally, for the local staff working with company products, nothing (in principle) should prevent the export executive from openly dis-cussing their organization, training and career evolution with the representative's executives.

Moreover, this can be an important source of dynamic devices, as a large sales increase can result from the reorganization of an agent's departments, especially the sales force, as illustrated by **Avon** in Japan[3]:

▶ *This American cosmetics giant had, at first, applied their sales tool, effective nearly everywhere else in the world: an army of saleswomen peddling door-to-door. However, this technique turned out to be less productive in Japan, where most women are too reserved to pitch to strangers.*

***Avon**, then, adapted their sales force organization so that the bashful ones could sell to acquaintances instead. This reorganization, strongly reinforced by pleasant and poetic themes diffused through media advertising, helped increase **Avon** sales at an annual rate of more than 25% during the following years.*

On the other hand, it can be more delicate to bring up professional incompetence on the part of one of the agent's executives by suggesting that a company specialist come on an assistance mission, or that this executive follow a training program. In this case, a more diplomatic approach will avoid any potential blunder, such as organizing 'a visit by a company specialist interested in exchanging points of view'. If well presented, this obvious tactic will enable the local executive to save face and, according to his field, become more familiar with modern techniques in organization, motivating sales teams, stock management, etc. In the same way, if it involves a training program, it should be presented as 'a conference, assembling executives from different markets, so they can discuss practical problems'.

This diplomacy, often necessary for assistance or training company agents' executives, is, moreover, always present in daily work relations with them. Field executives on a local visit have, in fact, a continuous 'helpmate' role, but must avoid a lecturing attitude when giving advice. On the other hand, they should take advantage of every occasion to bring out the complementary nature and productivity of their exchanges with the local executives. The results of these assistance and training actions will obviously be in direct relation with the competence of the person in charge:

▶   *Thus, for example, **RoC** trainers all have the equivalent of a physician's or a pharmacist's degree; therefore, the local representative's staff, or the saleswomen/demonstrators, are thoroughly trained and can better transmit the **RoC** product message, which reinforces the scientific background of the brand's image.*

It is important that the training programs, as well as the support material, are prepared by staff members who have real field experience, so that the content is not just theoretical.

According to the case, group training can be undertaken in a number of different ways:

■   *Training at headquarters*: obviously, this is the most productive formula, but the cost of bringing people to headquarters usually reserves this type of training for executives, at least those in faraway markets. In fact, headquarters normally has the best adapted materials and equipment for training, and visitors can also be impressed by the company's organization, infrastructure, etc.; and when applicable, with the domestic market position held by the company. Finally, receiving the local representatives' staff is an occasion on which to roll out the red carpet and cultivate their loyalty.

■ *Regional training*: this intermediary formula involves the organization of a training base, in several world regions, on the premises of a subsidiary or a local representative. This type of training benefits in part from the advantages of headquarters training, as well as local training.

■ *Local training*: this is the most inexpensive formula, since it only entails the travel expenses of the trainer(s)*. There is a trend to use it for training subordinate personnel, whose numbers would greatly increase travel expenses. These training programs, which do not benefit from all the facilities available at headquarters, can be rendered more attractive even though there is no trip involved: choice of pleasant premises, VIP welcome and treatment (participants' names on the tables; name badges; tables arranged conference-style, in a circle or rectangle, and not classroom-style, in rows; good food; gifts, etc.), and most important, trainers with international charisma.

▶ *These three types of training locations are used by **Potain**, who place a lot of attention on technical training, as much for crane operation and maintenance as for moving them (this equipment, in fact, cannot be set up or moved to another site without the assistance of technicians who are specialists in the setting up and taking down of such structures).*

*This has led **Potain** to develop a complete training system: two major centres, one in France, the other in Germany; training branches on the premises of their largest local representatives; and, of course, the possibility of complementary training for technicians on worksites every time a **Potain** technical specialist passes through.*

A well-conceived training program will generate a positive atmosphere for the exchange of ideas, experience and information. Because of this, the training program provides a rare opportunity to get to know all the participants, who have left their usual professional persona behind, and have a more authentic attitude thanks to the change of place and activity. A lot can also be learned about the internal operations of the local representative's company, and (in the case of non-exclusive representatives) precious information gleaned about competitors' methods and sales results.

For the same reasons, these training periods can create serious problems for a company which has assembled the executives of local representatives, who all have different sorts of agreements with the company. The participants will not take long in comparing transfer

---

*Or the setting up of a local training service, if market needs justify it.

costs, local prices, royalties, etc., and use this information to their best advantage.

5.2.1.5   Loyalty reinforcement

Loyalty can be considered as a way of strengthening the foundations of the local representatives' motivation, making them more amenable to a greater commitment and investment on their part for developing company business in the medium- and long-term . . . without forgetting that the local representatives' loyalty favours a much pleasanter working atmosphere.

Each of the above-mentioned means for improving communication obviously contributes to the growth of loyalty, but their impact can be reinforced.

First, it logically seems difficult to succeed in developing loyalty on the part of local representatives without first showing them a minimum of trust, particularly concerning the length of their contract. Thus, for example, a year's contract, tacitly renewable, is usually an acceptable way of getting to know and assessing the local representative's potential; but it cannot be reasonably hoped that the representative will make a great effort to push company products when he has such a short time in which to harvest the fruits.

As soon as a representative's willingness and aptitude to play the development game has been assessed, it is up to the company to perpetuate, to some extent*, agreements with him, prolonging the contract to three, even five years. This is often a fundamental condition for market expansion.

Showing the local representatives a promising future is logically another powerful loyalty factor:

▶   *For **Yoplait**, who built their international expansion on exclusive franchising agreements with local companies, franchise partner loyalty is based mostly on the brand's innovative capacity and success. Obviously, it is reassuring for the franchisees to see that the **Yoplait** R&D department are constantly coming up with new products, and that the most recently launched novelties, such as 'petit filou', a cottage cheese containing chunks of fruit, or 'ofilus', a fermented milk product containing bifidus, are selling quite well. What can be more natural than for the franchisees to support their brand with growing confidence?*

Representatives' loyalty is also based on the regular development of quality personal relations, which will lead to a highly privileged

---

*Indeed, contract terms should provide the company with different guarantees concerning the representative's activities: sales quotas, respect of rules laid down for international brand strategy, respect of (if applicable) an exclusivity clause and territorial limits for distribution, etc., which permit a possible break of contract in the case of any infringement.

cooperative relationship. One's attitude* and different, individualized attentiveness paid to the local representatives who have 'proved their worth' will make them feel part of the 'company family circle', whether they be second cousins from Venezuela or the Philippines.

5.2.1.6 Performance control

Checking up on local representatives' performance should be done regularly in the normal framework of communication, and understood as a legitimate interest in the realization of common objectives; however, 'checking up' should be adapted so that it does not run counter to the local way of doing things.

In previous sections concerning the motivation and loyalty of the local representatives' executives, the importance of creating a positive working relationship has been stressed. However, it is important to make sure that this attitude for assuring a more productive and agreeable cooperation with more friendly relationships, does not degenerate into casualness.

▶ *An export executive from a perfume company had a very unpleasant experience with a 'model agent' in a small country within his geographical zone. This agent had become a real friend, and his professional skills were widely cited as examples. The export executive, while on vacation in this country, had even agreed to be the godfather for one of the agent's daughters.*

Parallel to this, the export executive was having problems with a neighbouring micro-market. The local representative of this market complained that he regularly received returned perfume bottles from his retail outlets which leaked or were broken, as well as 'dummies' (filled with an odourless, coloured liquid and normally used as POP material) which inexplicably seemed to have been packaged and sold as the real thing.

This situation lasted for almost two years, before the origin of the mystery was discovered – 'the model agent'! It was true, the export executive had been careless to sign, without checking, certificates for the destruction of merchandise which was supposedly defective or which had been damaged during transportation. These defective perfumes and dummies, along with other brands, had enabled the agent's brother to carry out some smuggling operations, thus perturbing distribution in the neighbouring market.

Such examples demonstrate that friendship should not affect the rigour or efficiency normally required from each partner.

Regular performance checks should be carried out in two complementary ways:

- more of a quantity control, taken from the information sent to headquarters by the local representative (see section 5.2.1.3),

---

*Development of extra-professional relationships, personalized gifts, etc.

which will be broken down into more detail by the export executive whenever visiting his country.

▶ *Clarins have developed a log-book, used in each of their markets, which enables them to check up on local operations with great precision. According to the size of the markets, these log-books are filled in and sent on to* **Clarins** *every month, or every two, three or six months.*

Key recorded figures: units sold per reference; sales turnover; number of retail outlets; average turnover per retail outlet; number of salespeople; evolution of training, media advertising, POP material and public relations budgets; state of the stocks; orders on the books, etc. For all these indications, the yearly forecasts, as well as the current results, are shown. Performance checks can thus be made easily by comparing forecasts with results. This log-book allows the modification of the unfolding development plan, either during a local visit by the **Clarins** *Export Director, or by 'phone (see section 3.1.1.2) from the head office.*

■ more of a quality control carried out in the field, whose purpose is both to observe the attitude of the local representative's personnel and to be in direct contact with the local retail outlets.

▶ *In a European country where* **Perrier** *sales seemed to have reached a peak, it was thanks to a field survey rapidly carried out by an export executive that the Group realized they had to diversify the number of their retail outlets, whereas their local agent had never mentioned a word about this. With the high price of the green bottles, sales progression was slowing down in food stores. On the other hand, getting into hotel, bar, restaurant and club outlets seemed more promising. This resulted in a difficult negotiation with the local agent, who did not have a commercial organization to cover these new channels of distribution: he was quite satisfied with the sales volume in food stores, and was not particularly enthusiastic in investing in a larger commercial structure. However, in the end he preferred doing that rather than losing the* **Perrier** *contract altogether ... and he was quickly satisfied when the sales results of this new clientele demonstrated a clear success.*

Thus, of all the advice about efficient international market checkups, the most important is to get as close to the field as possible, as we are to see.

The representative's log-book figures and accompanying explanations should give a fairly precise market impression, but there could be inherent errors, intentional or not, by the local representative: analyses more or less objective, or even erroneous; doubtful figures and overly-optimistic or pessimistic trends.

All this falls into place with field visits, together with cross-checking the information gleaned elsewhere (see section 5.2.1.3) and the data provided by the local representative, which will give the export executive a coherent control basis, in parallel with general market trends. It is on the grounds of this comprehensive checkup that it is possible to appreciate the representative's real performance, by measuring the difficulties encountered and his capacity to resolve them.

It is quite frequent to see local representatives trying hard to erect a screen between the exporting company and their local clientele (distributors or end-users). This attitude can be explained by the desire to remain in control of their market, to prevent the company from either dealing directly with the clientele or replacing the local representative (thus risking a loss of the agent's customers who are unknown to the company). This screen can be felt in visits organized by the local representative, where the export executive only meets clients chosen with care to testify to the representative's performance. It is, however, fundamental for the company to remain in contact with the final clientele, not to short-circuit the local representative commercially, but to check up on him so that company products are not reduced to being hostages of the local representative – which makes any change or evolution perilous ('without me, Mr. Exporter, you are nothing on this market: you don't know who I sell to, the quantities sold, nor the selling price'). It is also useful to obtain direct feedback on product appreciation, requirements, ideas for new products, possible improvements, etc.

According to the professional field, it will be more or less difficult to break through this screen while avoiding direct conflict with the local representative: for products distributed in retail outlets, it is quite easy to survey a market by playing the 'tourist' and discreetly observing POP displays and the general attitude of the sales staff regarding the company's products.

For other products, direct contact with the end-users can be more difficult to establish, especially if the local representative is in a strong position in relation to the company. In this case, there are two main solutions: make the local representative more aware of the support direct company assistance could bring him during meetings with certain clients; or participate in trade shows and international congresses frequented by these clients, during which there will be numerous occasions to become acquainted and follow this up.

There is another point to emphasize concerning checking up on local representatives' performance: it is beneficial (in the majority of cases) to assess the representative's performance *with* him regularly. Before leaving the country, the export executive should, frankly but diplomatically, tell the representative the positive and negative observations that were made during the visit. This should lead to a more cooperative situation*:

---

*The opposite attitude is fairly common: many export executives leave their representatives on a firm handshake, without taking the time to make their observations known, reserving this for the Export or General Manager (a frequent case when the export executives do not have sufficient delegated authority to act directly in their markets). There is thus a time lag in dealing with problems, and delays can lessen the impact of solutions, as well as provoke market-headquarters conflicts.

- the local representative can see clearly that his efforts are appreciated: for example, the seriousness with which he is directing development plan operations;
- he can immediately justify the negative observations that will prove to be too fragmentary to have any real importance;
- any problems highlighted will be solved more easily thanks to a common effort;
- it is important for the representative to know any points of discordance with the company as they arise, so that he can adapt and organize so as to better conform to company expectations. It is also a smooth way to let him know, long beforehand, of a change in company strategy directly concerning him, or even of a possible replacement in the company's representative.

5.2.2.   Local representative replacement

Without doubt, this question is one of the most delicate problems in international development. The right to make a mistake is extremely limited by the risks of ruining company image on a market in the eyes of the involved professional sectors (agents, wholesalers, buyers, distributors) in the case of frequent changes, usually accompanied by gossip and inconvenience for the consumers and users: stockouts, after-sales service disturbances, etc.

Still, there are often good reasons for making mistakes in an unfamiliar market, if an irrefutable motive makes a 'quick divorce' unavoidable: the required continuity to keep local business running smoothly forbids 'living together before marriage' or 'engagement periods' where the future spouses live together to see if they are compatible in all domains. No, another marriage contract has to be arranged as quickly as possible, hoping this time for the better and not the worse!

However, most changes of local representatives are fortunately not leaps forward in the dark, as in many cases they are key conditions for a company's success in a market at decisive stages of local development.

This can also be true in the case of changing the local representative while keeping the same status, or in modifying the form of representation: for example, taking over from a commissioned agent to an importing agent, or even from an importing agent to a commercial subsidiary (see the **Zodiac** example in section 2.2.2.1), whose set up can be through a faithful agent, the takeover of a local company, or *ex nihilo*.

5.2.2.1   Opportunities for change assessment

This assessment should become automatic every time a parallel study of priority market potential and representatives' performance is carried out – during the study phase of a new development plan, for example.

Disappointing results in an expanding market provide a perfect opportunity to envisage changing representatives, but apart from this case, numerous reasons can lead to the replacement of local representatives:

■ changing in the heat of the action, when it becomes dangerous for the company's local or even international future to keep the representative in place any longer: an immediate action, then, for which one has to be prepared (see section 5.2.2.3);

■ changing after cold calculation, when it becomes more interesting for the company to change representatives; fortunately, this is the most frequent case, which allows the company time to prepare this delicate operation properly.

Among the following reasons mentioned briefly as examples, only the first few should lead to changing representatives in the heat of the action:

■ bankruptcy of the local representative;
■ prolonged suspension of payments;
■ violation of an essential contract clause (e.g. non-respect of the territorial limitations by deliberately participating in a re-exportation traffic);
■ non-respect of the company's international strategy (product positioning, type of distribution, price, advertising, etc.);
■ parallel representation of a rival brand despite an exclusivity agreement;
■ non-respect of sales quotas (it should be noted that these quotas usually represent a relative value, as their forecast proceeds less from the calculation of the local sales potential as from the balance of power existing between the two parties at the time of the agreement: a small company with unknown products will have to be satisfied with a symbolic quota, whereas the candidate representatives will be bending over backwards to get the exclusivity of a renowned brand);
■ inability of the representative to go beyond a certain growth level, for various reasons: inaptitude of his staff to master the orchestration of a more complex development; limited investment possibilities, etc.

Finally, assessing an opportunity for changing local representative would not be complete without knowing the answers to two essential questions:

■ What are the possibilities of improving the present representative's company structure? (For example, a technical assistance mission or a permanent local delegation of company executives; partnership or transformation into a subsidiary). Assessment of the probable outcome of any of these actions.

■ What other forms of local representation are possible? Advantages and drawbacks in relation to the present situation. Assessment of the probable outcome.

▶ *In the case of **Pepsi-Cola** in the United Kingdom, the necessity of changing the local representative made itself felt in a quite unexpected manner, in December 1985, when their bottler-franchisee announced (after 30 years of partnership) his intention of going into a joint venture as of January 1987 with . . . **Coca-Cola**!*

*When one thinks of the size and means necessary for bottling and distributing (with appropriate advertising backup) the range of products of one of the world's soft-drinks giants in a market this large, replacement partners are not numerous, and the commentary of Peter Kendall (then VP of **Pepsi-Cola** in Northern Europe) after he managed to deal with this problem successfully can be understood: 'What others thought might have been disaster for **Pepsi** in the UK has been turned into the biggest opportunity we have ever had to increase brand sales here.'*

*To succeed, **Pepsi-Cola International** were not satisfied with just franchising a replacement company, since the new partner was practically made to the measure for this market. In fact, as soon as it was announced that their bottler was going over to the enemy, in the 'Cola Wars', Peter Kendall started looking for the best alternative, but in doing that he found not only one but two . . .*

***Britvic Soft Drinks Ltd.** had an excellent position with bars, restaurants and caterers, whereas a division of the **Beecham Group** was remarkably well-established in the take-home side of the trade, in the food distribution channels.*

*The addition of these two complementary networks could give birth to the soft-drinks distribution leader in the UK, and **Pepsi-Cola** were able to accomplish this merger; **Britvic Soft Drinks** took over **Beecham**'s non-alcoholic beverage division to form a new company called **Britvic Corona**, in which **Pepsi-Cola International** had 10% of the equity.*

Let us leave the conclusion of this spectacular change of local representative to an impartial observer, with a few excerpts from a January 1987 article in Food Processing Magazine: *'Market analysts who thought that **Pepsi** had sustained a severe setback . . . were unprepared for the power and scale of **Pepsi**'s retaliation. By moving with the speed of light . . . **Pepsi** have tripled their UK sales potential at a stroke.'*

5.2.2.2   Psychological precautions

There have already been occasions to emphasize the importance of personal relations, and thus of psychology, for international business development. If it has been decided to replace a local agent* with another form of representation, serious psychological preparations are needed.

In fact, the separation of a company from its local representative resembles a divorce: there is often the serious risk of emotional reactions, particularly violent in 'hot blooded' latitudes, all the more difficult to calm if the marriage was long and the request for divorce unexpected.

In addition to this cold shower on those friendly feelings which existed until then, this implicit disavowal has a serious effect on self-respect and pride, especially in relation to one's professional and personal environment. Finally, outside the obvious parallel between the two situations, for all the practical questions which risk provoking explosive discussions, it is not exaggerating to say that many local representatives have a paternalistic attitude towards the brands and products they look after. Such remarks are often heard: 'It's scandalous to take this brand away from me . . . I've worked years guiding its first steps . . . it grew up under my watchful eye! . . .'

In the company's interest, and also in those of the future ex-representative, such emotional reactions must be sufficiently under control to permit a fair separation, in the best circumstances possible for the two parties (as much for their immediate interests as well as for their image in their own professional environment), and even, why not, to maintain amicable relations.

In this case, it is possible to adapt certain of the following attitudes to the situations encountered:

■ Above all, frankness; given that the local representative will always have been informed not only of the positive aspects of the relationship, but also of the unsatisfactory ones (see section 5.2.1.6), he will not think that his good faith was betrayed, since he could have regularly measured the mounting dissatisfaction with the evolution of local business.

■ A separation is always better tolerated when both parties retain the impression of having decided it together. Everything should be done to avoid giving the local representative the impression that he has been sacked. He could be told that if he had not wanted to adapt to company needs, it is because he had already felt that an eventual separation was inevitable. He and the company had been able to do very profitable business together, but the company now shares his analysis and thinks that now is the right time to separate.

■ Care should be taken to give the representative an elegant way out, emphasizing exterior factors more as reasons for the separ-

---

*Here, we will not go into the case where it is the representative who breaks the contract, either by a request on his part, or because of non-respect of his contractual obligations. Then, few psychological precautions need to be planned for, as the company is not directly at the origin of the rupture.

ation – market evolution, international economics, company policy, etc. – rather than those calling into question his personal qualities. Such explanations, to be quoted consistently on both sides, will enable him to save face in relation to the local professional environment.

■ Another very positive attitude will be for the export executive to keep an 'open door', by suggesting a possible future collaboration, which could happen one day if the company launches a new product brand in the same line and is looking for a local exclusive representative for it. Furthermore, the same applies more personally to export executives who leave their present company and go to work for a competitor.

■ At this point in the discussion, if the future ex-local representative has not leapt at the executive's throat, very discreet praise could be given, by expressing satisfaction that working with pragmatic businessmen is always a pleasure ... and by telling the terrible story of an export company and a local representative who were at war with each other for years because of a broken contract, resulting in total loss for both parties. Such live examples are numerous indeed.

5.2.2.3   Practical preparation

A few words have to be said first about defensive practical preparation. It is out of the question to be caught unaware, in one of the priority markets, by the sudden disappearance of the present representative – whatever the cause. Therefore, direct contacts in each market should be carefully cultivated, providing a local pool of potential collaborators for just this type of emergency. Here is another reason for regularly visiting priority markets, participating in important professional events, and insisting on meeting the local representative's clientele.

On this basis, preparing the desired change of representative will be made easier, particularly if the operation is carried out after cold calculation, leaving more time to plan things properly:

■ Before announcing the change, the local pool of potential collaborators, as well as any other interesting sources, should be contacted. Care should be taken to avoid divulging the real reason for getting in touch (a plausible explanation: the company wants a more in-depth market study). When the two or three best potential representatives have been identified, they should be approached with utmost discretion, under the seal of secrecy. At this point, a decision has to be made rapidly, as such secrecy if often illusory.

■ Another way of looking for a new local representative is to entrust the procedure to an outside consultant. He has the advantage of being able to carry out a much more detailed study of the potential candidates, while at the same time preserving the company's anonymity up until the final, face-to-face negotiations.

■ As soon as the new local representative has been selected, the future ex-representative should preferably be informed *verbally*, with the consideration and diplomacy mentioned above. The following negotiations will be easier to conduct if the representative gets the news from his usual (or privileged) contact rather than from an indiscretion, and certainly not by letter, even a well-formulated one. The official written confirmation will follow in the time period mutually agreed upon for the date of change.

■ The agreement to separate, as for the initial agreement to cooperate, must be satisfactory for both parties so as to avoid negative repercussions. According to the type of change, the classic negotiation on taking back the stock should be enlarged by the proposal to have the 'new' representative take on certain of the 'old' representative's employees who looked after company products. This may facilitate matters for the future ex-representative who then might not have to lay anyone off, and contribute to local business continuity.

Finally, if the divorce is concluded in a cooperative atmosphere, the 'ex' and the 'future' representatives could be encouraged to cooperate regularly to sort out practical details (stock transfers, commercial information on the clientele, etc.).

5.2.3   Product 'chain'

If we talk about products in a section dealing with local representatives, it is because products are the focus of physical distribution (here, essentially, we mean products distributed through retail outlets, where there is a regular flow from manufacturer to user/consumer).

Indeed, experience has shown that regular checkups and subsequent reorganization of an export product chain is a sure (and not very expensive) way to develop sales in many international distribution channels, often in incredible proportions.

The necessity of paying serious attention to the efficiency and rapidity of the product chain can only be amplified with the growing determination on the part of distributors to limit their financial costs; because of this, the level of stocks lessen at each distribution stage, and risks of stockouts grow in inverse proportion.

Thus, both the exporting company and the local representative have to ensure that there is a very efficient stock rotation, well adapted to the specific constraints for every link of the product chain.

5.2.3.1   Local chain control

The local chain begins with the order placed by the retailer or final user, which is transmitted to the local representative; in the case where the representative is not maintaining a regular stock, the local circuit is prolonged to the order's transmission to company head-quarters.

This part of the local circuit has already been dissected (see section 2.3.4.3) within the framework of communication organization for the development plan's practical preparation; then we cite only two examples to illustrate the ways of accelerating the taking and trans-mitting of orders:

▶ *The fantastic success of 'phone ordering in the USA with toll-free numbers gives the clientele (retailers or individuals) a simple and free order procedure which greatly reduces suppliers' delivery periods, especially if this latter is compared to that of mail ordering, or worse, to periodic visits of manufac-turers' agents who sometimes have geographically immense zones to cover.*

▶ *Order transmission takes a few seconds for companies using electronic mail, like **Schweppes**, whose Australian subsidiary equipped itself with very efficient material: each representative has a portable computer enabling him to 'phone in his orders directly to the central computer. In addition to the obvious advantages of this type of system for the clientele, as well as for stock management, accounting, etc., the representatives are relieved of a lot of time-consuming paperwork, and thus are free to spend more time in canvassing potential clients.*

The second part of the local chain starts up again with the local representative and his treatment of the local order from his stock or from the shipment delivered from headquarters. The different operations needed in handling this order, as well as the dispatching procedure, from the warehouse to the end-user, can be checked on and improved.

It is useful to mention here Express Transport services, which deliver international or local merchandise in record time, from the local representative or company's warehouse to the retailer or end-user. The cost of these services is largely compensated for by avoiding stockouts and accelerating the stock rotation.

▶ *It is by proposing such an express service that **Calberson** was able to profit from a big market opportunity offered by the German group **AEG**, who decided to delegate all deliveries in France for small household appliances and kitchen equipment to this transport group. There are more than 300 product references, more or less fragile and voluminous – like the new, vitro-ceramic cooking plates – that **Calberson** pick up at the Mayence German factory and deliver to retailers within a guaranteed two-day period, anywhere in France.*

*To accomplish this feat and totally relieve **AEG** of all logistics operations, the following system is adhered to:*

- in Germany, preparation of individual French orders received through electronic mail;
- immediate loading of tractor-trailers, making the Germany-France return trip daily;
- customs procedures by **Calberson** from 6:30am on in the eastern Parisian central hub;
- dispatching to the **Calberson** regional branches;
- subsequent **Calberson** delivery to the retailers;
- all this takes place within the contractual two-day period from the time of the order; **AEG** avoid all stock and logistics infrastructures in France, and can provide their clientele with a better and more economic service at the same time.

5.2.3.2   International order check

From the moment when the local representative indicates his stock needs by placing an order*, the company should make efforts to ensure delivery within a specified period so as to avoid loss of local sales:

▶   Contrary to many companies which give priority to urgent orders from national distribution channels, **CGH (Jaz and Yema)** as a rule are even more strict about scrupulously respecting delivery dates for their export markets.

It is unfortunate that this attitude is not more common, when the cost of mounting such an operation abroad and its fragility are considered, especially when importers are already exasperated by the lack of precision and punctuality of a fair number of exporters.

An urgent order, then, from an important market has to be given top priority, from its arrival (hopefully it will have been sent by fax, telex or electronic mail rather than by surface mail!) to its dispatching by the best-adapted means of transport.

However, internal organization rules sometimes lead to the accumulation of delays, as illustrated by the following examples:

- mail delivery in mid-morning: executives in meetings at this time will not see their letters and orders until after lunch; whatever system is adopted, mail has to be on desks at the beginning of the day;
- a director wanting to filter all company mail: this holds up getting the mail to the staff concerned, according to the hazards of the director's own timetable. Why not transmit the orders directly to

---

*It is to be mentioned in passing that a motivated local representative will not have to be pushed to reorder (unless he has a tendency to have insufficient stock); this explains why the export executive is less a pure salesman, but more of a commercial/marketing generalist whose job is to assure general market development.

the interested parties, leaving a copy, as information, for the director?

■ absence of the person in charge: it is usual to see orders presenting anomalies – wrong price, special requirements, etc. – held up until the executive has been contacted, if he is away on business, or simply await his return. It is fundamental to set up a system at headquarters for handling orders when the person looking after them is away (see section 5.1.1.6);

■ the forwarding of orders from the export department to the warehouse or factory can take one or two days more, even if distances are not great. In companies where handling orders is not yet electronic, an urgent order could be sent by fax or telex, could it not?

■ the staff in charge of preparing and dispatching the merchandise cannot know which orders to deal with in priority, without specific instructions. Moreover, it is not unusual to see an urgent order ready to go, but held up in the warehouse . . . because one or two missing parts (of minor interest) have not arrived yet. In the Export Service, daily contact between an administrative executive and field executives will allow the assessment of the importance of the orders as they come in, and they will indicate the priorities to the services interested; also order preparation progression should be followed up each day so that the alarm can be raised and a special procedure organized if an urgent order has been delayed in relation to its promised delivery date;

■ finally, international transportation still appears to be a badly performed activity by many exporting companies, making them lose 'competitiveness' points dearly-won elsewhere. Transportation is a specialist's job, and it can improve the company's international position considerably by bringing speed and reliability to deliveries, and by permitting better transport cost management.

As for transportation, more specifically, routine again appears as another factor to contribute to competitiveness loss for exported products:

▶ *As Gérard Wingel, Transport Manager for* **Parfums Christian Dior***, explains, 'Transportation facilities are constantly evolving. To get the most out of them, we have to update regularly the transportation organization towards our priority markets. For other markets, a checkup is necessary at least once a year to improve certain procedures.'*
This is how **Parfums Christian Dior** *were able to considerably accelerate the delivery time necessary for some major faraway markets, without having to raise their products' landed cost: using maritime freight for normal shipments and air freight for emergencies was the standard way of doing things until a detailed study of all transport costs, and a tough negotiation*

with freight forwarders, enabled **Parfums Christian Dior** *to just use air freight without increasing their prices. The effect this performance had on sales development with the trade can be imagined.*

In the same spirit, the regular review of transport cost calculations by land, sea and air enabled the company to tighten the FOB/retail price structure of several countries, where the local representatives purposely overestimated these costs so as to increase their margins.

It is thus thanks to real cooperation among exporters, freight forwarders and transport companies that logistics can become another important source of dynamic devices, as this 1988 **UTA** experience testifies:

▶   *The* **Optorg** *company had the problem of not being able to satisfy their clients in Mali, by delivering vehicles in good condition within the stipulated delivery period. Several means of transportation were tested, at first, without finding a viable solution:*

■   *sea freight to Dakar, then by rail convoy from Dakar to Bamako (1000km). Numerous problems were encountered: irregularities in supply shipments, frequent stops, breakdowns, theft (certain parts were particularly appreciated – batteries, starters, spare tyres, canvas covers for pick-up trucks);*

■   *another variation was tried: sea freight to Abidjan, then overland by convoy to Bamako: 1100km of asphalt roads and bush trails. The convoy drivers came from Bamako to Abidjan by 'plane and drove back to Bamako. There, as well, problems arose: irregularities in forwarding, damage, road accidents, and the vehicles were arriving in Bamako with 1100km on the odometer after a hard drive.*

Air freight was then envisaged, the exporter and the transporter engaging in serious discussion about the matter. The coming of the B747 Combi freight 'plane and the building of special kits for vehicle transportation enabled **UTA** *to reduce their tariffs, making air transportation possible.*

Very quickly, the **Optorg** *company noticed that their brand image improved, as well as client service, as the company now sell vehicles with '0' kilometers on the odometer and can respect delivery dates. Supply shipments have become regular, stock rotation ultra-fast, and interest payments considerably reduced: it is a 'plus' for the French manufacturers who were able to develop their sales, while other foreign vehicle manufacturers still used old-fashioned transportation methods.'*

5.2.3.3   Sales forecasts

In most professional fields, control and improvement of the product 'chain' are of interest only when there is sufficient stock to fill orders.

For this, sales forecasts* have to be made in time so that an adapted production program can be prepared.

This is another fundamental point which has to be worked on with the local representatives: they have to understand that these forecasts have no other purpose but to allow them to profit from their own development efforts, which would be rendered useless without stocks. Then, it might be necessary to help them make their forecasts (as well as with stock management and orders) which the company will check up on regularly for the purpose (among others) of keeping on a friendly footing with the factory manager.

▶ *In the automotive industry, the gigantic job of planning can easily be imagined. For **Renault**, as for their competitors, everything starts before the conception phase, by the continual study of each vehicle class's evolution on the major world markets. Before manufacturing, studies of each model on the drawing boards are carried out – for example, clinic tests, where panels of motorists are assembled to examine different models, among which the prototype being tested remains anonymous. All these studies taken together enable the company to quantify and establish the first production plan. Then, there follow a succession of five-year plans, regularly updated, in which each market defines its sales forecast by model and by version. Luckily, the cars' colours are not asked for at this stage . . . but at the actual moment of filling the orders!*

▶ *Unfortunately, such sophisticated methods are not applicable in all fields. For the **Commentryenne des Aciers**, whose majority of client-users can hardly make short-term guesses, especially since the beginning of the world economic crisis, forecasting has become a difficult but necessary exercise.*

*Obviously, being able to deliver from existing stocks is an enormous advantage in gaining markets. This medium-sized company's field executives have to count a lot on their own intuition for establishing forecasts for high-speed steel's different alloys, by cross-checking all the information they can gather through regular business trips abroad, and by frequent contact with their clients. These forecasts, along with an ingenious system of recuperating scrap material (see section 6.5.2.5), normally leave the **Commentryenne des Aciers** sufficient leeway for extremely urgent orders.*

▶ *Here is a change of scenery, with a planned production system in the fashion industry, which has the particularity of seeing two complete product lines come and go each year. The **Benetton** organization is basically composed of a nucleus around which many SMEs rotate (about 350 in Italy, employing more than 30,000 people). The essential tasks are carried out inside the company: colour and style studies, electronic cutting, dying, quality control. The intermediary production stages take place outside. This means that the company only directly produces 20% of the global turnover. This same system is applied within each country where **Benetton** manufacture, and*

---

*In all professional fields and in markets where local representatives can be persuaded to establish sales forecasts, these figures will be precious indications for defining company objectives (see section 1.3).

allows great flexibility with the possibility of adapting to even the most unexpected market trends.

The garment prototypes to be manufactured are drawn up by a team of designers (more than 20) from the globe's four corners. There are 1000 proposals for each of the two collections presented (spring-summer, fall-winter), among which about 600 are made in different colours and sizes. Given that the time necessary to create a collection is quite long, a very efficient program is established. For example, the 1988 spring-summer collection was planned for in the following way:

- *February-March, 1987: design of garment prototypes and selection of colours;*
- *April 1987: presentation of the collection and taking of orders;*
- *May-June, 1987: supply shipments for the manufacture of selected prototypes;*
- *June-November, 1987: production of garments;*
- *December 1987-April 1988: delivery.*

Afterwards, to respond to specific market requirements, the seasons' collections are concluded with re-order campaigns and the production of additional garments.

5.3 Local Distributors

Under this very general name we cover the two main categories of distributors who serve as go-between for our products, from the local representatives to the end-user*:

- the intermediaries, such as sub-agents, wholesalers, semi-wholesalers, etc., who distribute to retail outlets (e.g. consumer products, household appliances, etc.) or directly to the end-user (e.g. capital goods to professional users, services, etc.). It can be seen that this type of intermediary does not always exist, particularly in markets whose size does not justify the need for a distribution relay, and in fields where the local representative finds it more profitable to deal directly with the retail outlets or end-users;
- the retail distribution includes, in most countries, two main categories: general stores and speciality shops. The general stores

---

*It is to be remembered that certain distributors are the only relay between the exporting company and the end-user, without the presence of a local representative: for example, this is the case for exporters who deal directly with local wholesalers, or chains of department stores, rather than going through a local representative-type structure. This is also the case of franchised stores and Duty Free outlets which are stocked directly by the manufacturer without going through an intermediary. According to the situation, in such hybrid cases certain 'push' dynamic devices (listed for local representatives in section 5.2.) can be used, and will be reviewed for local distributors.

It is also to be noted that this section does not cover business done with buying centres like those used by certain department store chains or wholesalers, operating in the exporter's territory. For, in most cases, this system of exporting takes the initiative and control of local development out of the exporter's hands.

are subdivided into department stores, variety stores and super-markets. Speciality shops and boutiques make up the other major retail store category.

Given that these two distribution categories also buy products to resell them, certain 'push' dynamic devices designated for distributors resemble those already mentioned for local representatives (see section 5.2); they are thus reviewed very quickly here.

However, besides this common point, the export company's relationship with local representatives and distributors differs greatly:

■ with the local representative, there is a privileged relationship usually formalized by a contract committing both parties to a close collaboration in company product development – this makes it vastly different from the relationship with the distributors;

■ communication with distributors is more difficult for the company because of the screen erected by the succession of relays (company representatives and any other possible intermediaries). Moreover, truly personalized communication can only be established with a small number of distributors, whereas several hundred thousand are listed in the Food and Drug channels in the USA. In such cases, a system corresponding to the company's strategy has to be set up to communicate with the distributors;

■ the local representative preferably has to be exclusive, at least in the company's field of activity, contrary to distributors, whose vocation is also to sell the most dangerous competitors' products to satisfy their clientele. Distributors are thus in a strong position in relation to their suppliers, who are constantly being played off against each other.

This unlimited list of differences with local representatives leads to the search for an original approach to push company products through distributors all the way to the end-user. This is what we are going to come up with by going over the numerous and varied 'push' dynamic devices at our disposal.

5.3.1   Distribution dynamics

International business cannot possibly be developed without energizing distribution: this is the opposite of a static attitude, where the exporter settles for the same distribution channels that have been used since his products were introduced on the market, without regularly examining their suitability.

Indeed, a constant and often divergent evolution of distribution channels can be observed in each country, in parallel to lifestyle transformations and demand trends.

These big changes in commercial scenery are broadened by business reversals, particularly frequent in distribution channels due to mergers, new company policy or the arrival of new managers, etc.

All this, then, should lead the company, with the local representative, to follow distribution trends as a whole very closely and to modify the product positioning if necessary (within the limits of international distribution strategy) to keep them within the best possible channels for sales development.

5.3.1.1   Performance analysis

It is up to each local representative (with more or less close company assistance) to keep track of* the results of each channel through which company products are distributed.

For each channel, there should be parallel study of actual turnover and selling costs, transfer prices, special discounts, dynamic devices particularly committed (sales staff, POP material, media advertising, etc.).

The reasons for sales progression, stagnation or decline will be analyzed: are they due to the local representative action (positive or negative) and that of his sales force, distributor attitude, competition, or even to an evolution of end-user purchase motivations? Does it seem to be a lasting trend for company results, and what push dynamic devices could influence it? Next, the results and potential of the different channels should be compared; then the channels not yet used should be surveyed by observing competitors' results whose products are distributed on them. However, this comparative study of competitors' distribution channels, along with those of the company, is an essential parameter to introduce into the analysis . . . but it is not to be followed blindly!

In addition to this distribution channel analysis, the local representative should follow up the individual results of his distributors** so as to adapt incentive actions towards the major ones (see section 5.3.2).

▶ *In this field, **Air France** benefit from a privileged position in relation to other types of professional activities, since they have the sales results for each of their licensed travel agencies: sales by flight line or product type (First, Le Club/Business, Economy class), thanks to the computerized treatment of the ticket stubs and boarding passes. 'These figures are very useful for **Air France** sales representatives', emphasizes Jean-Michel Masson***,*

---

*In certain markets, this results verification is accompanied by a supervision of distributor activities, in case some wholesalers or retailers decide to organize local black-market or smuggling activities.
**This, obviously, cannot be applied to markets where the distribution is too scattered, or in countries where market statistics are not available.
***Then **Air France** Corporate Planning Vice-President, now **Air France** Group Vice-President and General Manager for United Kingdom and Ireland.

'especially as they enable them to study in parallel the specific devices used in canvassing, advertising, promotions, etc. Thus, the efficiency relative to these dynamic devices can be measured.'

5.3.1.2   Quality control

Distribution quality control will complete the information resulting from performance analysis by bringing in elements which might influence the decisions to follow.

In this way, a European or Japanese company marketing luxury products might be tempted to close their New York, Madison Avenue boutique, whose disappointing results are an expensive burden for the American representative, but finally decide to help keep it open with financial assistance, because it is a highly visible outlet, of great importance for developing brand awareness and prestige among opinion leaders, market influencers and the market as a whole.

This quality control will mainly be a control of those conditions in which the brand and products are presented at each stage in the distribution channel, and how they can attract the end-user's attention. Thus, it is to cover the image coherence between the retail outlets and the brand; the place and surface area reserved for the products' presentation, for the POP displays, average stock levels, competence of the sales personnel and their product knowledge, etc.

Furthermore, the development and cooperation potential of each channel has to be assessed, as well as the ways of motivating this potential.

This quality control of distribution channels, as well as parallel observation of other possible channels, is part of the local representative's responsibilities; however, it is of utmost importance for the export executive to keep an eye on the local distributors (or at least to keep informed), to make sure that they correspond well to the company's long-term development objectives in each market.

5.3.1.3   Distribution improvement

Performance analysis and quality control of a market's distribution, where the channels used by company products are compared to other possible ones, will allow export executives to periodically decide on modifications.

Thus, for example, it is frequent for export development to be slowed down by a bottleneck, caused by a particular type of channel used for certain products on a market:

▶   *In France, the exclusive distribution of **RoC** products in pharmacies reinforces their 'safe' image, but unfortunately this type of channel is not organized consistently everywhere in the world. For example, in Japan,* *medicines are given out both by doctors and pharmacists, and this double system did not allow sufficient sales development for **RoC** products; however, this brand did not want to join all the other cosmetic brands in their traditional retail outlets, department stores in particular, and become 'one of the crowd'. **RoC** then decided to use an unusual channel: beauty clinics and dermatology departments in Japanese hospitals, which corresponded perfectly to their image of safety and high technology . . . and which was far from that of the traditional cosmetic brands.*

A point has to be made, however: a big change in the local distribution network (any change which affects the totality of one or more channels) usually requires considerable investment and serious effort, both by the local representative and headquarters: product adaptation to the new distributors' needs; enlargement and/or restructuring of the local sales force; training of the distributors' personnel; adaptation of product services such as technical assistance and after-sales; rethinking (totally or partially) of advertising and promotions, etc.

This means that it is out of the question to change channels too often (which would project an unfortunate image of inconsistency for the company's professional environment), and this type of decision should be made only after measuring all the direct and indirect consequences.

Still, judicious modifications in local distribution channels are powerful dynamic devices for business development. Concerning intermediaries, one relay can be replaced by another so as to improve total performance; a channel which is too long can be shortened to become more efficient and profitable by eliminating one or more middlemen and thus get closer to the end-user . . . (a comparable action to that described in section 4.3.3.3. for the **Baccarat** local representative).

▶ *Again, in this case, prudence should be exercised as these modifications can be unwelcome, even for the distributors who benefit from them, as the American group **Warner-Lambert** found out in Japan. This group's divisions distribute their products through different wholesale organizations; **Schick** razors and razorblades have had spectacular success, controlling over 70% of the market for stainless-steel razorblades thanks to a powerful distributor and a vast network of very active, independent wholesalers who do the legwork of stocking racks in stores.*

*In comparison, the **Warner-Lambert** chewing gum division's results (**Chiclets**, among other brands) were less spectacular. They even started declining during the 1970s because the wholesalers were not working the retail outlets hard enough. This is why **Warner-Lambert** decided to set up their own sales force to sell directly to retailers without going through the wholesalers. Rapidly, this initiative proved to be a big mistake. Not only, as was foreseeable, did the wholesalers not appreciate being 'bypassed', but the retailers themselves found this way of doing things suspect: traditions are so strongly entrenched in Japan that the rules of the game are not easily changed. Finally, a compromise solution was found: the **Warner-Lambert** salesmen solicit orders from retailers and then pass them back to the whole-*

salers. *This is how the group's chewing gum sales increased in Japan up to a 17% market share, quite an honorable performance for such a scattered product category.*

Making the distribution channel longer can also energize sales, given that the addition of one or several relays can increase the number of outlets and reinforce market activity.

▶ *During the last 20 years where the development of leisure activities has given rise to, among others, spectacular increases in the sales of nautical equipment, the distribution channels have evolved in many markets. As a result, **Zodiac** followed this evolution by readapting their distribution structure: opening subsidiaries in certain markets (see section 2.2.2.1) and agreements with agents (importer-distributors) in others. Often, in fact, low demand in a country limited the number of retail outlets for boats, and in this case, **Zodiac** dealt directly with the best local retailers.*
*When there are enough retail outlets in a country, **Zodiac** deal with a local representative and bring him solid backup (in the form of motivating margins, technical and commercial training, public relations and advertising assistance, etc.) so that he can get off to a quick start and, thus, ensure satisfactory market share growth.*

Less conventional means to improve the distribution channel results can be used successfully, such as enlisting the help of market influencers (see section 6.4.3.1):

▶ *As the testimony of **Airelec Radial Distribution** illustrates: 'With our importer in a southern European country, we had decided to distribute our heaters through a dealer network. However, sales settled at an unsatisfactory level because the dealers were reluctant to push this new-concept product. This is why we decided to canvass in parallel engineering firms and real estate promoters, who are the decision-makers, so that they can impose a non-traditional product on a market. This enables us, at the same time, to stimulate sales in our dealer network and to make big deals directly with the promoters on some of their current projects.'*

In the same way, at retail outlets level, there is the choice among very different kinds of modifications.* Here are some examples:

■ Enlarging distribution within the same retail channel to cover a market better, thus immediately increasing turnover with the opening stock sell-in. Given the nature of the products and the degree of exclusivity held by the initial retailers, efforts have to be made to both preserve their motivation and the product image.

Companies within certain product sectors will benefit from enlarging their distribution, while at the same time keeping it under tight control, either by setting up a chain of franchised

---

*Conforming to the legislation in force and local commercial practices.

outlets through takeover of existing distributors, or by opening their own retail outlets:

▶ *According to 'Forbes', the Austrian company **Swarovski** controls 75% of the world's cut crystal market, with products as diverse as the giant chandeliers of Carnegie Hall and The Kremlin, or the very popular Silver Crystal line of animal figurines, and their crystal costume jewellery. Becoming a large shareholder (50%) in the American **Zale Group**, which has the biggest world retail jewellery network, enabled **Swarovski** to impose their name in a sector directly related to theirs. In the United States, **Swarovski** products are present in 700 of the 1125 stores of the **Zale** chain and in the up-market department stores. **Swarovski**, which have assembly plants in Brazil, South Korea and Germany, have already taken over 27 stores in Australia, which completes the number of boutiques already in the fold: 24 in Asia, 35 in Great Britain and one in Paris.*

▶ *Here is another example, for an SME, which presents an interesting innovation, the setting up of a hyper-specialized retail outlet: in 1987, in San Francisco, **Doublet** opened the only store in the world specializing in flags. This first flagstore has a turnover of $200,000 today. It is part of the **Doublet** strategy which aims at developing a line of products around the flag image (books, tableware, tee-shirts, boxer shorts (! . . .), etc. decorated with flags) as well as, obviously, the whole range of **Doublet** flags . . .*

■ Shortening the distribution by closing unproductive retail outlets so as to eliminate the 'dead wood' can make a higher turnover with fewer retailers; more dynamic devices can be concentrated on fewer outlets to back up their motivation to 'push' company products because of greater exclusivity. Among other problems to get under control in such a case are the lack of enthusiasm on the part of intermediaries whose vocation and organization are not always compatible with selective distribution, and the risk of losing end-users/clientele who will have to change their shopping habits to remain loyal to company products.

■ Investing in new retail channels: in particular, make 'the great leap' by extending a speciality shop distribution to include general stores (or the contrary); here again, efforts have to be made to keep up the motivation of the initial retailers, who will be accusing the company of treason.

■ Innovating, in distribution, can be a trump card, particularly for 'impulse purchase' products. In this case, it is fundamental to look for all means possible of exposing the products to potential consumers' eyes.

▶ *A spectacular and historic example of innovation in penetrating distribution channels concerns gas stations over 20 years ago.*
*At this time in the UK they only sold gasoline and automobile accessories. Three companies with complementary products, **Cadbury**, **Schweppes**** and*

---

*This initiative took place in 1965, before the merger of **Cadbury** and **Schweppes** into a single group.

Wrigley, joined to propose a better use of the gas stations' commercial premises and thus to increase their turnover.

These three companies* had designed display cases where their chocolates, tonic drinks and chewing gum were on view. The success was instantaneous. Today, many other brands of very different products have joined up with these three innovators all around the world: sales in the UK gas stations have attained such growth (almost $200 million just for sweets) that each of these three companies has their own distribution structure to deal with this channel.

▶ *More recently, when **Yoplait** was launched in Thailand (in August 1987), this brand also innovated by creating a new . . . mobile distribution channel! Dozens of young Thai women were trained in direct selling, dressed in pale pink uniforms on almond-green bicycles with a refrigerated container. Their mission was to sell **Yoplait** yoghurt in the street, in companies, and even in homes. The success of these attractive 'itinerant oases' can be understood better if the Thai climate is taken into consideration, as well as the visual attraction of these 'retail outlets on wheels', whose image of coolness is well accentuated by their colours, the shade offered by their big **Yoplait** umbrellas and the salesgirls' friendly smiles. 'Our launching in Thailand also took place in traditional distribution channels, supermarkets in particular, with strong editorial advertising support,' explains the General Manager of **Yoplait**, 'but there is no doubt that the impact generated by the very strong image of our cyclist salesgirls in the streets was one of the key driving forces of our success: in six months, we gained more than 50% of the yoghurt market, at the expense of the four brands already present in Thailand.'*

■ Rebalancing distribution, which is also the logical consequence of widening product positioning.

▶ *For **Lacoste** in Germany (as, in fact, more generally all over the world), the product overflowed the tennis activity, entering into sport/leisure and weekend niches. German distribution, then, accompanied this evolution: at present, exclusive distribution of **Lacoste** products in sports outlets is a far cry from reality, where more than half the sales are made in men's clothing shops.*

5.3.2   Actions on distributors

It is obviously very tempting to increase the distribution sales by bringing into play those dynamic devices which can efficiently stimulate the intermediaries and/or retailers. The local representative has to attend to this continually, and the export executives should contribute directly to this stimulation. The length of business trips in each market limits participation in this assistance quite a bit, and time investment has to be thought about carefully so as to find the most

---

*A good example of co-operation among companies with complementary activities (see section 2.2.2.5).

productive way for meeting a maximum of carefully selected distributors.

But what can best incite distributors to come running? Not very much: to receive delivery before they have even ordered, to sell only successful products with sole exclusivity, extra-comfortable margins, solid media advertising backup, all this bringing them crowds of customers; and finally, their suppliers should help them in all necessary fields – training sales personnel, POP material, etc. – and especially not have the nerve of wanting to be paid too quickly . . . simple, isn't it?!

It is out of the question to encourage this fantasy on the part of company distributors, but all actions which can be envisaged within budgetary limits should be examined so that distributors will participate more fully in product development.

5.3.2.1   Priority targets

In certain professional fields, the local representative and the export company can maintain individual relationships with their distributors and even with their big clients, given that there are very few of them on the market.

On the other hand, as soon as one enters the domain of a more scattered distribution, as for consumer products, contact becomes extremely difficult, both because of the number of retailers and 'screens' put up by the intermediaries.

▶   *This difficulty reaches its zenith in certain countries like Japan (see the* **Warner-Lambert** *example in section 5.3.1.3.), which holds the world's record for distribution density (agents, sub-agents, wholesalers, sub-wholesalers, retailers) in relation to the population; this can be explained partly by tradition, but is nevertheless surprising in such a highly developed economic context.*

'The mechanisms of our distribution system are a barrier to the entry of imported products on the Japanese market' admits Isao Nakauchi[5], president of the Keidanren Public Affairs Committee, the Japanese Employers' Federation.

Foreign exporters, who have encountered the Japanese market, have been saying this for years. They repeated it during the Toronto Summit Meeting. However, today the deregulation of trade has become a priority for Japanese managers. As a symbol of this project's importance, Isao Nakauchi, who is in charge of it, manages one of the major department store chains in Japan.

The Japanese retail trade is truly overprotected by a whole series of regulations. Drawn up during the 1950s, no fewer than 150 rules have basically served as an employment guarantee for the middle classes, and as a guard against competition.

As a result, this sector features overstaffed structures, a myriad of small companies and very low productivity, paid for by the client: in comparison with Europe and the United States, the extra charge paid for by the Japanese consumer is estimated at 80%.

According to the Ministry of Trade and Industry (MITI), Japan has

400,000 wholesalers and 1,600,000 independent shop operators. In the USA,
'for 100,000 inhabitants, 690 work in distribution channels. In Japan, there
are 1300. In the USA, independent traders handle 3% of the distribution
business. In the UK, they handle 5%, in Germany 11% and in Japan 57%
' continues Isao Nakauchi.

Faced with hundreds, thousands, even hundreds of thousands of distributors, export executives are going to have to allocate carefully – according to very selective criteria – the actions they envisage undertaking, from among those listed below: first, the characteristics and specific needs of each category of possible intermediaries have to be distinguished, and the different categories of retail outlets which distribute company products have to be classified into homogeneous groups. Then, within each category, the distributors have to be subdivided into several groups, according to their importance and potential, e.g. priority, important and secondary distributors.

This selectivity will avoid wasting effort, and be more efficient given that care will have been taken to identify the decision-makers and those in charge of the priority distributors, and the decision-makers of the important distributors.

The majority of dynamic devices will be concentrated on these distributors; export executives should check that they are on target by making sure the local representative is on good terms with them, and should themselves cultivate a direct relationship with their priority distributors, which can always be useful.

5.3.2.2   Interest stimulation

As for the local representatives, the distributors' essential motivation is based on their own interests; it is necessary to come to an agreement with them which reasonably satisfies their expectations, particularly concerning their margins, terms of payment, special commissions, and other various benefits.

However, there is an additional difference between local representatives and distributors: the latter will be less patient about sales taking off. Introducing a new brand or products brings them a new attraction for their clientele (especially if the company invests, in parallel, in well-adapted 'pull' dynamic devices), but sales of these products have to reach a satisfactory 'cruising speed' rapidly in relation to the time and space devoted to them.

▶   *This explains the failure, then the success, of **Mikli** in Germany, as explained*
by Alain Mikli, whose glasses – as everyone knows – are made to see with
as well as to be seen!
*   'In 1979, I tried to get positioned in Germany, our first export market,*
before conceiving and applying our present strategy: communicate with the
public in order to create a demand for the opticians. Result: two successive
flops, in 1981 and 1983, due to the simple fact that we were just selling a
handsome product without the adapted communication backup which should

envelop it in a fashionable aura of grace and mystery. Thus, opticians couldn't sell my creations, which were both expensive and unknown.

After a deliberate two year absence, to have these flops forgotten, we made a come-back on the market in 1985, with a real communication strategy and a know-how already tested in France and the USA.

*We made appointments with the major German newspapers to present our products and to give them our press file. After this, quite a few editorials appeared, introducing the brand to the German public. This modest invest-ment (DM 20,000 – see section 6.4.3.4) was enough to create demand for our product at the opticians, and sales followed along. This 'pull' dynamic device was obviously backed up by a 'push' action for the distributors, particularly **Mikli's** participation in trade shows and active development of privileged commercial links with opticians.'*

Exclusivity is a direct means to incite distributors to devote more time and space to a supplier: it will be in their own interest, logically, to feature a product (sufficiently competitive) and to push it if they feel that this helps to develop a relatively captive clientele in their region. On the contrary, products distributed in all the possible chan-nels and retail outlets will only benefit from a backup proportional to the spontaneous demand generated; if this demand is regular and strong enough, the company will then be in a more comfortable position to expect maximum distributor support, by emphasizing their interest in not losing a sure profit source with the 'pre-sold' product.

Whatever dynamic devices have been selected for mobilization, to undertake an action aimed at the distributors' own interests, they must appear well adapted to them to solve some of their problems, to help them reach their own objectives, and/or to satisfy their personal ambitions or needs. Here are some examples:

- general communication action (advertising, public relations, and/ or promotion) which will back up product demand. It is worth warning distributors about these actions beforehand, so they will bring in enough stock and 'feature' the products to get the most out of the campaign;
- 'tailor-made' communication actions specifically to stimulate product sales for one or more distributors. This type of action is particularly appreciated in variety stores/department stores where competition among suppliers is carefully maintained: pres-ence of a sales 'commando', promotions, cooperative advertising,* public relations action on a distributor's premises, etc.;
- various types of assistance: technical, commercial, merchandising, training, etc.;
- various incentives, bonuses, sales contests, window display con-tests, for the retailers themselves.

---

*An advertising action whose cost (in principle) is shared between the distributor and the supplier. In the USA, for example, a department store often used to accept to pay for 50% of a press ad where their name figured beside a product; today, such advertising is co-operative in name only . . . since in most cases the supplier has to pay for everything.

5.3.2.3   Communication and information

The more unstructured the local distribution channels, the scarcer*
are the occasions of communicating with them – and these few
occasions have to be fully taken advantage of.

Thus, every contact with a distributor really has to be prepared
and not just improvised, whether it concerns the local representative
or the company executives. Objectives have to be fixed for these
contacts, and adapted backup material planned for (professional
literature, sales presentations, etc.).

▶ *For example, a mid–1980s Cointreau development plan in Germany dealt*
with distributor information: Cointreau trained their local representatives
so they could have interesting information for the distributors, support
material to transmit this information efficiently, and on this basis, to know
how to negotiate so that the distributors would realize that promoting
Cointreau, by giving it a privileged position and more shelf space, would
serve their interests. Included among the information transmitted to the
distributors to incite them to promote Cointreau were:

- *Cointreau is the French liqueur most sold in Germany;*
- *Cointreau enjoys strong recognition;*
- *Cointreau is bought and consumed by women as well as men;*
- *in tests of image definition, consumers situate Cointreau with Rémy*
  Martin, Dimple and Veuve Cliquot;
- *in co-operative advertising, Cointreau is in fourth place for all alcohol*
  brands;
- *Cointreau is one of the most visible brands in TV and magazine*
  advertising.

As in the case of local representatives, it is most productive to promote the company and their products continuously, and thus
reinforce company image for distributors. But means well adapted to
the field must be selected: projecting a film on the advantages offered
by our products to a group of distributors will have more impact
than sending out the group's financial report(!), and the documents
and material furnished will be better accepted if they take into
account distributors' day-to-day problems, and thus have a direct
influence on the cash drawer.

▶ *This is the way Christaud (grindstones and abrasives) were able to increase*
sales by supplying their African distributors with an efficient training
document for their personnel: a sales presentation, very simple and clear,
which provides 'the Christaud answer' to problems caused by each type of
metal, thus making over-the-counter sales easier.

---

*As mentioned above (see section 5.3.2.1) in the case of scattered distribution channels, several categories
of distributors have to be distinguished (e.g. priority, important and secondary) and sufficient regular
communication has to be maintained with each of them.

Moreover, export executives should try to differentiate their visits to distributors, so that they stand out in relation to those of competitors (especially in professional fields where the companies in direct competition number several dozen or more), which can be done by the quality and originality of the contacts and the backup material used.

▶ *An exemplary demonstration of this was carried out by **PBI** (**Parfums et Beauté International, Groupe L'Oréal**) when they launched their development plan for airline Duty Free sales (see section 1.2.2.2): instead of presenting the plan over and over again, by successively visiting each airline, or for the occasion of one of the annual Tax Free conventions where all their competitors were present, **PBI** decided to innovate by participating in the IFSA convention (In-Flight Food Services Association). This convention brings together the 'cabin service/catering' executives from almost all the world's airlines (these people are often also in charge of Duty Free sales on-board), to speak about . . . food and beverages. **PBI** was outside the subject with their perfumes and cosmetics, but nevertheless received a warm welcome: being the only French perfume company participating in the convention, their presence brought an unexpected spin-off to the food and beverage suppliers; moreover, **PBI's** presentation of an original market study (the first ever done), on the needs and motivations of international passengers concerning in-flight purchases, was so successful that **PBI** were invited back the following year to the IFSA convention to lead a conference on Duty Free sales! It is clear that the desired objectives were reached: reinforcement of the brand's awareness; promotion of its perfumes' image to increase sales; all this, while catching the competition totally off guard.*

Concerning information, it must not be forgotten that the distributors are a major source: they can suggest ideas of capital importance for developing product lines, or 'hints' on results of actions undertaken or on competitors' projects, or even on general market evolution.

Moreover, as with the local representative, the company might envisage having an information bulletin for the distributors to complete and formalize the information transmitted by the sales representatives; this is an efficient way of broadcasting the successes and backing up the efforts of the company's priority and important distributors, and keeping in touch with the secondary distributors rarely visited. According to needs, this bulletin could be drawn up at headquarters for everybody (with one or two pages printed specially for each priority market) or directly in the different markets; an unusual format should be sought to distinguish the company from competitor 'house organs'.

Finally, note that 'pull' dynamic devices destined for the products' end-user can also have a 'push' effect on distributors . . . if they are aware of them. To this effect, the local representative's sales staff should have a portfolio containing all media advertising, and editorial articles where the company and its products are mentioned; this direct communication will be usefully extended by taking up the best elements and recycling them into the documents used to transmit information to the distributors.

Collecting all this various information into one file can be used on certain occasions when it is necessary to mobilize the distributors, particularly to launch a new product.

▶ *Launching a blond tobacco cigarette on a market where the company image is rather that of a specialist in dark tobacco is not easy. So, for launching* **Gauloise** *blond cigarettes in Belgium, the* **SEITA** *wanted to use a particularly well orchestrated push/pull campaign. Among other information tools, the sales force was given a portfolio for the distributors, which gave importance and credibility to this new cigarette to convince each retailer of his interest in backing this new product, because of the synergy of a strong communication campaign and active retail support. Associated with the* **Gauloise** *blond logo, the invitation 'Share our success' reinforced this message.*

The file's page format, well illustrated with very succinct text (key sentences and major figures), made up a very clear presentation guide, ensuring a better impact for these informative calls made by each salesperson on the retailers, who were doubly incited to order:

■ *by push arguments, benefiting them directly in their store ('For you: a very advantageous introductory offer . . . , attractive POP displays . . . , bonuses and gifts . . .').*

■ *by pull arguments, guaranteeing the creation of a* **Gauloise** *blond demand at the outlet ('* **Gauloise** *blond: the most important launching on the Belgian market in 1986. From April to December, an enormous advertising presence . . . more than 100,000,000 messages . . .' with details of the media used: billboards 36m², 20m² at bus stops and 2m² in underground/subway stations; coloured ads in daily newspapers and magazines, etc.).*

5.3.2.4   Assistance and training

The dynamic devices here are largely derived from those already described for local representatives (see section 5.2.1.4).

Export executives should invest in the possibilities offered by the development of their company hold on major distributors by assisting them in the fields where they lack experience or means: for example, advice for the concrete organization of sales, for the selection and display of their product range; specialized training (sales, stock management, etc.); assistance for arranging shops or shelves, merchandising, decoration, etc.

It is interesting to note that help and training can sometimes become export products in themselves, in parallel to company product lines:

▶ *Instead of jealously guarding their know-how, **Lenôtre** welcome foreign chefs in their school in Plaisir, a Parisian suburb, bringing technical assistance to restaurants in different countries, and Gaston Lenôtre regularly gives conferences to groups of professionals all over the world. This real exportation of services is not just a supplementary revenue source, but a particular reinforcement of **Lenôtre**'s world awareness, and confirms their image of quality and **savoir-faire**.*

5.3.2.5   Loyalty

The distributors' growing importance is obvious: almost everywhere in the world, distributors have taken the initiative on suppliers, and impose conditions all the more severe as their own position becomes difficult, by the cumulative effects of the international economic crisis and their country's more or less interventionist policy.

In parallel, it would be wrong to neglect the quality of direct relations with distributors, which is always an important source of business development means.

Among these means, those whose effects are multiple will be given priority:

▶ *In this way, **La Porcelaine Blanche** regularly organize study trips for their franchised distributors in countries having enterprising arts and crafts activities (or even an industry) in glass, china or stoneware. These trips to Poland, Portugal, Romania, Turkey and Spain strengthen the personal links between **La Porcelaine Blanche** and their distributors, bringing the latter practical knowledge of the history of manufacturing methods, as well as the specificities of each country's production. At the same time, a program of leisure activities is carefully planned to give them well deserved time to relax.*

Here again, export executives find themselves faced with numerous distributors (in comparison with the number of local representatives), even if they have just selected the most important in each of their markets.

There is only one solution for this: a diabolical personal organization, along with an efficient secretary and a computer: a file on each distributor with his professional, personal and family characteristics, the circumstances of meeting him, subjects of conversation, his taste, list of gifts given and received, the names of restaurants eaten in together, even a photograph, which helps to recognize him six months or two years later (we are wrong to laugh at Japanese businessmen who are constantly photographing their business acquaintances!).

Important dates (birthdays, contracts) should be recorded in a special diary for continuous updating and follow-up by the secretary, who can thus prepare letters adapted to these occasions: 'personalized' letters can also be sent out to super-distributors to announce an important 'scoop' for the development of common business.

Finally, export executives should not hesitate to benefit from their original geographic base to bring a 'plus' to distributor loyalty, by using the country's specificities according to their tastes (history, culture, various entertainments, gifts) during their visits, and also when export executives visit distributors' countries or when they write to them: a book or a record travel well and help keep up friendships:

▶ *Here is an example to conclude on communication, motivation and loyalty actions which show that it is possible to keep in touch with very unstructured distribution channels for a reasonable cost.*

*In the USA, all the managers of retail outlets selling **Spontex** products received information on a merchandising operation, and in this file they found a very 'communicative' sponge. Indeed, this compressed sponge (1.55mm thick) was printed like a one-dollar bill, except that the **Spontex** logo replaced the noble head of the founding fathers in the middle of this counterfeit dollar. A message printed at the top of the bill quickly caught the attention: 'Watch your profit grow!'. And to be sure that this motivating invitation was entirely credible, there was an instruction printed at the bottom of the bill 'Drop this bill in water – Watch it grow!', which reinforced the message. Many businessmen are still children at heart, so many of them must have dunked the sponge in water (by the way, so did I!) before converting their amusement into a growing interest for **Spontex** proposals.*

5.3.3   Actions on distributors' personnel

Why bother, if we agree with the management? We don't have time to spend on underlings!

However, the bigger a distributor, the more the personnel's desires will influence (positively or negatively) the agreements made with the company management. This is generally verifiable at all hierarchical levels dealing with company business, particularly at the last stage of retail distribution.

▶ *For example, a department store saleswoman, in charge of the section where company products are displayed; she can be quite a helping hand . . . if she wants. She can:*

■ *not turn demand away from company products to those of competitors;*
■ *emphasize company products and propose them spontaneously when a client is undecided . . . or even if he has preposterously asked for another brand!*
■ *use the POP displays well, keeping them clean and in working order;*
■ *warn the section head and/or the local representative's commercial service before being out of stock;*
■ *communicate information on purchasing trends, the clientele's attitude toward company products, even competitors' results and projects.*

This is why many companies give a lot of importance to motivation, as well as to the training and financial incentive schemes offered to their distributors' sales personnel, by regularly organizing actions intended for them:

▶ *Cristalleries de Baccarat managed to increase their sales spectacularly in Central American and West Indian markets (both visited by many American tourists) by combined training-profit sharing actions. The training program brings specific knowledge on Baccarat manufacture and quality control. By explaining the exceptional features of the product, this presentation provides the sales arguments which convince the client. In parallel, a point system on the articles sold incite the saleswomen to have the 'Baccarat reflex', by spontaneously suggesting these products.*

More generally, the personnel exercising an essential activity for company development within the local distribution framework have to be identified; it is the local representative's job to make them allies, with the occasional support that export executives can provide on their periodic visits.

5.3.3.1 Motivation

In this domain, it is possible to build up a strong motivation without necessarily having to play on the interests of distributors' personnel.

For this, during visits to their companies, elementary politeness requires that employees be greeted pleasantly, rather than being ignored like any number of robots. Then, occasions should be sought to talk with them*, showing that they are considered as responsible professionals, even if decisions are made over their heads; in any case, there is no hypocrisy in this attitude, since the importance of opinions, advice and information they can provide has been emphasized.

It can be useful, as for the distributors themselves, to help our memories by establishing an identification card for such key employees so as to personalize contacts with them (calling them by their name at each visit, indicating that we remember who they are and what they do; letters on special occasions or to congratulate them on good results; invitations, little gifts, souvenirs, etc.). As for major gifts or important material benefits, this is going beyond friendly motivation to enter into 'push money'.

Between these two means of stimulating sales results, there are

---

*Some distributors do not like their personnel establishing contact with the suppliers. Consequently, this point is to be dealt with very carefully.

contests* open to distributors' personnel (thus, distributors know about them and approve), whose forms and organization vary considerably from one country to another, and should be studied case by case.

5.3.3.2   Financial incentives

The quality of business relationships with distributor personnel is obviously a necessary dynamic device for motivation, but it is not always sufficient; their favourable attitude towards certain competitors is sometimes so evident that it can only be explained by some sort of 'push money' scheme.

In some countries or in certain cases, distributors encourage suppliers, more or less openly, to pay their personnel commissions on sales, which enables them to underpay their staff. However, in most cases, commission on sales is paid 'under the table', behind distributors' backs.

The decision to 'unofficially commission' certain distributor employees should be considered according to personal principles, ethics, the legislation in force . . . and one's liking for risks, since the discovery of such 'influence trafficking' on the premises can bring a distributor to get rid of both the employee and the supplier.

Because of this, a decision to make any sort of payment (commission and other forms of remuneration, payments in kind) should be accompanied by sufficient precautions to avoid leaks which can lead to disastrous consequences: in particular, the number of people who know about it should be limited, both within the company and at the local representative's** and have the actual payments looked after by a discrete, dependable person. For instance, it would be unfortunate for a commission payment to be sent to the person's office instead of his home!

Finally, given the situation and according to the possibility of contact within distributor structures, push money should only be offered (very prudently, and with allusive terms) to real decision-makers, or those having a direct influence on the sales volume of company products (buyers, sales staff).

In sectors where commission payments for distributors' personnel are official and considered normal, it can be noted that the methods used are often in the form of promotional actions:

---

*A remark has to be made about these 'sales' contests, which are valid at all levels of 'push', particularly for sales representatives who work for local representatives or distributors. It would be wrong just to limit prizes for only top sales reps: such actions must stimulate all salespeople, who should know that they have a chance of winning a prize geared to their efforts and performance level.
**To limit the risk of indiscretion, or even denunciation, by another employee who wants revenge for having been laid off.

▶ *In this way, the 'Méridien Challenge' offers travel agency, airline and tour operator personnel a free weekend for two in a Méridien hotel for every 20 reservations made in this chain. In ten years, this challenge has become an institution, with more than 6000 winners every year.*

▶ *Similarly, Evian organize contests in their export markets to stimulate sales staff. The objectives are calculated so that everyone can reach them and receive a prize by making a normal effort, whereas a trip to Evian for two is given to those who have the highest sales record beyond their fixed objective.*

5.3.3.3   Training

Training dynamic devices, already reviewed for the local representatives (section 5.2.1.4) and for distributors (section 5.3.2.4) are priority development actions in many professional sectors.

Since this concerns the distributors' employees, training provides an excellent occasion on which to motivate them to push company products, to create loyalty, even to interest them in the company and its products, as the training sessions encourage personal contact.

▶ *This is how it is for the Swedish group SKF, the world's leading manufacturer of ball bearings: 'We are determined to inform and train our distributors' sales personnel regularly, as if they belonged to our own company', explains Alain Gérard, General Manager of SKF Distribution in France.*

The training of the distributors' sales staff is not just centred on the product, but also deals with SKF commercial methods (marketing plan, sales plan, leading a sales force). About 3000 'trainee hours' are thus directly proposed to distributors each year.

The training is given by SKF personnel on company premises, sometimes transformed into real training centres, as exist already in Germany, the USA, the Far East, etc.

In addition, field training is also provided: SKF Distribution engineers spend several days a week on distributor premises (information, support staff training) or with the sales force where they accompany them on client calls.

'To get our ideas in place, I think the ideal field presence for our engineers is about a week a year, with each salesperson under their wing', concludes Yves Lagier, Marketing Director for SKF Distribution.

However, it is wise to assess the actual return on such training actions (often quite expensive) before triggering them; this is even more important in countries with high sales staff turnover, which shortens the training's positive effects on sales to a few months at the most.

There is another difficulty: the number of people to be trained might be largely beyond the capacity of the international training service.

A relatively satisfying solution to staff instability and the number of employees to train in certain professional domains can be found through pedagogical tools, such as films, manuals, etc., which will be used by the distributors' trainers after being prepared by the company. The advantage of this solution, proportionally inexpensive, is the ability to give the people thus trained a positive brand image, and to incite them to favour company products on the job.

▶ *The film made by* **PBI** (***Parfums et Beauté International*** *– see section 2.2.2.5) on the techniques for in-flight Duty Free sales, was used by different airlines for thousands of hostesses and stewards, for whom* **PBI** *could obviously never have provided direct classical training.*

According to the professional domain, training actions can be efficiently completed with various communication support materials in company colours (name, logo, etc), destined to facilitate the work of the distributors' personnel who specifically look after company business: desk diaries, notepads, summaries of sales presentations, writing instruments, tools, etc.

6

Stimulating international demand: 'pull' dynamic devices

After the 'product' and 'push' dynamic devices, we shall now look at the third category of ingredients that enter into the development plan mix. These are all the 'pull' dynamic devices, originating in communication, that are mobilized to inform and attract the clientele and their personal/professional circle, completing or replacing their direct contact with the 'push' dynamic devices, or with the product itself. After dealing with international communication as a whole, an inventory of the entire 'pull' dynamic range is given: advertising, public relations, and promotions.

6.1   International Communication Organization

Many exporters – mostly those involved in capital goods and industrial sectors – still appear insufficiently aware of the power of communication, when it is used professionally to reach well defined expansion targets. Furthermore, the communication arsenal proposes such varied dynamic devices that its effectiveness range goes far beyond basic sales development 'pull' objectives, offering adapted actions to face all kinds of situations encountered in foreign markets.

▶ *For the French **Ugine** group (world's largest producer of stainless steel) the choice of Thailand was quite logical in terms of strategy, as the springboard for their expansion plans in south east Asia. However, this Group's competitors had made the same market analysis which generated three industrial projects, all of them set up with local industrial partners and receiving the approval from the Thai Board of Investment.*

*'The key issue to succeed was to move faster than our competitors, because the Thailand stainless steel demand plus the export potential to other Asean zone countries could obviously not absorb the production capacity of the three projected plants', recalls Jean-Paul Thévenin, the **Thainox Steel Ltd**. Chief Executive. Consequently, he opened up this Thai **Ugine**'s subsidiary in 1991 and had the construction of the plant started immediately in Rayong*

(200 kms south east of Bangkok), a $240 million project with a yearly production capacity of 60,000 tons.

'This fast industrial start was not enough to discourage our contenders' continues Jean-Paul Thévenin. *'In addition to this threat, and even with the support of our Thai partner, the PM Group, our newly formed company was faced with the classical hindrances of any business starting from 'scratch', due to the lack of recognition and image when dealing with local administrations and suppliers. Another problem was to hire the best available staff: a very difficult task for an unknown newly formed company that required about a hundred highly qualified engineers and technicians, whose motivation had to be built up to join the starting Thainox as opposed to work for a well established group.*

This is why we decided to move fast as well into communication, immediately after the plant construction was implemented. We contracted a communication agency based in Thailand, Francom Asia, to deal with these problems'.

'Fairly soon afterwards, an adapted mix of a few communication actions, combining corporate advertising and public relations, helped Thainox overcome these establishment difficulties in Thailand', explains Paul Dumont, Francom Asia* Managing Director. 'At first, we launched a media campaign in both the English and Thai local press: 'Enter the world of stainless steel', explaining how Thailand's Thainox was entering into this sophisticated technology, with the support of the world leader Ugine, presenting the applications of stainless steel in most industrial fields, etc ... Then, we followed up with several recruiting campaigns, using the same concept, to invite engineers and technicians to enter into this appealing 'world of stainless steel'.

In parallel with media advertising, we developed a few P.R. actions, involving regular press relations and sponsorship (see section 6.4.1.1) which resulted altogether in having Thainox become a valid actor within Thailand economy, even before their factory opened'. Furthermore, concludes Jean-Paul Thévenin, 'The impact of this fast industrial and communication move was such that our Japanese and Italian competitors preferred to withdraw their projects to join Thainox original shareholders: we now are partners! ...'

However, it would be a mistake to underestimate the difficulty in organizing international communication, which is an area where most companies could improve their results.

Given that development plans are rarely successful *without* efficient communication support, it is necessary to start by checking one's organizational reliability and its adaptability to overall needs.

---

*Francom Asia (tel. contact in Bangkok: (66–2) 233 43 29 – is a branch of the French FRANCOM Group – contact in Paris: Daniel Verpeaux, tel.: (33–1) 49 44 30 00 – which offers as well international global communication services in Europe through ENTENTE INTERNATIONAL COMMUNICATION GROUP (Headquarters: Brussels, tel. (32–2) 514 34 04), one of the leading European networks. ENTENTE comprises a team of 250 consultants;
Contact in Athens: Michail Lavetzis, Tel: (30–1)364 15 11; in Brussels: Paul Luijten, Tel: (32–2) 514 33 00; in Budapest: Zsuzsa Zwitter, Tel: (361–1) 86 93 08; in Copenhagen: Vibeke Mestanas (45–33) 12 59 60; in Haarlem – The Netherlands: Wim Van Luyken, Tel: (31–23) 40 04 24; in Hamburg: Werner Bauch Tel: (49–4) 507 11 30; in Lisbon: Joao Tocha Tel: (351–1) 301 17 50; in London: Maureen Smith Tel: (44–71) 630 14 11; in Madrid: Mayda Alvarez Tel: (34–1) 521 48 36; in Milan: Luca Barabino Tel: (39–2) 72 02 35 35; in Prague: Ales Langr Tel: (42–2) 37 24 74; in Vienna: Wolfgang Rosam Tel: (43–1) 749 42 43.

Thus, we shall initially analyse the reasons for those problems that arise in international communication, and then survey their two extreme solutions, centralization and delegation, before giving detailed general practical advice.

6.1.1   Communication problem sources

International communication is a classic source of conflict between headquarters and local representatives; it is important to know the main origins of this conflict before trying to define the kind of organization that will best respond to one's development needs.

6.1.1.1   Psychological conflicts

Communication (more specifically, advertising communications) is one of those rare specialties in a company that nobody needs any specialization to discuss; from the night watchman to the CEO, everyone has an opinion and is ready to defend it against those of the so-called 'specialists'. Having established the background, let us see how all this works.

Communication's force of expression and evocation elicits a subjective response related to each person's psychological profile, where subconscious impulses may intervene, and generate a variety of reactions that is also multiplied by the international factor. This can logically provoke either rejection or supportive attitudes that are more violent than those observed, for example, for the presentation of a new product with which each person can freely establish an initial personal and professional relationship: indeed, advertising communication often goes further in proposing a specific relationship with the product.

In addition to the initial response provoked by one's own sensitivity, there are secondary reactions, particularly abroad, in the sense that local representatives are generally labelled according to their main activity ('he's the **L'Oréal** importer; well, well, here's Mr. **Air Canada** . . .'). Thus, they care very deeply about the way in which their brand is represented in relation to their professional and personal environment.

Furthermore, executive leadership qualities can broaden the sources of tangible conflicts, wherever they are based: at headquarters, the marketing managers feel they have legitimately fathered the brand/products and thus are invested with a sort of pontifical infallibility in communication matters. The local representatives, on the other hand, consider that they know better than anyone else how best to communicate with their own market.

It is always frustrating to have to approve ideas that are different from one's own, particularly when the international communication organization operates in one direction only, and local representatives have ideas imposed upon them without being able to propose their own; they are thus denied any creativity.

6.1.1.2   Divergent interests

Communication offers an ideal battleground for showdowns between headquarters and subsidiary executives, all wanting to justify the importance of their own jobs. Here, according to interpretations made of observations and surveys, opposing positions can be defended with the same relentlessness. International communication is not an exact science, and cannot be reduced to a simple equation.

In examining the adversaries' general interests, an obvious headquarters – local representative opposition can be distinguished:

■ headquarters are concerned with the brand's world longevity and their products' international image. One essential factor in this long-term strategy is the synergy effect resulting from homogeneous communication on all markets;

■ local representatives (especially when they are not company subsidiaries) often want to use the brand and products to achieve *their* own short-term targets: they are interested in *their* immediate profit, they want to use *their own* communication ideas for their business relationships with their distributors, and they wish to enjoy direct advantages by subcontracting tasks to *their* service agencies, etc. It should be noted, in any case, that it is in these agencies' interest to contest the communication proposed by headquarters, and to encourage the local representatives to act separately in this field, raising as a justification the market's specific needs. Their interest is twofold: a higher remuneration when they work autonomously, and greater prestige in handling the totality of the brand's communication on their market, instead of appearing as a 'lackey' while only locally adapting the communication concepts already drawn up at headquarters.

6.1.1.3   Deficient organization

As we have just seen, there are always causes for international communication problems, even within experienced groups.

If, *a fortiori*, an exporting company does not want to or does not go to the trouble of organizing and controlling their international communication, the result will be total chaos:

■ This will be the case when there is no coordination, leaving the initiative entirely to each local representative: 'you have to spend x% of your turnover on advertising; it's up to you to do your best...', as is often heard. It must not be forgotten that this is not a service rendered to the local representative, but an element in the contract, normally planned for in the market price structure; this element has too important a role to play in the brand's future on each market to leave communication up to the local representative, whose interests usually diverge from those of the company, and whose competence in communication has not been established.

■ This will also be the case when an international communication strategy has not been defined, and will not be followed up with sufficient continuity to be effective. Changes in direction every six months, according to the prevalent winds of the company's internal politics, can only wreck the best articulated development plans, for the absence of homogeneity among the different actions will engender negative effects that will be amplified by the international factor.

■ There will still be chaos if, even after the company has defined a valid international communication strategy, the executives do not check up on the conditions for its local adaptation.

6.1.2　Strategy and creation/production centralization

This is obviously the formula sought by most companies, although it is not applied successfully by all.

6.1.2.1　Principal advantages

As already mentioned, there are many advantages in centralizing the communication strategy, as well as creation-production at headquarters:

■ a thorough knowledge of the brand and its products, with both their strong and weak points, is a sure 'plus' for producing quality communication;

■ centralization provides the assurance of maintaining the best possible coherent brand image worldwide;

■ planning a mid- and long-term product strategy enables executives to define the positioning and communication of present products, while taking into account those which will be launched later on;

■ maximum exploitation of synergy effects is made possible by the unity and coherence of international communication, which in turn reinforces the company/brand/product image in each market. This is verifiable* both in professional product sectors such as capital goods and services, where trade magazines in leading countries are read by the buyers/users all over the world, as well as for consumer products, whose users travel and/or are in contact with international communication media;

■ the possibility of reducing creation and production costs by amortizing them on all the markets. Thus, creating POP material for each isolated market, in small quantities, would generate prohibitive unit costs in comparison to those engendered by centralizing POP needs at headquarters or elsewhere;

■ the ability to assemble, analyse and possibly re-exploit communication experience between home and foreign markets.

6.1.2.2   Major drawbacks

Centralizing communication can have disadvantages, particularly when it is exercised in a very rigid manner:

■ a communication strategy adapted to a company's general policy cannot always suit local needs exactly, given, for example, that the sales level reached in each market is rarely uniform, and purchase motivations for the same product vary greatly between markets;

■ there is such a variety of constraints** to be respected in the world today (habits, beliefs, lifestyles, legislation, etc.) that it is not easy to elaborate universal communication concepts that are 'acceptable', while at the same time retaining a sufficient force of impact:

▶ *In this way, the same cosmetic brand's press advertisement for an anti-stretch-mark cream provoked varied reactions, according to the market: in some markets it was unanimously praised for its visual beauty and purity (a naked, pregnant woman was shown through shadowing); in others, this 'shameless' nudity was considered as scandalous. Elsewhere, family groups were up in arms, not against the nudity, but because the young woman was not wearing a wedding ring! Not to mention, of course, those countries where this ad was not used as the legislation in force did not even allow a woman's unclothed shoulder to be shown.*

■ the arsenal of communication means proposed by headquarters does not always respond completely to overall market needs.

---

*Moreover, since the Second World War, a visible acceleration in unifying life and work styles, as well as of consumption habits, has been seen all over the world. This can be explained by the growing influence of major communication media – TV, press, radio – as well as by direct communication resulting from the spectacular expansion of international travel.

**We have only mentioned those constraints concerning the communication itself, but it is obvious that centralized communication can also run into constraints linked to the product: whenever certain visible features have to be adapted to standards or demands of various markets, it becomes difficult to use the same centralized communication for basically different product versions.

Experience proves that these specific needs (often urgent so as to be able to take advantage of local opportunities, or to modify an unfolding development plan) are not easily taken into account in the case of centralized communication. Two reasons are usually given for this: if headquarters does not have sufficiently specific information on these needs, its answer cannot correspond to market expectations; in the same way, these markets have to manage by themselves if the time necessary for the transmission of the request, dealing with the question, and dispatching the solution, appears to be too short. This drawback is one of local representatives' main pretexts for justifying possible schisms or variations in strategy and creation;

■ the communication means developed at headquarters are sometimes too sophisticated, and as a result, completely unsuitable for certain markets: four-colour transparencies with delicate hues which cannot be printed locally; POP displays whose size and use do not correspond to local market constraints; editorials destined for local newspapers whose intellectual style would pass way over the heads of the targeted average reader;

■ the high production and transportation costs of many communication dynamic devices (advertising printed material and POP displays, in particular) often place them out of reach of most overseas markets (see section 6.1.3.1).

6.1.2.3 Practical advice

A definitive reply cannot always be found for each of these drawbacks, but the implementation of a few recommendations (with more detailed general advice given in section 6.1.4) will enable export executives to satisfactorily organize and operate a centralized communication system for their foreign markets:

■ First, the local representative should have a contact person at headquarters in charge* of international communication whose professionalism and field experience are indisputable, and who is preferably very persuasive and patient as well. This executive will have to travel often enough to keep in touch with the main markets' evolution, and to gain credibility in the eyes of the local representatives.

■ At headquarters, a file should be drawn up containing all the important information on communication in at least the major export markets: various constraints and restrictions, as well as the addresses and 'phone numbers of the local representatives'

---

*In companies whose export structures are too small to justify a fulltime international communication specialist, another executive could be in charge of this activity in parallel to his own, if he has the competence and the time.

advertising and public relations agencies, along with the technical equipment they use.

■ The communication strategy has to bring off the difficult feat of backing up the company's general policy and development strategy for *all* the markets, while at the same time respecting local constraints encountered. Migraine headaches are guaranteed for the unfortunate marketing/advertising executives at headquarters!

Where strategic communication actions do not respond to the overall development needs of certain priority markets, tactical actions could be specifically planned to complement them, but care has to be taken to maintain sufficient unity for these actions as a whole.

It may be that a strategic communication action, full of promise worldwide cannot be used in one specific market for various reasons (e.g. a similar concept is being used for other products, competitive or not; legal prohibitions; negative interpretation of the concept for a motive that is specific to this market). If headquarters decides to follow this action through come hell or high water, it should prepare a special version of the action that is both acceptable to this market and which, nevertheless, resembles the original action used in the rest of the world.

This kind of difficulty can even pop up when a communication action is specifically designed for a region, and not the whole world:

▶   *This is what a European car manufacturer was able to verify when it prepared an advertising film (TV and cinema) for several African countries. The original scenario seemed workable, with an energetic hook line, a touch of humour, and the product strongly featured. The film started with an aircraft landing and a crowd of journalists waiting expectantly: out came a gorgeous black actress, delighted by the welcome. Suddenly, the Jumbo jet's freight doors opened, and all the journalists left the actress to admire and photograph the new model car which was being unloaded. Before shooting this film, the company prudently consulted their local representatives and their advertising agencies; the reaction was unanimous: there was a serious risk of a negative interpretation of this film as it could be considered an insult to African women. The scenario was then modified into a more classic form: the actress – brilliant example of success – got into the car and drove around, instead of being confronted with it.*

■ The local preparation of communication actions and means, previously created at headquarters, should be organized systematically together with the local representative and his/her advertising agency: the latter should be responsible for the adaptation (translations and checking details, essentially) which will assure a strong impact on the market without fundamentally changing the basic concepts. The local representative should then check his agency's work before sending it to headquarters to be printed, if it is a commercial or promotional document, or to be manufactured, if it is POP material, etc.

This gives us another opportunity to stress the importance of accurate translations. Attention in this matter has to be paid to all export functions (see, for example, section 4.2.2.2), but it is fundamental in advertising, public relations and promotions. In fact, errors here are not only expensive, but extremely harmful to both the product and brand image:

☐ spelling mistakes in copy will emphasize negatively the product's foreign origin, and give an impression of inefficiency and disorder;

☐ an awkward translation*, will undermine a product's technical credibility by creating doubt concerning its capacity to adapt to a market:

▶ *A German company's laboratory equipment (though presented in a magnificent catalogue) whose product names were ridiculously translated: Taumelgerät became a 'tottering machine'; Schüttelgerät a 'trembling machine', etc!*

☐ in addition to translation, the style can hold unpleasant surprises as well:

▶ *A large service company had this experience when they decided to have the French version of a training film for sales personnel dubbed in London: bad luck – the actor chosen to read the text must have been living outside France for a long time, for his diction – emphatic and propagandistic – reminded people of radio/newsreel programmes from the Second World War occupation period. Needless to say, this film's career in France was short-lived.*

It can be seen through these examples that the adaptation errors are mostly due to a lack of coordination with the individual markets: as we have just seen, it is *essential* to have the local representative and/or his advertising agency participate in the preparation of communication dynamic device actions. In addition to restoring this coordination between headquarters and the markets, it should be remembered that the quality and exactitude of international communication depend on the original message: it is important, then, to 'think multilingual' when writing crystal clear basic copy, where idiomatic phrasings, plays on words and obscure metaphors should be avoided:

■ A request has to be acted upon within a reasonable time limit, especially as companies now have the means for instantaneous communication by fax or express international mail delivery services: **GD Express Worldwide** (formed by **TNT** and their

---

*This is the appropriate time to apologize to readers if they have found the author and translator guilty of any such sin!

European partners, such as **Chronopost** in France), **DHL, Federal Express, UPS, XL**, etc.)

6.1.2.4   Centralized communication examples

▶ *RoC intend to keep their homogeneous world image, where safety is allied with beauty (be beautiful, but be safe). Consequently, their international communication, aiming at the long-term, had to be rigorously controlled to avoid any divergence: thorough advanced training for sales personnel by instructors having the equivalent of a physician/pharmacist diploma (see section 5.2.1.4): contractual obligation for local representatives to exclusively use the advertising messages provided by the company (the only adaptations allowed concern language, terminology constraints and local customs): press relations are limited to a reduced number of international medical magazines and the big women's fashion/beauty magazines so that the RoC message is not deformed or made 'common'; public relations concentrates on health professionals in general, whom RoC contact regularly by participating in most of the world's dermatology conventions. (For instance, at the World Dermatology Congress in Tokyo, RoC were able to become known by hundreds of doctors from all over the world, given that their Medical Director was invited to give a session on sun-bathing products).*

▶ *The determination of Méridien Hotels to impose their image in the minds of their targeted international clientele, getting a maximum out of the committed investment, has led logically to the choice of a communication strategy concentrated on the general theme 'the French art of living in the world'. However, this general theme is easily expressed everywhere in the world, thanks to its use as a press advertisement 'base line' which mentions the place, city or region 'The very soul of France. In the very heart of Boston'). Moreover, the presence of one of Ken Maryianski's original drawings on all Méridien advertising reinforces their impact and recall. Indeed, these highly recognizable drawings attract attention with their 1920s style sophisticated figures; make-up in page form is possible for all press advertisement formats; in addition, the huge choice and diversity of these drawings can illustrate all possible campaign themes: business or tourist clientele, quality service, restaurant, banquets, bar, special evening occasions (Christmas, New Year's, Valentine's Day), beach/pool, sports, musical evenings, weddings, business centres, fashion shows, exhibitions, conventions, etc.*

▶ *The IBM example is special, since it can be included both in centralized as well as decentralized communication, as explains Ronald Driesen, Advertising and Promotion manager for IBM Eurocoordination: 'Our advertising is based on a flexible approach to get the best possible efficiency. This means that we concentrate on strategic campaigns for our "pan-European advertising" such as the 1992 OS/2 operating system for personal computers, with this ad concept being used in most countries. Still, we have local campaigns too . . .' (to follow for decentralized communication, see section 6.1.3.4).*

▶ *Here is another successful example of centralized communication, with a* memorable **Qantas Airways** *campaign whose approach was both humorous and emotional. It featured a cranky (but adorable) Koala bear who grumblingly lists, in a series of messages, the numerous advantages offered by* **Qantas**. *This campaign was so successful on all continents in the mid–1980s that it was carried on by new messages, bringing this likeable marsupial into play again, to the great joy of his fans. But nobody is a prophet in his own country, not even a cute Koala bear: in Australia, where this animal is part of the every day scenery,* **Qantas** *preferred to launch a new campaign theme.*

▶ *Creating universal concepts is made easier by* **Waterman**'s *advertising style, which can generally be transposed to any market: this style, which is decidedly visual, attracts attention by the originality of the image, and captivates by magnifying the object. Little or no copy, then: at this stage of communication, the pen's beauty bypasses the need for text. Because of this, few* **Waterman** *campaigns do not have an international applicability. Among the rare campaigns with a limited geographical range, the 'Honorable* **Waterman**' *can be remembered, an advertisement where a Japanese woman in a kimono was practising the traditional art of calligraphy with a pen as big as she was; just as in the* **Qantas** *Koala case (see the preceding example), this theme is too typical to be applicable with success in its own country. Another example is one of the ads from the* **Watermania** *campaign, where a jewelled pen decorated the braided hair of a dark-haired woman on the background of her golden tanned back ... nudity is obviously a no-go in many Moslem countries.*

6.1.3   Strategy and/or creation/production delegation

Very different reasons can lead to delegating communication to local representatives. It can be sometimes explained by historic reasons (isolated markets left on their own because of war, an embargo or a crisis within the exporting company). Another explanation can be the adaptation to local regulations or constraints (see section 6.2.2.5), but usually delegating communication simply corresponds to different international development strategies.

6.1.3.1   Interest of delegating

Delegating may concern the whole communication strategy, just the creation and production, or the production only:

- For many 'mass market' products (a classic example is washing powders and cleaning products), international development depends largely on complete adaptation to each market's needs, which often calls for local manufacture, a specially chosen name and, of course, total delegation of communication. However, it is useful to maintain inter-market stimulation by regularly comparing methods, ideas and results in all domains – including communication.

- Sometimes the local representative's company in a leading world market is bigger than the exporting company, and it has a vastly superior competence and resources in the communication field. If the exporting company has not yet come up with a real communication strategy, they could enlist their representative's assistance in defining it, and in taking charge of creation-production for this market. This same strategy can sometimes be adapted to neighbouring market needs, enabling the company to save time and reduce the creation-production costs of certain dynamic devices (printed and POP materials, in particular) by amortizing them with larger quantities.

- Some countries want to protect their local industry, and do not authorize imported films and advertisements. In this case, production has to be handled locally (see section 6.2.2.5).

- As mentioned above, one of the drawbacks of centralized communication is the often high cost of production, which can be explained by different reasons: general labour and production costs, often higher in the country of origin, occasionally including participation in the operating costs of the communication service at headquarters, to which are added transportation costs (transport, insurance, customs duty and various other taxes). An exceedingly high cost of pull dynamic devices obviously reduces their use, and becomes a serious brake to business development; this hindrance can be eliminated by delegating the production of some of these dynamic devices to a few local representatives (it is often the case for printed material, POP displays, promotional material, etc.).

- Finally, some companies have deliberately decided to decentralize international communication to adhere perfectly to their markets' specific needs.

▶ *Sony, for example, do not deny their Japanese origins at all, but they are determined to become an integral part of each of their markets, as Dominique Demarquay from **Sony France** explains: 'No worldwide campaign for **Sony**, but national ones . . . The Americans are combining humour and emotion in an ad series, to provide major "reasons why", such as "London for under two pounds a day", which positions the camcorder Handycam TR5 as the ideal travel companion with emphasis on its light weight; or "**Sony** Handycam. For a lot of small reasons", which highlights this Camcorder's qualities for recording children's sports accomplishments. The Germans are promoting the Handycam's technical qualities: "System HI8. Because separate processing gives truer detail", with a concept that explains how two separately processed signals can offer greater picture detail as well as more vibrant colour. The Spanish propose the beautiful image of a harpist in concert for an invitation to "sharpen your sight and hearing", which emphasizes the sharper images and superior sound of the Handycam V700. No wonder, if by the time of the World Cup, the Brazilians are featuring their soccer star*

*Zico, to testify to **Sony**'s picture quality, or if Chileans are promoting the Black Trinitron TV set as "the best international stadium". As for the French, we developed a comprehensive campaign which is adaptable to every product advertisement, positioning **Sony** as 'The Creator', with the common headline "if you can dream it, **Sony** can do it", that resulted in extraordinarily high recall rates . . .'*

6.1.3.2   Essential risks

Delegating communication, in specific cases such as those just mentioned, has real advantages, and particularly the advantage of a better adaptation to local needs. However, the risks involved should not be forgotten:

- for most products marketed under a brand name, there is a great risk of leaving behind a deflected and scattered brand image, therefore weakening international awareness;
- this international drifting of the positioning-image-awareness entity, buffeted on all sides from one market to another, might in the long run deprive a brand of its very substance and originality. It is very difficult afterwards to consider returning to a world development strategy;
- insufficient supervision of delegated communication might lead to a loss in local creation and production quality, while facilitating malpractice, unofficial commissions, bribes, etc.

6.1.3.3   Advisable supervision

As for all other fields of delegation to the local representatives, a rather strict control* system has to be set up to minimize risks:

- in the case where only creation and production are delegated, this supervision will concern the respecting of the international communication strategy, as well as quality and costs;
- in the case where just production is delegated, it will be a matter of checking that the international creation standards have been respected. The only acceptable modification will be for details that better adapt 'pull' dynamic devices to local needs;
- the only efficient way in which to concretely impose this supervision is to tie budget approval for the creation and/or production of each 'pull' dynamic device to the presentation of the *proposal* in the form of a layout, model, storyboard, etc. (supervision has to occur, obviously, *before* commitment to production costs, so there is still time to rectify or improve a

---

*Such a strict control is, of course, not applicable to 'autonomous' markets which develop their own products, as mentioned in section 6.1.3.1.

proposal). Such a rule is easily applicable to company subsidiaries; for the other representatives, it should be made explicit in the agreements. This supervision (at headquarters, or directly exercised on the markets by visiting executives) can only function well if done rapidly, as production of 'pull' dynamic devices has one thing in common all over the world – it is always behind schedule!

6.1.3.4   Delegated communication examples

▶   *Grand Marnier's* *international communication uses different creations from one market to another, with the general objective to assure sales development, either by messages reinforcing brand awareness, or by messages inciting users to vary their **Grand Marnier** consumption habits. Thus, in the United States a series of advertisements on the theme 'it's **Grand Marnier** time' presented different ways of drinking this liqueur, which are well adapted to different times of day and night; another ad showed a small desert island with the caption 'There may still be places on earth where **Grand Marnier** is not offered after dinner', emphasizing with humour the brand's success and world awareness. In Australia, a campaign on the theme 'if Paris were a drink . . . it would be **Grand Marnier'** exploited the reputation of French good taste. In parallel, numerous other themes were used in other countries or regions, such as '**Grand Marnier**, a touch of class', '**Grand Marnier**, the seal of excellence', 'In **Grand Marnier** beats the heart of Cognac', '**Grand Marnier**, a certain idea of France', '**Grand Marnier**, the Entente Cordiale'.*

▶   *Moulinex* *advertising communication, very decentralized, is geared to their appliances' specific uses in each world region: there is a data bank at headquarters where all the available advertising material is collected, and **Moulinex** leave the choice to each subsidiary and agent as to whether to use it. In the latter case, **Moulinex** only supervise TV film creation, and recommend that their local representatives maintain the brand's general style for press and outdoor advertising.*

▶   *IBM* *subsidiaries have total freedom to define the best strategy for their market. 'They may choose to adapt the pan-European advertising concepts proposed to them,' says Ronald Driesen, Advertising and Promotion Manager for **IBM** Eurocoordination, 'or decide to develop more specific ones. For instance, **IBM** France is using in 1992 an original concept, stressed by a strong baseline, '**IBM**, c'est tout' (literally, **IBM** is everything). It is meant to please the French liking for witty messages, with its double meaning: **IBM** is all that I want . . . **IBM** provides all solutions . . . in information technology and related services.'*

▶   *Elida Gibbs Group's* *Impulse, which is both a deodorant and a fragrance, provides an interesting semi-delegated communication case, where international management define a strategy, then leave creation and production to each country. Thus, for example, TV and cinema film themes are imposed on all the world markets: a handsome man delightedly sniffs at the perfumed wake of a pretty woman; then, driven by an irresistible impulse, he offers her a bouquet of flowers. Only the creative guidelines have to be respected on the different markets (description of the man's reaction, having to find a bouquet of flowers near the place of the encounter, bouquet's composition, etc.). For the rest, the local advertising agency can adapt the theme quite freely, according to the product's positioning in its country; this enabled England and Denmark to emphasize the product's deodorant feature with illustrations of the pretty woman – lightly clad – spraying herself with* **Impulse***, whereas the French film insisted more on its perfume application during the corresponding sequence.*

▶ *For* **Peugeot Automobiles***, communication decentralization operates in different ways. In Europe, regular dialogue between subsidiary companies and headquarters provides overall coherence: part of the proposed communication action is applied successfully in most countries after possible adaptation (see section 6.1.4.1, a detailed explanation with the example of the 405 in Europe). Moreover, specific actions are launched in a few countries to respond to exclusively local needs.*

On the other hand, in the rest of the world divergence of needs is such that **Peugeot** *Overseas Export Management established five geographical communication zones: Latin America, Black Africa, North Africa/Middle East, Far East and Australasia. In each region, a central advertising agency coordinates activities between headquarters and the countries (where each* **Peugeot** *representative has his own local agency). Regional or local actions are undertaken all over the world, often in very different ways. This can be seen in the considerable variations in the dynamic device mix in each country, where priorities obviously differ among media advertising, POP displays, printed material, public relations and promotions. Each action's concept can also vary considerably from one country to another for the same car: for example, in a press ad in the Ivory Coast and Senegal, the 505's city/bush duality is insisted upon (its elegance could otherwise make potential clients wonder if it is sturdy enough off asphalted roads), whereas in Thailand and Indonesia, it is presented as a luxury status symbol.*

6.1.4   General advice

International communication is aligned so closely on each professional domain's specificities, on market needs and constraints, on the company's characteristics and general development policy, that it is not desirable to take sides here with either the partisans of centralization at headquarters or those of local delegation. This is a matter which can only be dealt with case-by-case.

Still, after studying in parallel centralized and delegated communication systems, it is worth concluding with some general advice, whose dynamic effect can be verified in the field.

6.1.4.1   Cooperative organization

In the general case of centralized communication, and for reasons already listed (see Section 6.1.1), top 'pull' dynamic device efficiency will be achieved if the local representatives can be convinced that it is in their own interests, rather than having them imposed.

This dialogue can initially be obtained by involving the local representatives in defining the international communications strategy; in any case, this is not too difficult to manage, and a coherent strategy should normally win general adhesion.

On the other hand, there are many more local stumbling blocks for creative aspects at the time when the proposals are presented. It is prudent, then, to plan this presentation far enough ahead, and to collect all the representatives' comments and suggestions; both objective and some subjective remarks should be taken into account in developing the final 'pull' dynamic devices:

▶ *Beyond looking for a consensus of opinion with the local representatives and their advertising agencies, presenting campaign proposals through layouts, models or storyboards helps avoid communication errors, often unforeseeable for a foreigner without advice from the 'natives' or a pre-test. Here are two examples from Africa, one dealing with style, the other with the message:*

■ *To launch a new beer brand in Nigeria, the picture in the poster ad campaign showed a man holding a glass in his left hand – which one of the ethnic groups considers a homosexual attitude.*

■ *A bank wanted to illustrate their efficient services with a hen laying dollar bills. Result: total incomprehension of this symbolic illustration, leaving the public indifferent since they did not feel concerned by the message.*

After this stage, the only concessions* made to local resistance could be possible minor modifications to facilitate the adaptation of strategic 'pull' dynamic devices by certain markets; the matter is to convince (more or less persuasively) everybody that their interests lie with the centralizing of forces around a mutual strategy and creation, rather than with individualistic behaviour:

▶ *An interesting illustration in this field is provided by the evolution of* **Peugeot's** *European communication strategy, which led to the successful organization of the launch campaign 'Un talent fou ! . . . /Take your breath away ! . . .' for the 405. Daniel Vasseur, then* **Peugeot Automobile's** *Central Marketing Director, tells the story: 'In 1972, when we started doing international advertising, we chose at first a centralized organization to launch the 104. One concept; one message, one illustration, translated into*

---

*Besides using tactical pull dynamic devices, specially developed for certain markets' specific needs (see section 6.1.2.3). It would be prudent to supervise the allocation of the pull budget to be sure that the strategic dynamic devices get the priority investment before the local tactical ones.

all languages: "104, all of **Peugeot** *in 3.58 meters. The shortest 4-door in Europe".'*

This message which meant, as you have understood, that all the **Peugeot** know-how already demonstrated by their intermediary and big cars, 203, 403, 404, was concentrated in this new compact, passed way over the heads of many Europeans, for whom **Peugeot** didn't mean very much at that time due to low market awareness. To be the shortest 4-door in Europe was, in 1972, not a client advantage either, for certain markets. I'm thinking of Belgium at that period, which was a market for big cars. As for the European banderole made up of mixed national flags, it was definitely ahead of its time.

Then, for the next ten years, we delegated communication. Each country looked after its own advertising, with headquarters assuming information and some coordination.

1980 was the merger of the **Peugeot-Talbot** networks and their sales teams. Then, we had to question everything. We established a single organization with HDM advertising agency subsidiaries in all the major European countries. A central advertising service was set up: to simplify, let's say that campaigns carried out in France were attempted in other European countries.

At this point, European harmony was attained or not, according to the degree of pressure maintained, the goodwill of local teams and especially the quality of the campaigns. For example, the James Bond style 205 GTI film went all around Europe. But we wasted a lot of time trying to sell typically French creations to Italians, English or Dutch, who rejected them. Their main reproach was, of course, that we made films for France that we were trying to 'pawn off' afterwards.

Concerning the 405, its European vocation seemed clear right from the start. Moreover, market studies all indicated that the profiles and motivations of the targeted clientele segment were identical or very close in all European countries. Finally, we counted a lot on the 405 to reinforce brand image, following along the energy and rejuvenation lines initiated by the 205 and the 309. It was, thus, of utmost importance to have a harmonious communication, while at the same time motivating our subsidiaries for a project in common. The procedure followed was:

- Starting from our marketing positioning, based on the market and motivation studies just mentioned, we established a European communications strategy, which brought forth a single creative brief. We worked hard on this, as it was the base on which we were going to build the rest, and we wanted it solid and irreproachable.

- This creative brief was exhibited at the same time as the car prototype, to the HDM agencies in four European countries, in the presence of the marketing directors of the four subsidiaries concerned: France, Germany, Italy and Great Britain. We asked the advertising agencies for these four countries to each prepare, one, two or three concepts from the creative brief, with the objective of launching a European campaign.

- One month later, they presented their proposals: 'animatic' story boards for TV films, layouts for press and outdoor advertising. Together with the four countries' Marketing Directors, the Director from France, and the Export Director, we selected one concept per country.

■   *These four concepts were tested in the four countries: 16 tests altogether, from which we chose one to become the European campaign.*

In retrospect, the organization of this campaign appears globally positive, but there are nuances. First of all, each country's campaign adaptation shows some differences. There is harmony around the concept 'talent', but not a rigid message. Then again, if the concept was accepted without protest by the three other rival countries, I am not sure they would appreciate being eliminated several times running. There were also countries which didn't compete at all. It was agreed there would be a rotation, but with France always included, as the home market supplies 50% of European sales. Finally, the procedure is long and complicated.

The positive aspect is that we considerably enriched our knowledge of the European market, and we managed to get people working together and broke down barriers. We used the same organization for the 309, to reposition this product, but only putting two countries in competition: France and Italy. This produced the '309, Toujours partante/You've never been here before' campaign.

But at the same time we keep on developing, in France, follow-up or product development campaigns, which are proposed to other countries because it's quicker and handier; as before, when the campaign is good, it crosses all borders. Two examples testify to this: the 205 GTI, **Peugeot** James Bond sequel, and the 205 film which has just won a European award.

Finally, there are several conclusions to be drawn from this experience:

■   *There is no miracle solution.*

■   *For a big exporting company like ours, we have to think 'European' resolutely, definitively and absolutely.*

■   *Openness is fundamental, along with mixing people and ideas, and breaking down routine arrangements.*

■   *Flexibility is it: such a solution for such a market will work for such a product at such a moment. Then, another might be necessary.*

■   *But, what is probable, is that our next launching campaign for a future product will be European, several subsidiaries will be involved in its elaboration, and it will be tested in several countries. But all this isn't easy and we'd like to lighten the organization. We need more than talent for that!'*

Open, flexible dialogue can also be sought for decentralized communication:

▶   *Yoplait's* International Division executives cooperate with their franchised partners in each country to prepare and finalize the local marketing plan, and can thus orient their communication projects. The frequency and closeness of the *Yoplait*-Franchisee relationship help the latter keep communication naturally in line with the brand's philosophy. In fact, *Yoplait* have the role of catalysts for their franchised partners all over the world. This enables the brand to adapt permanently to the ever increasingly rapid evolution of international communication networks, and to multiply inter-country synergy effects; for example, a recent TV commercial broadcast in the Ivory Coast was a direct adaptation of a film made by the Spanish franchisee.

▶ *In France, we know well the often humorous themes of **Perrier** communication, which are as gaily effervescent as the water's bubbles. But it has to be realized that this kind of communication necessitates an enormous brand awareness; in addition, the initial result of adapting a message like 'Ferrier, c'est **pou**' (a slogan sounding as a joke, with the inversion of the letters F and p, untranslatable into other languages), would provoke a nervous breakdown on the part of the unfortunate foreign advertising agencies. **Perrier**, as a result, adopted an attitude of open dialogue for their communication: the Group proposes to their subsidiaries and agents concepts specially developed for international markets, and encourage them to use these concepts, thus saving on local production costs and enabling them to invest more in media buying. However, **Perrier** also accept special concept development in certain countries, if they respect the international **Perrier** style. This is all the more justified as the visual impact of **Perrier** bottles maintains an intermarket synergy effect, even when the communication concepts are different.*

▶ *For **Club Med**, communication can be international or local, according to the development stage reached and each market's specific needs:*

■ *The corporate campaign 'Play, dream, love, sleep . . .' associating each verb with an evocative photograph, was well adapted to countries where the **Club** is solidly established.*

■ *Curiously, this same campaign was very efficient in Japan, even though it was being tested at a time when **Club Med** awareness was still weak. In fact, there was a strong attraction to these simple pictures, the verbs being replaced by the same caption in French 'Vacance, je t'aime' which differentiated the **Club** from the Japanese 'Travel Tours', and still remained comprehensible (in Japanese, the translation of 'vacation' is 'vacantsu'.*

■ *In the USA, there were many specific campaigns, such as '**Club Med**, the antidote for civilization' and '**Club Med** versus room and bored', which presented the **Club** advantages in comparison with traditional hotel stays, and whose purpose was to increase awareness of all the **Club's** facets.*

▶ *By 1992, 'the antidote for civilization' still appears in **Club Med** ads, as the end line under the **Club's** logo, while one of the major campaign concepts 'Take home a **Club Med** vacation' stresses the new way of looking at life, after such an experience.*

6.1.4.2 Information circulation

Although it can seem strange to talk about ensuring efficient communication for *company* communication, this subject deserves to be dealt with, given that there are a few obstacles to overcome and few effective dynamic devices to activate.

First, it is useful to select and use the surest and quickest means of transmitting/sending the proposals, layouts, models and such documents. Theoretically, the normal postal service should be enough, but delays are frequent in communication creation and production, which often makes the use of express services necessary; moreover, the postal service is not always dependable in many countries. For delicate cases, specially adapted means have to be planned for, such as using the fax and international courier services.

The exporting company should centralize all the information concerning the overall pull dynamic device needs felt in the markets so as to deal with them in a homogenous manner, consolidating creation and production costs, and thus giving the communication campaigns more clout.

Given the exporting company's structures, as well as those of the local representatives and their specialized agencies, simple procedures should be sought, best adapted to handling the different aspects of communication creation and production. For example, this could bring the public relations headquarters' agency to work directly with the local representatives' PR agencies to coordinate the preparation of a major international event according to specific instructions, in such a way that headquarters and the local representatives simply have to check up on overall progression from time to time.

Here is a final reminder to emphasize the importance of information circulation about communication experiences in all markets – including the home market. These experiences should be collected at headquarters, analysed and reexploited case-by-case with the local representatives to inform and stimulate them concerning a new product which they are to be launching soon, to warn them about a difficulty observed for a dynamic devices use in certain markets, etc.:

▶ *The **Sony** Corporation organized a 'marketing hot line' which issues a yearly '**Sony** ad exchange report', printed in Japan and distributed worldwide to all their relevant executives. This full-colour report has the size and almost the thickness of a news magazine; it features a reproduction of all new press advertisements launched in any country for **Sony** video, hi-fi and other electronic equipment, with additional details about the concept positioning, or results achieved.*

6.1.4.3   Communication bible

If the company has centralized communication, the organization and regular updating of a 'communication bible' is an important dynamic device, as it enables all the local representatives and their advertising agencies to work from the same standards. In this way, the homogeneity of international communication can be greatly improved, and the risks of erroneous interpretations or local deviations from standards avoided, which would not be the case if only a vague description of the pull dynamic devices to be used was provided.

However, the communication bible has to be constantly renewed and updated each time there is a new pull dynamic device, much more so than the bible mentioned in section 4.1.1.5, for preserving corporate brand image. Practically, the best way to go about this is to plan for a big binder to be available at each local representative's office and at each advertising agency, into which standard examples of communication campaigns are inserted as they come along. Thus, in the bible for press advertisements there will be the make-up in page form for each suggested format, duplicates of transparencies, colour and typography references, plus any other useful instructions. For public relations, the bible will include different types of press files as well as specific instructions for organizing various events, with the checklist for all the operations to be carried out according to a standard schedule. For promotional actions, a detailed breakdown of each action will be provided, as well as a model for the necessary material.

This communication bible, in fact, puts in the local representatives' hands all those elements they will need to use successfully the pull dynamic devices proposed by headquarters*, and to reinforce international image coherence.

▶ *For **Bull**, this bible is used within the framework of both a centralized and decentralized communication strategy. 'The choice of the tree as symbol and identification of the Group makes the implementation of such a strategy considerably easier: the tree concept and its wealth of expressions is perfectly adaptable to computer communication; moreover, its image is universally appreciated, which is another great advantage, given **Bull**'s international vocation.*

Our communication bible specifically defines the possible areas of expression, as well as those which are prohibited.

In each country, our subsidiaries can thus decide, with their advertising agency, which formula responds best to local needs: using a campaign already launched and tested elsewhere, or designing a specific campaign with a concept interpretation adapted exactly to their development strategy.

*In Germany, for example, the **Bull** Tree is usually presented in a drawing and not in a photograph, and in one campaign it was broken down into elements (trunk, big branches, smaller branches, leaves, fruit) developing the Tree-Computer parallel, in order to reinforce the didactic content of the message and respond better to the German user's considerable product information expectations.*

In the Netherlands, another campaign showed the interaction of our systems with an attractive illustration of an old tree helping a young tree to grow . . .'

---

*Only example concerning press advertising, public relations and promotional actions have been mentioned, but it is clear that similar instructions and models should be provided for all the other communication media likely to be used (TV, radio, cinema, outdoor advertising, printed material, direct mail and telesales, POP and merchandising material, etc.).

6.1.4.4   Agency assistance

A majority of companies do not have their own integrated advertising, public relations and promotions departments; periodically or regularly they use communication agencies at headquarters in the home country, and/or with local representatives in international markets.

The services performed by these agencies have a preponderant effect on business development, since they are responsible for the creation and production of most pull dynamic devices. We shall examine the main points which underlie the quality and productivity of their assistance.

We skip rapidly over the choice of headquarters' agencies, of which one of the deciding factors is international know-how (which presupposes linguistic capacities), and the faculty to adapt to international needs, as well as sufficient credibility in the eyes of foreign partners and clients, so as to look more closely at the selection of a new agency in foreign markets together with the local representatives.

Some exporters no doubt consider that this choice falls into the local representative's responsibility area, but I think it is important for the export executives to be implicated and to help make the selection. In fact, even in cases of very centralized communication, local agencies are not just simple executants who do what they are told, as their role is to be the communication message 'adaptors' between headquarters and their market, together with the local representative.

Then, if the export executives help the local representatives on priority markets choose their new communication agencies, a few guidelines will be useful, even if it is not a question of drawing here an identikit description of the ideal agency:

■ An independent agency or a local subsidiary of an international group? Both theses are defendable, and neither can be absolute decision-making factors:

  □ A local agency, a subsidiary of that working with the headquarters, should normally have solid links with the parent agency, which eliminates risks of misunderstanding and rivalry. However, one should check that the agency is run by local managers (and not by foreigners sent by head office, who might not have thorough market knowledge and perception), and whether its clients include national or only foreign companies (the latter case might indicate that the agency is not well adapted to the market).

  □ On the other hand, a local independent agency could be expected to be in perfect osmosis with the market, but one might run into a certain parochialism and a lack of enthusiasm to work with the export company's own agency.

  □ There is a hybrid solution: local agencies that are the correspondents or work in association with the company agency and which should, theoretically, present the advantages of both the above-mentioned examples; still, the real practical advantages* have to be measured, as this system sometimes only provides an efficient means for the communication agencies based in the exporting countries to collect an extra commission on their clients' international activities.

- The agency's size is not necessarily a determining factor either. What is more important is the competence of the executives who will *really* be working on the company account (who will be looking after our current business? Is the brilliant agency manager, who 'convinced' us to go with his agency, about to delegate this task to a junior advertising executive, whose professionalism has yet to be proven?).
- Another important element: the motivation of the candidate agencies to look after our business . . . and to keep our local representative and company within their clientele, which should be a clear indication of the availability and energy to be expected.
- To conclude this unlimited pre-selection checklist, here are a few supplementary points, both subjective and objective, which should also be taken into consideration:
  - ☐ the types of budgets making up the clientele of the interested agencies, as well as their experience in the company field of activity, distribution and/or end-users.
  - ☐ The quality of the relationship established between each agency, the local representative and the export executives, given that it can indicate the climate of future collaboration.
  - ☐ Contacts and information sources are an integral part of the added value in each candidate: contacts that public relations agencies have with the media, opinion leaders and trend setters; information sources the advertising agencies have on the market for company products, their distribution, the competition; privileged relationships that sales promotion agencies have with 'floor managers' in department stores, etc.
- Then, a visit to the premises of the two or three short-listed agencies will help make a final choice:
  - ☐ the strategic analysis and first recommendations (i.e. 'the pitch') presented by each agency will indicate the depth of their comprehension of the initial brief previously given, as well as the pertinence of the proposed solutions:

---

*Examples of items to be checked: how closely the agencies' managers are used to working together; is there a well-oiled communication network and data banks for mutual use which could rapidly provide some basic market information requested to test their system; can they organize package deals with international media, to buy the best advertising airtime or space at the most competitive rate, etc?

☐ further to this key meeting, such a visit will furnish the occasion to meet and size up the other agency staff members, and to see what equipment they have for production as well as for communications;

☐ an average talent for observation is enough to also get an impression of each agency's apparent qualities: for example, energy and enthusiasm, as well as overall organization.

■ There is still a last detail to be considered: paying for the agency services. This should be very clear right from the beginning, or else the company is in for a lot of future trouble. Generally, public relations and sales promotion agencies work for a fee previously fixed (annually or for each action) which has to be detailed: does it only include the agency fees, or are other expenses comprised? In the same way, all the supplementary costs will be checked closely: trips, production, receptions, etc., and it should be decided with the agency whether they keep the commissions possibly gained on technical costs or transfer them completely or partly back to the company.

■ For advertising agencies, the general rule of 15% commission on media space/time purchases and on production costs (printed material, POP display, etc.) is often found, but not in all cases:

☐ this system is normal for major advertisers and big agencies;

☐ payment by fees is more frequent for smaller budgets;

☐ in fact, nothing prevents the local representative or the export executives from negotiating a tailor-made payment system with an agency, both motivating for the latter and well-adapted for the company;

☐ it would be wise to foresee with the future agency what use will be made of possible extra-commissions obtained through media space/airtime purchase negotiations or subcontracting production; depending on the case, they could be transferred to the company, shared between the company and the agency, or left to the agency.

To conclude agency payment, it should be mentioned that the established commission system does not allow a perfect transparency, and sometimes even harms agency-company cooperation: despite all the experience and professionalism of ad-agencies, it is hard not to suspect that some of their advertising advice is influenced by their own interests. It requires a high degree of probity to encourage a company starting out in a market to invest in their sales force and retail outlets – which brings in no commission – rather than in a superb media campaign. Also, in media planning, it can be tempting to prescribe a medium which has the merit, among others, of providing the agency with a more generous commission.

Having chosen the agency, too many local representatives (and even export executives) consider that the initial brief, plus the more confidential elements transmitted once the agency has been hired, will be enough to come up with the sensational ideas that are expected. Of course this is not the case, and a new agency should receive more detailed instructions relating to its mission, which could include a history of company development (brand and product) in the world and in this particular market, well-founded information on the company's current local position (with strengths and weaknesses), positioning, distribution, priority targeted clientele and their purchase motivations, competitors' positions and actions, company strategy and quantitative as well as qualitative development objectives, description of product and push dynamic devices that the company plans on using in the development plan, and the communication constraints (size of available budget, brand communication rules, time limits, etc.). It is only after all of the above has been digested that the agency will be able to propose a coherent communication strategy with pull actions and dynamic devices suited to company needs.

Finally, when the local representative and/or the export executives have chosen quite a promising agency, which will be motivated by a stimulating remuneration and sufficiently briefed to be productive, care still has to be taken that the agency's efforts do not slacken:

- Given that the company works regularly with an agency, routine updating of information has to be seen (via the local representative or directly from headquarters) as indispensable for efficient output, just as it is done for the local representatives (see section 5.2.1.3).
- The organization of this regular information update and a good working relationship between the local representative, the headquarters communication agency and the export executives, should reinforce both the local agency's motivation and company recognition, as a communication agency is a powerful opinion relay. All activity turns around their clientele, who are talked about continually to a multitude of different publics; it would then be better for the company if the agency talks about their brands and products positively!
- 'You end up with the agency you deserve'. It is most important to be demanding on the creativity, quality, productivity, punctuality and finish of the work done. This will come naturally, as an agency knows very well how to adjust themselves to those of their clients they want to keep: they will be more than willing to do handstands for a dynamic and enterprising account ... and delighted to follow their own nose for a 'weakling'!
- Such is the complexity of international communication that an agency cannot be expected to be infallible. In practice, any major project should be submitted regularly during its preparation to the local representative, even sometimes to headquarters, so that changes and possible improvements can be carried out. This will

become easier, as after a time the agency's strong and weak points will be known:

▶ *If you are not constantly looking over your agency's shoulder to check up on things, anything can happen, explains* **Pronuptia** *founder Henri Micmacher:*[1] *'... Finally, after a thousand problems,* **Pronuptia-London** *opened its doors on Oxford Street ... The English advertising agent had required a free hand for the launch campaign. You can imagine my surprise and my concern when I saw our ad with a photograph in the press showing two brides accompanying one groom. 'Get married in the French style' said the caption. Or there was another ad, with a young woman entering a Rolls-Royce in an underskirt, her back bare: 'She's going to get married at* **Pronuptia**, *like in Paris'.*

■ If the company has finally decided to let an agency go because the work was unsatisfactory, it would be best to follow the advice already given for changing local representatives (see sections 5.2.2.2 and 5.2.2.3), so that this separation can be brought about to the best of everybody's interests.

6.2   Media Advertising

After dealing with communication in general, the difficulty of carrying off international advertising without blowing it (as is often said so elegantly at export meetings) can be imagined.

We shall now attack this particularly delicate and unstable* area to see how to use media advertising effectively by forging a solid advertising strategy that will be expressed through creation/production and media planning well adapted to foreign market needs.

6.2.1   International advertising strategy

Here, we shall only cover situations related to a centralized advertising organization formula; indeed, as for those cases when advertising strategy and creation are delegated to each market, we are only confronted by the addition of the usual national market advertising issues, which should simply be enriched by the necessary dialogue and cooperation between the company and its local representatives.

---

*This is the domain where the most 'special' cases and exceptions for establishing rules can be found.

6.2.1.1   Advertising strategy definition

This operation should start from a synthesis of development strategies and main objectives in priority markets; the largest possible common denominators in all these markets should be isolated at each stage of defining advertising strategy. This should lead to a rather specific general response to each of the following questions (which have deliberately been simplified) for international markets as a whole:

- *Who should the advertising be aimed at?*
  Identification of the major communication target(s);
- *What is the message?*
  Communication content to be transmitted.
- *How?*
  Choice of the most appropriate media to reach the target(s) with such a message.
- *What communication tone should be used?*
  Creative styles fitting both the major target(s) and the appropriate media.
- *What are the investment possibilities?*
  Range of media advertising budgets for each market, whose size will guide the dynamic device selection.
- *What are the constraints?*
  Inventory of rules not to be transgressed on the markets in general, and advertising themes to be avoided so as to be better distinguished from competitors.

If necessary, some of the answers may have to be slightly modified so that the advertising strategy which is defined corresponds well to the international development strategy and is therefore in line with the company's general policy. This particularly applies to activity sectors where it is desirable to keep the same strategic direction for several years. Because of this, some markets might not be quite ready to adhere completely or immediately to the new advertising communication. During a short transition period, different special formulae can be envisaged before these markets enter the ranks of the company's international strategy: temporary use of the preceding campaign's dynamic devices, in parallel with the introduction of the new campaign; initial investment in more non-advertising dynamic devices, with a moderate implication in the new campaign, then a progressive increase in the advertising budget until a satisfactory level is reached.

6.2.1.2   Complementary tactical actions

In the communication organization section, the necessity of sometimes using tactical pull dynamic devices in complement to strategic devices was highlighted; this same situation is found in media advertising, where a few rules have to be respected so as to avoid major dissonances:

■ The synthesis of company market development strategies, which leads to a definition of the international advertising strategy, will also provide the opportunity to detect and assemble similar tactical needs that are not already satisfied by the company strategy. However, it is better not to multiply tactical dynamic devices, as experience proves that their number can be limited.

■ The creation of tactical advertising dynamic devices should, of course, be well adapted to expressed needs, but it should also be complementary to the international advertising strategy, either in the message content and/or the tone.

■ Except for special cases, the strategic dynamic devices should logically benefit from the lion's share of the advertising budget for each market, whereas the tactical dynamic devices only play a secondary, supporting role.

▶ *Air France's advertising strategy, conceived after much exchange among those interested parties (international network executives at headquarters and expatriate local representatives), concentrates on large corporate or product campaigns, which normally take up most of the Air France media budget in each country. However, the local representatives can ask headquarters for a tactical campaign (or carry it out themselves locally) to back up their specific development needs. In this case, the creation will be directed in such a way that this local tactical campaign will produce a maximum synergistic effect with the international strategic campaign being used at the same time. This creative exercise is obviously made easier when a tactical campaign is directly complementary to the current strategic campaign. Thus, at the opening of the Air France Terminal at Roissy-Charles de Gaulle 2, its numerous advantages provided the focus of a major campaign all over the world; in parallel, a tactical campaign was launched in Asia on the theme (which could not be more complementary) of 'Paris, the Gateway to Europe', whose aim was Air France's sales development for passengers flying from this Far Eastern region to any European country, not only to France.*

6.2.1.3   Dissociation from the competition

All competitors' actions are of interest, especially in advertising, where their strategies and effects on the company's target market (as well as on distributors) should be studied closely* before defining any advertising strategy.

Then, one of this strategy's major objectives will be to stand out against the competition, whether it be by an original creation and/

---

*This task should be carried out continually by the local representatives and their advertising agencies.

or media planning, being careful all the same about errors of taste in creation and of targeting mistakes in choosing the media:

▶ *This is what **Potain** carried off successfully, bypassing what was usually done in industrial communication. Adapting the consumer product's more dynamic style to their needs, this company chose a clear, modern communication, both in media advertising (for example, the 'Jackpot' campaign which emphasized the very favourable running costs of their City Cranes) and their printed material.*

The 'Jackpot' campaign develops a message of profit – and not of savings – linked to the purchase of this kind of crane: gain on the price, on the cost of assembly labour, on transportation, on work space needed, on the time necessary to assemble or dismantle this equipment. It was the choice of the winning number!

Standing out against competitors leads the creative process in two directions:

■ If the company is lucky enough to have a product with an unparalleled 'plus', responding to target market expectations, the originality of the creation could be doubly felt in the message content as well as in the tone:

▶ *When the American tennis ball brand **Penn** got in touch with the **Concept Groupe** agency, the problem was how to confirm their position and promote their image as a leader in Europe.*

*The agency's solution was to create a transnational signature (used as a base line): '**Penn**, the Match Ball', and a campaign message, equally transnational: '**Penn** Precision', emphasizing this brand's added product value.*

*The message was diffused through a press campaign in nine languages in 20 countries. It featured those essential technical qualities obtained by **Penn** in the manufacture of their tennis balls for an efficient game.*

*In five years, **Penn** awareness increased considerably, and their image was reinforced in all European countries. Sales volume doubled.*

*The **Concept Groupe** communication set **Penn** apart from their competitors, mainly due to three factors:*

    □ *taking advantage of the synergy created by a brand signature and a campaign message circulated simultaneously in all countries,*

    □ *takeover of a communication 'territory', until then unoccupied by the competition: the technical qualities of a tennis ball (before this campaign, a tennis ball was an ordinary item whose advertising had never emphasized its technology),*

    □ *use of the same visual identity system and codes for colours, graphics, make-up in page form, in all communication expressions: logotype, packaging, press advertisements, POP material, product display units, tournament promotional material, giveaways, press files, etc.*

*The well-orchestrated coordination of actions and the construction of a strong, coherent image contributed to make **Penn** one of the most recognized brands in the world of tennis today.*

■ If the product does not have a decisive 'plus' over its competitors, an essential (even if non-exclusive) product promise is to be reinforced by the originality and strength of the creation's tone.

Finally, it is to be noted when dealing with advertising that not only does the company have to distinguish itself from the competitors, but it also has to avoid using advertising concepts too closely related or largely employed in other professional fields; this is a problem that is particularly complex on a world scale, where really good new ideas are becoming extremely rare. Despite the attention given to this by companies and their advertising agencies, verifying the originality of a campaign in preparation with their representatives in their major markets, there are regularly chance collisions of campaigns with very similar themes, for products in different professional domains; worse still, there are sometimes simultaneous launches of very similar campaigns for directly competitive products.

Given that the complexity of this problem is multiplied by the number of countries where company advertising creation will be applicable, it could be decided to disregard the above and to exploit an efficient theme, even though it has been used* more or less recently in a few markets for non-competitive products.

6.2.1.4   Efficiency rules

Exporters should take into consideration the difference that possibly exists between their home market and other world markets, where they will come up against advertising budgets, of both local and foreign competitor companies, that are substantially higher or lower than they are used to at home.

This gap can be clearly observed by comparing total advertising investments in several countries with their GNP; a parallel comparison of the same countries' advertising budgets per capita provides additional information, together with a few surprises (see Table 6.1).

After these figures, which enable us to assess the importance of advertising levels in different international markets, we shall investigate several more practical principles that can help to ensure the productivity of a media advertising budget:

■ Choose advertising actions in relation to the level of company development in each market. Thus, for example, its distribution level (number and density) is a major element in this choice: in normal market conditions, a national TV advertising campaign is justifiable only with a sufficiently dense distribution network to take advantage of local demand.

---

*Some particularly efficient advertising creations are even consciously copied in various professional fields, and reappear from time to time.

Table 6.1 Compared advertising investments

	Ratio of advertising budget with GNP (1991 in %)	Advertising budget per inhabitant (1991 in $)
Austria	0.62	128
Belgium	0.65	132
Denmark	0.86	207
Finland	0.95	238
France	0.73	153
Germany	0.84	165
Greece	0.84	55
Ireland	0.84	92
Italy	0.63	124
Japan	0.94	258
The Netherlands	1.04	197
Norway	0.79 (1990)	200 (1990)
Portugal	0.78	50
Spain	1.44	192
Sweden	0.76	200
Switzerland	0.94	326
United Kingdom	1.15	204
USA	1.30	292

Source: Philippe Legendre, Surveys Manager, AACC (Association des Agents-Conseil en Communication), 40 bd Malesherbes, 75008 Paris, France. Tel: 33 147 421342.

It would be useful for each company to establish a scale of priorities, which could guide actions in relation to the development stage reached in different markets. Figure 6.2 assembles all media, in a progressive manner, linked to the development of the distribution network. However, this general graph should be adapted further to each professional field, and to each market's specificities.

■ Invest in realistic advertising actions corresponding to the relative size of the available budget for the market. It is known that in the United States, an average consumer product budget for national advertising is between $5 and $10 million. If such a budget cannot be committed, a special strategy will have to be developed to get the most value out of the available investment (see section 6.2.1.5). It could even be possible not to plan any media advertising and still achieve successful sales in retail outlets by combining push dynamic devices, POP materials and promotional actions.

■ Avoid scattering resources: when there are several quality messages, one must resist advertising them all; in the same way, it is necessary to resist the temptation to attack the same target market with all the available media. In both cases this would

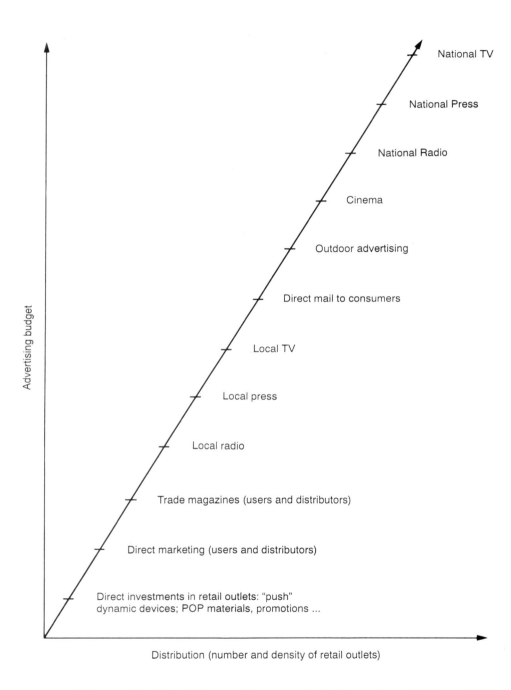

Figure 6.1 Advertising actions ranked in order of theoretical priority, according to the company development stage within distribution networks

require colossal budgets to ensure sufficient impact and recall. Moreover, it can be useful to define an average recall score for major media: if we give the cinema (a medium generally ensuring the best recall) a coefficient of 1 for a 30-second film, TV will follow with a coefficient of 2 for a 30-second spot, then the press with a coefficient of 3 for a full-page ad, and finally, radio with a coefficient of 4 for a 30-second commercial. These very *theoretical* figures indicate the approximate impact of each medium (obviously subject to local variations), and show that in principle, four times more radio commercials are necessary than cinema spots for a person to remember both messages.

■ Plan to have pre-tests done to secure major media investment. When a big advertising campaign is planned, these field test budgets are paltry compared to the cost of buying advertising space, which might be wasted if the message lacks the necessary impact, comprehension, credibility or recall capacities. After a campaign, post-tests will confirm whether the message really got through, and will help make the next campaign even more incisive.

▶ *Thus, after carrying out a market test in Munich, at the end of 1987, before launching blond Gauloise cigarettes in Germany, a communication post-test enabled the **SEITA** to modify the original message 'Heller Tabak-Französisches Flair' (French style clear tobacco). Indeed, there is no specific term to designate blond tobacco in Germany, where all cigarettes are normally blond. This message provided a strong image for the Germans, emphasizing the good French taste. But the product's blondness was not apparent enough, as the awareness of French cigarettes in Germany is directly linked to . . . dark tobacco.*

*Thanks to new tests, a more satisfying base line was successfully used, later on: 'Die andere **Gauloise**-international blend' (the other **Gauloise** international blend); the disappearance of 'French style' probably weakened the image, but the product's 'blondness' was obvious for the Germans, for whom a cigarette with an international flavour can only be blond.*

This example illustrates how important it is to carry out tests before and after launching a campaign. If there is total confidence in the advertising agency in charge of the campaign, the organization of such tests can be left to them. If not, these tests can be entrusted to specialized survey companies.

6.2.1.5 Productivity with small budgets

Since small advertising budgets make up the majority of cases, here are some ways of 'putting a tiger in the tanks':

■ Segment the market to get a better impact from the means committed on the selected target (generally, this segmentation is done geographically, according to distribution channels, or by targetting a more specific market, which allows better media planning, minimizing any waste of investment).

■ Concentrate the budget on certain periods of the year (this should be considered prudently for seasonal products, given that all the competitors will be investing their means during these same periods).

■ Concentrate the budget on the distributors, and/or the market influencers, and/or the trend setters.

■ Concentrate several actions on events gathering clients and/or prospects together (trade fairs, conventions, exhibitions, etc.). Competitors being also very active on these occasions, the effectiveness of such actions will depend on their originality.

■ Give priority to double action messages: for example, those which stimulate the demand of users/consumers as well as distributors' motivation.

▶ *Thus, in markets where demand remains limited, **Peugeot** decided to invest in advertising which concentrated on their distribution network. This kind of message, which emphasizes the technical qualifications and the good geographic coverage of the **Peugeot** network in each country is, of course, greatly appreciated by **Peugeot** agents and contributes to reinforcing their loyalty. It is also a powerful factor which makes the potential clientele feel secure, and consequently facilitates the decision to purchase.*

■ Finally, it can be useful to come back to a point already often mentioned, by a reminder to look for new ways of compensating for a small budget in the force and originality of the messages, and in the means of diffusing them.

*In this way, **Sève International** was able to develop their positions on world markets by using unconventional actions whose cost was minimal compared to that of a classical media advertising campaign: for example, this small company offered to decorate the lobby and restaurant of a big Abu Dhabi hotel with artificial plants and flowers. The very advantageous conditions offered by **Sève International** to this hotel were compensated by the possibility of leaving their 'business card' as a testimonial to this work. The beauty and freshness of these floral arrangements, especially in the Middle Eastern climate, were greatly appreciated by the high ranking officials and businesspersons passing through or staying at the hotel, which had excellent commercial repercussions for **Sève International**.*

6.2.2   Creation advice

As for dynamic device creation, the most difficult problems to solve are found in media advertising, particularly when international communication is centralized, as already mentioned.

The best way of letting each person find his way is not to impose directives that are too strict. It is better to stake out the field of advertising expression with the guidelines which will influence creation, by obliging art departments to slalom between them: advertising strategy with specific company and market requirements, media availability and quality, creation trends and legal constraints.

6.2.2.1   Conformity of creation to strategy

Getting a campaign from an advertising agency whose creation corresponds to expectations supposes that it has been fully briefed (see section 6.1.4.4), and that the two starting points of advertising strategy have been specifically defined (identification of the major target markets, and nature of the message to be transmitted).

This information as a whole is the indispensable basis for advertising creation, as it drives towards what should be the most adapted scope and tone of expression within the wide advertising field:

- corporate or product advertising;
- classic advertising or editorial advertisement;
- rational approach: featuring a promise the product offers to the consumer (supported by reasons-why), comparison, demonstration, additional product information or history... or, emotional approach: suggesting and enhancing a personal relationship of the consumer with the product, whether by seducing, flattering, shocking, reassuring.
- general atmosphere: serious or humorous, classic or modern, city or country, etc;
- visual style: produced by a photograph, a drawing; for a film, classic shooting or special effects; casting of actors, models or characters;
- choice of sound and musical illustration, for audio-visual media, as well as the definition of the voice's 'personality';
- hookline formulation: imperative, advice, question, information, etc.;
- with or without calling for action (response coupon, promotional offer, special price).

The scope and tone of advertising expression are greatly varied, as can be seen in this non-exhaustive panorama, which is fortunate, since constraints imposed by numerous foreign markets tend to limit some of their applications.

6.2.2.2   Media possibilities

Before getting down to international creation work, it is important to rapidly inventory the media possibilities in the markets concerned, to avoid wasting time. All media are not available everywhere: moreover, existing media in some countries are not always compatible with company image and/or standard advertising material.

Even besides the legal constraints that will be dealt with in the section on media planning (see section 6.2.3), other obstacles can lead to abandoning an advertising project. Thus, the production of TV films is not likely to be profitable when broadcast to market segments that are too narrow (example: the Middle East* for many product categories) or when linguistic problems (example: Belgium, Switzerland) fragment the possible audience, rendering the targets too small to balance the size of the investments.

6.2.2.3   Major requirements

The subjective response of each person to an advertising creation makes global evaluation very difficult to perform. It would thus be of interest to consider a project's qualitative criteria one at a time, to be able to carry out an assessment objectively so it can lead to improvements; in the case of centralized communication, the same approach is advised to 'sell' a campaign project to the local representatives' executives, with better chances of avoiding rejection motivated solely by personal taste (this phenomenon is generally referred to as NIH (Not Invented Here), often expressed by such reactions: 'No, I don't like it! . . .', or more subtly, 'Sorry, it will never catch on here!'), and of managing to convince them to use the campaign confidently.

These qualitative criteria correspond, of course, to various requirements which are adhered to by advertising agencies in their creative work:

- ■ conformity to the company's advertising strategy;
- ■ message clarity: concept universality (except in cases where the country of origin image has to be emphasized);
- ■ adaptability to major markets (creation constraints and media possibilities);
- ■ force of impact** (effectiveness of the ad to attract and hold people's attention);
- ■ concept exclusivity, originality and durability;
- ■ message credibility, power of persuasion and incitement to act;
- ■ satisfactory level of message recall (and not only concept recall, whose brilliance often eclipses even the brand and the product too!).

---

*This problem of profitability is one of the reasons why many TV ads used in the Middle East are shot in neighbouring countries (Greece, Cyprus, India) which offer very competitive production costs.
**It is useful to break down the impact quality of the main project's components; for example, in a press advertisement, hookline, illustration, body copy, base line.

► *As an example of an international campaign responding strongly to these criteria as a whole, in addition to those already mentioned, the **Benetton** 'United Colours' and 'United Fashions' campaigns can be cited, which have, moreover, won several professional awards, such as the European Advertising Oscar (these are obviously the campaigns launched in the 1980s, not the more controversial early 1990s ones). Besides other qualities, their proclaimed universalism can particularly be emphasized, which is expressed as an ideal or profession of faith. As the **Benetton** Marketing Director explains[2], 'The United Colours campaign, which gathers young people of all races, was conceived to promote an image of colours without borders and without racial discrimination; an image of peace and harmony.'*

Beyond the assessment of advertising creation according to these qualitative criteria, it is worth carrying out tests (whose cost usually represents about 2% or 3% of the overall budget) before and after a campaign launch, as illustrated in this example:

► *In 1987, the Swedish group **SKF** adopted a differentiation strategy, proposed by their consultant Michaël Porter, to establish a durable competitive advantage within the ball bearing market (of which they were already the world leader).*

*This strategic orientation enables **SKF** to set themselves apart on a world scale, by adapting their structure to that of their markets.*

	Market	*SKF*
Market 1	*Standard 1st assemblage*	*SKF Industry*
Market 2	*Standard spare parts*	*SKF Distribution*
Market 3	*Special bearings*	*SKF Special Bearings*

*As a result, the **SKF** company divided themselves into two or three independent companies according to the country; in France, **SKF** split into two companies, **SKF Industry** and **SKF Distribution**.*

*Then, **SKF** gave their communication agency, **MGTB Ayer Enterprise***, the mission to launch **SKF Distribution** and to give them a recognized personality rapidly. For Jacques Bely, president of MGTB Ayer, the path was narrow: 'They had to set themselves apart, while at the same time remaining in the **SKF** family, respect the company culture while bringing in a new tone, and still explain this strategic orientation. This is why the agency developed a rigorous methodological approach to ensure a smooth transition' (see Figure 6.2).*

---

*A department of **MGTB Ayer**, 20th largest French agency, associated with the American group **Ayer**, which is the 15th largest world network.

*As François Mandroux (General Manager of MGTB Ayer Enterprise)
explains: 'the first phase was necessarily informative, both for the agency
and for the company's internal communication. The matter was to explain
what a strategy of differentiation is, how it was to be implemented and what
SKF Distribution could get out of it. Then, the creative phase could get
started.*

*After defining the scope of communication expression, we organized a
meeting of SKF middle staff, which was conducted by a psycho-sociologist.
This procedure enabled us to test and verify the perception and comprehension of the information transmitted internally by SKF.*

*This verification being carried out, the agency was then able to inject into
the group the message axis (see Figure 6.3) and their creative expression.
Tested and enriched internally within the company, the message axis retained
by SKF Distribution (people/field) was reworked by the agency to come up
with the initial campaign. This first active phase gave priority to the people
working at SKF Distribution, as well as their desire to provide the market
with 'bearings without problems'. This act of faith is illustrated by the sign
OK which is shown as a rallying symbol on all the internal and external
communication visuals'.*

*A few months after the campaign, the agency went into a control phase,
followed by a correction phase.*

*The post-test results seemed positive, as much for samples of users and
non-users of SKF products, as for SKF Distribution personnel: SKF Distribution had forged their own personality, well perceived by internal
and external targets. 'However, existing isn't enough' continues François
Mandroux, 'and these tests showed us that we had to explain even more
clearly the vocation of SKF Distribution, as well as their mission. Then,
we found ourselves face to face with a real problem of content and information. We had six messages to communicate: SKF Distribution are in
the replacement part business, offer their clients a complete product range,
benefit from solid logistics backup, have an efficient distribution network,
ensure quality maintenance and plan on entering the car industry. As a
result, the retained communication approach can be drawn as shown in
Figure 6.5.*

*This strategic choice was turned into a communication creation aimed
internally as well as externally, joining two opposite approaches together:*

■ ***The emotional:*** *the creation of an imaginary character, the detective
Bill Rolling, on a secret mission: to discover SKF Distribution's reason
for existing. The mission's presentation medium: a comic strip.*

■ ***The rational:*** *each scenario of the comic strip finished with the hero's
investigative report, explaining SKF Distribution's vocation.*

*To this innovative procedure was grafted an original media investment. On
the agency's recommendation, SKF Distribution bought up all the space
in the July 1988 issue of* L'Usine Nouvelle *(an industrial magazine), to
publish all the Bill Rolling adventures.*

*The results of this double campaign, whose impact and effects were care-
fully tested at each decisive step with internal and external targets, are
eloquent: even before all the actions were committed (the* Usine Nouvelle
action, particularly), the sales figures for the first six months in 1988 had

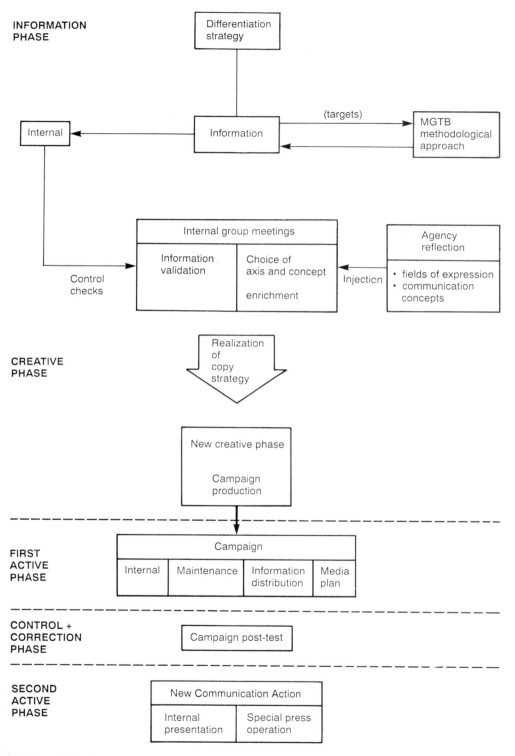

Figure 6.2   Methodological structure for launching SKF Distribution

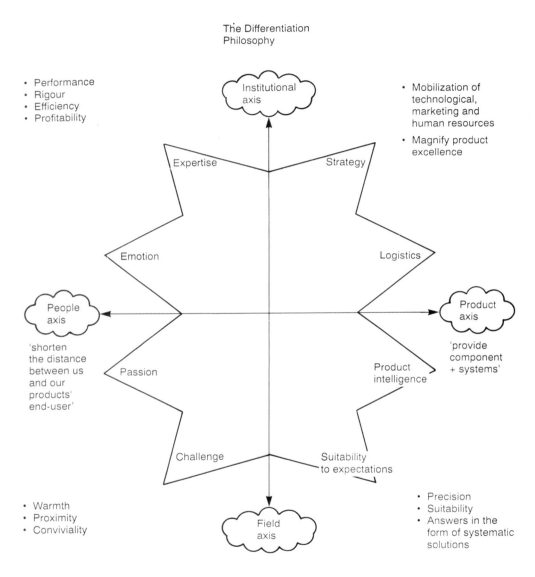

Figure 6.3   SKF's message axis

*increased by 19% in comparison to 1987, that's to say, 4% higher than the already very ambitious objectives set by **SKF Distribution.***'

The excellent synergy of internal and external communication can be observed in this example. It is a pity that so many companies do not take advantage of their advertising campaigns to mobilize all their personnel with these messages, which are sometimes misunderstood when discovered unexpectedly in the press or another medium. On the contrary, the personnel (who are the first prescribers of their company's products) should systematically get a preview of advertising campaigns, with all the necessary explanations. This can be done almost at no cost by the usual channels of internal communication, or – for strategic reasons – by a special internal communication operation.

6.2.2.4   International creation trends

Creation trends in each market are influenced by an unbelievable cocktail of factors – profound or superficial, stable or changeable, among which can be mentioned the nature, degree of evolution and size of the market; media possibilities, the size of advertising investments; legal restrictions, means of production; possible communication particularities linked to socio-cultural customs, as well as linguistic codes and even local fashion trends in advertising creation.

Under these conditions, it is impossible to draw up guidelines or a trend map to influence the preparation of international advertising communication: there are too many differences to take them all into account, and these trends can evolve very quickly.

Thus, we come back to the point that advertising creation* should basically avoid extremes, without necessarily trying to follow specific trends on major markets; the objective is to make company products stand out in positive comparison to the main international competitors.

Nevertheless, here are a few examples of advertising creation trends on a few markets, with quite diverging characteristics:

■ In France, the sophistication of messages, their often humorous style and aesthetic value aim at entertaining or creating fantasy more than informing the audience. Because of this, French creations have a hard time crossing borders, as can be observed by comparing two similar messages applied to the same consumer product, an electric battery:

---

*Reminder: this, of course, applies to centralized communication.

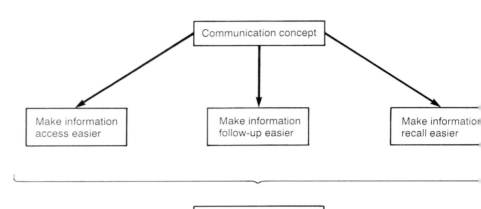

Figure 6.5   MGTB Enterprise's communication plan for SKF Distribution

▶   *Mazda emphasizes the long life of their batteries by putting them to work in a torture device, which forces various characters to listen to endless high-decibel music in a sinister torture chamber. In many countries, most people would take this message literally, and retain a negative product image, associating the brand with pain (unlike the French, who considered this dramatic ad tone as humour, and recalled the long lasting 'plus' of Mazda batteries).*

▶   *The Duracell message also deals with long life, but is more easily transposable for international markets: fluffy rabbits are seen (emotionally a strong childhood image), with their movements driven by electric batteries. They all stop moving after some time, because their batteries are dead, except the Duracell-powered rabbit (very effective rational information). This emotional/rational cocktail obviously appears adapted to consumers of all nationalities.*

■   In Germany, the role of advertising is not to attract or entertain, but rather to inform and explain. Through advertising messages, German consumers want to inform themselves, and compare the advantages of products and services they are thinking of buying. Hence, a very rational and informative message form, whose particularly dense body copy dominates the visual aspect.

- The emphasis on price gives the curious impression that we have come full circle in advertising creation, since the markets where this is most observed are found at both extremities of advertising sophistication: the United States and developing countries.

- Creation evolution in the United States deserves a few observations less superficial than certain notorious characteristics, such as the omnipresence of the jingle in audio-visual advertising. After being the Mecca of the world advertising creation, it seems that the US has lost some of its predominance in this field, to the benefit of Europe (the UK in particular). This can be explained to a large extent by the all powerful American marketing research, which imposes impact or recall standards to accept or reject creation, tending to favour short-term effects; creation is thus limited to middle-of-the-road scopes and tones which seriously level out more subtle communication.

  The relative banality of American advertising, together with advertising's invasion of all media (except the cinema), explains the public's lassitude, one of the driving forces of cable television's success.

- Japanese advertising agencies do not have any such worries: the public there is still receptive and well disposed to advertising, which is nevertheless omnipresent in the country. After being submitted to the strong influence of American creation trends since the post-war period, Japanese advertising now has a more national style, with a return to traditional expression (a form dominated by the spontaneity of the messages, which are not very aggressive towards competitors: the public's comprehension and confidence are sought, in a harmonious atmosphere). The American creative influence is, however, still discernible, as well as that of Europe, which is more recent.

6.2.2.5   Legal restrictions

Legal restrictions are imposed on advertising creation in very different ways according to the country. There are four main restriction areas which apply directly to products, themes, form or origin of the creation. Just a few examples are given here, since frequent changes make it necessary to check on the legislation in force before investing again in creation-production, especially in traditionally restricted fields.

Some countries forbid or limit advertising on various product categories; the most affected are tobacco, alcohol, pharmaceutical products and certain kinds of services; also, these constraints sometimes differ according to the type of media.

Similarly, representing certain themes or characters is regulated or even censured in many countries: women, children, religion, politics and violence, in particular.

These restriction types, applied to creation, can be extremely varied:

▶ *In Spain, all references and incitations to speed are forbidden in automobile advertising. The words 'holy' or 'sacred' are not to be used in this market, so as not to provoke hostile reactions on the part of a traditionally Catholic population, who would be shocked by their involvement in an advertising campaign.*

▶ *In Austria, a film showing a car driving on a beach was considered to be an attack on environmental protection.*

▶ *In the UK, advertisements for alcoholic beverages cannot present people under 25 drinking.*

The message form can also be specifically restricted, as illustrated by the following examples:

▶ *Comparative advertising, used a lot in the USA but still forbidden in many countries, enables a company to position a product by comparing it to another, obviously chosen from among the product leaders.*

▶ *The use of certain expression forms: in Canada, advertising cartoons are illegal because they exercise too strong an influence on children.*

Finally, it should be noted that some countries, like Australia, regulate the use of advertising material (film, photographs, etc.) not made in the country so as to protect local advertising agencies and production companies.

Advertising control is generally administered by supervisory viewing or censorship commissions, whose decisions form a sort of jurisprudence. These commissions are often assisted by autodisciplinary professional associations, made up of advertising agencies, advertisers and media representatives.

6.2.3   Media selection

Obviously, media planning is the key factor, both in foreign and home markets, to get the most out of advertising investment by transmitting the message with precision and force to the selected target segment . . . at the lowest cost.

Foreign markets, however, present specific difficulties due to the fact that not all countries offer the same media possibilities; moreover, the image, audience and tariffs of each medium vary greatly from one market to another, often making a different media selection necessary to reach the targeted clientele.

Sometimes, as well, the lack of really controllable media in some countries leads advertisers to use international means:

▶ *For example, covering a wide part of the Middle East by using Radio Monte Carlo, which broadcasts in Arabic from Cyprus. In these countries, difficult to penetrate with classical advertising actions, this solution offers both good market penetration and the possibility of real control.*

6.2.3.1   Media planning organization

For an appropriate selection to be made, according to a really effective media plan, it is worth checking how seriously the local representatives take this operation, and how closely they work with their advertising agencies:

■ The media planners should attend the agency's briefing (see sections 6.2.2.1 and 6.1.4.4) so they can become familiar with the advertising strategy elements that will directly condition their search for the best adapted media, given the target market, the message form to be transmitted, the coverage period, the approximate budget size planned on, etc.

■ The media plan's preparation has to be carried out in tandem with the creation, given that a creative idea's force or style can be expressed better with one medium than with another, thus influencing the final choice to be determined for each market:

▶ *In this way, the very visual style of **Waterman** advertisements (see section 6.1.2.4) expresses itself strongly in outdoor advertising; however, this French brand can only use it within a limited number of export markets (Belgium, Germany, Italy and the UK, particularly). Elsewhere, posters do not lend themselves well to luxury product presentations, or their location is unsatisfactory, in terms of visibility and density, to achieve sufficient impact.*

■ At the moment of assessing the selection possibilities, before deciding upon the definitive media plan it is best to give priority to those which bring a certain originality to the communication with the target market, especially if the budget is low compared to that of competitors; in such a case, the choice of traditional media (which are often the most expensive) might lessen the effects of a too limited number of message repeats, in the middle of competitors' advertisements.

■ More generally, innovation in media selection often generates good results if it produces a better impact on the targeted clientele without provoking negative repercussions*; for example, this is what was verified by perfume brands who audaciously were the first to advertise in the austere Anglo-Saxon financial dailies before Christmas and Mother's Day.

▶ *The same goes for **Grand Marnier**, who voluntarily include a good dose of innovation in their media cocktails, as International Director Philippe Revenu confirms: 'For our advertising campaigns, we want to add a few original media to the traditional ones. So, in 1986, for the Vancouver World's Fair, we managed to get the advertising space exclusivity on the electric trains transporting visitors in the Fair. This highly visible medium hit 13 million people, most of them North Americans – a priority market for **Grand Marnier**. As for the other visitors from the rest of the world, the cost of the trip to Vancouver obviously situated them in the income brackets which could potentially consume an up-market liqueur. This unconventional medium, whose impact was reinforced during the Fair by **Grand Marnier** tastings, proved to be of a particularly favorable cost/effectiveness.'*

▶ *In the early 1970s in North Yemen, **Moulinex** went even further by convincing local television managers that TV advertising could be profitable. One of the Yemeni television directors, a newcomer to advertising, who was already delighted to be offered a film, found it strange that **Moulinex** even proposed paying for this broadcast! Consequently, the inauguration of commercial spots by **Moulinex** on Yemeni screens was obviously quite noticeable, and helped make the French brand market leader.*

■ After deciding on the media plan and budget, when space buying is being negotiated, executives can sometimes get a better deal for their company, as a multinational advertiser, in the international media possibly selected.
■ Finally, the media plan's actual implementation has to be checked on, both in terms of quantity and quality, as well as the preferred positions and any other special advantages which might have been specifically negotiated at the moment of purchase.

6.2.3.2   Media evaluation criteria

In most developed countries, a clear media sophistication can be observed, as well as the appearance of new media which come from high technology: satellites, cable, electronic information services. In parallel, the media information means on these markets are progressing spectacularly along three main lines:

■ better definition of audience composition (socio-economic criteria, lifestyles, etc.);

---

*For instance, in countries where outdoor advertising is considered as a mass-market medium, using posters for luxury product brands will be noticed, but it might alienate their traditional clientele.

- a finer approach to the relationship between each individual and the media (place of each medium in daily life; thus, for example, different radio listening times for people driving their cars, women working at home, etc.);
- more precise media comparative analysis concerning their content: qualitative and quantitative studies of advertising and non-advertising contents.

Outside these developed countries, as a contrast, the exporter can only experience the difficulty in finding trustworthy information allowing him to assess the media, even when his local representative benefit from a well-established local advertising agency's help.

Consequently, it is useful to have an inventory of major media assessment criteria that can help to avoid overlooking any of the rare available information on the markets, so as to be able to draw up a media shortlist responding to essential needs:

- *Audience*: size, specific characteristics, stability, seasonality, lifestyles, time available; possibility of tests and complementary studies.
- *Profile*: does the media audience suit the company's target? Degree of adaptation to the strategic objective (according to the case, to inform, familiarize, compare, remind, overcome resistance, make secure, make credible, make the product stand out), and to the form (quality requirements) as well as the message type (an event, a technical argument, for example).
- *Coverage*: audience of a medium expressed as a theoretical percentage of the target market (households, companies, etc.).
- *Repetition*, or average frequency: adequate number of contacts to be directed towards the target, according to the media type.
- *Speed* of message penetration, on which depends market response rapidity.
- *GRP number* (Gross Rating Points): in more and more countries, it is becoming possible to assess a media plan according to GRP points (number of exposures to 100 individuals, or 100 people from the target market).
- *Recall factor*: the theoretical average mentioned previously (see section 6.2.1.4) has to be readjusted to correspond to the situation observed in each market and will be a valuable indication in calculating the frequency to plan on for each medium.
- *Attrition factor* (message life span): optimum message life expectancy, which can vary according to medium; in most markets, the cinema 'wears out' commercials more slowly than television, whose penetration is much faster.
- *Medium source effect*: in every country each medium has its own image (serious, classic, trendy, etc.), and executives should look for those media which can give the best credibility and reinforce their message towards the specific target market. Here can be included the importance of vicinity (preferred positions opposite

Table 6.2 Major media investment evolution (percentages of total media investment per country) (NK = not known)

	Year	Press	TV	Radio	Outdoor	Cinema
Austria	1980	53.6	33.1	13.3	NK	NK
	1991	54.6	26.1	12.2	7.1	NK
Belgium	1980	75	8.3	0.3	14.6	1.8
	1991	53.6	28.6	3.9	12.6	1.3
Denmark	1980	96.4	-	-	2.3	1.3
	1991	80.7	17.3*	*	2	*
Finland	1980	83.6	14	-	2.2	0.2
	1991	77.5	15.5	4.3	2.6	0.1
France	1980	60	14.3	10.03	14	1.4
	1991	53.7	27.2	6.5	12.0	0.6
Germany	1980	80.7	10.5	3.8	4	0.9
	1991	74.1	17	4.3	3.5	1.1
Greece	1980	44	49.6	6.4	NK	NK
	1991	39.7	55	5.3	NK	NK
Ireland	1980	55.2	33.4	10.8	NK	0.6
	1991	50.2	31.3	11.2	7.3	NK
Italy	1980	57.6	26.7	6.9	6.8	2
	1991	40.9	50.9	3.3	4.7	0.2
Japan	1980	48	45.3	6.7	NK	NK
	1991	40.2	38.9	5.6	15.3	NK
The	1980	84.7	7.8		7	0.5
Netherlands	1991	67.9	16		15.8	0.3
Norway	1980	97.6	0	0	1.4	1
	1990	93	2.6	1	2.2	1.2
Portugal	1982	26	54.4	15.4	4.3	NK
	1991	37.8	43.4	7.6	11.2	NK
Spain	1980	47	32	12.2	6.3	1.6
	1991	52.8	29.9	10.8	5.6	0.9
Sweden	1980	95.7	0	0	3.7	0.6
	1991	90.4	4.6	NK	4.4	0.6
Switzerland	1980	85	8	0	6	1
	1991	77.7	6.9	2.0	12.5	0.9
United	1980	62.8	29.5	2.3	4.6	0.8
Kingdom	1991	58.5	34.6	2.2	4.1	0.6
USA	1980	53.4	33.9	11.2	1.7	NK
	1991	49.9	37.1	11.5	1.5	NK

*17.3% = TV, radio and cinema

a specific heading in the press; broadcast time on TV or radio, chosen according to the best program to be associated with).

■ *Competitive environment*: it can be reassuring to appear in the same media as the competitors; moreover, there is often no choice, although it can seem that the company message may get lost in the crowd. But with a bit of luck and patience, a miracle medium can sometimes be found which offers a good target market coverage, and corresponds well to overall needs, including that of being set apart from the competitors.

■ *Cost*: (at last!): has to be considered on two levels: both the gross cost and the cost per thousand targeted readers, listeners or viewers, to compare media charges and assess their cost-effectiveness; negotiated possibilities should also be compared (space, time, volume, discounts, etc.).

6.2.3.3   Compared international media potential

Table 6.2 shows the relative importance, over 10 years, of the major media in 18 countries; although too general to provide direct relevance for practical purposes, it presents quite interesting comparisons.

Despite the diverse situations of the major media throughout the world, certain general characteristics can be observed which are found in almost all markets, to which will be added a few particularities interesting enough to be mentioned:

■ *Daily press*
Daily newspapers are very flexible in their use: short-term space purchase; possible geographic selection in many countries by choosing national or regional papers; good general coverage; highspeed penetration inducing a possible very rapid market response.

Major drawbacks: a precise audience selection is possible only with few specialized dailies; life-span normally limited to one day; messages wear out rapidly; limited reproduction possibilities due to a mediocre printing quality and the rare use of colours; these characteristics explain why this medium is more largely used throughout the world for event-type ads (special offers, new products, etc.) than for image campaigns.

▶   *In the USA, where three out of four Americans buy a newspaper every day, the dailies go from a few dozen pages during the week to a few hundred on Sundays, with 80% or 90% of the space covered in ads . . . the daily press is the priority medium for retail selling.*

■ *Magazines*
In many countries there is a wide enough magazine choice* to find some which have an audience corresponding closely to the sought-after target market; good quality reproduction and general use of colour which makes the product stand out satisfactorily; the message life-span is long and there are often 'late effects' due to second readings and the passing of the magazine from one person to another.

Among the drawbacks for magazines, there is a slow market response; the lead-time needed for space purchase and handing in printing documents; the difficulty in obtaining a high frequency, except with several insertions in the same issue; a very average adaptation to a demonstration (in comparison with television).

▶ *More than daily newspapers, the number of magazines confirms the level of market development: no surprise, then, at the incredible magazine proliferation in the USA, which covers all lifestyles as well as the most obscure industrial sectors and professional services (often associated with the organization of the traditional annual business convention).*

■ *Television*
This powerful mass penetration medium can ensure almost immediate market stimulation, somewhat variable according to the country; the product can stand out, and demonstrations are highly convincing.

Its high cost and the difficulty in selecting a specific audience, despite certain programming possibilities, make TV a medium chiefly adapted to mass consumer products. There are other drawbacks: generally, a long lead-time is necessary for air-time purchase, and messages wear out easily. More than 100 countries now accept television advertising, the most recent noteworthy stronghold to open up being Eastern Europe. Logically, this medium has a stronger influence on audiences of countries where it has been more recently introduced.

▶ *If we come back to the United States for a moment, as the extreme standard of comparison, a clear lassitude on the part of the public can be observed (cable TV equips about 70% of American households), and advertising executives have to take into consideration the loss of a percentage of the audience during the commercial breaks, who go off about their business, only coming back to the TV when the program starts up again (this is referred to under the generic name of the 'flush' factor)**; another major cause for audience evasion are remote control devices, which allow viewers to zap back and forth between channels to their hearts' content.*

---

*Not to be forgotten are other printed media, such as yearbooks, almanacs, 'phone directories, and guides in certain professional sectors, especially for services.
**A poetic evocation of the massive migration of TV viewers who take advantage of commercials to visit the bathroom.

■ *Radio*

This medium provides a rapid market response, and reaches a large audience, particularly in developing countries where television is not yet strongly established and the press is ineffective because of a low literacy level; its cost is generally affordable, permitting a regular message frequency; the existence of regional and local radio makes geographic audience segmentation easier.

Not very selective in audience terms, radio does not benefit from steady attention, and the absence of visual aids considerably reduces the recall factor. This medium then, is better suited to event-type advertising rather than image campaigns.

▶ *The importance of radio advertising differs greatly from one country to another, without necessarily having anything to do with their level of development: in the UK, radio seems to be a recent, local medium, often used for promotional actions; in the United States, as in France, radio has been established for a long time, and exemplary campaigns have ensured the success of products in the most varied categories; in Mexico, radio is in second position, far behind television, but this medium is considered to have an excellent cost effectiveness for mass market campaigns (95% of Mexicans own a radio, whereas only 80% a TV). In the Middle East, where radio is very popular, it is often advisable to deal with pan-Arab stations (RMC in Cyprus, for example) which offer the advantage of having a large audience simultaneously in most of the region's countries. This simplifies air-time purchase.*

■ *Cinema*

The cinema most often ensures a very good quality product presentation; the possibility of selecting the audience varies greatly from country to country; recall is very good thanks to the audience's relative 'captive' receptivity.

The coverage and penetration are quite slow with this medium, whose cost per thousand spectators is generally high. In any case, air-time purchase can be long and difficult in countries where the movie theatres are not managed by a small number of distributors.

▶ *The absence of flexibility and the immensely variable importance of this medium in different countries make it difficult to use for international campaigns: thus, for example, cinema advertising is very weak in the UK, almost non-existent in Scandinavia and the United States, and limited to local advertisements in Japan.*

■ *Outdoor advertising*

Outdoor advertising provides good geographic flexibility, high frequency, and makes the product stand out.

The audience selection possibilities are obviously very limited, and force of impact is ensured only with visually strong messages. This medium's brevity of exposure time per passage by a poster (6–8 seconds) has to give priority, logically, to simple and clear communication.

▶ *Like the cinema, outdoor advertising is not an easy medium to use for international campaigns. Regulations vary greatly from one country to another; also, local usage of this medium can strongly 'categorize' it: in many markets, the almost exclusive use of posters for mass market products makes it dangerous to use for luxury products whose image might be seriously deteriorated. Posters often have the advantage of a weak competitive environment, except in major city centres, and in certain countries like Japan, where illuminated signs are reaching a saturation point and consequently have less impact. In the Middle East, posters have been established strongly for a long time due to the underdevelopment of other media; there have even been foreign public works or heavy equipment companies using this medium to develop their awareness, and literally fighting over positions and sites in the neighbourhoods where all the Ministries are located. After this unbridled development, poster use is now settling down to normal in this part of the world.*

▶ *Apart from posters, there are a few small budget outdoor dynamic devices which can be very effective for developing brand awareness: in Australia, IPEC used a stationary balloon in their colours a few dozen metres above their agencies as a fixed advertisement; some companies use the inactive periods of their fleets* to organize small parades of a few trucks or vans; parking an unused truck in certain highly frequented places (roundabouts, intersections, bridges crossing over motorways) can stimulate brand awareness at an unbeatable cost.*

■ *Direct marketing*
According to the techniques used and existing possibilities – extremely varied according to the country – it can be a matter of another communication medium and/or a direct distribution network (particularly direct mail advertising or telephone, fax and computer selling, catalogue sales, direct sales transmitted by the classic media).

Direct marketing techniques, especially direct mail and 'phone selling, can provide an effective communication with a well targeted audience, as well as geographic flexibility; they also furnish a timetable tailored to needs, quite a rapid market response, and a very precise results analysis.

Direct mail or 'phone selling penetration and coverage cannot be compared to those of media having a huge audience that we have just enumerated; these latter media cannot, then, be used as primary media in a campaign for mass market products, but rather as tactical support**. In this form, such techniques are to

---

*On this subject, it has to be mentioned that too many companies neglect effective communication opportunities which come from 'decorating' their vehicles to be used as mobile posters.
**Concerning consumer products, direct mail is not addressed by name, but often in the form of more massive direct advertising: handbill distribution in the streets, in large meeting places (fairs, sports events), in letterboxes, etc.

be applied particularly to products whose potential clientele can be identified with precision, such as professionals*, distributors, or highly targeted consumer categories. It goes without saying that these actions can only be considered in countries where there exist recent and trustworthy files of targeted consumer categories, and whose postal service operates satisfactorily!

▶ *This is the case in the United States, where computer files and databases have reached an unbelievable precision in target definition: companies by activity type, turnover, number of employees, etc. Consumers by social/ professional categories, by purchase type, etc. Moreover, consumer defence organizations are opposed to this growing deluge of direct mail (annual average of 250 pieces per person compared to less than 50 in France) by demanding each person's right to get himself crossed off these files. In Japan, major media saturation has favoured the growth of direct mail and mail order. In Sweden, the long absence of TV and radio advertising was compensated for by direct marketing (25% of total advertising expenses). In developing countries where other media do not always provide satisfactory communication, it is possible to send direct mail to potential clients, identified by index or 'phone directories; but it is better to send the mail directly to their post office boxes rather than to their personal addresses, given post office distribution problems that exist in most countries.*

▶ *The **Doublet** company has been using direct marketing since 1982, sending out 100 000 catalogues per year, translated into seven languages, to three different continents. This communication action's commercial follow-up can be ensured in record time, despite the distances, thanks to a systematic use of fax, and to computer-managed technology for the flag manufacturing procedures (computer assisted conception, laser cutters, programmable robots). 'Using fax enables us to reduce delivery time considerably,' explains Luc Doublet. 'Thus, we can make delivery to our Japanese clients four days after receiving the order of a model to be made.'*

6.2.3.4   Legal restrictions

Given the constant legislation evolution in each country, regulations, limitations, possible duty on advertising in different media, this book cannot precisely list all this information, much of which will be out of date by the time it is published.

However, it is useful to illustrate the variety of constraints so as to emphasize the importance of making sure, with the local representatives and advertising agencies concerned, that it is possible to under-

---

*As for direct mail to companies, it is important to have the name of the person concerned by the product, so that a personally addressed letter can be sent to him, otherwise there is very little chance of the letter reaching its destination. In the case of a small targeted clientele, 'phone selling can be effective in parallel or in place of the direct mail to prepare for the sales force's intervention.

take any advertising action *before* committing any investment to creation and production.

▶ *In countries with 'open' economies, examples of media where all advertising is prohibited have become rare. Still, TV and radio advertising has been authorized only from 1990 in Sweden, and radio advertising from 1992 in Norway.*

Different kinds of limitations for media use can be observed: particularly, a strict broadcast time limitation for TV and radio advertisements exists in many countries; commercial interdiction on television during the weekend in Germany, very strict ethical code for advertising in children's magazines in Denmark, a minimum distance of 100 metres between posters presenting the same message in Germany, etc.

There can also be constraints concerning the presentation of certain product types according to the media; usually TV and radio are affected the most.

▶ *For example: alcohol and tobacco advertising is becoming illegal in more and more countries; pharmaceutical product advertising is not allowed in Greece, nor bank ads in Japan; in Holland, children cannot perform in TV commercials for candy and sweets, and these ads must have a toothbrush shown as a guest star.*

These legal constraints become even more arduous when restrictions appear unexpectedly, making a rapid media adaptation necessary:

▶ *'A few days before launching **Löwenbräu** in Turkey' remembers Dr. Johann Daniel Gerstein, 'a new law made all beer advertising on TV and radio illegal. To confront this situation, we developed a four-part strategy with our agent:*

- *As posters were still permitted, we used this medium widely, trying to occupy the key sites all over the country, especially in the main cities.*
- *In addition, we used an original medium which is quite important in Turkey: video films which are watched by the whole family, on which we were able to include an advertising film.*
- *To reinforce this campaign we organized press conferences to make our beer's features known, so as to take advantage of positive editorial support.*
- *Then we decided that these measures were not enough to get us the level of brand awareness we wanted; this is why we developed a **Löwenbräu** beer without alcohol (see section 4.4.2.2) whose television and radio advertising was possible, to broadcast the **Löwenbräu** name widely to the public. It is the totality of these actions which enabled us finally to get firmly established in Turkey, despite the difficulties encountered at the beginning.'*

6.3   Other Advertising Tools

After media advertising we take a look at the international adaptation of other advertising dynamic devices: some, like merchandising and point-of-purchase (POP) material, are essentially applicable to consumer products as well as to a limited number of capital goods and services; others, such as the various applications of sales literature, concern all fields of activity.

6.3.1   Merchandising and POP material

Merchandising, as well as its major component POP material, can take many varied forms according to the product types, but their basic function is to attract attention, to make products stand out, to inform, to convince. This is clearly confirmed in an Anglo-Saxon definition of POP material, which is considered as a 'silent salesman'; this old formula has now been left behind by technical progress, since POP signs and displays which move, produce sounds or provide audio-visual presentations have become common in most world markets. There is even POP equipment capable of having a dialogue with customers.

▶   ***Philip Morris*** *use a robot (called Philip, of course, who resembles a character from* Star Wars*) in high potential retail outlets, essentially airport duty free shops, to stimulate sales. Philip takes the initiative in striking up conversations with people, to convince them to buy **Philip Morris** 'Super Lights'.*

6.3.1.1   Potential and limits

It is considered on the average that purchase decisions for usual consumer items are made in retail outlets up to 50% (even 60%) of the time, according to the country and the product type. This includes impulse buying and changes in purchase intentions provoked by the attraction of one product, the absence of the desired product (not available or not visible), or the influence of the sales personnel.

▶   *A study carried out in the United States by the Point of Purchase Advertising Institute (**POPAI**) reveals that 66.1% of consumer purchases correspond to a decision made in the retail outlet. The figure was 64.8% in 1977.*

   Of these figures, impulse buying represents 52.6% instead of 47%. But what this American study really indicates is that the association of POP displays and media advertising can almost triple the chances for a product to be purchased.

All this reinforces POP material defenders, who emphasize the fact that this advertising form intervenes when the client is in the retail outlet, in front of the display, about to buy something; this is one of the rare moments when the client is not only open to advertising and product information, but is actually looking for them.

▶   *A comparative study on the average cost of 'productive contact' was carried out in 1986 by the **POPAI**, for 1000 exposures (opportunities to see or to hear):*

Magazine	*$16.55 (full-page in colour)*
TV	*$2 to $10 (30-second commercial, according to broadcasting time)*
Daily Press	*$10.83 (full-page)*
Radio	*$6.53 (30-second commercial)*
POP display	*$0.05 to $0.10 (a cardboard floor display)*

▶   *Another interesting view about POP material effectiveness should logically come from retailers. The results of a more recent study (1988) conducted by **POPAI** in the United States in various types of outlets show very similar support to those recorded by a 1990 study of French pharmacies, made by **POPAI** Europe*:*

Question: How effective are manufacturer-supplied point of purchase signs and displays in increasing sales?

Answers in the USA: (cumulative of 'extremely, very and somewhat effective') given by the store level managers: supermarkets 96%; convenience stores 94%; home improvement stores 93%; liquor stores and chain drug stores 92%; mass merchandisers 88%.

Answers in France: given by pharmacists, produce a 95% global effectiveness factor for POP material.

With these figures and the preceding remarks, it would be tempting to do away with all media advertisement! This would be a hasty reaction, as only common, everyday products and/or impulse purchase products can be sold with an exclusive POP pull, without any other dynamic device reinforcement. In fact, POP material is much more effective when it reactivates, on the client's part, the effects of previous contacts with the brand and product, particularly through media advertising and/or public relations (also when it serves as a salesperson's product presentation aid).

■   confronted with multiple POP displays for competitive products

---

*These figures were kindly released by Michel Devin, Chairman of POPAI Europe; this promotion centre for point of purchase advertising, launched in 1986, now gathers professionals from a dozen European countries. Contact: POPAI Europe, 5 rue Cochin, 75005 Paris. Tel: 33 146 333093.

in a retail outlet, a client is naturally attracted by brands he has already had a visual relationship with (thus, the importance of visual unity for media advertising and POP material).

■ A positive previous relationship with the brand and product helps the client justify his purchase decision; the bigger the purchase, the more necessary this 'seen before' guarantee becomes.

■ For all products which are said, rightly or wrongly, to reflect or influence the image of their owner (clothes, fashion accessories, cars, etc.), it is a must (!) that their featuring in the retail outlet be preceded by a certain recognition that will reassure the client in his choice: 'It's a product which is talked about' ... better still, if the POP material reminds the potential purchaser of an advertising message he enjoyed identifying with.

In relation to the trade, POP material is an effective selling aid, but is not sufficient on its own: providing it cannot guarantee that it will be set up in the retail outlets. Indeed, distributors, both in variety and specialty stores, do not readily accept* pushing a product which is only advertised by POP displays: for the same mark-ups, these distributors prefer to ensure success, and reserve the available space for brands and products whose awareness was already established for their clientele by other communication actions and which are thus almost 'pre-sold'. The programme of such actions is, moreover, one of the trump cards of these brands' sales force to incite the trade to feature their products and their POP material.

According to the country and type of distribution – general stores and specialty shops, in particular – the possibilities of setting up POP displays are limited, sometimes even non-existent; merchandising as a development means will then be reduced to negotiating the best available locations and the amount of shelf space.

6.3.1.2   Specific international difficulties

Despite some of these limits to effectiveness, merchandising in general and POP advertising in particular are an indispensable dynamic device source for many areas of professional activity, and often represent a considerable investment in an export development's budget. Thus, it is worrisome to observe that POP material use in the field can sometimes be a great waste.

The root of the problem can be found, with no surprise, in the difficulty of adapting to international needs, made even more complicated in this case by various practical obstacles. Thus, lots of POP material used at home cannot be transposed to all export markets, even after such matters as translations have been dealt with, and managing POP material all over the world is not so simple:

---

*A notable exception is distributors' brands.

- POP regulations, possibilities and usage vary according to country and the different distribution channels;
- integrating POP material into retail outlets continually runs into unexpected technical problems of standard, voltage, etc.;
- the weight and size of certain material can make transport costs too high, and many countries cannot manufacture them locally to a satisfactory standard;
- in the case where the POP material is not charged, and ordered from a catalogue by the local representative, it is frequently the exporting company which furnishes it for free, in proportion to a determined percentage of each order's value. When these orders are handled in the absence of the person in charge, or without specific instructions, the support staff who deal with filling orders might send off an assortment of POP material which is not adapted to market needs;
- it is rare for anyone to really take the time to check up on POP material use and study the improvements which could be introduced so as to transmit them clearly to the designers responsible for POP material's conception. In foreign markets, the export executives and local representatives complain how certain material is not adapted to their needs, and they 'make do' with it nevertheless; back at headquarters, the export executives have so many other urgent matters to attend to that they forget to speak to the POP material specialists, who carry on working in their ivory tower with insufficient market feedback.

6.3.1.3   Suggestions for effectiveness improvement

Since everyone agrees that POP material has a major importance and represents a huge, sometimes even considerable investment in the development budget, creation and management control should not be neglected; every sign or display should be a really effective dynamic device whose performance is well adapted to international markets.

- whether the staff in charge of POP material's creation and manufacture are part of the company or belong to an outside subcontractor, or are decentralized on certain markets, there is no question of letting them work in the dark. If, for reasons of a limited budget, POP specialists cannot be sent out into the field, they have to be thoroughly briefed to work in the right direction, with specific information on:

  □ the exact function that each POP display will have to fulfil, the desired life-span, the number of units foreseen, and a unit cost price bracket;
  □ the nature and characteristics of the different places in which the material is to be used;

☐ the target clientele's specific purchase habits;

☐ size and weight restrictions, regulations to be respected;

☐ competitors' POP displays, if possible with photographs. Analysis of their advantages and drawbacks;

☐ the specific problems to be taken into consideration (technical adaptations to foresee, specific risks of deterioration or theft, maintenance possibilities where the material is displayed).

It is up to the specialists to pool all this information, of which some will differ widely from one country to another, to try to respond with POP display creations that can be used successfully in most markets, and easily adaptable to others.

▶ *It is with this in mind that* **CGH** *internationalized all their POP material and thus reduced their costs: a simple concept, without text (just the mention* **Jaz Paris** *or* **Yema Paris**) *that can be used anywhere, in France as well as in almost all the export markets. Its impact is in the strength and beauty of the photographs used (like those of the North Pole expeditions led by Jean-Louis Etienne, with a prototype* **Yema** *watch – see section 6.4.3.3.), which energizes the POP material's presentation of these brands' lines of watches and alarm clocks.*

For priority markets whose needs will not be satisfied by standard materials, tailor-made solutions will be considered at headquarters or locally whenever development potential justifies this special investment.

■ There is no hope for improvements in new POP material unless their designers and manufacturers are regularly informed of the performance of the material currently being used in the field: strong and weak points, suggestions made by the sales personnel, remarks that they have heard from distributors, competitors' POP material novelties. The only sure way of ensuring that this information is getting through is by organizing one or two POP meetings a year, with the active participation of the field staff.

■ Each display's design should be carried out with the purpose of getting maximum effectiveness at all application levels, for example:

☐ all the different POP materials used within the same product line should be compatible (signs, display cases, dispensers, dummies, testers, samples) so that they can be used together or 'solo';

☐ each POP material should be exploited to its maximum. Thus, for a cardboard sign (a small poster on a cardboard base) the front should inform the customers, but it is a shame to leave the back blank when it can be used to inform the sales personnel; when the sign is placed on a counter, between the customers and the sales assistants, the back can provide reminders for the sales staff, with a short product presentation, or just a summary of product advantages, using key words;

- [ ] each POP material should be designed to maximize application opportunities. Taking up the cardboard sign example again, its dimensions are to be calculated for possible fastening to all display cases used; its adaptability should be such as to be used alone in most places (on a counter or in a window display, as well as hung on or placed against a wall, a counter or any other base; for this, on the back of the sign there should be a fold-out tripod and a ring, plus an adhesive band).

- ■ Attentive observation of the habits and needs of retailers can suggest ideas for POP articles that offer distributors added value, and which will logically get a better welcome and a preferred position. This can be seen almost everywhere in the world for seasonal consumer products: some companies do not hesitate to make giant display cases, bearing their names and colours, proposed as moveable gondolas to present all brands of the same product type (sun-tan items, for example), with, however, a strong visual impact advantage for their own products.

- ■ Generally, fragile POP material should not be used for export, nor material with a complicated* set up, or needing constant maintenance; an exception can be made for companies having direct assistance within their retail outlets: exclusive distribution by a franchised chain, specific counter and sales personnel in department stores, or other such cases.

- ■ We have already mentioned the problem of checking how POP material is used (see section 2.2.2.3), for which there is no miracle solution. What has already been said will be reinforced by some additional advice, which should further limit wasted investments.

  - [ ] As a first step, all the personnel using POP material have to be made aware of the situation, starting with the company's field staff, the sales staff of the local representatives, and also that of the distributors. The message to be passed along contains three points: why POP material is important as a dynamic device; its high cost and the fundamental necessity for all POP materials to be used properly for business development, and the good health of all the companies concerned. This information probably will have no effect on the hardcore 'couldn't care less' crowd, but it may affect those who waste POP materials through negligence: it can be hoped that a salesperson will not dump and abandon in the trunk of his car the 50 signs printed in full colour on glossy cardboard that were just given to him if he knows what impact they

---

*If instructions on how to install the POP material are necessary, they should be clear and comprehensible to give an extra chance for the display to survive abroad. Illustrations are usually better than large amounts of text, and these reduce the need for lengthy translations.

can have on his best customers, that they cost $7 each, and that he will not receive any more for another six months. This awareness can be heightened by instructions for use: what kinds of POP material to be used in priority in what kinds of retail outlets; how to present the material and give it importance in the eyes of distributors; how to influence the use made of it in retail outlets etc.

☐ Then, sufficiently precise POP material management has to be ensured. This begins with a knowledge of the needs at each level: export zone, market, distribution channel, retail outlet. In most cases, needs go beyond possibilities; priority markets will be taken care of first, as well as the most dynamic and dependable distribution channels; a double-check of POP material use should be set up if possible at each level mentioned above: both destination and results.

A destination check will lead to each sales representative, who will be asked what ultimately happened to the POP material in the various outlets he looks after. Thus, he will be more attentive to the POP material's use when he knows that anything he says can be verified at any time by his superiors when they visit the various retail outlets. Destination checks also provide relatively exact knowledge on how the material is used in each retail outlet, and what results it generates, which can be studied in parallel: for example, sales progression can be compared among the different outlets after a campaign where samples were given out. In this way, those in charge can be alerted by an insignificant sales progression that in certain retail outlets the personnel might have used the samples and testers for their own ends.

■ Merchandising in general is still a field where distributors on many markets lack experience, and will welcome specialists' advice gladly. In some professional sectors, an itinerant merchandiser's help would be greatly appreciated in the outlets. This will bring about a favourable treatment for POP material and their brand's products.

6.3.2 Printed material

Of all forms of advertising communication, advertising and sales literature is the only dynamic device applicable to all professional activities, without exception.

6.3.2.1   International use

Printed material plays an even more important role abroad than at home: far from headquarters, it is capital backup support, with a strong credibility, to present, inform, enhance the company and its products, convince and sell.

▶   *For example, the importance of presenting references of projects carried out in other parts of the world can easily be imagined for general engineering and turnkey projects. **Inter G** put a lot of care into the edition of data cards, fully illustrated and detailed, to describe their references in different domains: factories, hospitals, hotels, office and apartment buildings, etc. These cards are of a standard size and removable, which makes it possible to assemble a custom-made file corresponding to needs, to show the group's capacity to carry out a project in a specific domain. This literature is circulated extensively abroad to reinforce **Inter G's** awareness and credibility, which generates spontaneous demands for construction project advice all over the world.*

In most cases, printed material users and recipients are found at each level of international distribution:

- ■   *The company export executives.* Well adapted printed material is just as vital for them as a rifle is for an infantryman. Their needs focus around two main poles: corporate literature, where the company is introduced and situated in their professional context; and product literature, which should be sufficiently detailed when the product cannot be transported or presented directly.
- ■   *The local representatives.* The same remarks can be made as above; still, in addition to direct commercial use, advertising and sales literature can also serve to inform local official services, banks, service companies, as well as being used for public relations purposes.
- ■   *The local distributors.* This passes through the hands of the local representatives' sales staff, who must be shown how to use the sales literature effectively: too many just act as 'postmen', passively handing out documents instead of using them as a sales aid, to help emphasize the specific information which interests their clients. It might be useful to look for inspiration in the methodology used in the pharmaceutical industry, where medical service representatives often have only five minutes to convince the prospective client:

▶   ***Laboratoire Roger Bellon**, for example, are not just satisfied only with developing sales presentations adapted to each country's particularities, but they also make sure such presentations are performed well by their medical service representatives, and help them perfect their techniques by showing them training films and getting them to simulate client calls.*

■ *The final clientele*, in general, whether they be consumers or end-users (services, capital goods).

The form of the printed material, its presentation and volume can vary not only according to its uses and the people who receive it, but also according to the way in which it is to be circulated, in most cases:

■ directly, through one of the intermediaries that have been cited above;

■ by mail, either in a direct mailing, or in response to information requests;

■ picked up directly by prospective clients when left on a counter in retail outlets, or in booths at trade shows and exhibitions;

■ by direct distribution, in retail outlets, in the street, in letterboxes.

6.3.2.2   Main formats

To simplify this detailed review of printed material dynamic devices, three major categories will be examined successively: brochures, catalogues and folders:

■ *Brochures*
This type of literature can be all the more prestigious and effective if it is printed on thick paper and illustrated by well selected photographs, drawings and graphs to attract the reader's interest. The brochure is the classic aid used for company corporate presentation, with a few of the leading products, whereas the product presentations themselves will be made in a catalogue and/or folder. Due to its high cost, the brochure is usually reserved for important clients, and is only given out to individual consumers for expensive products (cars, HI-FI, travel).

▶ *In industry, brochures play an even more important role, and will take special forms adapted to each activity sector's needs. Thus, besides general presentation booklets, **Airbus Industrie** give each prospective airline literature corresponding to their individual requirements, which means that this aircraft manufacturer publishes specific brochures for each potential client.*

■ *Catalogues*
A direct sales aid, catalogues present the products and should provoke an order if placed in the right hands: buyers, sales personnel, users or consumers, given the situation (e.g. the **Facom** catalogues discussed in section 2.1.2.3).

■ *Folders*
With their light cost and volume, folders are excellent tools whose flexibility is greatly appreciated in exporting. They are used mainly for product information and promotion towards sales personnel and clientele. They can also be aimed at presenting a company and its

main products or services: they are less prestigious* sales aids than brochures, but their cost is lower, which allows for a greater distribution (quickly amortized over a short period) and frequent renewals; in addition, the weight and format make transportation easier, both during a trip and for post-dispatching.

▶   *For example, **Perrier** publish a wide assortment of folders: some have a corporate content, presenting the Vergèze springs, their history which goes back to Hannibal, explaining their natural origins, etc. Others offer sophisticated cocktail recipes, using **Perrier** water; the impact of these brochures in the USA can be imagined, where cocktail preparation is almost considered an art, the pride and joy of those who have mastered such techniques.*

6.3.2.3   Conception and writing/editing advice

It will not come as a surprise that the first point here is a serious briefing, which includes the users' and the target clientele's needs, as well as the way in which the printed material is to be employed. This will lead to practical decisions for the conception and presentation of the various literature:

■   The format and weight should be calculated in relation to the use and means of transmission: for example, not only suitable for the export staff's luggage, but also for not falling into an airmail postal category ruinous for the operation (the weight of the envelope and a possible cover letter should not be forgotten, either!). It is better to choose standard sizes to facilitate stocking the documents on shelves; unusual formats can be advantageous because they set the documents apart from competitors, but they are inconvenient to file, which shortens the life expectancy of a large percentage of giant or 'arty' brochures and catalogues.

■   On the other hand, the cover has to be distinctive, so the creative artists can let their imagination run riot here. For thick brochures and catalogues, the company name and/or logo appears on the spine, so it can be found quickly on office or library shelves. The cover's strength will obviously correspond to the life-span foreseen for each document type, as well as to the conditions and frequency of use.

■   The importance of all printed material quality for the brand or product image (especially if the products are still relatively unknown), means that budgets must not be too limited here, and executives should not try to scrimp on carefully done page make-up, impeccable typesetting, attractive paper, and well selected illustrations (use of colour is a highly recommended investment)

---

*Except for large format folders (e.g. A4) or those printed on heavy paper, which have an impact almost comparable to that of a brochure, for a lower cost.

to maintain interest, which helps message transmission as well as giving a favourable impression of company's activities.

■   If the life-span of the brochure/catalogue is to be prolonged, only stable information should be mentioned while changing figures, as well as tariffs and other variable elements, can be presented on a loose sheet or in a folder to be inserted and easily replaced.

■   Some documents can be designed to bring a 'plus' to the readers:

▶   *In this way, a **PBI (Parfums et Beauté International – L'Oréal Group)** products catalogue for Duty Free shop buyers provided certain practical information which could encourage them to consult it often: a discrete invitation to order. Among this information was a perfume classification according to scent family, an ingenious planisphere where a cursor system indicated the exact time in every time zone, a table presenting all the legal holidays in main countries, etc.*

The greatest difficulty in writing international documents lies in language adaptations. Many companies avoid the problem by providing their local representatives with the basic elements and having them produce their own printed material; it is the simplest solution, but has the drawbacks of uneven homogeneity and production quality, as well as of increasing technical costs in each market.

Two centralized formulas can be mentioned in parallel: the easiest is to produce printed material in two, three, or even four basic languages to be used all over the world; in addition to simplicity, this formula reinforces the company's international image, but will not be completely satisfactory in countries where some of the users/ readers do not know any of the proposed languages.

The other formula, more restrictive but adaptable to each market at a competitive cost, is to print a different version for each language, with the same page make-up and print setting; this operation is not too difficult for a limited number of languages, but as soon as there are more than eight or ten there has to be meticulous coordination and a rigorous respect of delivery deadlines; the person in charge must also have a saint's patience! He will have to orchestrate a high number of shuttles with the different countries for the transmission of the original text, its translation, proofreading, etc . . . and all those specific modifications which will intervene at each stage that could compromise the general production schedule.

As for writing this literature, it would be better to set forth information which is likely to interest the readers, rather than what the writer himself likes to read about: the company presentation should be incisive and not humdrum. Only a selection of important facts should be cited to establish company awareness, consolidate image, emphasize production quality, reinforce the credibility of the proposed advantages by introducing clientele testimonials, etc.

Whereas, the company founder's complete biography is not really a must for the brochure's introduction, nor are the President's greetings . . . in six pages, unless they bring a breath of innovation or a visionary concept to their professional world!

In the same way, product or service presentations will be better received if introduced after taking the clientele's preoccupations and problems as a starting point, then arriving naturally at company solutions with an emphasis (in synthetic form) on the products' specific advantages – thus creating a purchase motivation.

Going further, oriented towards client needs rather than on systematic product emphasis, it can be of interest to also produce non-classic literature which positions itself between public relations and advertising:

▶   *Clarins offer new mothers a guide to get back into shape, where practical information and advice are given, exercises suggested, and the best adapted beauty products indicated, with instructions on how to use them.*

Finally, here is another reminder that considerable attention has to be paid to translations. Speaking a language well is no guarantee of being a competent writer-translator, as already mentioned in section 4.2.2.2 using the example of a German cosmetics company.

Here are the main points to check, along with some advice from Jonathan Mandelbaum and Jeremy Wilson, two American experts in 'linguistic auditing' (*Le Moci*, No 636):

■ *Linguistic*
  □ misprints (frequent when a foreign text is entered into the typographical process)
  □ 'false friends' (words which resemble each other, but do not have the same meaning in the two different languages)
  □ words or expressions based on the original language and translated directly into the second language
  □ clarity of writing (vocabulary and sentence simplicity; logical syntax and idea development. If it concerns a document written in English for multinational audiences, it must not be 'over the heads' of readers whose mother tongue is not English).
■ *Marketing and presentation*
  □ company profile and brand image (are they well defined, does the company's international vocation clearly stand out?)
  □ emphasis on promotional arguments (too much said, not enough, were pertinent examples used?)
  □ easy to read (page make-up, typography)
  □ coordination between text and illustrations (very important, but often neglected, as the writers of the foreign texts rarely work, it seems, with the paste-up artist).

6.3.2.4   Audio-visual aids

It is not an exaggeration to say that the impact and persuasive support that audio-visual aids provide the export executive with are often the decisive ammunition, particularly when he is far from home base at the other end of the world; with these aids, he can give his company life and breath, and bring an extra dimension to his products in Quito, Kuala Lumpur or Harare.

Having a good product and mastering efficient advanced technologies is no longer enough. The company must show them off to their advantage. In addition to traditional sales aids such as catalogues, audio-visual techniques offer a range of means which can be used not only for promotion of the company's global image, but for their demonstration know-how as well.

It is estimated that the recall score of an audio-visual program content is about 65%. This is three times higher than that of a visual communication alone, and six times higher than just a verbal communication.

Showing a film is, then, an extremely effective presentation device, both for the brand image as well as the products; a film can lead to a conference, a meeting or a public relations action, but it cannot always be projected everywhere. These limitations can be solved by using a projection system which can be carried – screen included – in a suitcase, making it particularly well adapted for field use by the sales representatives. However, making a film is sometimes considered too costly to be included in development budgets, especially since this cost has to be amortized rapidly before information presented is out dated.

▶ *'But there are audio-visual solutions adapted to almost all budgets,' explains Maïté Mareschal*, 'to respond to exporting companies' communication needs: from a computer company that has just invested $70,000 in a 15-minute corporate film, or a perfume house who presents the marketing positioning of his new men's line with a 4-minute prestige film for a $40,000 budget, to a shoe manufacturer who had a real 5-minute video clip made on his company for $16,000. In this last case, of course, we used the cheapest shooting and montage procedure, which didn't stop us from making a very convincing film!'*

Presenting slides with a portable projector is flexible and inexpensive, but does not lend itself as favourably to all professional fields because its lack of sophistication may give a 'holiday picture' style to an important meeting. On the other hand, slides can be used for sumptuous multi-projector shows, yet this cost and the technical difficulties involved are sometimes dissuasive.

---

*WMP Communication, Paris, France. Tel: (33)–1 –43213434

▶ *Baccarat* have a lot of audio-visual aids (slide and video programs in French, English, German, Italian, Spanish and Japanese) to present their history, the spectacular crystal manufacturing procedures showing all the hot and cold work stages, between which come quality control and the destruction of flawed articles. This material is equally adapted to sales personnel training as to distributors' or journalists' meetings, and it is completed by a whole assortment of multi-lingual brochures and folders, renewed every two years.

As in the case of printed material, the conception and creation of audio-visual documents cannot be improvised without running the risk of provoking negative effects on the part of the target audience. Most advice concerning the conception and creation of printed material can be transposed to audio-visual devices.

6.3.3   Advertising items and gifts

If advertising items and gifts are presented together here, it is basically to simplify the book's organization, as they are two types of dynamic devices more different than common.

Advertising items can either be given away, or sold; their basic purpose is to be a more or less visible advertising medium. The object itself is only limited by imagination: from traditional lighters, calendars, desk diaries or pens, to surfboards and hot air balloons.

Gifts propose an even wider range of opportunities: an advertising item or a regular company product, also a sum of money in the form of a bonus, an allowance or gratuity, etc. It can be an 'unsigned' object as well, having no link to the company*, or a service, mostly in the leisure domain: trips, shows, various types of invitations.

In the case of advertising items, the choice has to take sometimes dissimilar aims into account (satisfy and reinforce loyalty; emphasize a brand image, and thus develop its awareness using this unconventional medium). But these aims *can* be reached simultaneously:

▶ *For example, we all remember the extraordinary fashion accessory fad in the 1970s (particularly handbags, umbrellas, scarves and tee-shirts) featuring the ostentatious signature of the designers and couturiers: thanks to snobism, it was considered good taste all over the world to buy these articles and to be transformed into walking 'advertising billboards', thus enabling the designers to make a profit on all sides!*

Advertising items and gifts can be linked either to 'push' or 'pull' operations, according to the recipient and the use that is made of them; however, it is specifically difficult internationally to direct them

---

*Which the receivers can even choose from a catalogue, similar to those companies specializing in motivating staff in relation to their sales objectives.

successfully towards the planned receivers, to choose the items and gifts best adapted to the targets, and to limit their unproductive use.

Recipients to privilege

The necessary coherence for a development plan's success also has to be applied here, just as for any other dynamic device. Advertising items and gifts being backup dynamic devices, the decision to use them depends primarily on the development strategy that is being applied to international markets.

In other words, it is only in the case where investment in advertising items and/or gifts is considered as a solid complement to the company's development effort that the operation should be implemented. It seems logical that the best way of anticipating this investment's impact is to be found in the specific identification of the targeted clientele to be reached, together with a forecast of attitudes after their having received the object in question:

- In chronological order, the first receivers to be privileged can be found within the company, as there is no doubt that the international team's motivation (field staff, support staff and expatriates) will be stimulated by well selected incentives, from the standard gift to profit sharing schemes.
- The same can be applied to local representatives and distributors, as mentioned earlier (see sections 5.2.1.5 and 5.3.3.1).
- Other possible recipients are obviously the company products' consumers and users themselves. At this point, things start getting really complicated:
  - ☐ For mass consumer products, among other difficulties, articles have to be found with a low unit cost to reach a significant number of potential consumers, but with a sufficient impact on sales development to justify their use. In practice, the usual solution is found within the framework of promotional actions (see section 6.5).
  - ☐ For capital goods (household or professional) and services, where the higher unit price can justify having recourse to advertising items and gifts, the main difficulty – particularly abroad – lies in identifying the real users and decision makers, as well as ensuring that the gifts really reach their final recipient.

▶   *No difficulty of this kind, of course, for **Sofitel Hotels** (Accor Group) in the United States, when offering French bread baked on their own premises to their departing guests. Such a crusty, tasty 'baguette' that it is a real treat to accept this slightly cumbersome souvenir! It can be added that this gastronomic, loyalty-creating gift, with a low unit cost, also has the advantage of being a highly visible communication medium, since it is presented* *in a red-white-and-blue bag, bearing the **Sofitel** name and logo.*

*I still remember an early morning in 1977 when I was waiting for an appointment in the Minneapolis **Sofitel** lobby: several dozen businessmen had left the hotel treasuring the **Sofitel** triple-coloured bread bag under their arms. There is also the following day's memory, when I easily picked out several other **Sofitel** clients in the airport departure hall who, like me, were waiting to board different domestic flights. An exchange of looks at our bread bags, followed by smiles and acknowledgements in the middle of a crowd. I never imagined that anyone would ever ask me about this case, during a lecture, why **Sofitel** offers their clients a long baguette rather than a croissant!*

■ In certain professional sectors, the importance of the role played by market influencers, opinion leaders and various trend-setters can be seen. Their support can be fundamental as a catalyst for success. The difficulty here also lies in identifying the targets, and the adapted gift choice.

■ Journalists are another example of recipients to be favoured (see section 6.4.3). Considerable caution is to be recommended here: most journalists intend to maintain their independence in what they write or say, and do not appreciate receiving a gift whose excessive value may appear as a payment for services, hoped for or already rendered. According to custom in the countries concerned, and the journalists' personalities, the correct attitude to adopt* should be determined – ranging from the symbolic, small gift, a friendly souvenir for a story/editorial, to a princely present, if that is what it takes.

6.3.3.2   Adequate selection

The recent difficult economic situation caused most companies to considerably limit their investments in advertising items and gifts abroad. This naturally stimulated the search for more incisive ideas that could best serve overall development strategy.

Here, again, it is originality that counts, but without endangering image coherence of the brand or the products.

▶ *The gifts of tennis and golf balls are directly coherent with the **Perrier** image, since these sports are natural and non-polluting, and they enjoy a positive image all over the world. In addition, such gifts bearing the **Perrier** name discreetly remind the players of the brand in their club houses when, after playing a game, they are ready for refreshment.*

Limiting the number of different advertising items and gifts to be used for most company needs is a sure way of reducing their unit

---

*A gift, even symbolic and of little value, is in any case not an obligation: a word of appreciation on the article that has been issued can be enough to thank the journalist for the quality of his work.

cost, and getting more of them into circulation. But this standardization requirement should not be overdone, especially when it is a matter of relatively expensive gifts for very important recipients: custom-made gifts should win here.

For a custom selection, one should not hesitate to collect as many ideas as possible both at headquarters and from the export markets, so as to have the widest available choice with which to compare prices according to supply sources.

Here are two examples of gifts, both having an interesting cost-effectiveness ratio, but whose value ranks at opposite ends of the spectrum:

▶ *Luggage tags in the form and size of credit cards) stamped with the user's name and bearing the company's name and colours (**Air France, American Express, Camel**) are greatly appreciated as they respond to a need, in a flattering form, for the traveller: moreover, these luggage tags are a small, eye-catching advertising medium, with a unit cost of less than $2. This gift is waste resistant: the names printed on them guarantee a minimum of misappropriation, and their recipients use them very often (most people do not like throwing away objects bearing their name).*

▶ *Who has not dreamt one day of being a racing car driver? And what better gift than making such an inaccessible dream come true? This observation explains the impact of quite an original and expensive gift that the **Hesnault Transport Group** offered some of their clients passing through France: a sports weekend at the **Renault-Elf-Winfield** driving school at Magny-Cours, during which they were able to learn the basics of driving a one-seater racing car, and experience the thrill of making the engine roar on the circuit. Of course, a photographer is present to record the event, taking close-up shots of the drivers helmeted and strapped into their 'Formula **Renault**'. With the exceptional atmosphere that is generated among participants, and their memories of it, such a gift is highly effective; moreover, its cost is lower that what many companies pay for a typical Parisian evening out on the town, offered to major foreign clients (expensive restaurant, cabaret show, nightclub ... a tour which has become quite classical, and which is consequently quickly forgotten, even if made spicier by the skills of talented hostesses!)*

6.3.3.3   Destination and use control

If investment in advertising items and gifts is limited, as just mentioned (see section 6.3.3.2), it is all the more important to check up on their proper use. Virtually the same principles can be applied here as for POP material (see sections 6.3.1.3 and 2.2.2.3). Two points, however, have to be emphasized:

■   It is absolutely necessary to record a description of gifts offered to important clients and contacts: first, this provides an indispensable memory aid so as to avoid offering someone the same gift twice, even several years apart; it is also an efficient way of making sure that the most expensive gifts, in which the company invests every year, actually reach their destination.

▶ *No surprise that an avant-garde group like **Matra** have a sophisticated organization, even in a relatively secondary area such as this: advertising items and gifts are managed by computer. Each executive can consult a catalogue with photographs and prices, and refer to a list (kept in the computer's memory) of gifts he has made the years before.*

■ It is also important to keep a few samples of items and gifts used all over the world, with their prices and manufacturers' references. Experiences proves that they can often be reused a few years later in other markets, or even sometimes in the same ones.

6.4   Public Relations

It is remarkable to observe the lack of interest generated by international public relations in many professional sectors, where executives undoubtedly seem to believe that their application is only adapted for highly visible products, those exclusively linked to more spectacular occurrences in everyday life. However, there is no field in which well organized public relations cannot be an effective dynamic device source.

6.4.1   International public relations potential

Public relations' importance for export market development is reinforced by the difficulty of international communication. The influence of public relations can simultaneously back up and guarantee the direct communication means used on foreign markets (the local sales force), as well as support and give credibility to advertising communication.

Hence, certain companies, even large ones, prefer to concentrate their communication investments on public relations:

▶ *'Even though **Descamps** is already leader in Europe, it is only in France that we are able to invest rather heavily in media advertising, in order to create a strong enough "pull" effect on our sales to justify the cost of purchasing space. So, we've placed our bets on public relations, and have employed an exclusive press relations manager on each priority market. We are lucky that there exist, like in France, columns where our products can be talked about in many magazines, even in some newspapers and on television: with such opportunities, success is due to the effectiveness of our public relations organization, as well as, of course, the interest and quality* *of the messages suggested to the press. In a field like ours, directly linked to fashion, it's the originality and abundance of our creations that enabled us to benefit from a very wide editorial coverage, usually accompanied by product photographs. Obviously, our public relations budget converted into advertising space purchasing power, would have been far from assuring us comparable visibility and such a strong impact . . .', confirmed Yves Carcelle when he was CEO of **Descamps**.*

It should be emphasized, with this testimony, that a public relations organization like that of **Descamps** is possible for most companies, if necessary adaptations are made for their field, on condition that they be really 'professional' (a must in this high risk domain where 'flops' are memorable).

Thus, for example, the press relations managers have to be 'over-informed' to be credible in specialized journalists' eyes; this is why they often go to Paris to revitalize their information with the stylists in the **Descamps** studios.

Another example: when it is a matter of organizing a major public relations event, like the creation contest launched with the Fashion Institute of Technology (see Section 2.2.1.2), **Descamps** make sure they have assembled a maximum number of trump cards so as to multiply the positive effects in the press and among distributors:

■ *Although it takes place in New York, this is a very international contest because of the world awareness of the Fashion Institute of Technology, the variety of nationalities present on the judges' panel and the prestigious department store chains participating: Bloomingdale, El Corte Inglès, Harrods, Le Printemps, among others.*

■ *This contest is credible because it assembles only the leaders: a leading manufacturer + the leading design school + leading distributors + leading designers and journalists (on the judges' panel), without forgetting the patronage of the French Ministry of Culture.*

■ *This contest is universal, as everyone all over the world can buy the design of the prizewinning student, reproduced in bedsheets, pillow cases and quilt covers in 180 **Descamps** boutiques and other selected stores.*

■ *The contest grew out of an attractive and generous idea: although not lacking in talented professional designers in their studios, **Descamps** try to promote young designers' textile creations worldwide. Here, then, is a quotation (taken from the press file) of Susan Rietman, Chairperson of the Fashion Institute of Technology's textile/surface design department: 'We think the best training for students is to treat them like professionals. This is exactly what the **Descamps** contest provides, offering a marvellous opportunity to integrate a training exercise into market reality.'*

■ *Last but not least, this contest is unique in the world, which is another trump card to mention in this obviously incomplete list; one can imagine how the strength of these cards, often multi-facetted, make it easier to approach each journalist with the best adapted angle for responding to his audience's expectations (see the IPEC example in section 6.4.3.3 on this subject), and thus to reinforce the potential for editorial coverage of this event.*

It appears, then, that international public relations is quite an effective communication device, accessible to all companies wanting to accelerate their development.

Better still, it is not only companies that can use public relations to improve their image and awareness: many governments have tried, with varying degrees of skill, particularly by inviting foreign journalists to visit so they can report on the country, which will hopefully then attract investors and funds and thus benefit from a better political backup or tourist industry development.

▶ *The biggest flop ever seen in this domain was in the 1970s, when the President of the Democratic Republic of Korea, Kim Il Sung, launched an all-encompassing public relations campaign in several western countries; full page advertisements (these were paid for, of course) containing outrageous praise for the President were so badly adapted to their free-world target audience that the expected awareness was attained: people talked about North Korea a lot . . . but not in the way the President was hoping for!*

6.4.1.1   Advantages to develop

An imported product is usually confronted with various difficulties and restrictions. However, a foreign product has a few advantages too, such as being surrounded by a certain mystery, enjoying a more or less favourable preconception, and creating curiosity (this latter effect is rarely capitalized upon). In its various forms, public relations can be a dynamic device arsenal, whose advantages and effects can be observed and used at all levels: clientele, distributors, administrative organizations, banks, service companies, subcontractors, as well as the local representative's personnel, who can only be energized and motivated by a flattering emphasis on the brand and the products they distribute.

International public relations can efficiently achieve four main aims: announcing events, creating credibility, improving image and developing awareness.

■ Thus, it can be very productive to 'pre-condition' a market by announcing beforehand the brand or product's arrival. This novelty angle can be played on to inform, to stimulate interest and to prime demand all the way up to the official launch.* During and after the launch, press relations actions are often very effective, when backing up other committed dynamic devices, to help sales progression.

The campaign launched by **Thainox Steel Ltd.** *(subsidiary of the* **Ugine Group***) with their communication agency,* **Francom Asia***, started almost*

---

*In this case, the main difficulty is to pace the public relations program so as to avoid a short-lived infatuation, and to make sure that the launch takes place when the provoked demand is at its peak.

as early as the building of their factory, more than two years before their production began.

*Obviously, the communication strategy was not meant to stimulate sales, but to establish a strong recognition and image of this newly formed company in Thailand. As a result, several objectives could be reached, so varied as deterring **Ugine's** Japanese and Italian competitors to implement their own industrial project in this country, or motivating highly qualified engineers and technicians to apply for a job with Thainox.*

*Together with the media advertising campaign 'Enter the world of stainless steel' already described (see the introduction of Chapter 6.1). **Francom Asia** set up a public relations program which produced strong synergy effects.*

*This very simple and relatively inexpensive program consisted of regular press relations actions that confirmed **Thainox** as a valid actor within Thailand's economy. For instance, these actions for which **Thainox's** chief executive Jean-Paul Thévenin was personally meeting the press, could make all concerned audiences aware of this project importance for the country's industrial development: Thainox's factory in Rayong, opening in October 1993 and employing 400 people, is making Thailand the first producer of stainless steel among Asean countries. Also, **Francom Asia** completed Thainox's public relations program with the sponsorship of Thailand's Athletic Sports Association and with the support of several charities, which accelerated the integration of this new company within the Thai community.*

*As a solid part of the whole corporate communication campaign, this public relations program contributed to a promising start of **Thainox** commercial activities which are to be backed up as well with product advertising.*

■ The natural curiosity surrounding a novelty which has 'come from somewhere else' that was played on to announce the product's launch is sometimes accompanied by certain reservations which can affect the decision to purchase; for example, relative skepticism on the product's genuine qualities, on its abilities to respond to specific market needs, on the after-sales service efficiency, etc. Public relations actions can be fundamental in providing credibility to a foreign product:

　□ Direct public relations actions facilitate a closer relationship with distributors, users and consumers, thus creating a client-product communication (see section 6.4.2).

　□ Indirect public relations actions, essentially through the press, can further reinforce product credibility (see section 6.4.3). The clientele's opinion is willingly based on journalists' professionalism and natural critical sense, which serve as a filter. Thus, information published in an editorial appears assuredly more powerful and credible than that found in an advertisement.

On this subject, it should be mentioned that it is effective to organize a press relations operation after a product launch to assess its market performance. This is a way of giving the product a second wind, by bringing it a 'plus' in extra credibility derived from obtained results, clientele testimonials, demonstrations of the specific product advantages.

■ Moreover, public relations offers a vast choice of actions likely to improve a brand or product image according to observed needs in international markets as a whole, or in certain specific markets.

■ Finally, all public relations actions taken together affect the development of brand and product awareness. In all professional fields, some companies manage to be talked about internationally all the time: they multiply and vary the approaches while emphasizing any new features of interest, or even creating an event by a specific action. Setting up a precise calendar of these actions (see section 6.4.3.3) allows the PR staff to alternate those domains where the company will be featured:

□ information on product innovations: in most developed countries there are many media having columns for such news, services, etc;

□ commercial information: new subsidiaries, spectacular successes on the market under consideration or on foreign markets can be mentioned in press releases;

□ information on special methods or techniques used by the company;

□ information on the overall financial results, on new stock holdings in other groups, on subsidiary activity throughout the world which is liable to interest business publications in many countries;

□ information on top company executives which can be found in different media having a 'People' section; a director's nomination, a company innovation, the successful conclusion of a project whose interest is general, and even a hobby that an executive excels in – all these subjects enable journalists to present these persons at a different angle from the usual corporate portrait;

□ nothing should stop the local representatives of company X, having efficient public relations services, from proposing to some of their client companies, not very organized in public relations, to prepare some press releases or public relations actions for them where their name and products will be featured; this provides the pretext for mentioning (tactfully!) company X's important role in their clients' success;

□ besides business, other means can develop awareness and improve company image, such as patronizing events (humanitarian, artistic, social, economic activities) or sponsoring (sports events, in particular).

In conclusion, let us again emphasize a basic public relations advantage: most actions, particularly press relations, offer a very attractive cost-effectiveness ratio which can often bring a rush of energy to a development plan with a very reasonable investment.

▶ *For example, we can imagine the impact of televised cooking classes in Latin America, organized by **Moulinex**, in relation to such an operation's low cost.*

6.4.1.2   Risks to foresee

First, public relations possibilities must not be overestimated: some exporters, enthusiastic over a public relations action's results, start thinking they can concentrate all pull development efforts in this domain 'instead of investing in advertising, which costs a fortune'. In reality, the markets and professional sectors are rare for which public relations actions alone are sufficiently effective. On the contrary, it is usually necessary to define for each case an advertising/ public relations mix to which will be possibly added a promotional action program.

This same desire to define an effective mix will help executives avoid the risk of dispersion, frequently observed when the public relations specialists* are not working exactly according to the development strategy's communication guidelines: then, public relations actions only bring in a reduced complementary impact to sales staff efforts and other push dynamic devices, as well as to the advertising program. This is what can be seen, for example, when a public relations action is orchestrated around an inadequate product image concept, or when one of the action's basic elements is not in harmony with the product mix. Direct and indirect public relations use the same unconventional communication channels to attain either a very exclusive audience, whose attitude will be decisive for company development in a market (important clients, major influencers), or a vast audience among which are found many potential users/consumers. Any failure can thus rapidly generate effects all the more dangerous, even catastrophic, since many public relations dynamic devices are no longer controllable after being launched:

■ Indeed, press relations are far from being an exact science, and there is no question of guaranteeing – outside specific circumstances – that a journalist will write or say exactly what is wanted: using his critical judgment is part of the mission, which is to report to his readers/viewers/listeners what corresponds to his personal convictions. It is useless, then, to expect much from press relations for a product that does not have solid qualities,

---

*A classic case of a badly chosen or underbriefed public relations agency.

as a real journalist will not write a laudatory story just because the local representative brought out the champagne, or even if payment in kind was discreetly suggested. Before meeting the press, the product has to be convincing, and it has to be materially possible to explain its specific advantages. There also have to be enough reasons to convince journalists to encourage readers/viewers to use it; in the case of a newly launched product, documents proving product performance on other comparable markets, will obviously be welcome.

■ Journalists are often specialists in different fields, but they cannot be expected to know everything, especially when it is a matter of sophisticated technical products;* the frantic pace of their jobs very rarely allows them the time to find out everything about some product before writing their commentaries. This can sometimes lead to publishing divergent or inexact interpretations of product information, very difficult to make up for afterwards. Public relations staff should be sure that the press file is crystal clear (see section 6.4.3.3).

■ There is a tendency to underestimate the talents necessary to organize really successful public relations actions, and it is fundamental to make sure that local representatives realize how important attention to detail is for preparing and carrying out programmed events. We shall see later (in section 6.4.3.3) how to minimize the main causes of flops.

6.4.2   Direct public relations

International public relations can follow two separate paths: aimed directly at the clientele in a more or less personalized form according to the number of client segments to be hit; and indirectly aimed at the clientele, using different communication relays to retransmit and amplify messages (see section 6.4.3).

6.4.2.1   Customized PR actions

Made-to-measure public relations actions are mainly justified where international development is based on the agreement, the goodwill and the support of a small number of decision makers. When the number of clients/users is very low, on each market, personalized public relations actions are more effective and profitable than most

---

*When the subject is difficult, it is not unusual for journalists to have their articles checked, before publication, by the company specialists they interviewed, to have any inexactitudes corrected; generally, it is preferable to leave this initiative to the journalists, or maybe to suggest a re-reading with a lot of tact to avoid giving the impression that their work is to be censured.

other communication dynamic devices. Thus, in the heavy equipment sector, organizing a study trip to headquarters for a market's few potential customers will have a much stronger impact than an expensive media campaign, whose effects will be quite limited in comparison.

▶ *This is the case for* **Potain***, who often organize trips for groups of users and potential clients in France. Welcomed with traditional Burgundy hospitality, they go back home convinced by the quality and performance of the cranes they have tried out at the Testing Centre, then seen manufactured and quality-controlled in the factories.*

Customized public relations actions regularly run into the difficulty of identifying the real decision makers, particularly in administrations or interministry buying commissions where titles do not always indicate a person's importance. This identification is not made any easier by the worldwide inclination to let it be understood that nothing can be decided without one's own agreement. However, it would be premature and even dangerous to start customized public relations actions without carefully identifying the key targets. In fact, besides the waste of time and investment in organizing tailor-made actions for 'small fry', the big wheels can only have a bad opinion or even feel slighted that the company is letting the 'big ones' get away, while going after an undersized catch.

Made-to-measure actions are so important that they must be prepared in relation to their targets; it is a question of following up the relationships established with major decision makers to know their personality, style, tastes and how to act to best influence them concerning company interests.

This does not discount using some basic recipes (modifiable according to visitors' importance) that can be applied successfully in most cases:

- General welcome: help in organizing business and private journeys, as well as an entertainment program adapted to each person, availability of a hostess-interpreter, a chauffeur, gifts and flowers at the hotel, etc.
- Welcome at headquarters or at a company subsidiary: raise the foreign visitor's flag; listing their names on the bulletin board at the entrance might seem childish to some, but few people welcomed this way abroad are insensitive to this kind of attention, even if they seem not to notice anything.

▶ *Luc Doublet, CEO of the* **Doublet Co.***, the world leader in flag manufacturing, and author of the book The Flag Adventure, is well placed to remind us that 'the flag, at the same time symbol of recognition, brand image and link between people and nations, is the oldest medium in the world.' And* *his company, itself a big exporter, is at the disposal* of all other exporters who would like to equip themselves in national flags to welcome their foreign clients, or in company flags with their logo (their cost also makes flags the cheapest medium in the world!).*

■ Such an 'international conference' style can also be reinforced by the presence, on the table, of each participant's name and a small national flag.

■ Some big companies have basic programs, according to the importance and professional specialty of the visitors; this concerns the pomp of the reception to be planned, and the different possible stages of the visit: demonstration of material/equipment (see the **Krebs** example in section 6.5.2.4), meeting VIPs, visiting retail outlets where company products are prominent etc. This precaution, easily transposable for SMEs, enables company executives to be prepared and always have at hand a program which can be modified to suit certain visitors expectations precisely, or used exactly as it is for others.

■ If a company wants to be fully effective, why not plan a few activities for the visitors' spouses as well? Suggestions for places to visit, boutiques to shop where these guests will be warmly welcomed, and any other thoughtful considerations can only be appreciated.

▶ *Over the years, **Waterman** have perfected their welcoming procedures for foreign visitors at their model factory in Nantes, France. Everything is planned, from raising the flags for the welcome to the visit of each service or manufacturing department, where the presentation is looked after by a person working there to ensure more precision in explaining processes or answering questions. This last procedure makes communication easier between visitors and visitees (see the Favi factory visit example in section 5.1.2.3), and helps motivate the support staff for the company's international development. Another thoughtful **Waterman** attention: postcards (already stamped!) of their beautiful factory.*

6.4.2.2   Operations on specific groups

The organization of public relations operations on a larger scale is often necessary to attract and develop loyalty among all or part of a company's clientele. This type of operation's effectiveness will be all the more strong when each person gains the impression that he has been selected from among the mass as part of a privileged group, and that he is receiving relatively customized treatment:

■ These operations can be carried out regularly, as the well-known and still quite successful 'club' examples:

---

*For more information: **Doublet**, 67 rue de Lille-Avelin, 59710 Pont-à-Marcq, France. Tel: 33 2049 4847.

▶ *Air France's* Club 2000 and *Hôtels Méridien's* Carte Noire develop loyalty among the most important clients, bringing them privileges and various advantages, having them benefit from special assistance in case of need, keeping them informed as a priority of new products liable to interest them.

■ Such operations do not necessarily require a colossal investment, as it is possible to have other companies participate – which are also interested in these client groups – whose products and services can fill out the whole offering; thus, an international package of privileges, introductions, benefits and services adapted to targeted client needs can be proposed. To embody such an action, club cards have to be prepared in company colours, with each member's name embossed on them, and there has to be an up-to-date index file to maintain and keep up regular communication.

■ These operations can also be periodic, organized for certain occasions, particularly at the time of fairs, conventions and trade shows. There is imaginative competition to attract, interest and charm clients and prospective clients in the booth or outside the exhibition's premises, with parties in carefully selected places: up-market restaurants, fashionable nightclubs, yachts, etc. (see section 6.4.2.4).

■ Other types of periodic actions can also be adapted to any activity:

▶ A system of birthday cards, used by the jeweller *Stern* in Brazil: each client's birthday is recorded, and a date index file seconded by an effective administrative follow-up ensure dispatching the cards in time – which creates a solid link, over the years.

■ Furthermore, nothing should stop a company from creating an event (convention, information days, for example) tailor-made for the target clientele aimed at:

▶ Thus, after perfecting a new process for chemical product extraction, *Krebs* organized a series of technical conferences for their existing and prospective American clients. It can be noted that the conferences' success was multiplied by the choice of location: in this case, there was no sun and palm trees, as *Krebs* had situated their conferences in a high-tech centre, the Colorado School of Mines, in Denver, which had in the past successfully tested their new chemical process. The backing provided by this centre, enjoying an excellent image in the eyes of American specialists, thus gave a lot of credibility to the *Krebs* innovation; the company was able to assemble their target audience easily, and demonstrate their technical capabilities.

6.4.2.3   General public campaigns

According to the case, these campaigns can be considered as public relations, in addition to being promotional or advertizing activities.

As for the implementation of any major dynamic device, but even more so in this instance where the budgets are considerable, a clear strategy must be defined whose objectives have to be in strong synergy with the company's development policy.

Then the task is to launch an action or use an existing event to captivate and charm all those who are part of the target market, whether by direct contact or indirectly through media coverage of such actions.

▶ *In the international hotel business, where the major chains are in constant competition for imaginative ideas, Méridien often manage to launch spectacular actions at low cost. Among these, a snow storm can be mentioned, in the middle of summer (December 31) in Rio de Janeiro: this phenomenon, provoked by . . . a laser beam 'shattered' by a sphere covered with thousands of tiny mirrors, attracted crowds in front of the Méridien Copacabana, and made the first page in all the press. In Abu Dhabi, Méridien received permission to have a fireworks display, which was a first, since this kind of explosive spectacle is normally forbidden. This presentation was followed by a laser show during which the Prince Emir's portrait was drawn in the sky! This evening was such a success that Méridien's banquet reservations book for the year was filled in record time.*

The purpose of these campaigns, then, is to reinforce general awareness, and to improve the image by creating an aura of goodwill around the brand and products. Such actions – in the case of foreign companies – will accelerate their local integration. Here are some examples of very different styles:

■ Artistic patronage, which issues from a company's desire to get closer to the public by rooting itself in a country's culture:

▶ *IBM were undoubtedly one of the great (if not the great) pioneers of company patronage. Hence, in France, everyone remembers Big Blue's activities in various artistic domains, both in Paris and outside the capital: Cézanne and Bonnard exhibitions, impressionism and the French countryside, Renoir, French sculpture in the 19th century, Gauguin at Pont-Aven, five centuries of Spanish art, and also in Lyon the first performance ever given of Berlioz's Requiem according to the composer's exact instructions: 800 choir members and two symphony orchestras for this awe-inspiring work.*

In 1991, these 'institutional programs' involved a Sevrat exhibition, followed in 1992 by Sisley.

'However,' confides Micislas Orlowski, who started and has been directing IBM France's corporate communication programs for a dozen years, until 1992, 'these actions in artistic areas only represent about 20% of the company institutional budget (about $4 million in 1991). We intervene in many other less spectacular sectors where our support is, for that reason, all the

more necessary, from help to developing countries and training tetraplegics in the Paris suburb Garches Hospital, to environmental protection . . . In this field, here is an anecdote concerning the promotion of national parks: we organized a helicopter air-lift for mountain goats over the French Alps, from Italy to the Mercantour Park, where the species was extinct; since then, park visitors have had opportunities of seeing these superb animals, thanks to an Argos emitting-collar that the animals wear, which enable visitors to localize them approximately on electronic maps, thanks to computer screens set up in the park . . .

Through these examples, it can be noted that our interventions are characterized by a desire for quality and continuity, and that they take different forms according to the case: financial help, of course, but also seconding of engineers and executives for periods up to two years, loans of equipment, participation in projects or studies, etc . . .'

■ Artistic sponsoring is also a communication medium, all the more powerful that it concerns the targeted clientele's most appreciated artists:

▶ *Hence, the extraordinary impact of actions launched by **Pepsi-Cola** with such stars as Tina Turner and Michael Jackson, whose fans can be counted in the hundreds of millions all over the world. In addition to the 30- or 60-second commercials that TV viewers watch with almost the same pleasure as a video clip, the concert tours sponsored by **Pepsi**, in exclusivity on the five continents, enable their bottlers-franchisees to cross promotional, public relations and press actions. Thus, the Tina Turner tour 'Break Every Rule' gathered enthusiastic crowds: more than a million spectators in the 14 countries visited. As one of **Pepsi-Cola International's** directors, Rod Malcolm, emphasizes, 'this tour has helped dramatically improve our image as a contemporary brand . . . Our aim is to identify **Pepsi-Cola** with the very best of today's music and to identify ourselves as a vital contributor to local entertainment and enrichment.'*

■ General interest services brought to the community:

▶ *Creation of foundations in many different domains: from help for children and medical research, to installation of useful, public equipment such as the emergency telephones set up on roadsides, with the mention 'donated by **Fiat**', that can be seen in many countries.*

■ Other initiatives take the form of enriching the historical patrimony of a professional sector:

▶ *Following up this idea, **Grand Marnier** (whose origins go back to 1827) have a permanent exhibition of old bottles in the Eiffel Tower cellars, a very popular place for visitors from all over the world.*

▶ ***LU** (biscuit brand of the **BSN Group**) organize exhibitions of their collections of advertizing posters, dating from the beginning of the century, as already mentioned in studying their Scandinavian development plan (see section 2.2.3.1).*

▶ *Here is another example, showing an energetic defensive patrimony action:*

Cartier emphasize, in a spectacular way, the distance that separates a prestigious jeweller, with over a century's experience to their credit, from their pale imitators, by organizing exhibitions of *Cartier* copies or destruction of such copies by steamrollers, obviously covered avidly by the media.

▶   It would be wrong to believe that this type of patrimony action is applicable only to luxury or consumer products. After taking over **Coplay** (an American company whose plant is 150 km away from New York), **Ciments Français International** knocked down almost all the old facilities to build an ultra-modern plant, totally automated, with the capacity to produce one million tons a year. However, knowing the interest Americans have for their own history, **Ciments Français International** knocked down almost all the old facilities to build an ultra-modern plant, totally automated, with the capacity to produce one million tons a year. However, knowing the interest Americans have for their own history, **Ciments Français International** kept the oldest buildings and installations to make an American industrial cement museum. Nothing very much need be said about the positive effects this initiative had for this company's image in the United States.

▶   Publishing a professional book can also be a solid public relations action, to the extent that it emphasizes one's know-how and products, directly or indirectly (plus another appreciable advantage: it is one of the only dynamic devices which pays off, in the form of royalties!). Hence, some of the Gaston Lenôtre recipe books published by Flammarion, Faites vos pâtisseries comme Lenôtre, Faites vos glaces et vos confiseries comme Lenôtre and Faites la fête comme Gaston Lenôtre have been translated and published in several countries, including the USA[3], Japan and Germany, where they have contributed to making Mr. Lenôtre's talents better known.

■   Sponsorship, sports events in particular, often brings a substantial 'plus' to a company's image, and there is no shortage of examples in most professional disciplines:

▶   First, an example that is already almost 20 years old; Jean-Luc Lagardère's decision to commit **Matra** to the world's most prestigious automobile race, 'The 24 Hours Le Mans', was a particularly audacious gamble on his part. But the means invested matched the Group's ambitions, and three victories* spectacularly illustrated **Matra's** technical know-how and energy, and greatly contributed to their international development in varied fields of activity.

▶   Today, depending on the country, sports such as sailing, automobile races, soccer and cycling can be communication relays of various importance. Formula One racing has a great variety of sponsors (among which the **Benetton Group** made a colourful and noticeable arrival) where cigarette brands predominate (**Marlboro, Camel, John Player Special, Gitanes**), since legal restrictions in advertizing can only encourage them to invest in this type of communication relay with worldwide media coverage.

---

*In 1972, 1973 and 1974; moreover, **Matra** won the title of World Champion Carmaker in 1973 and 1974.

■   However, sports sponsorship can be even more effective when a company provides, above and beyond a check, specialized assistance in its own professional field, thus reinforcing coherence between image and communication.

▶ *This is how **Rhône-Poulenc** invented 'technology sponsoring': this means the Group intend the sports world to benefit from their advance in many high-tech areas, even to the extent of opening up collaboration applied to these actions, notably with their research centres.*

*'Rather than content ourselves with financial backing in exchange for sticking our logo on a racing car or boat, we decided to develop research for high level sports activities', explains André de Marco, **Rhône-Poulenc** Communication Director, who decided to set himself apart from traditional sponsoring by following an original path better centred on the Group's communication strategy. This is also what Igor Landau, Executive Committee member and Group Communication Supervisor, emphasizes: 'Sponsoring and patronage have to illustrate and reinforce the image that **Rhône-Poulenc** hope to give of themselves: high technology and a contribution to improvement of everyday life and scientific progress'.*

*This is why **Rhône-Poulenc** have been involved with Formula One racing since 1988 in various ways. At first, their physicians participated in the medical preparation of several champions, in collaboration with the CERMA (Centre d'Etudes et de Recherche de Médécine Aerospatiale), because the physiological problems of Formula One drivers are very similar to those encountered in a jet. 'By recommending an appropriate diet and physical conditions, we are trying to improve the champions' performances,' specifies André de Marco. 'All this without forgetting their safety, which is crucial, as the spectacular accident in the 1988 Mexico Grand Prix demonstrated, from which Philippe Alliot escaped unscathed thanks to the progress made in automobile construction techniques and materials.'*

*Furthermore, **Rhône-Poulenc** bring their inflammable fibre experience to the pilots' suits, as well as composite material experience to reduce the car body's air penetration resistance and reduce the weight of different car parts.*

*Beyond the goal of image enhancement, this progress in competitive fields leads to better performance and safety in tomorrow's passenger cars. This is one race that **Rhône-Poulenc** do not want to miss.*

Finally, rather than associating their name with a participant or a team, some companies prefer to create or sponsor the sporting event itself; investment becomes all the more substantial, but the event is then totally controlled by the sponsor, which – among other advantages – reduces considerably the risks of failure linked to the hazards of direct participation in the competition.

▶ *The **Louis Vuitton** Cup is awarded to the winner of elimination races among the challengers for the America's Cup, the oldest sporting trophy in the world. From 1851 until 1983, the Cup remained firmly in the hands of the United States. In 1983, in response to the arrival of a growing number of challengers, the first **Louis Vuitton** Cup was organized. This was to be a historic year of the America's Cup. For the first time in 132 years, the Americans did not take the Cup. The Australians were victorious,* *and the next cup was disputed four years later in their waters at Fremantle. All the world breathlessly followed the final stretch between the Australian Kookaburra III and their American sworn enemy, Stars and Stripes. Ronald Reagan bet his cowboy hat with the Australian Prime Minister that Dennis Connor was going to bring the Cup back home.*

*The **Louis Vuitton** Cup became a fundamental element of the public image of the famous Paris manufacturer of travel goods, whose firm originated as trunk-makers in the same era as the America's Cup. As Yves Carcelle, Chairman of **Louis Vuitton Malletier** declares, 'Since 1854, there has been in **Louis Vuitton** a taste for competition, a need to excel, a demand for perfection, a desire to be in the forefront of research and creation, at the same time as there has been a deep attachment to tradition, all virtues that are expressed equally in the America's Cup competition. This explains why we regard the **Louis Vuitton** Cup as an essential element in our communication, as a reflection of the state of mind, of the ambition and the generosity of our company.*

Furthermore, from a purely strategic point of view, no other sporting event combines the same advantages as the America's Cup, the third world event, so far as the media are concerned, after the Olympic Games and the football World Cup. This is the first event in the world, in terms of image, at the same time elitist, national and international.'

*For the second **Louis Vuitton** Cup in Fremantle, Western Australia, 2800 journalists sought accreditation and more than 20 countries relayed the event by television, while the American TV network ESPN beat all audience records. The entry of new countries such as Japan, hitherto absent, broadened the media coverage of the **Louis Vuitton** Cup even further. A new naval battle took place in San Diego, California, from January to May 1992, gathering more than 4000 journalists and 28 television networks, until the final American defender/Italian challenger confrontation.*

There is, however, a drawback to sponsoring a sports event: it requires solid investments and perseverance to impose the sponsor's name on the event:

▶ *Many years went by before the **Lancôme** Golf Trophy was no longer called 'The Trophy of Champions' in articles by many ultra-discreet journalists, to become 'The **Lancôme**'. Then, with the event's success, now one of the world's classic golf tournaments, came the full circle in an original manner: **Lancôme** had launched the Trophy . . . and in return, this event gave birth to 'Trophee **Lancôme**', a resolutely sporty unisex perfume line!*

Through these examples, it can again be seen that successful operations are not due to luck, but after only a subjective or intuitive choice. If it has been determined that such a public relations action is adapted to communication needs within the framework of the development strategy for one or several markets, it is essential that the choice is guided by the desire to choose the activity that best corresponds to these objectives: in particular, its coherence with the brand and product image that is projected, the interest that it elicits on the part of the targeted clientele, the impact of various means which can make it more profitable, etc.

▶ *This type of analysis led* **Yema (CGH Group)** *to be one of the sponsors for Jean-Louis Etienne, who successfully completed a solitary trek to the North Pole in 1986. For this expedition,* **Yema** *designed a specially adapted watch, made of state-of-the-art materials, with a 24-hour face, always indicating North, operational in cold temperatures (down to –58°C) and very light. Passing this difficult test showed this product's great reliability and provoked significant commercial repercussions in Japan and the United States, since as a result the American army were convinced to order* **Yema** *watches.*

▶ *To conclude on the necessity of remaining coherent with the brand image that is projected when investing in public relations, here is* **Cartier's** *Chief Executive, Alain-Dominique Perrin's expert view: '. . . we have to make communication reinforce our brand image continuously, while at the same time respect market uses and regulations.*

So, for **Cartier,** *sponsoring is elitist: polo at Windsor, Mexico, Munich or Palm Beach, as for patronage, it's contemporary art, art freed from this constantly changing world in which we clearly position ourselves by giving the image of a modern, up-to-date, dynamic company, which is also a world recognized brand. For that matter, of the four* **Cartier** *products launched this year, only one was in France.'*

Since most of the examples given for general public campaigns involve large groups and well-known finished products, I suspect that SME executives, especially those who intervene as industrial subcontractors, will not feel concerned by this type of action; here, then, are two examples that demonstrate how effective such actions can be, no matter what the size, means or activity of the company.

▶ *The fast-growing SME* **Axon** *(1991 turnover: $25 million; 350 employees) manufacturing cables for advanced technologies (satellites, computers and various other electronic equipment) is already an old hand at patronage.*

The **Axon** *'formula' is the following: the company organize an exhibition of a contemporary artist, and for this occasion invite their clients to technical seminars. They also contact the general press (for the cultural aspect) and the professional press (for the seminars), convinced that, in any case, art and enterprise are made for one another.*

For their first operation in Germany, **Axon** *had the good taste to choose a French-German artist, Gloria Friedmann – a German living in France – whose sculptures were exhibited for a month in a historic cloister in Frankfurt, Germany's financial capital.*

As **Axon's** *CEO Joseph Puzo recalls: 'In our speciality Germany is a market three times bigger than France. We wanted to find a means of getting our German subsidiary (10 employees) off the ground. Up to 1986, it was just managing to survive. For us, the first stage was getting our name known here. Patronage seemed a good solution, as it corresponded to our products' style, which is technically highly sophisticated.'*

At present, **Axon** *make half their sales abroad, 25% of this in Germany. To expand on the German market,* **Axon** *use other weapons in parallel: the translation of all their sales literature into German, the adaptation – product by product – to the technical DIN standard and the enlargement of their marketing department.*

The cost of the operation? Mr. Puzo releases a figure: 'For the first German PR event, we spent a $40,000 budget.' Finally, to give more sparkle to these technical seminars, **Axon**, whose headquarters are in Montmirail (Champagne region), convinced a champagne house, Nicolas Feuillatte, to go along with them on their German adventure.' Another lovely example of a joint development action (see section 2.2.2.5).

▶

The second example is told by Henri-François Dubois, Deputy CEO of the 70-employee **Monin** Company, which specializes in the manufacture of liquor and syrups with 40% of their production exported and a total turnover of $20 million in 1991. 'To make up for limited investments, given the company's size, we carry small budget public relations campaigns, which can nevertheless have effective impact and enable us to get our return on investment quickly.

In 1984, we launched a completely new product, **Monin** Original Triple Lime, which is the only alcohol based lime drink in the world.

In cooperation with our Australian importer, the **Elders IXL Wine and Spirits Division**, this liquor was introduced for the occasion of the Australian barmen's competition. The Australian national champion won his title with a new cocktail, using Monin Original Triple Lime as a mix.

The event was covered by professional media, which helped our product become a 'must' in the fashionable bars. Two years later, it was sufficiently anchored for a general public approach, using radio commercials in Melbourne and Sydney, with the financial assistance of two selected liquor store chains.

In 1987, with our importer, we launched a new operation to promote the consumption of Monin Original Triple Lime by emphasizing the esthetic feature of 'new cocktails', which was the start of the 'Liquid Art' concept. It was a series of artistic photographs of cocktails using **Monin** Original Triple Lime, signed by Australian photographers and presented to the public in various forms, mostly in that of a travelling 'Liquid Art Gallery' in Australia's major cities.

For this operation, we played on synergy at each level:

- **Monin's** total financial participation: $22,000
- the importer's equivalent participation
- voluntary participation of the photographers who, in exchange, benefitted from public awareness and recognition
- support from the artistic community
- public relations operations in professional media, and echoes directed towards the general public thanks to editorial write-ups.

The innovative aspect of our initiative charmed the columnists on the watch for unusual events. For **Monin** in terms of results: development of our products' public awareness. Today, we are in third position on the Australian market for French liquor, just after **Grand Marnier** and **Cointreau**.

Furthermore, international magazines, as well as foreign trade journals, spontaneously took up the event in their columns, in the form of editorials with photographs.

Later on, we used the 'Liquid Art Gallery' again in our booth at the world wines and spirits trade show, Vinexpo Bordeaux, as well as in art gallery exhibitions in several European countries.'

In conclusion, it should be stressed that general public campaigns are rarely effective without the backup of other communication devices (from press relations, to stickers, premiums, clothing, etc) that have to be organized and orchestrated, particularly when the company is committed to a group action (example: sponsoring one of the 124 participants in a car rally); specialists consider empirically that the additional support communication budget to foresee should correspond at least to 50%, if not 100%, of the operation cost itself.

6.4.2.4   Fairs, exhibitions, trade shows

These three designations to which can be added symposium, convention, congress ... cover extremely varied categories of gatherings, professional or not. The presence of these dynamic devices in this book's public relations section is purely arbitrary, and can be explained by my perplexity on deciding where to deal with them: according to customs in force in different professional fields, and each company's strategy, they also belong to sales promotion, advertising communication and local distribution actions, among others.

Given the circumstances, it is worth listening to two specialists, Patrick Marant and Benoît de Guernon, directors of **EAG Volume***, to clarify our ideas on this multi-facetted subject:

▶ *'Fading out is the image of nails, pieces of wood and the overall boredom of the event! Today, trade shows have become a medium in themselves. As such, they are to be included in the company's commercial, marketing and communication strategy for export markets.*

There is no other place quite as captivating as that of a trade show dealing with a specific economic sector, given that all the visitors are directly interested in the exhibitors' activities. That's a lot to say, especially when it's your own booth and products which are attracting attention!

A trade show is a highly effective marketing tool, conceived to respond to the objectives and targets defined by company strategy; it is an exceptional observation platform, rich in feedback. It is also an excellent medium, the only one really interactive with the market, a relay and accelerator of the company corporate or product communication.

Finally, trade shows should no longer be considered as a source of expense, boredom or wasted commercial time, if their impact is prepared beforehand by operations making the target clientele aware of the brand or products, by motivating the sales force and informing the users, then reinforced afterwards by direct marketing and follow-up actions on the recorded contacts. Thus, trade shows become a highly profitable investment in export market penetration.'

---

*EAG Volume offer a complete worldwide exhibition service: advice for an 'expo-strategy', conception and production of display booths (modular or customized). The other divisions of this Group should be indicated as well: communication advice, graphics, merchandising, video (filming, production, post-production services) and public relations. In France, Tel: 33 1 49 46 47 48.

Although nobody will question the fact that an exhibition is profitable, if it is well targeted and prepared, this investment still remains considerable (direct participation costs include creation, transportation, assembling and dismantling the booths and the material to be presented, as well as the products to be exhibited; mobilization of company personnel, plus their travel expenses, etc.). The first question to be asked, then, is: fairs, conventions, trade shows, symposia, congresses, exhibitions (whew! . . . *) to accomplish what? To this simple question there are many answers, varying according to professional fields, markets and company strategies:

- to meet a maximum number of clients in a minimum time span, for one or more of the reasons mentioned below.
- to present company products, to launch a novelty (a trade show is often the only place where most heavy equipment can be exhibited and demonstrated outside the company)
- to close deals, or make sales directly on the spot.
- to create or stimulate demand, which will be felt after the trade show, by an increase in turnover for the local representatives and distributors
- to initiate or maintain client contact (and thus keep a direct link with the market so as not to be too dependent on the local representatives)
- to develop brand awareness and improve company image
- to establish personal relationships with business aquaintances (in American conventions, golf and tennis tournaments, as well as cocktail and dinner parties, often propose contact opportunities which can efficiently complete those of seminars and conferences)
- to offer a few pleasant days in a nice place to company executives, local representatives and distributors, using 'business' as a pretext. (This extreme case for a motivational objective should not overshadow the majority of trade shows, where company executives knock themselves out, literally working day and night.)
- to study client needs, their reactions to company products, proposals and development actions
- to study the competitors' products and proposals, to compare them with the company's and thus increase competitiveness.

The interest of investing in trade show participation will be in direct relation to the chances of attaining those above objectives which are considered to be priorities for a market's development.

Observing a few rules will reinforce this interest:

- Keep a record of and regularly assess the trade shows and other professional and public events likely to interest the company. Innovation is possible in this field, as well as by an original media plan: sometimes a professional event can be found in a

---

*To avoid this fastidious listing, the generic term 'trade show' will be used to designate all these events.

parallel activity, in which company clients and prospects participate . . . but no competitors! (see the **PBI** example in section 5.3.2.3.).

■   Stick to a specific definition of objectives that the company fixes for participating in a specific trade show; this induces those people in charge to make an inventory of the means to be engaged, both in personnel and material, and of ideas to be used to energize the whole organization.

■   Among those criteria for assessing the interest in participating in a trade show, the inventory of clients and other contacts to be met should figure prominently, as well as confirmation of their presence at the event. Indeed, too many companies monopolize two or three field executives for a couple of days, plus all the necessary logistic backup (booth, etc.) just to have rapid contacts with clients of minor importance, met recently during regular business trips. In this case, the basic activity of these field executives is to chat with their competitors, which can be of interest but hardly justifies the investment committed.

■   Thus, it is worth preparing meetings with the most important clients, and to make sure not to miss them: by sending them an invitation to come to the company booth where they are expected to see or hear something of great interest; by even making an appointment a long time in advance with super-clients; by organizing a 'social event' during the trade show, or a succession of events whose originality will attract all the interesting people to be met, etc.

▶   *In this way, the **Lainière de Picardie** were able to multiply their 'qualified traffic' by sending a 'passport' to all those people they hoped to meet at the European men's clothing trade show. Looking very official, this passport included each person's name and carried the **Lainière de Picardie's** logo; the text (in five languages) was not only an invitation to the company's booth, but also for two round table discussions; one about the 'economic use of fabrics', the other about 'fashion perspectives and trends for spring and summer', followed by a cocktail party at the nearby **Holiday Inn Hotel**.*

*'We were pleasantly surprised by the number of participants this public relations initiative attracted' remembers Gilles Bassi, General Director of the **Lainière de Picardie**, at the time. 'This illustrates well that from an original idea, even a small company can communicate with their targeted clientele, without necessarily having access to huge promotional budgets.'*

▶   *Here is another example whose originality was the key to success, but which is chosen in the aeronautics sector where the size of the contracts at stake intensifies competition and inflates communication budgets in consequence. As a participant in the Paris Air Show at Le Bourget, **Tracor** (an American group based in Austin, Texas, specializing in electronic equipment for civil and military aviation), wanted to organize a 'social event' that would be remembered. But what to do, when the main aircraft and jet engine manufacturers had already reserved all the top Paris restaurants and cabarets where* *they held 'open table' every night for those Air Show regulars who attended every two years?*

*Solution: have the guests discover places they did not know, and for that, invite them to several restaurants, carefully selected, the same evening. And this was the **Tracor** Gastronomic Cruise', which brought the guests, thanks to a riverboat, to four gourmet stopovers along the Seine banks, from 'l'Ecluse' to the 'Vieux Galion' in the Bois de Boulogne, without forgetting a cheese tasting session (with the participation of Pierre Androuet, the 'Pope of Cheese' himself) on the way to the 'Vieux Galion' for a round of desserts, dancing and champagne bubbles . . .*

*To be successful, this exceptional evening entertainment had to be announced in an exceptional way: for that, **Tracor** called on their own graphic artists and printers in Austin, who designed a splendid 16-page program-invitation on glossy, parchmented paper, with watercolour drawings of each restaurant to be visited, a map with the cruise itinerary, including the major sights to be admired on the Seine's banks, along with information on the gastronomic stopovers and what was going to be served: it was at 'l'Ecluse' that Zola wrote L'Assommoir and that the mime artist Marceau started his career . . . The Sauternes that are served there with the home-made foie gras have a history going back to the Crusades . . . The comments of Eleanor Roosevelt, Brigitte Bardot or Valéry Giscard d'Estaing about Pierre Androuet's creations are almost as savoury as his cheeses . . .*

*Of course, these selective invitations (about 250) were personalized, with each name written in old-fashioned calligraphy on the cover. Quantifiable results: more than 150 guests embarked on this '**Tracor** Gastronomic Cruise', an astonishing result given the competition of the many other invitations made to the same top people on this very evening. Qualitative results: the tone was given, on board, by the guests' remarks, such as that made by the Editor-in-Chief of a major aviation magazine: 'This is the most exciting party I've been to in my 20 years of the Paris Air show!'*

*The appreciation of Benny Jay, then **Tracor Aerospace** Marketing Vice-President: 'Not only were the contacts with our clients, prospects and press of a very special quality on this cruise during the Air Show, but the effects continued long afterwards: our guests are happy to talk about this incredible evening for a few minutes with us, when they welcome us in their offices, before getting down to business . . .*

Finally, the overall cost of this gastronomic cruise, including supplementary expenses (such as a mini-bus, for example, which was 'the sweep' following the riverboat between the restaurants: just in case a VIP guest got left behind in the restrooms!) was less than that of a classic 'Parisian evening', since each restaurant wanted to 'play the game' by participating in this première cruise, and proposed very reasonable prices.

■ Ways have to be found to attract a maximum of 'qualified traffic' to the company booth: effective visual presentations, with possibly (especially for a general public fair) a 'catchy' sound track; games, promotions, demonstrations, tastings, etc.

▶ *On this subject, an historic visit to the **Pepsi-Cola** booth at the Moscow Fair in 1959, can be mentioned – by a 'heavyweight' opinion leader, Nikita Khrushchev himself. Not only did this visit and tasting of several goblets of **Pepsi** by Mr. K, who was escorted by President Voroshilov and Richard*

*Nixon – then Vice-President of the United States – provoked intense interest on the part of the Russian public for this unknown drink (10,000 goblets served an hour, on average, during the 42 days of the Fair!) but they were the origin of many other contacts which concluded in 1974 with an agreement for bottling **Pepsi-Cola** in the USSR; moreover, the sensational photograph of the Soviet Leader sipping one of the symbolic products of capitalism made the world tour! So, it is not necessary to emphasize that before a VIP is enticed into the company booth, a lot of thought has to be given to how this visit can best be used to the company's advantage: choice of the few memorable words to say to him, of a product to put in his hands and/or have him try, as well as organizing an ambush of some photographers (and even a few film cameramen, if necessary) to make sure to be able to broadcast the event. Studying Mr. K's. historic photograph, we can imagine how the scene was set, with two **Pepsi-Cola International** directors naturally positioned on either side of their guest, each holding a **Pepsi** bottle, with the label facing the camera . . . Well done, gentlemen!*

■ The practical preparation for a trade show obviously has to begin in time, foreseeing a few days extra, just in case, to make sure that everything is in order before D-day so as not to risk having to sit stupidly on the floor in the empty allotted spot, for the usual reasons (problems in the production or transportation of the booth, blockage at customs for the products and samples, delays in putting up the booth, loss or theft of material . . . or worse still, because of faulty communication follow-up with the company organizing the trade show, the company spot is already occupied by another company, or the spot's dimensions are too small for the size of the booth, and other such joyous incidents!).

■ During the trade fair itself, every contact opportunity should be exploited to the full in this limited time. For this, the booth's organization has to be designed and adapted to the company's objectives and the tasks clearly specified for each team member. The welcome must be warm, but selective, and the red-carpet treatment reserved for visitors identified as 'qualified contacts' so that they can be dealt with in the professional way they expect (they do not want to waste their own time, either!)

▶ *Here, Americans, professionals at discerning hot-shots from the 'tourists', usually introduce themselves and ask visitors four or five standard questions (Who are you? Which company?). The 'window shoppers' are nicely dismissed with some sales literature. Clients and prospects are gently led to centre stage, where the lead actors are to be found. Even an artisan baker, like Guy Heumann, from Alsace, uses the same techniques: 'My wife knows how to detect the right kind of visitor. In two minutes, they are coded A, B or C on our client index cards.' Professional! Detection, selection, but also welcome: 'Americans like coffee; in machine tools, people like sandwiches and pretty hostesses, and when weather is hot, most visitors prefer water to any alcoholic beverage!'*

■ As after any client contact, a fast trade show follow-up should be implemented, carrying out what was decided and promised, and using the opportunities which were detected: this self-discipline will be the best way to set the company apart from most competitors!

▶ *As an example of a rapid follow-up of trade show contacts, here is a letter I received from the President of **Generation Publications**, a Swedish survey company based in Ornsköldösvik, a few days after a symposium. Passing by their booth, I had asked him for information on the kinds of publications available, without any immediate purchase need; after questioning me about my own business activities, he asked me for my card, probably to have it filed afterwards in the category 'influencers'. It can be imagined that contacts with more directly promising potential must have been followed-up even more dynamically.*

> Dear Mr. Giordan,
>   It was a great pleasure for me and my company colleagues to make your acquaintance in Cannes, at the Tax Free World Exhibition.
>   I hope you had an enjoyable time, found the business rewarding and that you had a safe return home.
>   Please let us know if we can be of further assistance and we look forward to meeting you again, etc . . .

*Practical result of this letter: it reminded me of this Swedish company's very interesting publications and Mr Yngve Bia's warm welcome, and confirmed their efficient organization. I then thought of recommending certain **Generation Publications** surveys to several companies . . . and I even cite this company here by name as an example: **CQFD**. A fast follow-up pays!*

■ Finally, a rigorous assessment has to be made as soon as possible, to evaluate the results gained from participating in the given trade show, to detect weaknesses in the company organization and to decide whether to invest or not in its next venue.

6.4.3   Indirect public relations/press relations

Indirect public relations allows the company both to spread a message and to reinforce its credibility; indeed, this credibility will depend a great deal on the communication relay used.

6.4.3.1   Identification of communication relays

We have already looked at two such relays (local representatives and distributors) who are normally won over to the company, but whose motivation has to be maintained and information kept up-to-date so that they can continue diffusing the good word on the brand and products.

Additional communication relays consist of opinion leaders taken as a whole, who are more easily identifiable when their influence on a given market is played in specific positions: administrators, doctors, architects, engineers, bankers, etc.

Other communication relays have an 'influencer' role because of the hold they have on the people around them, or more generally, on the public. They are usually referred to as opinion leaders or 'locomotives'; they are not always easy to identify, nor to be approached and convinced to support the company cause, as they are very often asked for help and swamped with requests. Here again, the originality of the approach, along with the quality and interest of the message, is what will help acquire these market influencers' backing.

▶   *This is how the **Laboratoire Roger Bellon** carried off very successful public relations actions, starting from the principle that the best way of interesting and convincing market influencers (professors, medical doctors and pharmacists) would be to organize seminars with the French specialists, authorities in their field. With their local agents' help, the **Laboratoire Roger Bellon** invited several well known specialists to give conferences in many countries so as to transmit to the audience the message of a highly technical product, and generate a maximum credibility.*

▶   *Here is another example, with **Grand Marnier's** launch of the 'Association des Jeunes Restaurateurs de France', one of the objectives being to incite these young French 'chefs' to promote their own creativity: **Grand Marnier** organize trips where they transmit their know-how (often delicately flavoured with this liqueur!) on television, radio and in the press . . . It is also because one of the chefs, Michel Pasquet, had been invited to preside over a dinner for the heads of state at the Versailles Summit Meeting that the world's media, which presented the different courses, thus announced for dessert: 'Velours de Versailles au **Grand Marnier'**.*

*In Japan, French chef Claude Pouget (who works exclusively for **Grand Marnier**) regularly demonstrates recipes in the two biggest cooking schools in Tokyo and Osaka using one of the brand's liqueurs. Moreover, **Grand Marnier** sponsor the national Japanese French cooking contest. To conclude this list of public relations actions on market influencers in a sporting way, **Grand Marnier** sponsor the annual Chefs Ski Race in the USA, which brings together the best American chefs every year, with – as a plus – a heavy press and TV coverage. This event was recently organized in Taos, New Mexico, where **Grand Marnier** welcomed over 200 chefs in March 1992.*

Finally, the press being the major communication relay in most professional fields, we shall now concentrate on press relations within this indirect public relations section.

It should first be emphasized that press relations are not reserved for luxury products, or to those linked to fashion and artistic activities. In the big industrialized countries, particularly Germany, the UK, France, the USA and Japan, there are many quality, technical magazines. Company directors, engineers and technicians of these neighbouring countries keep informed through this type of medium. For example, a German executive spends an average of one and a half to two hours a day tracking, recording and exploiting such information.

The organization of press relations* in an export market logically begins by an inventory of all media likely to be adapted to the type and image of company products, and which are supposed to be interested in reporting about them. According to the case, the company should approach the written and/or spoken press, the national and/or regional press, the trade and technical press, or the press as a whole, if the global importance of the message justifies it.

▶ *This is what was done to announce* **Calberson's** *takeover of the German transit company* **Hermann Ludwig GmbH** *in 1987, as recalled by Bruno de Segogne,* **Calberson** *Communication Director: '. . . it was unusual for a French company to take over a German company of this size (***Hermann Ludwig*** *have 1500 employees in Germany, as well as in their 28 subsidiaries and 60 offices based in Europe, North America and Asia/Pacific) and we decided to take advantage of this operation to reinforce* **Calberson's** *dynamic image. For that we approached each type of French and foreign press medium with an adapted message, both in form and content. Thus, it was an interview destined for the general public that our President gave to the German daily* Die Welt; *for the* Financial Times, *on the contrary, the interview was about our new international development perspectives, with more information likely to interest a finance-oriented audience.*

We had a different approach with the professional specialized press, such as the Swiss Journal du Transport International, *for which we revealed certain technical aspects of* **Calberson's** *world expansion strategy'.*

It is also possible to get international press coverage without even travelling, thanks to foreign correspondents who are based in one's own country.

Of course, their mission leads them to be more interested in major political and economic news, or in the activity of big groups rather than in SMEs; however, an unusual piece of information, an innov-

---

*Since press relations are made easier by personal contacts with the journalists, this task should generally be entrusted by the local representatives to public relations agencies. However, the company must know what is going on at all times, and be ready to intervene directly, if necessary, as well as to provide an additional plus, with the exotic flavour naturally expressed by foreign company executives, in relation to the local media and public.

ative product or a spectacular photograph, for instance, can catch their eye and be relayed to their countries. For example, there are about 500 foreign correspondents in Paris, of which 77 are German, 45 Italian, 32 Swiss, 27 American, 25 Japanese, etc.

6.4.3.2   Usable message inventory

To hook onto a communication relay, journalists especially, messages to diffuse have to be collected: what is new or special about our company, the products, the personnel, the local representative, which can interest the public or a professional audience? According to the markets and their importance, even relatively innocuous events can be highlighted such as a company anniversary (see section 3.3.2.1), a subsidiary opening in the country, the building of a factory, or the visit of a headquarters director.

It is regrettable that so many company directors, on visits abroad, tend to neglect or flee public relations events for fairly unconvincing reasons (from 'I haven't got the time' to 'It doesn't do any good') which do not stand up to serious analysis. In fact, rare are those trips where one or more public relations actions cannot be squeezed in somewhere. Executives should get used to considering these public relations activities as one of top priorities for their foreign travels.

▶ *Gaston Lenôtre would never have become one of the great ambassadors of French gastronomy if he had not been a communication man as well. For example, here is a list of public relations events he participated in during a recent week's stay in Japan, where he was also scheduled to attend many meetings with his Japanese partner:*

■ *several interviews with the written press, as well as with the 4th and 12th TV channels, in the **Lenôtre** boutique at Shibuya in Tokyo.*
■ *master of ceremonies for a pastry contest (covered by the press)*
■ *visit and address made to a professional Japanese cooking school (covered by the press)*
■ *reception organized by the directors of the **Seibu Group** (one of the top distribution groups, which is **Lenôtre's** Japanese partner) in honour of Gaston Lenôtre; this was also an internal communication event, meant to stimulate the motivation of the **Seibu-Lenôtre** team.*

▶ *An impressive performance, too, in the style of a public relations marathon, for the launching of the 1988 Muscadet 'primeur' wine, the very day that 'new wines' can be officially put on the market: Muscadet presentation by the **Sauvion** House, on the same Thursday November 17, for breakfast in Hong Kong, for lunch in Bangkok, for dinner in Singapore, held in each city by Jean-Ernest Sauvion for the press and local distributors. Good health to him!*

In the case of shortage or inconsistencies in the available messages, there is the possibility of creating the event: organize a symposium on a 'touchy' subject, with the invitation of a well-known dignitary, for example.

In the domain of consumer products or household appliances, the calendar can also be used to bring out the press files, whose informative qualities will have been carefully prepared: before Mother's Day, Father's Day, Christmas. Practical advice on the choice and purchase of perfume and other gifts can discreetly remind the readers of the brand products; the same approach for a brand of furniture or appliance could propose, in the form of serial stories or comic strips, suggestions and advice for fixing up and decorating interiors, as well as guiding the choice of products.

6.4.3.3   Practical organization advice

Some still think of public relations as an activity for any talkative person, ideally suitable for young ladies of good family who are looking for a pleasant and fashionable occupation. Such 'clichés' are quite outmoded, mostly for international PR, where nothing can be taken care of with a few 'phone calls, and where only a rigorous and detailed organization gets any valid results:

- ■ In cases where the local representatives do not employ an executive who has both the time and skill to take care of public relations, a specialized agency could be taken on, either for periodic actions, or even retained for a year if the planned program of events justifies it. A good public relations agency also has the advantage of having its own awareness and credibility within the press, which considerably reinforces the impact of messages coming from a still relatively unknown company.
- ■ The selection of media to be approached has to be carefully checked: there is no point in dispersing efforts with interviews in media that do not address the targeted clientele.
- ■ The most delicate moment in press relations is how to approach the editorial staff. According to the style and quality* of this approach, the company may be pushed aside, and superhuman efforts will be required to get back on the rails, or the journalist's interest will be awakened and things will be off to a start. Just how to do this merits serious thought:
  - ☐ Initially approaching a journalist who is a specialist in the company's professional field will be all the more effective if the first steps taken have enough strength to get through

---

*It should be remarked that, in practice, it often happens that the solidity of the relationships between the public relations agents and the editors-in-chief render the 'technical' part of the message secondary; thus, connivance takes over for the approach phase: 'Hello, sweetheart? . . . , who can you send me Thursday, the 9th at noon, for the presentation of a new, absolutely fa-bu-lous shampoo?! . . .

possible obstacles, and have an originality likely to whet the curiosity.

▶ *Thirty years ago,* **Qantas Airlines** *did not hesitate to use . . . carrier pigeons, to announce the opening of their Sydney-Tokyo route to the Japanese press.*

▶ *More simply, approaching American TV stations' Newsdesks to cover the presentation of the* **Léonard Fashion** *collection was made a lot easier by a sibylline telephone introduction, reinforced by a slight French accent: 'This is X . . . , of* **Léonard Fashion** *from Paris'. Most switchboard operators and secretaries thought this call came from France and hurried to connect it to the right journalist, who for once appreciated being contacted directly by a person in charge of a French fashion house, and not by a local public relations agency.*

  □ According to the perception of the journalist's style, at the beginning of a 'phone call, a sense of humour can be an extremely efficient tool to set oneself apart from the dozens of other callers he will have had during the day.
  □ In the same way, it has to be realized that some journalists get hundreds of messages, letters, files and packages all in the same day, and that they just do not have the time materially to open them all if they do not have help. Result: after sorting things out very hastily, most of this mountain of mail is classified vertically into enormous waste-paper baskets. Hence, the importance of a follow-up 'phone call, necessary but also as fastidious for the press attachés as for the journalists: 'Did you get our invitation?' It would be better to give company mail more of a chance of being favourably noticed and opened and then read. Here again, the originality of the approach will make the difference.
  □ In cases where the first approach can be custom made (especially by 'phone), care should be taken to present the message from the best adapted angle to catch the attention of each medium, according to its specificity, and the type of information which is liable to interest its readers or listeners.

▶ *This is the method that the* **IPEC*** *Group followed, when starting operations, to organize press conferences and interviews all over Europe successfully: the general press (daily newspapers and magazines) were invited to the presentation of a revolutionary, door-to-door freight express system, faster and cheaper than air transport; each time, the president and founder of* **IPEC** *passed through a European country, a small number of journalists from dailies and magazines were invited to interview Gordon Barton, to draw the portrait of the world pioneer in door-to-door express freight, which got started in the 1950s in Australia, with three Peugeot vans!*
  With the economic and export press, it was the new benefits that the

---

*IPEC Europe have since joined the TNT Group.

IPEC system brought to companies which were focused on: possibilities of offering a faster and safer service to the European clientele, making company products more competitive by reducing certain transport costs (see section 5.2.3.1), knowing in advance the exact total cost of sending a shipment, customs included, and the time necessary to deliver it door-to-door, etc.

The transport press were invited to observe the new methods used by IPEC for their unique system, and many specialized journalists followed a shipment from the moment it was picked up at the exporter's all the way to its delivery at the recipient's, and were thus able to verify IPEC's affirmations of rapidity and dependability.

☐ Continually receiving invitations by mail, and being harassed by 'phone, journalists often promise to go everywhere without intending to go anywhere, just to get rid of certain solicitors . . . in order to avoid a disagreeable surprise on the day of the press conference (such as the number of journalists who said they were coming = 57, the number who really showed up = 6!), the journalists should be contacted again just beforehand. Not to annoy them, brevity is everything, and a last bit of important information is necessary to serve as a pretext for the call, as well as reinforcing the journalists' interest at the moment when they are deciding their final schedule on the company's D-day.

■ Together with an efficient press approach, the determining element of a successful public relations action will be, in parallel, the choice of a form, context and moment, all well-adapted to the communication of the message: exclusive interview, press conference, show, possibly accompanied by a lunch, a cocktail party, a dinner, or even breakfast; there are many possibilities – according to country and local customs – to find the most appropriate formula, which can be rendered even more effective by a touch of originality concerning the place of the meeting.

There are many examples, especially in the world of haute couture and perfume, where companies are compelled by permanent public relations competition to outdo each other.

▶ *To this day in Mexico, people still remember the **Jean Patou** fashion show which took place at the airport, in a brand new, immense **Mexicana** hangar, where dinner for the 1500 guests was served. It was followed by a surprise, the size of which matched that of the hangar: the majestic entrance of an **Air France** Concorde (it was just at the beginning of the supersonic Paris-Mexico routes), out of which came the stewardesses, whose uniforms had been designed by **Jean Patou**, followed by the designer's own models.*

▶ *For the international launch of **Lancôme's** 'Magie Noire', **Parfums et Beauté International** had an original modern dance show created on this theme, which was presented all over the world, and powerfully reinforced this perfume's mysterious and haunting image.*

■ At the moment when the press have been successfully gathered, it is out of the question to risk a 'flop' by an improvised or insufficiently prepared presentation. The conception of certain public relations actions has to begin several months beforehand, and a check list of tasks to be carried out should be made, coupled with a precise calendar where the necessary material elements are written, as well as any required training for those people having to intervene; the whole should be usefully completed by one or more rehearsals. Of course, not all public relations actions can be prepared a long time in advance, which means foreseeing emergency procedures to allow rapid exploitation of an unexpected event, even when it comes at a 'bad' time.

▶ *It was the 31 December 1987 when the takeover of the **Chase Manhattan Bank's** subsidiary in The Netherlands by the **Crédit Lyonnais Bank Nederland** was signed. There was no question of going away for the weekend or to a New Year's party for the Communication department of the **Crédit Lyonnais Bank** in Paris; simultaneously, they had to inform the whole bank network on five continents and broadcast the news worldwide (press agencies and editors of the major press media), in coordination with the event's other participants, in The United States and The Netherlands. The existence of well-oiled emergency procedures was of paramount importance for the media repercussions of this end-of-the-year banking scoop, which profited greatly from the New Year's political truce and its traditional news shortage.*

■ For the press conference itself, one should not scrimp on the welcome, and care should be taken to give a rhythm to the events which keeps the guests' attention at a satisfactory level: speakers should be varied, their speech time limited, and different audio and visual tools used (any quality audio-visual aid is certainly to be considered as a 'plus').

After the message presentation is completed, as quickly as possible, there could be a debate where an experienced public speaker could take advantage of the questions asked to draw attention to the few important points not yet mentioned. It is an elementary safety procedure to have a couple of questions prepared, to be asked by guest-friends, in case of need.

Then will be the moment to go to the dinner table, or the buffet (this type of press conference model is, of course, one among many) where informal conversations will be carefully cultivated. Before their departure, a small gift, or better still, a souvenir, which rarely constitutes an obligation, could be given to the journalists along with the press file, as it is important not to give the impression of buying their support; when promoting a low value consumer product, there will be no problem in giving them a sample to test, as opposed to a car or a steam shovel: then, one has recourse to . . . models, or premiums of little value, preferably bearing the company brand logo.

■ Solutions to fall back on should also be held in reserve to deal with possible unforeseen situations. Such as the press attaché's nightmare: a presentation where most of the journalists who had confirmed their participation do not show up ... This kind of unfortunate occurrence sometimes happens, even after prior good press relations work: such an incident is usually caused by a very important event happening just before the company conference, obliging all the journalists to be on the spot, or right back in their offices to deal with the subject while it is 'hot'.

A few simple measures can be taken to save the situation: if the conference depends on the intervention of a VIP who cannot be easily replaced (the President of the Group or one of the company directors, for example), or on the presentation of a unique show or equipment, their participation or appearance should not be scheduled at the next stopover (in the case of a trip where there are several stops) for one, two or three days, according to the time needed to get them to this destination; a 'remake' could be proposed to the press the next day, or several presentations could be improvised for small groups of journalists of the major media, at times convenient for them.

■ More generally, the importance of preparing a Public Relations Bible cannot be stressed enough, for companies willing to use public relations seriously to develop international business. In principle, this bible is similar to those already mentioned for other fields of activity (company and product image; advertising communication). This bible, destined for the local representatives and their public relations agencies, will reduce risks of failure considerably. In it should be found:

☐ The company public relations principles, with precise descriptions of the kinds of actions that the company does not want to get involved in (sports sponsoring, for example; theoretically, this should prevent a local representative, crazy about soccer, from allocating a part of the company's communication budget to help along his local club).

☐ A choice of actions and public relations recipes already tested, whose effectiveness has thus been confirmed, along with detailed and specific operating instructions, and models of the necessary documents (invitation cards or letters, programs, etc.), possibly including photographs giving examples of how to decorate a hall using the brand's logo and colours.

☐ A selection of short introductory speeches, adapted to different audiences, and a list of standard questions that are usually asked, along with the outline of the most pertinent answers, to help prepare for press conferences.

☐ Finally, a press file specimen, that should include – depending on the message – the presentation of the company, the staff, the products, the specific qualities that users/consumers benefit from, and the significant results already obtained ... All this should be introduced by a specific list of contents, presented clearly and succinctly, enabling the reader to get a quick overview. The file should be illustrated in an interesting and pleasant manner, with the possible additional documents included at the end, to be consulted by the journalists needing to go further into the subject.

▶ *For example, **Perrier's** public relations pack contains several press files: '**Perrier**, a miracle of nature'; 'From Hannibal's troops to the hordes at Regine's, **Perrier** has slaked the thirsts of 85 generations', among other titles . . . **Perrier's** public relations principles are also to be found, as well as real examples taken from all over the world in each field of activity: Sports (organization of tennis, squash and golf tournaments . . .); presence in fashionable places, and in specialized gastronomic conventions; there is also advice and ideas for relations with the press, local distributors, and opinion leaders (a list of 'Special **Perrier** aficionados' is included in the press file, for that matter, with dozens of well-known names, in politics, arts, show business, gastronomy).*

6.4.3.4   Follow-up systematization

Experience proves that it is the public relations actions' follow-up that is usually the most neglected, which can be easily explained: the company field executive who might have participated in or assisted at an event will have left the market in question to go on to other destinations, whereas the local representative and possibly his public relations agency have other matters on their minds!

However, finishing and following up a public relations event are the best means of ensuring valid results:

- First, a press file *must* be given to the journalists present at the conference (and sent to those who were absent). Nothing is stopping the company from completing this file with summaries of the speeches and debates, if they have access to the technical means of getting this done in a few hours and sending the complementary documents off to the interested parties.
- A 'phone conversation with each journalist can help anticipate the specific information requirements or complementary specifications required, or even the need for a private interview; this telephone follow-up is also a delicate way of making sure the hoped for articles are in the works.
- When the reports have been published or broadcast, if it is acceptable to express appreciation on the quality of the reporting, in most cases, confusion should not be created by offering thanks or gifts. Unfortunately, this only applies to countries where journalistic ethics are still a reality.
- It is remarkable to observe how little advantage companies take of secondary use possibilities of the reports and editorials they went to so much trouble to get: once the narcissistic pleasure of

reading about company products and activities has passed, and the direct repercussions on the target market have been maximized, the exporter and the local representative do not always have the reflex to study what dynamic effects can still be extracted. If a report does not contain any major error, and if it is sufficiently positive, it could be a communication tool of interest to circulate: the local sales force can possibly include it in their sales pitch; similarly, it could be included in an information letter sent to the clientele, along with other positive articles focusing on company business (see section 5.3.2.2).

Moreover, it is of the utmost importance to keep a press book containing all the articles published on the company and the products, both at headquarters and on the local representatives' premises. Experience shows that selections of these documents are always needed for various reasons . . . and that few companies archive them as they should.

▶ *After carrying out a press relations operation to relaunch the **Mikli** brand (see section 5.3.2.2.) in Germany, with a very reasonable investment ($1200 for making up these press files, visits to the different newspapers and magazines, loans of glasses and dispatching costs), the best published stories were sent to opticians (example: 3000 offprints of the* Stern *article were mailed with a cover letter) to encourage them to distribute and prescribe **Mikli** glasses.*

■ Finally, regular contact with the press is to be maintained: this is the local representative's role. Headquarters, however, may reinforce this action from time-to-time by sending an interesting information letter, a funny greeting card or a gadget-souvenir. Remaining present in journalists' memories is a two-way street: they sometimes need information or testimony in our professional fields, and they will save time by immediately thinking of contacting us; and it is infinitely preferable to see the company brand mentioned or presented, rather than those of competitors, in a professional feature prepared by a magazine or during a TV debate!

6.5   Promotional Actions

The number and diversity of promotional actions have made a lot of headway in most countries with a market-led economy during the last ten years, along with the evolution of distribution.

This has engendered a trend for customers to think more carefully about what they purchase, and to be more receptive to special offers; this receptivity is often transformed into an active search for promotions, whose existence will then be an important factor in the purchase decision, to such a point that in certain fields the purchase will be put off until such times as a special offer appears.

It can also be noted that the decline or stagnation of sales progression, felt in many sectors, has logically led to an intensification of aggressive competitiveness of which promotional actions have formed one of the main weapons, both for distributors and manufacturers.

Promotional actions are thus not only a source of effective dynamic devices in the general arsenal of international development means, but they become all the more necessary to keep one's clientele from being gradually poached by the competition, and, at the same time, to reinforce distributors' loyalty.

From one country to another, the importance of promotional actions can be found in the same sectors: mainly in consumer products and household appliances. On the other hand, as for raw materials, components, heavy equipment or even services, there is clearly a certain reticence towards using promotional techniques, almost as if such methods were improper.

Thus, we shall now analyse the opportunities and dangers offered by promotional actions, then see how to keep up the effectiveness of their dynamic effects by a detailed organization and a dose of flexibility for each market. Finally, we will inventory the promotional arsenal, and give practical examples in different markets and professional sectors.

6.5.1 Promotions and international development

One of the advantages of promotional actions is to permit the assessment and verification of results with more precision than for any other pull dynamic device, given that these results can be isolated during a specified period by outlet, city, region, country or market and compared with the results from a normal period.

To open this section in an exemplary way, there are at least three reasons to mention the **Pepsi Challenge**:

■ First, its particularly rich concept, which combines two promotional techniques: tasting and a game, since it requires participants to taste **Coca-Cola** and **Pepsi-Cola** one after another from covered bottles. After this blind tasting, the bottle of the preferred drink is unveiled.

■ Its international application, very rarely as wide in the promotional sector: in twelve years more than 24 million people participated in the **Pepsi** Challenge in 23 countries from its 1975 launch in Dallas, Texas. Global results: 60% preferred the **Pepsi** taste.

■ Rarer still, beyond the impact on the public, the **Pepsi** Challenge provoked an unexpected reaction from **Coca-Cola** in 1985, with their controversial decision to change their product's formula. This decision, often referred to afterwards as one of the major marketing blunders of the 1980s, is explained this way by Thomas Oliver, in his book *The Real Coke, the Real Story:*[4] 'The **Pepsi** Challenge challenged the heart and soul of the **Coca-Cola** Company . . . their sacred cow, their secret formula . . . The Challenge threatened **Coca-Cola's** heritage . . . The company, and some of their bottlers simply overreacted.'

Let us see in practice how the **Pepsi** Challenge is launched on a market; the Australian example, described by the **Pepsi-Cola International** magazine, appears as being particularly instructive:

▶ *October 1982 saw the advent of another summer activity – the **Pepsi** Challenge. Launched in Sydney, the most populous city in the country, **Pepsi Cola** and their Australian bottler, **Cadbury Schweppes**, started their challenge at a time when **Pepsi** had only 5% share of the total cola market and **Coca-cola** a massive 75%.*

*This national distribution of the product opened up the whole Australian market for **Pepsi-Cola** – a market of 15 million in a country the size of the USA. Compounding the problem of size (the distance from Perth, the capital of Western Australia, to Sydney is comparable with that from New York to Los Angeles) are the problems inherent in co-ordinating a marketing and promotional program when all six states in the country have different laws.*

*Planning for the **Pepsi** Challenge began in late 1981 with the decision made in June 1982 to launch in Sydney, the strongest and largest **Pepsi** market. There were, however, many problems to solve, and there was an intensive period of preparation between June and October for the **Pepsi** Challenge team:*

■ *Obstacles: firstly, because of **Coca-Cola's** massive 75% share of the cola market, there was concern that the Australian consumer might tend to choose the taste with which he was familiar. The national taste test conducted by an independent market research company reassured the **Pepsi** team that the great taste of their product was preferred in Australia just as it is everywhere else in the world. Figures showed a 54% preference for **Pepsi** with 46% for **Coke**.*

*The next problem was to tailor the **Pepsi** Challenge to the Australian market in a way that made the Challenge a fun thing to do. To do this, the Challenge was taken to different locations during the summer months, capturing the target market, Australian youth, in their typical summer environment. The 'beach culture' of young Australians is a reflection of the country's unique population distribution, where 85% of the people live within six miles of the beach. Other areas used for Challenge sessions included rock concerts (some of which were run by **Pepsi-Cola** on the beach), schools, entertainment centres, supermarkets and community festivals.*

*According to Alan Tooth, Sydney Manager of **Cadbury Schweppes**,*

'Australians enjoy a good challenge, especially when issued by an underdog. And with **Pepsi-Cola's** market share at 5% compared to **Coke's** 75%, we knew the Challenge would attract a lot of interest. We also knew that the Challenge had been successful in other countries where **Pepsi** had a minor share and low brand awareness. Also, the Challenge market strategy relied on growth of the take-home market and this is one of our strong areas,' he added.

■ **Trade promotion**: prior to the Challenge launch, every major buyer and merchandiser from the key chain stores in Sydney was invited to a series of trade presentation nights. A ten-minute film called The Cola War in Australia was produced for these presentations, and Challenge booths were set up so that buyers could 'let their tastes decide'.

'We were delighted that all the trade who took the Challenge showed figures that substantiated our claims,' commented Tom McCarter, Managing Director of **Pepsi-Cola**. 'We were really able to show them how well it worked.' The **Pepsi** Challenge program was promoted to the store as a way of complementing and strengthening the regular scheduled trade deals during the summer months, and resulted in bigger and better displays of **Pepsi** in all stores.

The trade press also followed the Challenge and gave it extensive coverage. The Challenge attracted the attention of the economic and consumer page editors. In one of their programs broadcast all over the country, a Sydney television station featured a documentary on the 'cola wars' theme.

During an interview in this documentary, Tom McCarter had offered to provide free samples of **Pepsi** for the **Coca-cola** tasting booths set up as a counter offensive, which apparently were offering just their own product for the taste test. This generous offer was politely refused by the **Coca-Cola** public relations officer!

■ **The Challenge Team**: to direct the kiosk promotion, we called in **Market Place**, a big marketing company. In collaboration with **Cadbury Schweppes** and **PepsiCo** personnel, this company set up the **Pepsi** Challenge team.

In 600 'kiosk days' altogether, more than 100,000 people took up the challenge; 54% of them preferred the **Pepsi** taste, which corresponded exactly to the results of the national survey. During the Challenge, **Pepsi** sponsored 15 rock concerts on beaches and in parks for the Christmas season. The tasting booths were literally taken by storm by the teenagers, as numerous as they were enthusiastic.

At the peak of the campaign, tasting kits were delivered by **Pepsi** Challenge girls to the Disc Jockeys of morning drive-time radio shows. Three of the DJ's took the Challenge on the air and all chose **Pepsi** as the taste they preferred.

■ **Advertising campaign**: to support the launch, the television advertising campaign began on October 10th, featuring Australian youths in typical summer environments (such as beaches and fun parlours) taking the Challenge. 'We wanted to use real people in Australian settings so that Australian audiences could identify with them,' said Frank Swan,

Managing Director of **Cadbury Schweppes**.

All the people used in these commercials were filmed with hidden cameras to further enhance their authenticity. The TV campaign covered 23 weeks and consisted of six 30-second TV commercials that featured **Pepsi** and did not show the competition. These were geared to encourage trial by teenage consumers and to encourage women to increase their take-home purchases of **Pepsi** at the expense of other colas.

In conjunction with TV, two radio campaigns were used. One was geared to the teenage market and was run on the top radio station for that audience, and the other campaign was targeted at housewives. This campaign encouraged women to take the Challenge themselves at their local supermarkets.

■ **Competitor's reaction: Coca-cola** reacted promptly to the Challenge launch by broadcasting three anti-Challenge television commercials featuring American comedian Bob Cosby. **Coke** ran these commercials throughout the summer season, doubling their advertising budget, and outspending **Pepsi** six to one. In addition to their advertising campaign, **Coke** also mounted the most extensive radio, billboard and consumer promotion campaign ever seen in the Australian market.

Always aggressive in their trade deals, **Coke** became even more so, and subsequently launched a mixer range and two new soft drinks in direct competition to **Cadbury Schweppes**.

■ **Results**: in terms of sales results, prior to the Challenge launch, **Pepsi-Cola's** packaged goods sales were down 17.1% compared to the same period a year ago. The Challenge reversed that trend and sales from October to December were up to 28.1%. Packaged goods sales have averaged an increase of over 25% each month since the Challenge began. These sales increases are even more encouraging when one realizes that between October and December 1982 the Sydney cola market was down almost 9%, with consumer spending in food stores down 3 to 5% compared with the previous year.

The first six months of the Challenge saw an average 53% share increase in the take home segment, but the effects of the Challenge have been much more far-reaching. According to Don Saunders, National General Manager of the Carbonated Beverages Services Division of **Cadbury Schweppes**, 'The **Pepsi** Challenge has certainly created a lot of community awareness. Our rate of acquiring new postmix accounts is up 30% over the pre-Challenge period.'

■ **Tracking study**: from September 1982, **Pepsi-Cola**, in cooperation with their advertising agency **John Clemenger** (an affiliate of **BBDO International**) undertook a weekly brand development monitor in which 150 housewives and 150 soft drink consumers were interviewed to gauge attitude changes prior to, and during the Challenge program.

This tracking study revealed that **Pepsi's** level of awareness has increased from 13 to 90% since the Challenge started, and the level of repeat buying has increased from 3 to 20%. While prior to the Challenge there were 4.2 times as many people who preferred **Coke** to **Pepsi**, the Challenge has reduced that ratio to 2.4. Prime consumers' purchases of

Pepsi have also increased from 2 to 20%.

The tracking study also monitored the impact of the Challenge advertising campaign, and enabled the team to modify their television advertisements for greater believability. The second series of television advertisements, which aired in January, was less structured and used peer group approval as a means of selling the Challenge.

'We are delighted with the Challenge's success in increasing sales and in building up a consumer preference based on taste,' commented Alan Tooth from **Cadbury Schweppes**. 'Challenging **Coca-Cola** was rather like David taking on Goliath, but we believe that David has made Goliath more than a little bit nervous,' he concluded.

It can be observed that Goliath was right to be worried, since the **Pepsi-Cola** Australian market share increased at his expense, going from 5% –11.2%.

Let us emphasize, as a conclusion to this introduction, that promotional actions are not only adapted to consumer product development, but can often be applied successfully to industry and services, as demonstrated further on.

6.5.1.1   Interest in promotional actions

For an export director willing to take the offensive, or confronted by a slowdown of sales in a market, promotions can be a powerful striking force, with a remarkable rapidity and flexibility of intervention that is practically unique among the dynamic devices in his development armory:

- A well prepared promotion can have very spectacular effects on sales:

▶ *The free offer of a **Guy Laroche** chain and pendant with the purchase of a perfume quadrupled Fidji sales on-board **Qantas** Airways literally overnight.*

- Promotional actions should be taken into consideration within the strategic framework of a company's international development policy, with the same importance as the other product, push and pull dynamic devices, but their rapid intervention capacity make them an emergency tactical force which can be used on those fronts threatened suddenly, particularly to resist a new product's successful launch or to combat other competitors' promotional actions.
- The precision and great geographical flexibility of promotional actions enable them to be used in 'made-to-measure' situations, even in just one retail outlet (a major department store in a big American city, for example), with more freedom than media advertising and public relations whose visibility cannot be con-

trolled; however, one should ensure that promotional actions will not have negative effects on the brand image (see section 6.5.1.2).

■ The variety of the promotional arsenal enables export executives to stimulate desired targets with precision by proposing well-adapted offers: local representative's sales force, the trade (wholesalers and retailers), and the sales personnel in the different outlets (already mentioned), as well as the final consumer/user.

Schematically, the actions that address the final customer are meant to develop sales in two different ways:

■ by inciting the existing clientele to consume or increase the use of the company's products (example: special offer of a giant size, or an attractively priced multi-pack);

■ by making a sufficiently tempting offer so as to attract a new clientele and have them buy company products (example: trial offer at a special price).

In retail sales, promotional actions provide a privileged means of cooperation between suppliers and distributors; the latter definitely feel the promotion's actual results, which concern and implicate their sales outlets directly, far better than the more diffuse effects of media advertising and public relations.

A tempting promotion will attract 'qualified traffic', a highly appreciated clientele into a department store, a variety store or a boutique; in exchange, the supplier can expect solid distributor support (at least during the promotion) by featuring his POP displays, by a favourable and enlarged shelf positioning, and by special instructions given to the sales personnel, etc. Some promotional actions plan for extra complementary incentives to further reinforce this support: for example, by having the distributors and/or their sales personnel participate to win prizes or other benefits.

These few general applications for promotion give an idea of their positive effects, another of which could be that of projecting a dynamic company image for the benefit of the trade; there is also the advantage of bringing an anonymous brand into the limelight and stimulating sales with a reasonable development budget; not to be forgotten, either, is that of making up a regular or occasional user index for personalized mail (which could even be sold to certain non-competitive companies that have an identical target market.)

Thus, it can be said that promotional actions do not necessarily have sales as a direct aim, but they can be an indirect sales stimulation:

■ this is the purpose of promotions that create brand loyalty (making up collections, reductions offered on the next purchase, etc.);

■ similarly, in certain fields a promotional action's aim can be to prompt potential clients to try a product without any purchase obligation;

▶ *As explained by Jean-Paul Lafaye, President and CEO/worldwide of* **Wund-erman Cato Johnson***, in the automobile industry, advertising attracts attention to a car by making it known to the public and having people dream, whereas promotions should incite people to try it out; as for the purchase decision, it is influenced by the salesperson's capacity to demon-strate the car's qualities that respond to client needs, as well as to his conscious and unconscious motivations. These sales efforts are backed up by promotional offers which have become common practice (such as purchase of the old vehicle, credit, special services), given the toughening of competition.*

■ here is another example, which combines client loyalty, identifi-cation of new clients and a product demonstration, and which proves that promotional actions can also be used for a business-to-business clientele:

▶ *The magazine* Transport Actualité *and* **Calberson** *decided to implement a joint promotion based on the offer of bottles of Beaujolais Nouveau. This operation was obviously greatly appreciated by the readers and client recipi-ents selected by the two companies. Furthermore, it enabled each one to enlarge their impact by contacting new prospects coming from the index files of the other. When one takes into consideration today the importance of the annual appearance of Beaujolais Nouveau, launched like a car rally in the middle of the night on the French roads in Burgundy, and its speedy transportation to each recipient in Europe, this action appears as an excellent demonstration of the* **Calberson** *service efficiency.*

6.5.1.2 Dangers to consider

There is always the other side of the coin, and promotional actions are no exception. The first danger would be (as for public relations) to consider promotions as the 'answer to all ills', as there are obvi-ously limits to their effectiveness, as well as certain risks:

■ When a product does not offer a 'plus' or a specific advantage over its competitors, promotional actions can only stimulate sales for a very short time, and they will fall back to their previous level as soon as the promotion is over. Very quickly, promotions for this kind of product will only temporarily attract a 'floating' and unfaithful clientele, who are always on the lookout for special offers on any brand.

■ A promotional campaign's visibility is generally weaker than that

---

*Wunderman Cato Johnson-Action Marketing, with 50 offices on five continents, is one of the rare agencies specializing in promotional activities to offer a world network. Contact: New York head-quarters: +1 212 941 3000. Paris Headquarters: +33 1 46 84 34 07.

of a media advertising campaign, which means there can be a fair amount of liberty in promotional activity from one market to another, so there can be a better adaptation to local constraints and needs. However, the dynamism and dimension of certain actions, as well as for the importance of the advertising means (promotion of the promotion), are sometimes such that they can considerably affect the product and/or brand image: some types of action will have very positive effects on this image (contests and games, for example), whereas others such as price reduction offers can provoke various interpretations, often negative: 'Is the normal price artificially inflated? Is the product of inferior quality? Sales must be way down for them to sell off the goods like this!'

It is better, then, to be attentive not to sacrifice future sales for those of today, and to really check on the projected promotional actions planned for international markets, even *before* these activities are in the preparation stage; there is no question of letting each market do what it wants for promotions without running serious risks concerning the image and product mix coherence.

■ The clientele's reactions, like those of the trade, regarding promotional actions can vary greatly from one country to another, and prudence incites export executives to test any new promotion concept on a market where such an action has not yet been proven successful for another company. Such prudence with new promotion concept launches is not only recommended to prevent any lack of interest from the target market. The worst danger may come, on the contrary, from underestimating the demand triggered by the proposal of a too appealing offer.

▶ *This is the painful experience that was suffered early in 1993. The **Hoover** top executives in the UK who were sacked because of a 'gift with purchase' promotion that went out of control. Indeed, the offer of two airline tickets for any American or European destination, with a £100 minimum purchase of a Hoover appliance was even more stunning that − surprisingly − no further obligation was requested. Then, **Hoover** was faced with 200,000 demands in a few weeks, as opposed to their forecasted 10,000. A first cost estimation for this 'successful flop', amounting over £20 millions, can explain the speedy dismissal decision that came from the US Hoover mother company to change some directors of their British subsidiary, and even the President of **Hoover Europe**.*[5]

■ The variations in legal constraints are considerable, even within the EEC (legislation is supposed to be harmonized since 1993, and there will be a lot of changes towards liberalization). This partially explains why, despite the multitude of promotional activities observed in most countries, examples of international promotion campaigns (like that of **Esso** and the tiger's tail, or the **Pepsi** Challenge) are fairly rare. This should not prevent exporting companies from offering 'kit' campaigns to their international markets, as we shall see.

6.5.1.3   Implementation

■ The organization* of an effective promotional action is based on close collaboration between the field executives, who know the market needs, and the company staff in charge (along with the possible assistance of an outside specialist/agency).

☐ This collaboration begins with a brief where the problem to be resolved will be carefully outlined (for example: back up support for the launch of a new product; sales stagnation because of reduced activity in retail outlets; decrease in turnover following competitors' promotions), in the overall presentation framework of the company's position in the market to be considered (see section 6.1.4.4).

☐ Promotion objectives will be sought that are best adapted to deal with the problem (it is out of the question to be satisfied with an objective as vague as to stimulate sales). It is important to be specific: attract new buyers, or on the other hand, incite present company clientele to buy more; motivate sales personnel; reinforce company presence in retail outlets by obtaining more shelf space, etc.

☐ From these objectives, the definition of one or several targets will be specified (for example: working women; enterprises using company services within the car industry; sales staff in department stores) within a specific geographic zone.

☐ The most effective actions to reach the predefined targets should then be pre-selected from the promotional arsenal (see section 6.5.2), while at the same time respecting market regulations, constraints and specificities.

☐ After getting this far, creativity can be unleashed . . . but at the same time it should not be allowed to get out of control. Obviously, original ideas are what is being looked for, to distinguish company actions from those of the competition. At the moment of choosing one or several of these ideas, their originality will be one of the main decision-making criteria.

☐ According to the type of action and the nature of the idea retained, the length of the 'event' will have to be determined (necessarily long enough to 'hit' the target, and short enough to prompt it to react rapidly to benefit from the proposed

---

*This is the case where proposals for promotional actions originate at headquarters. In the event that the organization of these actions is delegated to local representatives, the company could simply indicate the limits of promotional communication (see 'promotion bible' further on, and make sure that the framework has been respected *before* starting on the preparation of these actions.

advantages) as well as which advertising dynamic devices will have to be committed to back up and promote this operation efficiently.

☐ Finally, the whole promotion project has to be fitted into a calendar (preparation and implementation) and a budget, which will help in making the final decision.

■ In promotional actions, as everywhere else, we have just mentioned that creative research should aim for clear originality; this does not mean coming up with complicated ideas that will be disappointments or flops on the market, where only simple ideas are well received.

▶ *In this regard, we can mention the example of **Winston** in England, where a brief and detailed objective definition with **Cato Johnson UK** enabled the company to determine the key to development for the brand, which found themselves featured in pubs where cigarettes for a great part are both bought and consumed; a difficult task for a brand that had held, until then, only secondary roles to the 'American cigarettes' category. **Cato Johnson**, however, were able to find an original means of carrying out their mission by launching the **Winston** 'Hands across the sea' twin pubs campaign, a twinning operation among several thousand British and American pubs. These twinnings are embodied in each pub by a big **Winston** plaque where the names of the two 'twinned' pubs are engraved in gold by **Winston** bar accessories and by organizing different contests and lotteries, which offer as prizes trips to the USA to visit the 'twin' pub. The results corresponded to the energy invested in the implementation, and sales progressed accordingly . . . despite the general market tendency towards a decrease in cigarette sales!*

*This example clearly confirms the possibility of innovation within simplicity: each material element in this promotion (decorative plaque, bar accessories with the **Winston** brand logo, contest and lottery) had all been largely used and had proved their effectiveness before. It was only the overall concept of the twinning operation that was new, and which provided the link among all these elements.*

■ According to the markets, adaptations might have to be planned so as not to go against certain regulations, constraints or local specificities. A test on a large or small scale could also be carried out, if necessary, to be sure of the reactions of the clientele and the trade. Thus, for a contest, it might be wise to verify in the major markets if the clientele perceive the two variables as being positive: attractive prices and the chance of winning, while associating the theme of the contest with the brand image in a positive way.

■ No error of appreciation or improvisation can be tolerated for the preparation of a promotional action and its support material, particularly when dealing with mass market products that have to confront the competitor's multitude of tempting offers in supermarkets. Moreover, for two comparable products, the difference between success or failure is played out in a few seconds, and can depend on the choice of a word or the colour of a drawing.

■ The staff in charge will try to tie the promotional action to the other dynamic devices planned in the development mix, so as to obtain better overall effectiveness in a market concerning the calendar of events and general organization, as well as the material used: for example, to plan on using in synergy the same photograph as that of media advertising; to take advantage of a promotional event to transmit interesting and useful positive information on the brand (example: a recipe with the promotion of a food product) so as to retain and create loyalty within that section of consumers who had only bought to benefit from the special offer.

■ The constant results follow-up by the local representative's sales manager is another success factor, given that, according to the types of promotional actions and their application, certain modifications can be made during the events (this is the case for demonstrations organized in retail outlets whose results should be systematically checked so that they can be modified or reorganized to produce the expected effects).

■ After each promotional action, results assessment is essential, because it will lead to a refinement of techniques used to promote company products in other comparable markets. Thus, for promotion X on a specific market, the adoption of an already tested type of organization can be advised, with specific doses of different variables. Advertising means which should be committed can also be suggested to ensure the operation's success.

■ In any case, it will be to the advantage of companies wanting to energize their promotional actions to regularly propose to their local representatives a bible (this is the last in our series!) containing general recommendations (what to do and what not to do, how to organize well in advance a promotion program with their main distributors, etc.), and a choice of different kinds of promotions on descriptive cards, with a detailed explanation of the operating instructions for each, as well as a description of all the necessary ingredients:

☐ objectives, expected effects, for each kind of promotional action;

☐ sample (or photograph) and price of promotional articles (if they are provided by headquarters);

☐ minimum quantities to be ordered, and the lead time necessary to have them on hand;

☐ sample, photograph or detailed description of promotional articles (in the case where they have to be manufactured locally);

☐ suggestions for advertising actions that are generally the most efficient for announcing and backing up each kind of promotion;

☐ models of the different support material; special wrappings, invitations or letters, leaflets, various press ad formats, even TV or radio commercials;

☐ presentation of a premium or gift selection, with their cost price from the company's own suppliers;

☐ indicative number of necessary staff per outlet, specifying their required qualifications and training.

Given that all export markets are never at the same level of development, as for the company's penetration there, and given that local regulations, constraints and specificities vary greatly from one country to another, it would be wise to include in this bible a sufficiently wide choice of promotional actions so that all local representatives can reasonably find something that suits their purposes: according to the case, certain actions can be directly transposed, or adapted to local needs.

6.5.2   Promotion arsenal inventory

This inventory includes about 20 kinds of promotional actions, whose features enable them to be grouped into four families. After reviewing this promotional arsenal, illustrated by a few international examples, we shall conclude with a table indicating those kinds of actions that best correspond to the different development objectives.

6.5.2.1   Lotteries, contests and games

Sweepstakes
Sweepstakes, one of the most controversial promotion activities, are forbidden in many countries. Participants in this promotion must buy a product to obtain a ticket (or another document) that qualifies them for a lottery draw. Sweepstakes are often forbidden because the participant is obliged to buy a product. This difficulty can be overcome by allowing participation in the lottery without a purchase obligation; this manoeuvre does not take too much revenue away from the event, given that in practice not too many people come to a sales outlet to ask for a lottery ticket without buying anything.

Here are three sweepstake examples from the USA, a sales promotion wonderland. In these actions, which have become classics, it can be seen that each company elegantly leaves the possibility of participating without a purchase obligation, but that it is much easier and more tempting to participate after a purchase thanks to the combination of sweepstakes ticket with a discount coupon (in these cases, the discount varies from a few cents to a few dollars, according to the product).

▶ *General Foods*, one of America's food giants, offered 'a dream house'; to win this house, the participants had to fill in one or more discount coupons for the purchase of the group's many products (*Sanka* coffee, *Tang* instant fruit juice, *Minute Rice*, etc.); or, without buying anything, they could fill in a simple sweepstake ticket. However, such simple sweepstake tickets had to be sent in individually, whereas while doing their shopping, a family could take advantage of several discounts (sent on by the retailer to *General Foods*), as well as having extra chances of winning.

▶ *Kodak* offered $1000 a week . . . for life!!! to a sweepstake winner, without purchase obligation, based on the comparison of a photograph appearing on each sweepstake ticket with those presented on a large display case in all retail outlets. A discount coupon for a 'colorburst instant camera' was given with this sweepstake ticket.

▶ *Aqua Fresh* toothpaste (*Beecham Group*) proposed several cash prizes (first prize: $50,000) by combining – like *General Foods* – a sweepstake ticket and a discount coupon. There were two particularities: to have a chance at having one's ticket drawn, a simple crossword puzzle had to be filled in, whose words were part of the product's sales pitch; to participate, *Aqua Fresh* purchasers only had to join a part of the package to the ticket, whereas non-purchasers had to recopy the *Aqua Fresh* slogan within a rectangle, whose dimensions were very strict (3" × 5").

Free draws

This is a simpler version of a sweepstake, without a purchase obligation: they can easily be organized individually in each retail outlet, whereas a sweepstake generally has a regional or even a national coverage, and will often be reinforced by considerable advertising means.

Participants simply have to write their names and addresses on a card and put it in a sealed ballot box; a winner/winners will be drawn every day, week, or at any other frequency. Sales stimulation in this kind of promotion is essentially based on featuring the brand:

▶ In supermarkets, for example, *Schweppes* set up special counters for their lotteries, whose visual impact is obvious: simultaneously, announcements are made by microphone to present the lotteries and inform shoppers where they are located in the store.

Contests and games

Contests and games are favourite promotion activities in many countries for different reasons: this kind of promotion proposes unlimited opportunities to imagine original concepts for distinguishing the brand; everywhere in the world, the same fascination is felt for playful activities (most daily newspapers and news magazines offer games) whether there are prizes or not; this natural trend can be further exploited by brands that retain the possibility of using participants' contest answers: suggestions for cooking recipes, helpful hints for handymen, ideas on how to use a product, a search for a new product name or slogan, a photograph or film sequence where a product is consumed or used, etc.

▶ *Jacobs Club offered holidays in Florida for participants who determined the number of their chocolate biscuits that would have to be placed end-to-end, to link their head office in England to the Miami hotel where the winners would be staying.*

▶ *In Germany, **Kaba** launched a children's contest: participants had to guess the sports played by a bear in several drawings to have a chance of winning one of 100 children's bath robes, printed with portraits of this gentle beast.*

▶ ***Black and White** (the whisky brand symbolized by two scotch terriers that have always militated for racial equality!) organized a 'pub of the year' contest in Ireland. This was an original promotion concept, placing the outlet itself in the spotlight, since the customers of each Irish pub were invited to fill in an evaluation questionnaire.*

6.5.2.2   Gifts and bonuses

Gifts with purchase (GWP)

Used a lot in Anglo-Saxon markets, this kind of promotion has been a warhorse for companies as different as **Estée Lauder**, whose cosmetics and perfumes have made a grand entry into the world's department stores thanks to stunning gift offers, or major oil companies that often work on creating client loyalty using gifts because of the difficulty of differentiating a common product like gasoline. It must be said that in many domains, GWP adaptations have been sought to reduce the cost, which is relatively high since it is carried by each sale: sometimes a minimal purchase is imposed to receive a gift, or the customer is required to collect a certain number of coupons to be cut out from the package of each purchased product, which are then sent in to receive the gift (this transforms the GWP into send-away gifts; see below).

GWP offers can be found in all professional fields:

▶ ***Spontex** frequently use this promotional technique on vastly different markets, either with their own products, or with an offer combined with a complementary product:*

- ■ *In Portugal, there was the offer of a compressed sponge which expanded when in contact with water, into the form of a Walt Disney character (undoubtedly, very effective to propel the kids into their baths!), with any purchase of another **Spontex** product.*
- ■ *In Italy, the tender union of a **Nivea** Bath bottle and an oval **Spontex** sponge, offered in GWP, probably generated lots of impulse purchases. The same results were seen in Chile, where a gorgeous flower sponge was given with the purchase of two bars of **Lux** soap.*

▶ *Here is another example from Italy, where a **Lego** toy was offered with the purchase of **Ovomaltine** (GWP + combined promotion).*

▶ *In Africa, many SMEs and craftsmen send a driver to buy their supplies. This is why some manufacturers like **Christaud** (grindstones and abrasives) and **Fop** (handtools), addressed free gifts to their African distributors: tee-shirts, caps, etc. The drivers are very interested in these premiums, which is logically to the advantage of the brands making this offer.*

▶ *To increase the occupancy of their Caribbean beach resorts – Aruba, Nassau-Paradise Island, Montego Bay and Grand Cayman – **Holiday Inn** offer a Honeymoon package of a minimum three days, where couples receive, in addition to classic hotel services, attractive honeymoon features such as those offered at the **Holiday Inn** Aruba: an upgraded room, welcome cocktails and a tropical fruit basket, a bottle of champagne, candlelight dinner, snorkelling cruise, honeymoon T-shirts, and a free night at the hotel each wedding anniversary.*

In-pack gifts

This is a variation of GWP that consists of putting the gift inside the package at the time of manufacture. This kind of promotion is based on an ever renewable imagination for finding low cost items, which are, nevertheless, attractive; many such gifts are thus destined for children, whether the products concern them directly or not: breakfast cereals, desserts, as well as washing powder.

Send away gifts

An immediate gift offer with a purchase is quite attractive in comparison with the necessary wait for a gift sent for and delivered by post; however, this gift can be of greater value for the simple reason that the company will give away fewer items: indeed, many purchasers will neglect to complete or send in their order form, even if they intended to at the moment of purchase, and sometimes even if this purchase was greatly influenced by the idea of receiving a gift.

▶ *Here again, gifts are often aimed at children, whether it be a plastic boat to assemble and paint (**Kellogg**), a **Walt Disney** album where the child's name is included in the story (**Lenor** fabric conditioner), or more seriously, in Germany, an ABC of the bank and stock market, published in collaboration with the **Commerzbank (Kellogg)**.*

Shareouts

This promotional action combines a sure win with a relative 'luck' factor: a sum of money is the jackpot that will be shared at the end of the promotion by all those participants sending in proof of purchase. This kind of promotion has almost never been tried out in continental Europe; moreover, this typically Anglo-Saxon promotion would only be authorized in a minority of European countries.

▶ *As an example, in Great Britain there was the **Oxo** shareout, where £500,000 was offered to all those who sent in proof of purchase of two 24-cube **Oxo** multipacks.*

Extra product

This kind of promotion is based on the logical observation that one of the most attractive offers to make a regular client (loyalty reinforcement), or even a potential client, is to give more of the product at the normal price. Simply, it is to be said that each sale bears the extra cost of the additional product, whereas it could often have been made without this special offer.

The effect of such a promotion, relatively common in many fields of activity, can be carried further by crossing it with a free trial offer (see section 6.5.2.4) to incite the clientele of one company's product to use another as well.

▶   *For example, **Yoplait** successfully organized such 'bonus' promotions in several countries (Spain, in particular),by adding to a yoghurt pack a free mousse or dessert, whose sales were naturally stimulated as a result.*

This kind of promotion can also be well adapted to the service business-to-business sector:

▶   *__Méridien__ guests are identified during their first stay at one of the Chain's hotels and offered membership in the 'L'Invitation' program, which includes several attractive advantages. Furthermore, after five stays in at least two __Méridien__ hotels in different cities within a two-year period, these guests receive a complimentary night (during the weekend) at the __Méridien__ hotel of their choice.*

Alternative use packs

This is perhaps the oldest kind of promotion, if we go back to prehistoric man, who probably used shells as spoons, after eating their contents. Nowadays, this kind of promotion remains quite popular, mostly in the food industry:

▶   *Mustard jars become glasses (__Amora__), __Grandos__ coffee packaging turns into multi-purpose jars, etc. Too bad that this kind of promotion is not readapted more often in other domains, where excellent results can be obtained (see section 4.2.2.3, the example of the reusable mini-container developed by the __Hesnault Transport Group__).*

6.5.2.3   Premiums and discounts

Cash-back offers

This promotional action offers to send back a sum of money in exchange for one or several proofs of purchase. This is, then, a delayed reduction in price that particularly addresses regular clients. As in the case of send away gifts, many purchasers will neglect to follow-up, which lowers the cost of such promotions.

Money-back offers for unsatisfied clients can be associated with this kind of promotion – very effective for launching new products

– because it eliminates any hesitation concerning a first purchase, with a negligable return rate if the product lives up to its promises.

Price reductions

This kind of very simple, easily organized, generally effective promotion can sometimes elicit suspicion (see section 6.5.1.2), which can be dangerous for the brand image. Moreover, since the reduction is applied to each sale (generated by the reduction offer or not), the cost of this kind of promotion can be high.

Collector items

This is one of the best activities for creating loyalty, used a lot by oil companies: collections of maps, glasses, tool kits, etc.

▶ *In this way, **Heinz** organized a promotion (**Heinz** Schools Foundation) in Great Britain, for which children collected coupons on different **Heinz** product packagings to obtain sports equipment for their schools in exchange. About 45 million labels were gathered in this way, which enabled English schools to receive more than £500,000 in various sports equipment/ accessories.*

Purchase with purchase (PWP or self-liquidating premiums)

This kind of promotion, very popular in Anglo-Saxon countries, consists of proposing (after the purchase of one product, sometimes with a minimum purchase amount) the opportunity of buying another product at an extremely attractive price. Whether this product is part of the usual company product range or not, the purchase price is usually close to its cost price; generally, there is no commercial mark-up on the PWP, so the client only pays for its actual cost price. As for the company and distributors, their return comes from the increase in sales of the initial product, sold with a normal mark-up.

▶ *Promotions of this kind were carried out by most perfume and cosmetics brands in the USA, Canada, UK, Australia, etc, with their catalogue products as well as with items ordered in large quantities (often in the Far East), such as umbrellas, bags, change purses, raincoats, etc.*

Cross product offers

The basis of this kind of promotion is found in the common interest of two companies for the same target market and in the advantages they will have in collaborating to reduce their promotional costs.

▶ *A very successful cross-promotion offer was carried out in the UK by **Lever Brothers** and **British Railways**: in exchange for four proofs of purchase from any of these products, the customers could obtain a voucher giving them the right to buy two train tickets (any destination) for the price of one, to any train station in the country.*

Money-off next purchase
A savings coupon can be printed on a product's packaging, and upon its presentation it will give a price reduction on the purchase of the same product. This is another efficient means of creating client loyalty.

Money-off vouchers or savings coupons
This kind of promotion is very effective for consumer products, whether used alone or crossed with a sweepstake, as previously mentioned. This can be explained by the client's feeling to practically have cash in hand, with a savings coupon of $x.

▶ *In the USA*, marketing specialists of mass consumer products are using the system of vouchers and coupons more and more.*

*The offers, which range from a 20 cent reduction on cheese to $500 discount on a car, are the basis of success for this new kind of consumption-promoting formula. According to one of **Kraft Inc.**'s vice-presidents, marketing budgets for coupons might now pass those of classic advertising. Markets are already invaded, even overwhelmed, by an infinite variety of products sold under different brands, and manufacturers have to come up with new arguments to attract and keep the consumer.*

*Instead of investing for years in their products' brand image, many companies have found it to be more immediately profitable to dynamize their sales by investing in coupon distribution. It is much easier to offer the consumer an instant discount than to differentiate a product from the competition. In proportion, investments devoted to coupons by mass consumer product manufacturers such as **Nabisco** or **Kraft** have increased in the 1980s, whereas those of 'classic' advertising have gone down.*

Generally presented within an advertisement, coupons can be distributed in shops, sent to homes, put in letterboxes, or printed in the press.

This kind of promotion is relatively expensive, but its effects are very rapid and quite exactly foreseeable: thus, for a staple consumer item for which an attractive price reduction has been offered, a response rate of 1.5–2% can be expected in stores, based on the circulation of the daily newspapers in which the coupons were published.

▶ *Some products lend themselves to a combined sampling transmission; this is the case for **Johnson and Johnson** small Band-Aids, of which one is given out with each 25 cent off coupon. In this kind of promotion, we can also mention the generalization of subscription offers at reduced prices for most magazines all over the world. But this can also be considered a full-size sample at a lower price, since these offers usually have a limited period before the promotion expires.*

*Source: Fortune Magazine, June 13 1986.

6.5.2.4   Sampling and trial offers

Free samples

There was a time when samples were considered an efficient means of promotion, but nowadays, budgets in this field have been seriously reduced because of the unavoidable heavy loss on the part of sampling to potential non-purchasers. Sample offers, obviously encouraged by the trade, still continue in the perfume-cosmetics sector (with, however, serious efforts to control their use), especially for personalized distribution in the retail outlets, with direct mail, or after sending in a coupon.

In mass distribution, a sample is often accompanied by other promotional techniques to obtain maximum profitability:

▶ *In Great Britain, a small sample flask of Jif was offered with the purchase of two **Spontex** 'moppet' sponges. This sampling of Jif which was also a gift with the purchase of **Spontex** sponges, was further reinforced by the offer of a money-off voucher (10p off coupon) printed on the **Spontex** packaging, to be redeemed on the next Jif purchase.*

Demonstrations/tastings

An in-store demonstration is surely the most direct method for enhancing a product's strong points and inciting a purchase. This kind of promotion obviously has a high cost, but its advantages balance the scales favourably, even more so given that the trade greatly appreciate the qualified traffic generated by this type of action; proposing a demonstration program is, then, a proven method for convincing a chain of distributors to launch a new product.

This can also be the best way of getting a new kind of product off the ground where it would not generate any demand otherwise.

▶ *Thus, **Yoplait** organized many yoghurt tastings in Japanese supermarkets, where such a product had never been sold. Moreover, it should be noted that **Yoplait** do not limit these tastings to retail outlets, and organize them in different countries (USA, Australia, and Japan, particularly) in the streets with special vans: for the occasion of sponsored cycling challenges in the USA, of course, but also at the exits of movie theatres, and at other heavy pedestrian traffic centres.*

▶ *But it is without doubt **Grand Marnier** which get the prize for being one of the first to try out brand product tastings. Their promotion also went down in history: having come to Paris in 1889 for the World Fair, the Prince of Wales (the future Edward VII) tasted a dessert created especially for him by the great master chef, Escoffier. It was a crepe with **Grand Marnier** which was then called 'Crepe Suzette', in honour of the lady accompanying the Prince. He was won over by this novelty, after seeing it flipped and flambéed, and relishing its flavour. The Crepe Suzette became famous, and this is one more reason why **Grand Marnier** remain so faithful to the British royal family (see section 4.4.2.3).*

▶ *Some professional sectors, particularly those industries that have remained small and craftsmanlike, have the opportunity of presenting their activities as a show. Thus, the **Vanneries Ardenaises** (a wickerworks in the east of France) sent one of their craftsmen to Japan for a week's demonstration in a department store; this activity was warmly welcomed by the Japanese, who are always attracted by such traditional skills.*

▶ *Concerning turnkey projects, the most effective dynamic device is to propose technical references with existing facilities built by the company, and to present testimonials of satisfied customers. For **Krebs**, former clients are their best salesmen, and this 'turnkey' specialist does not hesitate to have them meet their prospective clients during a negotiation. So, for example, when dealing with the study of a chlorate factory, **Krebs** will invite their prospective clients to visit a similar plant in Spain, to finally convince them of the quality of their know-how.*

▶ *From turnkey projects to handtools, the transition is easy! **Facom** have a 130 truck fleet of demonstration vehicles crisscrossing the world, to which can be added 150 similar trucks belonging to their local distributors. Within prospective or existing client facilities, they make a high-impact product presentation: the **Facom** sales technicians can accommodate four or five potential users on-board, have them try out all the different kinds of tools, and finish off the show with various sales films.*

Free trials

This is the equivalent of a sample for household equipment (example: automobile) or company equipment (example: data processing systems).

▶ *Sometimes, a trial can take a special form and become a real wager, such as putting four **Airbus Industrie** aircraft at the disposal of the American carrier **Eastern Airlines** in 1977 for a six-month period, during which the aircraft were operated on their domestic networks. This historical promotion action brought off a resounding success, since **Eastern Airlines** bought 34 Airbus A300s in 1978.*

Certain types of sales, on approval, could possibly be included under this heading, since they allow the sending back of a product whose try-out has not been convincing *before* having to pay for it.

6.5.2.5   Other kinds of promotions

A detailed inspection of all promotional actions would take a whole book; thus, this inventory is limited to a rapid look at the main ones.
    Among promotions which cannot be assimilated into a family, two deserve to be mentioned briefly:

Trade-in offers

These apply especially to consumer products and durable heavy equipment, and are made in the form of a reduction for the purchase of a new product in exchange for trading in an old product, or even one that is decrepit (of the same brand or not, according to the case). It is a good way to attract a clientele who do not like waste, by proposing a disguised price reduction, because the product traded in is often good for nothing, except the junkyard.

▶ *Who would imagine a specialist in high-speed steel concocting a promotional offer like* **L'Oréal** *or* **Moulinex***? And, however, the system of recuperating manufacturing scraps that the* **Commentryenne des Aciers** *offer their clients resembles a trade-in premium: when the latter machine-finish the precious steel alloys of tungsten, molybdenum, vanadium or cobalt, they inevitably produce a certain quantity of waste which they usually get rid of by selling at a low price to local scrap metal dealers. The* **Commentryenne des Aciers** *equipped themselves with unique machinery to recuperate and treat these scraps with a totally automated process: analysis, separation, stocking and removal. This 'promotion' is a powerful factor for developing client loyalty: indeed, buying back the scraps at a reasonable price is interpreted as 'an extra service', and even as a kind of counter-trade, which is greatly appreciated in countries where strong currency is rare. For the* **Commentryenne des Aciers***, it is also an efficient means of partially mastering their production costs, by stabilizing the price of a fraction of their supplies (the price of rare metals is a very speculative area, and as a consequence can be highly irregular). Finally, the return of these scraps serves as a buffer stock that leaves the company some space in which to manoeuvre, in addition to forecasts, so as to be able to deliver urgent orders more rapidly.*

▶ *Trade-in premiums have become frequent in the car industry; but even after a few years Operation 'Usatissimo' is still remembered in Italy today. It offered 700,000 lira for a traded-in vehicle – no matter what condition it was in – to be put towards the purchase of any new* **Peugeot***. This promotion activity was all the more successful as it was the first time that such an offer had been applied to a vast choice of vehicles. It should be noted that the cost of this kind of operation is quite heavy for the manufacturer and dealers; more than profitability, the sought-for objective is developing brand awareness and capturing new market share rapidly.*

Referral premiums
This promotional technique (also called 'use-the-user') offers gifts or motivating rewards to current clients to incite them to introduce potential customers to the company within their social environment.

▶ *This kind of promotion is being developed a lot, especially for service activities such as credit cards (***American Express***) and banks, but nothing is preventing the application of this technique – with tact – to other professional sectors.*

6.5.2.6   Compared promotional action effectiveness

Table 6.3 compares the effectiveness of promotional actions on a general marketing scale. This scale should be reviewed and adapted to each market's specific case, and to each product type.

Table 6.3   **Effectiveness of promotional actions.** +++: extremely effective; ++: very effective; +: effective; -: rarely effective.

Inventory of promotional actions	- Enlarge clientele - Incite first purchase - Back up new product launch	- Obtain sales progression rapidly - Counter attack the competition	- Distinguish product image - Contribute to client behaviour evolution	- Reinforce client loyalty - Develop average purchase level per client	- Carry off product promotion at low cost
			Objectives		
Sweepstakes	+	++	+	++	++
Free Draws	+	++	+	+	+++
Contests & Games	+	+	+++	+	+++
Gifts with Purchase	+++	++	++	++	+
In-Pack Gifts	++	+	+	++	++
Send Away Gifts	+	+	+	+++	++
Shareouts	+	+	+	++	++
Extra Product	++	++	+	+++	+
Alternative Use Packs	+++	+	++	++	++
Cash Back Offers	++	+	+	+++	++
Price Reductions	+++	+++	-	+	+
Collector Items	+	+	++	+++	++
Purchase with Purchase	++	++	++	+	+++
Cross Product Offers	++	+	++	+	+++
Money-Off Next Purchase	+	+	+	+++	++
Savings Coupons	+++	+++	+	+	+
Free Samples	++	++	+	+	-
Demonstration/ Tastings	++	+	+++	++	++
Free Trials	+++	+	+++	++	+
Trade-In Offers	+++	++	+	++	-
Referral Premiums	++	+	++	+	++

Conclusion

Why a conclusion?
Rather than formally closing this book with a few vibrant recommendations, I prefer leaving it open-ended, so that a dialogue can be established.

To illustrate **Expand!** ... with sufficiently varied examples, I met many other international development specialists; with them all, I felt the same passion for comparing methods and exchanging ideas or practical information, which are often transposable, after adaptation, to any other field of activity.

Given that this book is primarily meant for export professionals, I hope it will enlarge the communication circle further: all those who have comments, suggestions and criticisms to make, or exemplary case studies to propose for the next edition of **Expand!** ... , should not hesitate to write to me.

In thanking for their interest those readers who have reached the end of this book ... without taking too many short cuts, I also wish them a good wind for sailing on the seas of foreign development, and excellent international business!

Alain-Eric Giordan
116 Avenue des Champs-Elysées
75008 Paris
France

References

Chapter 1
1 Henri Micmacher, *The Most Beautiful Day in My Life*
2 Kenneth Labich, in *Fortune International*, April 14, 1986

Chapter 2
1 Sandra Snowdon, *The Global Edge*, Simon & Schuster, NY
2 *Wall Street Journal Europe*, June 24, 1992

Chapter 4
1 Christian Regouby, *Global Communications*, Editions d'Organisation
2 Dominik Barouch, in *L'Exportation Magazine*, No. 13
3 Louis S. Richman, in *Fortune International*, April 27 1987
4 Catherine Chatignoux, in *Les Echos*, January 28 1988
5 Didier Gout, in *Les Echos Industrie*
6 *Crédit Lyonnais International*, April 1987
7 Kenneth Labich, in *Fortune International*, April 14 1986

Chapter 5
1 Peter Danton de Rouffignac, *How to Sell in Europe*, Pitman, London
2 *Le Point Magazine*, September 14 1987
3 Kenneth Labich, in *Fortune International*, April 14 1986
4 Françoise Kostolany, in *Les Echos*, September 2 1988
5 *Les Echos*, August 4 1988

Chapter 6
1 Henri Micmacher, *The Most Beautiful Day in My Life*
2 Leigh Bruce, in *International Management Magazine*, November 1987
3 *Lenôtre's Desserts and Pastries/Lenôtre's Ice Creams and Candies*, Editions Barron's, New York
4 Thomas Oliver, *The Real Coke, the Real Story*, Random House, NY
5 Michel Roland, *La Tribune*, April 21 1993

Detailed Contents List

SELECTING WAYS TO EXPAND: INVENTORY AND PRACTICAL ADVICE

CHAPTER 6   Stimulating International Demand: 'Pull' Dynamic Devices 287

Building and Maintaining a European Direct Marketing Database

Graham R Rhind

This book is not only a guide to the building and maintenance of a database but also a handbook of direct marketing information pertaining to 33 European countries. The book takes the reader through the stages of database management, and warns against common, but potentially expensive, pitfalls. It moves from general principles to the specifics of database management, including deduplication and merge-purge. The second part of the book includes chapters on each European country and provides a mass of valuable information not available in any other single source, ranging from language information and job title translations, through address structure systems and forms of salutation, to postal code systems and variants of town names.

Written for anybody involved in building or maintaining a European address-based database, the book will drastically shorten the learning-curve involved in building or improving their direct-marketing database.

Contents

Introduction • Why bother? • The database and its structure • The principles of good database management • Deduplication and Merging • Handling the data in practice - General principles • Handling the data in practice - Data types • Outputting the data • Accents and ASCII codes • Job titles • Country Information • Andorra • Austria • Belgium • Bulgaria • Cyprus • Denmark • Finland • France • Germany • Greece • Greenland • Guernsey • Hungary • Iceland • Ireland • Isle of Man • Italy • Jersey • Liechtenstein • Luxembourg • Malta • Monaco • The Netherlands • Norway • Poland • Portugal • Romania • San Marino • Spain • Sweden • Switzerland • The United Kingdom of Great Britain and Northern Ireland • Vatican City • Appendix 1 - Returns • Bibliography • List of Maps Used.

1994   500 pages   0 566 07471 0

Gower

Licensing
The International Sale of Patents and Technical Knowhow

Michael Z Brooke and John M Skilbeck

This book is designed to take the reader through the maze of activities necessary for the successful selling of technical expertise internationally. It therefore provides a comprehensive review of licensing for the practitioner: how and where licensing is used, the kinds of business supported, the opportunities, the problems and their solutions, together with other relevant issues.

After part 1, which summarizes current usage, part 2 examines the strategic aspects of licensing as a method of operating outside the home country; the relevant decisions are listed as are other options such as investment and franchising.

In part 3 the authors turn to legal and political issues and this part includes a specimen agreement. Part 4 deals with the managerial issues – it looks in turn at organizing, planning, financing, marketing, staffing and other issues; and concludes by examining the vexed question of relationships between licensor and licensee.

Part 5 looks at special considerations for particular nations and regions (including the developing world) while part 6 summarizes and looks to the future.

The result is a comprehensive and up-to-date view of the issues and questions that face the licensing executive, together with practical guidance on dealing with these issues effectively.

1994   350 pages   0 566 07461 3

Gower